The Vehement Flame

by

Margaret Deland

The Vehement Flame
by Margaret Deland

Copyright © 2024

All Rights reserved.

ISBN: 978-93-68090-96-0

Published by

DOUBLE 9 BOOKS

2/13-B, Ansari Road
Daryaganj, New Delhi – 110002
info@double9books.com
www.double9books.com
Tel. 011-40042856

ABOUT THE AUTHOR

Margaret Wade Campbell Deland (1857–1945) was an American author, known for her works of fiction, short stories, poetry, and her two-volume autobiography. Born in Pennsylvania, Deland became an important figure in American literature, particularly within the literary realism movement. Her writing often centered around the intricacies of domestic life, human relationships, and the social constraints of the late 19th and early 20th centuries. She was particularly interested in the roles and struggles of women, which was a major theme in many of her works.

Deland's novels are known for their psychological depth and their exploration of the challenges faced by individuals within the context of societal norms. Her most notable works include The Awakening of Helena Richie (1906), The Way to Peace (1910), The Iron Woman (1911), and The Voice (1912). Throughout her career, Deland's stories reflected her keen observations of the emotional and moral dilemmas faced by her characters, particularly women navigating complex family and social expectations.

CONTENTS

TO LORIN

Together, so many years ago—seven, I think, or eight—you and I planned this story. The first chapters had the help of your criticism ... then, I had to go on alone, urged by the memory of your interest. But all the blunders are mine, not yours; and any merits are yours, not mine. That it has been written, in these darkened years, has been because your happy interest still helped me.

MARGARET
May 12th, 1922

CHAPTER I

Love is as strong as death; jealousy is cruel as the grave: the coals thereof are coals of fire, which hath a most vehement flame

THE SONG OF SOLOMON, VIII, 6

There is nothing in the world nobler, and lovelier, and more absurd, than a boy's lovemaking. And the joyousness of it!...

The boy of nineteen, Maurice Curtis, who on a certain June day lay in the blossoming grass at his wife's feet and looked up into her dark eyes, was embodied Joy! The joy of the warm earth, of the sunshine glinting on the slipping ripples of the river and sifting through the cream-white blossoms of the locust which reared its sheltering branches over their heads; the joy of mating insects and birds, of the whole exulting, creating universe!—the unselfconscious, irresponsible, wholly beautiful Joy of passion which is without apprehension or humor. The eyes of the woman who sat in the grass beside this very young man, answered his eyes with Love. But it was a more human love than his, because there was doubt in its exultation....

The boy took out his watch and looked at it.

"We have been married," he said, "exactly fifty-four minutes."

"I can't believe it!" she said.

"If I love you like this after fifty-four minutes of married life, how do you suppose I shall feel after fifty-four years of it?" He flung an arm about her waist, and hid his face against her knee. "We are married," he said, in a smothered voice.

She bent over and kissed his thick hair, silently. At which he sat up and looked at her with blue, eager eyes.

"It just came over me! Oh, Eleanor, suppose I hadn't got you? You said 'No' six times. You certainly did behave very badly," he said, showing his white teeth in a broad grin.

"Some people win say I behaved very badly when I said 'Yes.'"

"Tell 'em to go to thunder! What does Mrs. Maurice Curtis (doesn't that sound pretty fine?) care for a lot of old cats? Don't we *know* that we are in heaven?" He caught her hand and crushed it against his mouth. "I wish," he said, very low, "I almost wish I could die, now, here! At your feet. It seems as if I couldn't live, I am so—" He stopped. So—what? Words are ridiculously inadequate things!... "Happiness" wasn't the name of that fire in his breast, Happiness? "Why, it's God," he said to himself; "*God.*" Aloud, he said, again, "We are married!"

She did not speak—she was a creature of alluring silences—she just put her hand in his. Suddenly she began to sing; there was a very noble quality in the serene sweetness of her voice:

> "O thou with dewy locks, who lookest down
> Through the clear windows of the morning, ten
> Thine angel eyes upon our western isle,
> Which in full choir hails thy approach, O Spring!"

That last word rose like a flight of wings into the blue air. Her husband looked at her; for a compelling instant his eyes dredged the depths of hers, so that all the joyous, frightened woman in her retreated behind a flutter of laughter.

"'O Spring!'" he repeated; "*we* are Spring, Nelly—you and I.... I'll never forget the first time I heard you sing that; snowing like blazes it was,—do you remember? But I swear I felt this hot grass then in Mrs. Newbolt's parlor, with all those awful bric-à-brac things around! Yes," he said, putting his hand on a little sun-drenched bowlder jutting from the earth beside him; "I felt this sun on my hand! And when you came to 'O Spring!' I saw this sky—" He stopped, pulled three blades of grass and began to braid them into a ring. "Lord!" he said, and his voice was suddenly startled; "what a darned little thing can throw the switches for a man! Because I didn't get by in Math. D and Ec 2, and had to crawl out to Mercer to cram with old Bradley—I met you! Eleanor! Isn't it wonderful? A little thing like that—just falling down in mathematics—changed my whole life?" The wild gayety in his eyes sobered. "I happened to come to Mercer—and, you are my wife." His fingers, holding the little grassy ring, trembled; but the next instant he threw himself back on the grass, and kicked up his heels in a preposterous gesture of ecstasy. Then caught her hand, slipped the braided ring over that plain circle of gold which had been on her finger for fifty-four minutes, kissed it—and the palm of her hand—and said, "You never can escape me! Eleanor, your voice played the deuce with me. I rushed home and read every poem in my volume of Blake. Go on; give us the rest."

She smiled;

"…. And let our winds
Kiss thy perfumed garments; let us taste
Thy morn and evening breath!…"

"Oh—*stop*! I can't bear it," he said, huskily; and, turning on his face, he kissed the grass, earth's "perfumed garment," snow-sprinkled with locust blossoms….

But the moment of passion left him serious. "When I think of Mrs. Newbolt," he said, "I could commit murder." In his own mind he was saying, "I've rescued her!"

"Auntie doesn't mean to be unkind," Eleanor explained, simply; "only, she never understood me—Maurice! Be careful! There's a little ant—don't step on it."

She made him pause in his diatribe against Mrs. Newbolt and move his heel while she pushed the ant aside with a clover blossom. Her anxious gentleness made him laugh, but it seemed to him perfectly beautiful. Then he went on about Mrs. Newbolt:

"Of course she couldn't understand *you*! You might as well expect a high-tempered cow to understand a violin solo."

"How mad she'd be to be called a cow! Oh, Maurice, do you suppose she's got my letter by this time? I left it on her bureau. She'll rage!"

"Let her rage. Nothing can separate us now."

Thus they dismissed Mrs. Newbolt, and the shock she was probably experiencing at that very moment, while reading Eleanor's letter announcing that, at thirty-nine, she was going to marry this very young man.

"No; nothing can part us," Eleanor said; "forever and ever." And again they were silent—islanded in rippling tides of wind-blown grass, with the warm fragrance of dropping locust blossoms infolding them, and in their ears the endless murmur of the river. Then Eleanor said, suddenly: "Maurice!—Mr. Houghton? What will *he* do when he hears? He'll think an 'clopement' is dreadful."

He chuckled. "Uncle Henry?—He isn't really my uncle, but I call him that;—he won't rage. He'll just whistle. People of his age have to whistle, to show they're alive. I have reason to believe," the cub said, "that he 'whistled' when I flunked in my mid-years. Well, I felt sorry, myself—on his account," Maurice said, with the serious and amiable condescension of youth. "I hated to jar him. But—gosh! I'd have flunked A B C's, for *this*. Nelly, I tell you heaven hasn't got anything on this! As for Uncle Henry, I'll write him to-morrow that I had to get married sort of in a hurry, because Mrs. Newbolt wanted to haul you off to Europe. He'll understand. He's white. And he won't really mind—after the first biff;—that will take him below the belt, I suppose, poor old Uncle Henry! But after that, he'll adore you. He adores beauty."

Her delight in his praise made her almost beautiful; but she protested that he was a goose. Then she took the little grass ring from her finger and slipped it into her pocketbook. "I'm going to keep it always," she said. "How about Mrs. Houghton?"

"She'll love you! She's a peach. And little Skeezics—"

"Who is Skeezics?"

"Edith. Their kid. Eleven years old. She paid me the compliment of announcing, when she was seven, that she was going to marry me when she grew up! But I believe, now, she has a crush on Sir Walter Raleigh. She'll adore you, too."

"I'm afraid of them all," she confessed; "they won't like—an elopement."

"They'll fall over themselves with joy to think I'm settled for life! I'm afraid I've been a cussed nuisance to Uncle Henry," he said, ruefully; "always doing fool things, you know,—I mean when I was a boy. And he's been great, always. But I know he's been afraid I'd take a wild flight in actresses."

"'Wild' flight? What will he call—" She caught her breath.

"He'll call it a 'wild flight in angels'!" he said.

The word made her put a laughing and protesting hand (which he kissed) over his lips. Then she said that she remembered Mr. Houghton: "I met him a long time ago; when—when you were a little boy."

"And yet here you are, 'Mrs. Maurice Curtis!' Isn't it supreme?" he demanded. The moment was so beyond words that it made him sophomoric—which was appropriate enough, even though his freshman year had been halted by those examinations, which had so "jarred" his guardian. "I'll be twenty in September," he said. Evidently the thought of his increasing years gave him pleasure. That Eleanor's years were also increasing did not occur to him; and no wonder, for, compared to people like Mr. and Mrs. Houghton, Eleanor was young enough!—only thirty-nine. It was back in the 'nineties that she had met her husband's guardian, who, in those days, had been the owner of a cotton mill in Mercer, but who now, instead of making money, cultivated potatoes (and tried to paint). Eleanor knew the Houghtons when they were Mercer mill folk, and, as she said, this charming youngster—living then in Philadelphia—had been "a little boy"; now, here he was, her husband for "fifty-four minutes." And she was almost forty, and he was nineteen. That Henry Houghton, up on his mountain farm, pottering about in his big, dusty studio, and delving among his potatoes, would whistle, was to be expected.

"But who cares?" Maurice said. "It isn't his funeral."

"He'll think it's yours," she retorted, with a little laugh. She was not much given to laughter. Her life had been singularly monotonous and, having seen very little of the world, she had that self-distrust which is afraid to laugh unless other people are laughing, too. She taught singing at Fern Hill, a private school in Mercer's suburbs. She did not care for the older pupils, but she was devoted to the very little girls. She played wonderfully on the piano, and suffered from indigestion; her face was at times almost beautiful; she had a round, full chin, and a lovely red lower lip; her forehead was very white, with soft, dark hair rippling away from it. Certainly, she had moments of beauty. She talked very little; perhaps because she hadn't the chance to talk—living, as she did, with an aunt who monopolized the conversation. She had no close friends;—her shyness was so often mistaken for hauteur, that she did not inspire friendship in women of her own age, and Mrs. Newbolt's elderly acquaintances were merely condescending to her, and gave her good advice; so it was a negative sort of life. Indeed, her sky terrier, Bingo, and her laundress, Mrs. O'Brien, to whose crippled baby grandson she was endlessly kind, knew her better than any of the people among whom she lived. When Maurice Curtis, cramming in Mercer because Destiny had broken his tutor's leg there, and presenting (with the bored reluctance of a boy) a letter of introduction from his guardian to Mrs. Newbolt—when Maurice met Mrs. Newbolt's niece, something happened. Perhaps because he felt her starved longing for personal happiness, or perhaps her obvious pleasure in listening, silently, to his eager talk, touched his young vanity; whatever the reason was, the boy was fascinated by her. He had ("cussing," as he had expressed it to himself) accepted an invitation to dine with the "ancient dame" (again his phrase!)—and behold the reward of merit:—the niece!—a gentle, handsome woman, whose age never struck him, probably because her mind was as immature as his own. Before dinner was over Eleanor's silence—silence is very moving to youth, for who knows what it hides?—and her deep, still eyes, lured him like a mystery. Then, after dinner ("a darned good dinner," Maurice had conceded to himself) the calm niece sang, and instantly he knew that it was Beauty which hid in silence—and he was in love with her! He had dined with her on Tuesday, called on Wednesday, proposed on Friday;—it was all quite like Solomon Grundy! except that, although she had fallen in love with him almost as instantly as he had fallen in love with her, she had, over and over again, refused him. During the period of her refusals the boy's love glowed like a furnace; it brought both power and maturity into his fresh, ardent, sensitive face. He threw every thought to the winds—except the thought of rescuing his princess from Mrs. Newbolt's imprisoning bric-a-bràc. As for his "cramming" the tutor into whose hands Mr. Houghton had committed his ward's very defective trigonometry and economics, Mr. Bradley, held in Mercer because of an annoying accident, said to himself that his intentions were honest, but if Curtis didn't turn up for three days running, he would utilize the time his pupil was paying for by writing a paper on "The Fourth Dimension."

Maurice was in some new dimension himself! Except "old Brad," he knew almost no one in Mercer, so he had no confidant; and because his passion was, perforce, inarticulate, his candid forehead gathered wrinkles of positive suffering, which made him look as old as Eleanor, who, dazed by the first very exciting thing that had ever happened to her,—the experience of being adored (and adored by a boy, which is a heady thing to a woman of her age!)—Eleanor was saying to herself a dozen times a day: "I *mustn't* say 'yes'! Oh, what *shall* I do?" Then suddenly there came a day when the rush of his passion decided what she would do....

Her aunt had announced that she was going to Europe. "I'm goin' to take you," Mrs. Newbolt said. "*I* don't know what would become of you if I left you alone! You are about as capable as a baby. That was a great phrase of your dear uncle Thomas's—'capable as a baby,' I'm perfectly sure the parlor ceilin' has got to be tinted this spring. When does your school close? We'll go the minute it closes. You can board Bingo with Mrs. O'Brien."

Eleanor, deeply hurt, was tempted to retort with the announcement that she needn't be "left alone"; she might get married! But she was silent; she never knew what to say when assailed by the older woman's tongue. She just wrote Maurice, helplessly, that she was going abroad.

He was panic-stricken. Going abroad? Uncle Henry's ancient dame was a she-devil, to carry her off! Then, in the midst of his anger, he recognized his opportunity: "The hell-cat has done me a good turn, I do believe! I'll get her! Bless the woman! I'll pay her passage myself, if she'll only go and never come back!"

It was on the heels of Mrs. Newbolt's candor about Eleanor's "capableness" that he swept her resistance away. "You've *got* to marry me," he told her; "that's all there is to it." He put his hand in his pocket and pulled out a marriage license. "I'll call for you to-morrow at ten; we'll go to the mayor's office. I've got it all fixed up. So, you see there's no getting out of it."

"But," she protested, dazzled by the sheer, beautiful, impertinence of it, "Maurice, I can't—I won't—I—"

"You *will*," he said. "To-morrow's Saturday," he added, practically, "and there's no school, so you're free." He rose.... "Better leave a letter for your aunt. I'll be here at five minutes to ten. Be ready!" He paused and looked hard at her; caught her roughly in his arms, kissed her on her mouth, and walked out of the room.

The mere violence of it lifted her into the Great Adventure! When he commanded, "Be ready!" she, with a gasp, said, "Yes."

Well; they had gone to the mayor's office, and been married; then they had got on a car and ridden through Mercer's dingy outskirts to the end of the route in Medfield, where, beyond suburban uglinesses, there were glimpses of green fields.

Once as the car rushed along, screeching around curves and banging over switches, Eleanor said, "I've come out here four times a week for four years, to Fern Hill."

And Maurice said: "Well, *that's* over! No more school-teaching for you!"

She smiled, then sighed. "I'll miss my little people," she said.

But except for that they were silent. When they left the car, he led the way across a meadow to the bank of the river; there they sat down under the locust, and he kissed her, quietly; then, for a while, still dumb with the wonder of themselves, they watched the sky, and the sailing white clouds, and the river—flowing—flowing; and each other.

"Fifty-four minutes," he had said....

So they sat there and planned for the endless future—the "fifty-four years."

"When we have our golden wedding," he said, "we shall come back here, and sit under this tree—" He paused; he would be—let's see: nineteen, plus fifty, makes sixty-nine. He did not go farther with his mental arithmetic, and say thirty-nine plus fifty; he was thinking only of himself, not of her. In fifty years he would be, he told himself, an old man.

And what would happen in all these fifty golden years? "You know, long before that time, perhaps it won't be—just us?" he said.

The color leaped to her face; she nodded, finding no words in which to expand that joyous "perhaps," which touched the quick in her. Instantly that sum in addition which he had not essayed in his own mind, became unimportant in hers. What difference did the twenty severing years make, after all? Her heart rose with a bound—she had a quick vision of a little head against her bosom! But she could not put it into words. She only challenged, him:

"I am not clever like you. Do you think you can love a stupid person for fifty years?"

"For a thousand years!—but you're not stupid."

She looked doubtful; then went on confessing: "Auntie says I'm a dummy, because I don't talk very much. And I'm awfully timid. And she says I'm jealous."

"You don't talk because you're always thinking; that's one of the most fascinating things about you, Eleanor,—you keep me wondering what on earth you're thinking about. It's the mystery of you that gets me! And if you're 'timid'—well, so long as you're not afraid of me, the more scared you are, the better I like it. A man," said Maurice, "likes to feel that he protects his—his wife." He paused and repeated the glowing word ... "his wife!" For a moment he could not go on with their careless talk; then he was practical again. That word "protect" was too robust for sentimentality. "As for being jealous, that, about me, is a joke! And if you were, it would only mean that you loved me—so I would be flattered. I hope you'll be jealous! Eleanor, *promise* me you'll be jealous?" They both laughed; then he said: "I've made up my mind to one thing. I won't go back to college."

"Oh, Maurice!"

He was very matter of fact. "I'm a married man; I'm going to support my wife!" He ran his fingers through his thick blond hair in ridiculous pantomime of terrified responsibility. "Yes, sir! I'm out for dollars. Well, I'm glad I haven't any near relations to get on their ear, and try and mind my business for me. Of course," he ruminated, "Bradley will kick like a steer, when I tell him he's bounced! But that will be on account of money. Oh, I'll pay him, all same," he said, largely. "Yes; I'm going to get a job." His face sobered into serious happiness. "My allowance won't provide bones for Bingo! So it's business for me."

She looked a little frightened. "Oh, have I made you go to work?" She had never asked him about money; she had plunged into matrimony without the slightest knowledge of his income.

"I'll chuck Bradley, and I'll chuck college," he announced, "I've got to! Of course, ultimately, I'll have plenty of money. Mr. Houghton has dry-nursed what father left me, and he has done mighty well with it; but I can't touch it till I'm twenty-five—worse luck! Father had theories about a fellow being kept down to brass tacks and earning his living, before he inherited money another man had earned—that's the way he put it. Queer idea. So, I must get a job. Uncle Henry'll help me. You may bet on it that Mrs. Maurice Curtis shall not wash dishes, nor yet feed the swine, but live on strawberries, sugar, and—What's the rest of it?"

"I have a little money of my own," she said; "six hundred a year."

"It will pay for your hairpins," he said, and put out his hand and touched her hair—black, and very soft and wavy "but the strawberries I shall provide."

"I never thought about money," she confessed.

"Of course not! Angels don't think about money."

"So they were married"; and in the meadow, fifty-four minutes later, the sun and wind and moving shadows, and the river—flowing—flowing— heralded the golden years, and ended the saying: "*lived happy ever afterward.*"

CHAPTER II

It was three days after the young husband, lying in the grass, his cheek on his wife's hand, had made his careless prophecy about "whistling," that Henry Houghton, jogging along in the sunshine toward Grafton for the morning mail, slapped a rein down on Lion's fat back, and whistled, placidly enough.... (But that was before he reached the post office.) His wife, whose sweet and rosy bulk took up most of the space on the seat, listened, smiling with content. When he was placid, she was placid; when he wasn't, which happened now and then, she was an alertly reasonable woman, defending him from himself, and wrenching from his hand, with ironic gayety, or rallying seriousness, the dagger of his discontent with what he called his "failure" in life—which was what most people called his success—a business career, chosen because the support of several inescapable blood relations was not compatible with his own profession of painting. All his training and hope had been centered upon art. The fact that, after renouncing it, an admirably managed cotton mill provided bread and butter for sickly sisters and wasteful brothers, to say nothing of his own modest prosperity, never made up to him for the career of a struggling and probably unsuccessful artist—which he might have had. He ran his cotton mill, and supported all the family undesirables until, gradually, death and marriage took the various millstones from around his neck; then he retired, as the saying is—although it was really setting sail again for life—to his studio (with a farmhouse attached) in the mountains. There had been a year of passionate work and expectation—but his pictures were dead. "I sold my birthright for a bale of cotton," he said, briefly.

But he still stayed on the farm, and dreamed in his studio and tried to teach his little, inartistic Edith to draw, and mourned. As for business, he said, "Go to the devil!"—except as he looked after Maurice Curtis's affairs; this because the boy's father had been his friend. But it was the consciousness of the bartered birthright and the dead pictures in his studio which kept him from "whistling" very often. However, on this June morning, plodding along between blossoming fields, climbing wooded hills, and clattering through dusky covered bridges, he was not thinking of his pictures; so, naturally enough, he whistled; a very different whistling from that which Maurice, lying in the grass beside his wife of fifty-four minutes, had foreseen for him—when the mail should be distributed! Once, just from sheer content, he stopped his:

> Did you ever ever ever
> In your life life life
> See the devil devil devil
> Or his wife wife wife—"

and turned and looked at his Mary.

"Nice day, Kit?" he said; and she said, "Lovely!" Then she brushed her elderly rosy cheek against his shabby coat and kissed it. They had been married for thirty years, and she had held up his hands as he placed upon the altar of a repugnant duty, the offering of a great renunciation. She had hoped that the birth of their last, and only living, child, Edith, would reconcile him to the material results of the renunciation; but he was as indifferent to money for his girl as he had been for himself.... So there they were, now, living rather carefully, in an old stone farmhouse on one of the green foothills of the Allegheny Mountains. The thing that came nearest to soothing the bruises on his mind was the possibilities he saw in Maurice.

"The inconsequence of the scamp amounts to genius!" he used to tell his Mary with admiring displeasure at one or another of Maurice's scrapes. "Heaven knows what he'll do before he gets to the top of Fool Hill, and begins to run on the State Road! Look at this mid-year performance. He ought to be kicked for flunking. He simply dropped everything except his music! Apparently he *can't* study. Even spelling is a matter of private judgment with Maurice! Oh, of course, I know I ought to have scalped him; his father would have scalped him. But somehow the scoundrel gets round me! I suppose its because, though he is provoking, he is never irritating. And he's as much of a fool as I was at his age! That keeps me fair to him. Well, he has *stuff* in him, that boy. He's as truthful as Edith; an appalling tribute, I know—but you like it in a cub. And there's no flapdoodle about him; and he never cried baby in his life. And he has imagination and music and poetry! Edith is a nice little clod compared to him."

The affection of these two people for Maurice could hardly have been greater if he had been their son. "Mother loves Maurice better 'an she loves me," Edith used to reflect; "I guess it's because he never gets muddy the way I do, and tracks dirt into the house. He wipes his feet."

"What do you suppose," Mrs. Houghton said, remembering this summing up of things, "Edith told me this morning that the reason I loved Maurice more than I loved her—"

"What!"

"Yes; isn't she funny?—was because he 'wiped his feet when he came into the house.'"

Edith's father stopped whistling, and smiled: "That child is as practical as a shuttle; but she hasn't a mean streak in her!" he said, with satisfaction, and began to whistle again. "Nice girl," he said, after a while; "but the most rationalizing youngster! I hope she'll get foolish before she falls in love. Mary, one of these days, when she grows up, perhaps she and Maurice—?"

"Matchmaker!" she said, horrified; then objected: "Can't she rationalize and fall in love too? I'm rather given to reason myself, Henry."

"Yes, honey; you are *now*; but you were as sweet a fool as anybody when you fell in love, thank God." She laughed, and he said, resignedly, "I suppose you'll have an hour's shopping to do? You have only one of the vices of your sex, Mary, you have the 'shopping mind.' However, with all thy faults I love thee still.... We'll go to the post office first; then I can read my letters while you are colloguing with the storekeepers."

Mrs. Houghton, looking at her list, agreed, and when he got out for the mail she was still checking off people and purchases; it was only when she had added one or two more errands that she suddenly awoke to the fact that he was very slow in coming back with the letters. "Stupid!" she thought, "opening your mail in the post office, instead of keeping it to read while I'm shopping!"—but even as she reproached him, he came out and climbed into the buggy, in very evident perturbation.

"Where do you want to go?" he said; she, asking no questions (marvelous woman!) told him. He said "G'tap!" angrily; Lion backed, and the wheel screeched against the curb. "Oh, *g'on!*" he said. Lion switched his tail, caught a rein under it, and trotted off. Mr. Houghton leaned over the dashboard, swore softly, and gave the horse a slap with the rescued rein. But the outburst loosened the dumb distress that had settled upon him in the post office; he gave a despairing grunt:

"Well! Maurice has come the final cropper."

"Smith's next, dear," she said; "What is it, Henry?"

"He's gone on the rocks (druggist Smith, or fish Smith?)"

"Druggist. Has Maurice been drinking?" She could not keep the anxiety out of her voice.

"Drinking? He could be as drunk as a lord and I wouldn't—Whoa, Lion!... Get me some shaving soap, Kit!" he called after her, as she went into the shop.

When she came back with her packages and got into the buggy, she said, quietly, "Tell me, Henry."

"He has simply done what I put him in the way of doing when I gave him a letter of introduction to that Mrs. Newbolt, in Mercer."

"Newbolt? I don't remember—"

"Yes, you do. Pop eyes. Fat. Talked every minute, and everything she said a *nonsequitur*. I used to wonder why her husband didn't choke her. He was on our board. Died the year we came up here. Talked to death, probably."

"Oh yes. I remember her. Well?"

"I thought she might make things pleasant for Maurice while he was cramming. He doesn't know a soul in Mercer, and Bradley's game leg wouldn't help out with sociability. So I gave him letters to two or three people. Mrs. Newbolt was one of them. I hated her, because she dropped her g's; but she had good food, and I thought she'd ask him to dinner once in a while."

"Well?"

"*She did.* And he's married her niece."

"What! Without your consent! I'm shocked that Mrs. Newbolt permitted—"

"Probably her permission wasn't asked, any more than mine."

"You mean an elopement? How outrageous in Maurice!" Mrs. Houghton said.

Her husband agreed. "Abominable! Mary, do you mind if I smoke?"

"Very much; but you'll do it all the same. I suppose the girl's a mere child?" Then she quailed. "Henry!—she's respectable, isn't she? I couldn't bear it, if—if she was some—dreadful person."

He sheltered a sputtering match in his curving hand and lighted a cigar; then he said, "Oh, I suppose she's respectable enough; but she's certainly 'dreadful.' He says she's a music teacher. Probably caught him that way.

Music would lead Maurice by the nose. Confound that boy! And his father trusted me." His face twitched with distress. "As for being a 'mere child,'—there; read his letter."

She took it, fumbling about for her spectacles; halfway through, she gave an exclamation of dismay. "'A few years older'?—she must be *twenty* years older!"

"Good heavens, Mary!"

"Well, perhaps not quite twenty, but—"

Henry Houghton groaned. "I'll tell Bradley my opinion of him as a coach."

"My dear, Mr. Bradley couldn't have prevented it.... Yes; I remember her perfectly. She came to tea with Mrs. Newbolt several times. Rather a temperamental person, I thought."

"'Temperamental'? May the Lord have mercy on him!" he said. "Yes, it comes back to me. Dark eyes? Looked like one of Rossetti's women?"

"Yes. Handsome, but a little stupid. She's proved *that* by marrying Maurice! Oh, what a fool!" Then she tried to console him: "But one of the happiest marriages I ever knew, was between a man of thirty and a much older woman."

"But not between a boy of nineteen and a much older woman! The trouble is not her age but his youth. Why didn't she adopt him?... I bet the aunt's cussing, too."

"Probably. Well, we've got to think what to do," Mary Houghton said.

"Do? What do you mean? Get a divorce for him?"

"He's just married; he doesn't want a divorce yet," she said, simply; and her husband laughed, in spite of his consternation.

"Oh, lord, I wish I was asleep! I've always been afraid he'd go high-diddle-diddling off with some shady girl;—but I swear, that would have been better than marrying his grandmother! Mary, what I can't understand, is the woman. He's a child, almost; and vanity at having a woman of forty fall in love with him explains him. And, besides, Maurice is no Eurydice; music would lead him into hell, not out of it. It's the other fool that puzzles me."

His wife sighed; "If her mind keeps young, it won't matter so much about her body."

"My dear," he said, dryly, "human critters are human critters. In ten years it will be an impossible situation."

But again she contradicted him: "No! Unhappiness is possible; but *not* inevitable!"

"Dear Goose, may a simple man ask how it is to be avoided?"

"By unselfishness," she said; "no marriage ever went on the rocks where both 'human critters' were unselfish! But I hope this poor, foolish woman's mind will keep young. If it doesn't, well, Maurice will just have to be tactful. If he is, it may not be so *very* bad," she said, with determined optimism.

"Kit, when a man has to be 'tactful' with his wife, God help him!—or a woman with her husband," he added in a sudden tender afterthought. "We've never been 'tactful' with each other, Mary?" She smiled, and put her cheek against his shoulder. "'Tactfulness' between a husband and wife," said Henry Houghton, "is confession that their marriage is a failure. You may tell 'em so, from me."

"You may tell them yourself!" she retorted. "What are they going to live on?" she pondered "Can his allowance be increased?"

"It can't. You know his father's will. He won't get his money until he's twenty-five."

"He'll have to go to work," she said; "which means not going back to college, I suppose?"

"Yes," he said, grimly; "who would support his lady-love while he was in college? And it means giving up his music," he added.

"If he makes as much out of his renunciation as you have out of yours," she said, calmly, "we may bless this poor woman yet."

"Oh, you old humbug," he told her—but he smiled.

Then she repeated to him an old, old formula for peace; "'Consider the stars,' Henry, and young foolishness will seem very small. Maurice's elopement won't upset the universe."

They were both silent for a while; then Mary Houghton said, "I'll write the invitation to them; but you must second it when you answer his letter."

"Invitation? What invitation?"

"Why, to come and stay at Green Hill until you can find something for him to do."

"I'll be hanged if I invite her! I'll have nothing to do with her! Maurice can come, of course; but he can't bring—"

His wife laughed, and he, too, gave a reluctant chuckle. "I suppose I've got to?" he groaned.

"*Of course,* you've got to!" she said.

The rest of the ride back to the old stone house among its great trees, halfway up the mountain, was silent. Mrs. Houghton was thinking what room she would give the bride and groom—for the little room Maurice had had in all his vacations since he became her husband's ward was not suitable. "Edith will have to let them have her room," she thought. She knew she could count on Edith not to make a fuss. "It's such a comfort that Edith has sense," she ruminated aloud.

But her husband was silent; there was no more whistling for Henry Houghton that day.

CHAPTER III

Edith and her fourteen-year-old neighbor, Johnny Bennett, had climbed into the old black-heart cherry tree—(Johnny always conceded that Edith was a good climber—"for a girl.") But when they saw Lion, tugging up the road, Edith, who was economical with social amenities, told her guest to go home. "I don't want you any longer," she said; "father and mother are coming!" And with that she rushed around to the stable door, just in time to meet the returning travelers, and ask a dozen questions—the first:

"*Did* you get a letter from Maurice?"

But when her father threw the reins down on Lion's back, and said, briefly, "Can't you unharness him yourself, Buster?" she stuck out her tongue, opened her eyes wide, and said nothing except, "Yes, father." Then she proceeded, with astonishing speed, to put Lion into his stall, run the buggy into the carriage house, and slam the stable door, after which she tore up to her mother's room.

"Mother! Something has bothered father!"

"Well, yes," Mrs. Houghton said; "a little. Maurice is married."

Edith's lips fell apart; "Maurice? *Married?* Who to? Did she wear a veil? I don't see why father minds."

Mrs. Houghton, standing in front of her mirror, said, dryly: "There are things more important than veils, when it comes to getting married. In the first place, they eloped—"

"Oh, how lovely! I am going to elope when I get married!"

"I hope you won't have such bad taste. Of course they ought not to have got married that way. But the thing that bothers your father, is that the lady Maurice has married is—is older than he."

"How much older?" Edith demanded; "a year?"

"I don't just know. Probably twenty years older."

Edith was silent, rapidly adding up nineteen and twenty; then she gasped, "*Thirty-nine!*"

"Well, about that; and father is sorry, because Maurice can't go back to college. He will have to go into business."

Edith saw no cause for regret in this. "Guess he's glad not to have to learn things! But why weren't we invited to the wedding? I always meant to be Maurice's bridesmaid."

Mrs. Houghton said she didn't know. Edith was silent, for a whole minute. Then she said, soberly:

"I suppose father's sorry 'cause she'll die so soon, she's so old? And then Maurice will feel awfully. Poor Maurice! Well, I'll live with him, and comfort him."

"My dear, I'm fifty!" Mrs. Houghton said, much amused.

"Oh, well, *you* —" Edith demurred; "that's different. You're my mother, and you—" She paused; "I never thought of you being old, or dying, *ever*. And yet I suppose you are rather old?" She pondered. "I suppose some day you'll die? Mother!—promise me you won't!" she said, quaveringly.

"Edith, don't be a goose!" Mrs. Houghton said, laughing—but she turned and kissed the rosy, anxious face, "Maurice's wife isn't old at all. She's quite young. It's only that he is so much younger."

Edith lapsed into silence. She was very quiet for the rest of that summer morning. Just before dinner she went across the west pasture to Doctor Bennett's house, and, hailing Johnny, told him the news. His indifference—for he only looked at her, with his mild, nearsighted brown eyes, and said, "Huh?"—irritated her so that she would not confide her dismay at Maurice's approaching widowerhood, but ran home to a sympathetic kitchen: "Katy! Maurice got eloped!"

Katy was much more satisfactory than Johnny; she said, "God save us! Mr. Maurice eloped? Who with, then? Well, well!" But Edith was still abstracted. Time, as related to life, had acquired significance. At dinner she regarded her father with troubled eyes. He, too, was old, like Maurice's wife. He, too, as well as the bride, and her mother, would die, sometime. And she and Maurice would have such awful grief!... Something tightened in her throat; "Please 'scuse me," she said, in a muffled voice; and, slipping out of her chair, made a dash for the back door, and ran as hard as she could to her chicken house. The little place was hot, and smelled of feathers; through the windows, cobwebbed and dusty, the sunshine fell dimly on the hard earth floor, and on an empty plate or two and a rusty, overturned tin pan. Here, sitting on a convenient box, she could think things out undisturbed: Maurice, and his lovely, dying Bride; herself, orphaned and alone; Johnny Bennett, indifferent to all this oncoming grief! Probably Maurice was worrying about it all the time! How long would the Bride live? Suddenly she remembered her mother's age, and had a revulsion of hope for Maurice. Perhaps his wife would live to be as old as mother? "Why, I hadn't thought of that! Well, then, she will live—let's see: thirty-nine from fifty leaves eleven—yes; the Bride will live eleven years!" Why, that wasn't so terrible, after all. "That's as long as I have been alive!" Obviously it would not be necessary to take care of Maurice for quite a good while. "I guess," she reflected, "I'll have some children by that time. And maybe I'll be married, too, for Maurice won't need me for eleven years. But I don't know what I'd do with my husband then?" She frowned; a husband would be bothering, if she had to go and live with Maurice. "Oh, well, probably my husband will be so old, he'll die about the time Maurice's wife does." She had meant to marry Johnny. "But I won't. He's too young. He's only three years older 'an me. He might live too long. I must get an old husband. I'll tell Johnny about it to-morrow. I'll wear mourning," she thought; "a long veil! It's so interesting. But not over my face—you can't see through it, and it isn't sense not to be able to see." (The test Edith applied to conduct was always, "Is it sense?") "Of course I shall feel badly about my husband; but I've got to take care of Maurice…. Yes; I must get an old one," she thought. "I must get one as old as the Bride. If they'd only waited, the Bride could have married my husband!"

But this line of thought was too complicated; and, besides, she had so entirely cheered up that she practically forgot death. She began to count how much money her mother owed her for eggs—which reminded her to look into the nests; and when, in spite of a clucking remonstrance, she put her hand under a feathery breast and touched the hot smoothness of a new-laid egg, she felt perfectly happy. "I guess I'll go and get some floating-island," she thought. "Oh, I *hope* they haven't eaten it all up!"

With the egg in her hand, she rushed back to the dining room, and was reassured by the sight of the big glass dish, still all creamy yellow and fluffy white.

"Edith," Mrs. Houghton said, "you won't mind letting Maurice and Eleanor have your room, will you, dear?"

"Is her name 'Eleanor'? I think it's a perfectly beautiful name! No, I'd love to give her my room! Mother, she won't be as old as you are for eleven years, and that's as long as I have been alive. So I won't worry about Maurice just yet. Mother, may I have two helpings? When are they coming?"

"They haven't been asked yet," her father said, grimly. "I'm not going to concoct a letter, Mary, for a week. Let 'em worry! Maurice, confound him!—has never worried in his life. Everything rolls off him like water off a duck's back. It will do him good to chew nails for a while. I wish I was asleep!"

"Why, father!" Edith said, aghast; "I don't believe you *want* the Bride!"

"You're a very intelligent young person," her father said, scratching a match under the table and lighting a cigar.

"But, my dear," his wife said, "has it occurred to you that it may be as unpleasant for the Bride to come, as for you to have her? *Henry!* That's the third since breakfast!"

"Wrong for once, Mrs. Houghton. It's the fourth."

"*I* want the Bride," said Edith.

Her mother laughed. "Come along, honey," she said, putting her hand on her husband's shoulder, "and tell me what to say to her."

"Say she's a harpy, and tell her to go to the—"

"Henry!"

"My dear, like Mr. F.'s aunt, 'I hate a fool.' Oh, I'll tell you what to say: Say, 'Mr. F.'s aunt will send her a wedding present.' That's friendly, isn't it?"

"Better not be too literary in public," his wife cautioned him, with a significant glance at Edith, who was all ears.

When, laughing, they left the table, their daughter scraping her plate, pondered thus: "I suppose Mr. F. is the Bride's father. I wonder what present his aunt will give her? I wonder what 'F' stands for—Frost? Fuller? Father and mother don't want the Bride to come; and mother thinks the Bride don't want to come. So why should they ask her to come? And why should she come? I wouldn't," Edith said; "but I hope she will, for I love her! And oh, I *hope* she'll bring her harp! I've never seen a harpy. But people are funny," Edith summed it up; "inviting people and not wanting 'em; and visiting 'em and not wanting to. It ain't sense," said Edith.

CHAPTER IV

In spite of his declaration of indifference to the feelings of his guardian, the married boy was rapidly acquiring that capacity for "worry" which Mr. Houghton desired to develop in him. *What would the mail bring him from Green Hill?* It brought nothing for a week—a week in which he experienced certain bad moments which encouraged "worry" to a degree that made his face distinctly older than on that morning under the locust tree, when he had been married for fifty-four minutes. The first of these educating moments came on Monday, when he went to see his tutor, to say that he was—well, he was going to stop grinding.

"What?" said Mr. Bradley, puzzled.

"I'm going to chuck college, sir," Maurice said, and smiled broadly, with the rollicking certainty of sympathy that a puppy shows when approaching an elderly mastiff.

"Chuck college! What's the matter?" the mastiff said, putting a protecting hand over his helpless leg, for Maurice's restlessness—tramping about, his hands in his pockets—was a menace to the plastered member.

"I'm going into business," the youngster said; "I—Well; I've got married, and—"

"*What!*"

"—so, of course, I've got to go to work."

"See here, what are you talking about?"

The uneasy color sprang into Maurice's face, he stood still, and the grin disappeared. When he said explicitly what he was "talking about," Mr. Bradley's angry consternation was like the unexpected snap of the old dog; it made Eleanor's husband feel like the puppy. "I ought to have rounded him up," Mr. Bradley was saying to himself; "Houghton will hold me responsible!" And even while making unpleasant remarks to the bridegroom, he was composing, in his mind, a letter to Mr. Houghton about the helplessness incidental to a broken leg, which accounted for his failure in "rounding up." "*I* couldn't get on to his trail!" he was exonerating himself.

When Maurice retreated, looking like a schoolboy, it took him a perceptible time to regain his sense of age and pride and responsibility. He rushed back to the hotel—where he had plunged into the extravagance of the "bridal suite,"—to pour out his hurt feelings to Eleanor, and while she looked at him in one of her lovely silences he railed at Bradley, and said the trouble with him was that he was sore about money! "He needn't worry! I'll pay him," Maurice said, largely. And then forgot Bradley in the rapture of kissing Eleanor's hand. "As if we cared for his opinion!" he said.

"We don't care!" she said, joyously. Her misgivings had vanished like dew in the hot sun. Old Mrs. O'Brien had done her part in dissipating them. While Maurice was bearding his tutor, Eleanor had gone across town to her laundress's, to ask if Mrs. O'Brien would take Bingo as a boarder—. "I can't have him at the hotel," she explained, and then told the great news:—"I'm going to live there, because I—I'm married,"—upon which she was kissed, and blessed, and wept over! "The gentleman is a little younger than I am," she confessed, smiling; and Mrs. O'Brien said:

"An' what difference does that make? He'll only be lovin' ye hotter than an old fellow with the life all gone out o' him!"

Eleanor said, laughing, "Yes, that's true!" and cuddled the baby grandson's head against her breast.

"You'll be happy as a queen!" said Mrs. O'Brien; and "in a year from now you'll have something better to take care of than Bingo—*he'll* be jealous!"

But she hardly heeded Mrs. O'Brien and her joyful prophecy of Bingo's approaching jealousy; having taken the dive, she had risen into the light and air, and now she forgot the questioning depths! She was on the crest of contented achievement. She even laughed to think that she had ever hesitated about marrying Maurice. Absurd! As if the few years between them were of the slightest consequence! Mrs. O'Brien was right.... So she smoothed over Maurice's first bad moment with an indifference as to Mr. Bradley's opinion which was most reassuring to him. (Yet once in a while she thought of Mr. Houghton, and bit her lip.)

The next bad moment neither she nor Maurice could dismiss so easily; it came in the interview with her astounded aunt, whose chief concern (when she read the letter which Eleanor had left on her pincushion) was lest the Houghtons would think she had inveigled the boy into marrying her niece. To prove that she had not, Mrs. Newbolt told the bride and groom that she would have nothing more to do with Eleanor! It was when the fifty-four minutes had lengthened into three days that they had gone, after supper, to see her. Eleanor, supremely satisfied, with no doubts, now about the wisdom of what she had done, was nervous only as to the effect of her aunt's temper upon Maurice; and he, full of a bravado of indifference which confessed the nervousness it denied, was anxious only as to the effect of the inevitable reproaches upon Eleanor. Their five horrid minutes of waiting in the parlor for Mrs. Newbolt's ponderous step on the stairs, was broken by Bingo's dashing, with ear-piercing barks, into the room: Eleanor took him on her knee, and Maurice, giving the little black nose a kindly squeeze, looked around in pantomimic horror of the obese upholstery, and Rogers groups on the tops of bookcases full of expensively bound and unread classics.

"How have you stood it?" he said to his wife; adding, under his breath, "If she's nasty to you, I'll wring her neck!"

She was very nasty. "I'm not a party to it," Mrs. Newbolt said; she sat, panting, on a deeply cushioned sofa, and her wheezy voice came through quivering double chins; her protruding pale eyes snapped with anger. "I shall tell you exactly what I think of you, Eleanor, for, as my dear mother used to say, if I have a virtue it is candor; I think you are a puffect fool. As for Mr. Curtis, I no more thought of protectin' him than I would think of protectin' a baby in a perambulator from its nursemaid! Bingo was sick at his stomach this mornin'. You've ruined the boy's life." Eleanor cringed, but Maurice was quite steady:

"We will not discuss it, if you please. I will merely say that I dragged Eleanor into it; I *made* her marry me. She refused me repeatedly. Come, Eleanor."

He rose, but Mrs. Newbolt, getting heavily on to her small feet, and talking all the time, walked over to the doorway and blocked their retreat. "You needn't think I'll do anything for you!" she said to her niece; "I shall write to Mr. Houghton and tell him so. I shall tell him he isn't any more disgusted with this business than I am. And you can take Bingo with you!"

"I came to get him," Eleanor said, faintly.

"Come, Eleanor," Maurice said; and Mrs. Newbolt, puffing and talking, had to make way for them. As they went out of the door she called, angrily:

"Here! Stop! I want to give Bingo a chocolate drop!"

They didn't stop. In the street on the way to Bingo's new home, Eleanor, holding her little dog in her arms, was blind with tears, but Maurice effervesced into extravagant ridicule. His opinion of Mrs. Newbolt, her parlor, her ponderosity, and her missing g's, exhausted his vocabulary of opprobrious adjectives; but Eleanor was silent, just putting up a furtive handkerchief to wipe her eyes. It was dark, and he drew her hand through his arm and patted it.

"Don't worry, Star. Uncle Henry is white! She can write to him all she wants to! I'm betting that we'll get an invitation to come right up to Green Hill."

She said nothing, but he knew she was trembling. As they entered Mrs. O'Brien's alley, they paused where it was dark enough, halfway between gaslights, for a man to put his arm around his wife's waist and kiss her. (Bingo growled.)

"Eleanor! I've a great mind to go back to that hell-cat, and tell her what I think of her!"

"No. Very likely she's right. I—I have injured you. Oh, Maurice, if I *have*—"

"You'd have injured me a damn sight more if you hadn't married me!" he said.

But for the moment her certainty that her marriage was a glorious and perfect thing, collapsed; her voice was a broken whisper:

"If I've spoiled your life—she says I have;—I'll ... kill myself, Maurice." She spoke with a sort of heavy calmness, that made a small, cold thrill run down his back; he burst into passionate protest:

"All I am, or ever can be, will be because you love me! Darling, when you say things like—like what you said, I feel as if you didn't love me—"

Of course the reproach tautened her courage; "I do! I do! But—"

"Then never say such a wicked, cruel thing again!"

It was when Bingo had been left with Mrs. O'Brien that, on their way back to the hotel, Maurice, in a burst of enthusiasm, invited his third bad moment: "I am going to have a rattling old dinner party to celebrate your escape from the hag! How about Saturday night?"

She protested that he was awfully extravagant; but she cheered up. After all, what difference did it make what a person like Auntie thought! "But who will you ask?" she said. "I suppose you don't know any men here? And I don't, either."

He admitted that he had only two or three acquaintances in Mercer—"but I have a lot in Philadelphia. You shan't live on a desert island, Nelly!"

"Ah, but I'd like to—*with you*! I don't want anyone but you, in the world," she said, softly.

He thrilled at the wonder of that: she would be contented, *with him*,—on a desert island! Oh, if he could only always be enough for her! He vowed to himself, in sudden boyish solemnity, that he *would* always be enough for her. Aloud, he said he thought he could scratch up two or three fellows.

Then Eleanor's apprehension spoke: "What *will* Mr. Houghton say?"

"Oh, he's all right," Maurice said, resolutely hiding his own apprehension. He could hide it, but he could not forget it. Even while arranging for his dinner party, and plunging into the expense of a private dining room, he was thinking, of his guardian; "Will he kick?" Aloud he said, "I've asked three fellows, and you ask three girls."

"I don't know many girls," she said, anxiously.

"How about that girl you spoke to on the street yesterday? (If Uncle Henry could only see her, he'd be crazy about her!)"

"Rose Ellis? Well, yes; but she's rather young."

"Oh, that's all right," Maurice assured her. "(I wish I hadn't told him she is older than I am. Trouble with me is, I always plunk out the truth!) The fellows like 'em young," he said. Then he told her who the fellows were: "I don't know 'em very well; they're just boys; not in college. Younger than I am, except Tom Morton. Mort's twenty, and the brainiest man I know. And Hastings has a bag of jokes—well, not just for ladies," said Maurice, grinning, "and you'll like Dave Brown. You rake in three girls. We'll have a stunning spread, and then go to the theater." He caught her in his arms and romped around the room with her, then dropped her into a chair, and watched her wiping away tears of helpless laughter.

"Yes—I'll rake in the girls!" she gasped.

She wasn't very successful in her invitations. "I asked Rose, but I had to ask her mother, too," she said; "and one of the teachers at the Medfield school."

Maurice looked doubtful. Rose was all right; but the other two? "Aren't they somewhat faded flowers?"

"They're about my age," Eleanor teased him. As for Maurice, he thought that it didn't really matter about the ladies, faded or not; they were Eleanor's end of the shindy. "Spring chickens are Mort's meat," he said...

The three rather recent acquaintances who were Maurice's end of the shindy, had all gaped, and then howled, when told that the dinner was to celebrate his marriage. "I got spliced kind of in a hurry," he explained; "so I couldn't have any bachelor blow-out; but my—my—my wife, Mrs. Curtis, I mean—and I, thought we'd have a spree, to show I am an old married man."

The fellows, after the first amazement, fell on him with all kinds of ragging: Who was she? Was she out of baby clothes? Would she come in a perambulator?

"Shut up!" said the bridegroom, hilariously. He went home to Eleanor tingling with pride. "I want you to be perfectly stunning, Star! Of course you always are; but rig up in your best duds! I'm going to make those fellows cross-eyed with envy. I wonder if you could sing, just once, after dinner? I want them to hear you! (Mr. Houghton will love her voice!)"

Eleanor—who had stopped counting the minutes of married life now, for, this being the sixth day of bliss, the arithmetic was too much for her—was as excited about the dinner as he was. Yet, like him, under the excitement, was a little tremor: "They will be angry because—because we eloped!" Any other reason for anger she would not formulate. Sometimes her anxiety was audible: "Do you suppose Auntie has written to Mr. Houghton?" And again: "What *will* he say?" Maurice always replied, with exuberant indifference, that he didn't know, and he didn't care!

"*I* care, if he is horrid to you!" Eleanor said "He'll probably say it was wicked to elope?"

Mr. Houghton continued to say nothing; and the "care" Maurice denied, dogged all his busy interest in his dinner—for which he had made the plans, as Eleanor, until the term ended, was obliged to go out to Medfield to give her music lessons; besides, "planning" was not her forte! But in the thrill of excitement about the dinner and in the mounting adventure of being happy, she was able to forget her fear that Mr. Houghton might be "horrid" to Maurice. If the Houghtons didn't like an elopement, it would mean that they had no romance in them! She was absorbed in her ardent innocent purpose of "impressing" Maurice's friends, not from vanity, but because she wanted to please him. As she dressed that evening, all her self-distrust vanished, and she smiled at herself in the mirror for sheer delight, for his sake, in her dark, shining eyes, and the red loveliness of her full lip. In this wholly new experience of feeling, not only happy, but important,—she forgot Mrs. Newbolt, sailing angrily for Europe that very day, and was not even anxious about the Houghtons! After all, what difference did it make what such people thought of elopements? "Fuddy-duddies!" she said to herself, using Maurice's slang with an eager sense of being just as young as he was.

When the guests arrived and they all filed into the private and very expensive dining room, Eleanor looked indeed quite "stunning"; her shyness did not seem shyness, but only a sort of proud beauty of silence, which might cover Heaven knows what deeps of passion and of knowledge! Little

Rose was glowing and simpering, and the two older ladies were giving each other significant glances. Maurice's "fellows," shepherded by their host, shambled speechlessly along in the background. The instant that they saw the bride they had fallen into dumbness. Brown said, under his breath to Hastings, "Gosh!" And Hastings gave Morton a thrust in the ribs, which Morton's dignity refused to notice; later, when he was at Eleanor's right, the flattery of her eagerly attentive silence instantly won him. Maurice had so expatiated to her upon Morton's brains, that she was really in awe of him—of which, of course, Morton was quite aware! It was so exhilarating to his twenty years that he gave his host a look of admiring congratulation—and Maurice's pride rose high!—then fell; for, somehow, his dinner wouldn't "go"! He watched the younger men turn frankly rude shoulders to the older ladies, who did their best to be agreeable. He caught stray words: Eleanor's efforts to talk as Rose talked—Rose's dog was "perfectly sweet," but "simply awful"; then a dog story; "wasn't that *killing*?" And Eleanor: she once had a cat—"perfectly frightfully cunning!" said Eleanor, stumbling among the adverbs of adolescence.

At Rose's story the young men roared, but Eleanor's cat awoke no interest. Then one of the "faded flowers" spoke to Brown, who said, vaguely, "What, ma'am?"

The other lady was murmuring in Maurice's ear:

"What is your college?"

Maurice trying to get Rose's eye, so that he might talk to her and give the boys a chance to do their duty, said, distractedly, "Princeton. Say, Hastings! Tell Mrs. Ellis about the miner who lost his shirt—"

Mrs. Ellis looked patient, and Hastings, dropping into agonized shyness, said, "Oh, I can't tell stories!"

After that, except for Morton's philosophical outpourings to the listening Eleanor, most of the dreary occasion of eating poor food, served by a waiter who put his thumb into things, was given up to the stifled laughter of the girl and boys, and to conversation between the other two guests, who were properly arch because of the occasion, but disappointed in their dinner, and anxious to shake their heads and lift shocked hands as soon as they could get out of their hostess's sight.

For Maurice, the whole endless hour was a seesaw between the past and the present, between his new dignity and his old irresponsibility. He tried—at first with boisterous familiarity, then with ponderous condescension—to draw his friends out. What would Eleanor think of them—the idiots! And what would she think of him, for having such asinine friends? He hoped

Mort was showing his brains to her! He mentally cursed Hastings because he did not produce his jokes; as for Brown, he was a kid. "I oughtn't to have asked him! What *will* Eleanor think of him!" He was thankful when dessert came and the boys stopped their fatuous murmurings to little Rose, to gorge themselves with ice cream. He talked loudly to cover up their silence, and glanced constantly at his watch, in the hope that it was time to pack 'em all off to the theater! Yet, even with his acute discomfort, he had moments of pride—for there was Eleanor sitting at the head of the table, silent and handsome, and making old Mort crazy about her! In spite of those asses of boys, he was very proud. He had simply made a mistake in inviting Hastings and Brown; "Tom Morton's all right," he told himself; "but, great Scott! how young those other two are!"

When the evening was over (the theater part of it was a success, for the play was good, and Maurice had nearly bankrupted himself on a box), and he and Eleanor were alone, he drew her down on the little sofa of their sitting room, and worshiped. "Oh, Star, how wonderful you are!"

"Did I do everything right?" She was breathless with happiness. "I tried so hard! But I *can't* talk. I never know what to say."

"You were perfect! And they were all such idiots—except Mort. Mort told me you were very temperamental, and had a wonderful mind. I said, 'You bet she has!' The old ladies were pills."

"Oh, Maurice, you goose!... Maurice, what will Mr. Houghton say?"

"Hell say, 'Bless you, my children!' Nelly, what *was* the matter with the dinner?"

"Matter? Why, it was perfect! It was"—she made a dash for some of his own words—"simply corking! Though perhaps Rose was a little too young for it. Didn't you enjoy it?" she demanded, astonished.

He said that if she enjoyed it, that was all he cared about! He didn't tell her—perhaps he didn't know it himself—that his own lack of enjoyment was due to his inarticulate consciousness that he had not belonged anywhere at that dinner table. He was too old—and he was too young. The ladies talked down to him, and Brown and Hastings were polite to him. "Damn 'em, *polite!* Well," he thought, "'course, they know that a man in my position isn't in their class. But—" After a while he found himself thinking: "Those hags Eleanor raked in had no manners. Talked to me about my 'exams'! I'm glad I snubbed the old one, I don't think Rose was too young," he said, aloud. "Oh, Star, you are wonderful!"

And she, letting her hair fall cloudlike over her shoulders, silently held out her arms to him. Instantly his third bad moment vanished.

But a fourth was on its way; even as he kissed that white shoulder, he was thinking of the letter which must certainly come from Mr. Houghton in a day or two. "What will *he* get off?" he asked himself; "probably old Brad and Mrs. Newbolt have fed oats to him, so he'll kick—but what do I care? Not a hoot!" Thus encouraging himself, he encouraged Eleanor:

"Don't worry! Uncle Henry'll write and *beg* me to bring you up to Green Hill."

The fifty-four minutes of married life had stretched into eight days, and Maurice had chewed the educating nails of worry pretty thoroughly before that "begging" letter from Henry Houghton arrived. There was an inclosure in it from Mrs. Houghton, and the young man, down in the dark lobby of the hotel, with his heart in his mouth, read what both old friends had to say—then rushed upstairs, two steps at a time, to make his triumphant announcement to his wife:

"What did I tell you? Uncle Henry's *white*!" He gave her a hug; then, plugging his pipe full of tobacco, handed her the letters, and sat down to watch the effect of them upon her; there was no more "worry" for Maurice! But Eleanor, standing by the window silhouetted against the yellow twilight, caught her full lower lip between her teeth as she read:

"Of course," Mr. Houghton wrote—(it had taken him the week he had threatened to "concoct" his letter, which he asked his wife if he might not sign "Mr. F.'s aunt." "I bet she doesn't know her Dickens; it won't convey anything to her," he begged; "I'll cut out two cigars a day if you'll let me do it?" She would not let him, so the letter was perfectly decorous.)—"Of course it was not the proper way to treat an old friend, and marriage is too serious a business to be entered into in this way. Also I am sorry that there is any difference in age between you and your wife. But that is all in the past, and Mrs. Houghton and I wish you every happiness. We are looking forward to seeing you next month." ... ("Exactly," he explained to his Mary, "as I look forward to going to the dentist's. *You* tell 'em so.")

As Mrs. Houghton declined to "tell 'em," Eleanor, reading the friendly words, was able to say, "I don't think he's angry?"

"'Course not!" said Maurice.

Then she opened the other letter.

> My dear boy,—I wish you hadn't got married in such a hurry; Edith is dreadfully disappointed not to have had the chance "to be your bridesmaid"! You must give us an opportunity soon to know your wife. Of course you must both come to Green Hill as usual, for your vacation.

"*She* is furious," said Eleanor. "She thinks it's dreadful to have eloped." She had turned away from him, and was looking out across the slow current of the river at the furnaces on the opposite bank—it was the same river, that, ten days ago, had run sparkling and lisping over brown depths and sunny shallows past their meadow. Her face lightened and darkened as the sheeting violet and orange flames from the great smokestacks roared out against the sky, and fell, and rose again. The beauty of them caught Maurice's eye, and he really did not notice what she was saying, until he caught the words: "Mrs. Houghton's like Auntie—she thinks I've injured you—" Before he could get on his feet to go and take her in his arms, and deny that preposterous word, she turned abruptly and came and sat on his knee; then, with a sort of sob, let herself sink against his breast. "But oh, I did so want to be happy!—and you made me do it."

He gave her a quick squeeze, and chuckled: "You bet I made you!" he said; he pushed her gently to her feet, and got up and walked about the room, his hands in his pockets. "As for Mrs. Houghton, you'll love her. She never fusses; she just says, 'Consider the stars.' I do hope you'll like them, Eleanor," he ended, anxiously. He was still in that state of mind where the lover hopes that his beloved will approve of his friends. Later on, when he and she love each other more, and so are more nearly one, he hopes that his friends will approve of his beloved, even as he used to be anxious that they should approve of him. "I do awfully want you to like 'em at Green Hill! We'll go the minute your school closes."

"*Must* we?" she said, nervously.

"I'm afraid we've got to," he said; "you see, I must find out about ways and means. And Edith would be furious if we didn't come," he ended, chuckling.

"Is she nice?"

"Why, yes," he said; "she's just a child, of course. Only eleven. But she and I have great times. We have a hut on the mountain; we go up for a day, and Edith cooks things. She's a bully cook. Her beloved Johnny Bennett tags on behind."

"But do you like to be with a *child*?" she said, surprised.

"Oh, she's got a lot of sense. Say, Nelly, I have an idea. While we are at Green Hill, let's camp out up there?"

"You don't mean stay all night?" she said, flinching. "Oh, wouldn't it be very uncomfortable? I—I hate the dark."

The sweet foolishness of it enchanted him (baby love feeds on pap!) "Pitch dark," he teased, "and lions and tigers roaring around, and snakes—"

"Of course I'll go, if you want me to," she said, simply, but with a real sinking of the heart.

"Edith adores it," he said. "Speaking of Edith, I must tell you something so funny. Last summer I was at Green Hill, and one night Mr. and Mrs. Houghton were away, and there was a storm. Gee, I never saw such a storm in my life! Edith has no more nerves than a tree, but even she was scared. Well, I was scared myself."

He had stretched himself out on the sofa, and she was kneeling beside him, her eyes worshiping him. "*I* would have been scared to death," she confessed.

"Well, *I* was!" he said. "The tornado—it was just about that!—burst on to us, and nearly blew the house off the hill—and such an infernal bellowing, and hellish green lightning, you never saw! Well, I was just thinking about Buster—her father calls her Buster; and wondering whether she was scared, when in she rushed, in her night-gown. She made a running jump for my bed, dived into it, grabbed me, and hugged me so I was 'most suffocated, and screamed into my ear, 'There's a storm!'—as if I hadn't noticed it. I said—I could hardly make myself heard in the racket—I yelled, 'Don't you think you'd better go back to your own room? I'll come and sit there with you.' And she yelled, 'I'm going to stay here.' So she stayed."

"I think she was a little old for that sort of thing," Eleanor said, coldly.

He gave a shout of laughter. "Eleanor! Do you mean to tell me you don't see how awfully funny it was? The little thing hugged me with all her might until the storm blew over. Then she said, calmly: 'It's cold. I'll stay here. You can go and get in my bed if you want to.'"

Eleanor gave a little shrug, then rose and went over to the window. "Oh yes, it was funny; but I think she must be a rather pert little thing. I don't want to go to Green Hill."

Maurice looked worried. "I hate to urge anything you don't like, Nelly; but I really do feel we ought to accept their invitation? And you'll like them! Of course they're not in your class. Nobody is! I mean they're old, and sort of commonplace. But we can go and live in the woods most of the time, and get away from them,—except little Skeezics. We'll take her along. You'll love having her; she's lots of fun. You see, I've *got* to go to Green Hill, because I must get in touch with Uncle Henry; I've got to find out about our income!" he explained, with a broad grin.

"I should think Edith would bore you," she said. Her voice was so sharply irritated that Maurice looked at her, open-mouthed; he was too bewildered to speak.

"Why, Eleanor," he faltered; "why are you—on your ear? Was it what I told you about Edith? You didn't think that she wasn't *proper*?"

"No! Of course not! It wasn't *that*." She came quickly and knelt beside him. "Of course it wasn't *that*! It was—" She could not say what it was; perhaps she did not quite know that her annoyance at Maurice's delight in Edith was the inarticulate pain of recognizing that he might have more in common with a child, eight years his junior, than he could have with a woman twenty years his senior. Her eyes were suddenly bright with frightened tears. In a whisper, that fear which, in these days of complete belief in her own happiness, she had forgotten even to deny, came back: "What really upset me was the letters. The Houghtons are angry because I am—" she flinched, and would not utter the final word which was the hidden reason of her annoyance at Edith; so, instead of uttering it, she said, "because we eloped."

As for Maurice, he rallied her, and pretended to scold her, and tasted her tears salt upon his lips. He felt very old and protecting.

"Nonsense!" he said. "Mrs. Houghton and Uncle Henry are old, and of course they can't understand love. But the romance of it will touch them!"

And again Love cast out Fear; Eleanor, her face hidden on his shoulder, told herself that it really didn't matter what the Houghtons thought of ... an elopement.

CHAPTER V

The cloud of their first difference had blown over almost before they felt its shadow, and the sky of love was as clear as the lucid beryl of the summer night. Yet even the passing shadow of the cloud kept both the woman and the boy repentant and a little frightened; he, because he thought he had offended her by some lack of delicacy; she, because she thought she had shocked him by what he might think was harshness to a child. Even a week afterward, as they journeyed up to Green Hill in a dusty accommodation train, there was an uneasy memory of that cloud—black with Maurice's dullness, and livid with the zigzag flash of Eleanor's irritation—and then the little shower of tears! ... What had brought the cloud? Would it ever return? ... As for those twenty dividing years, they never thought of them!

In the train they held each other's hands under the cover of a newspaper; and sometimes Maurice's foot touched hers, and then they looked at each other, and smiled—but each was wondering: his wonder was, "What made her offended at Edith?" And hers was, "How can he like to be with an eleven-year-old child!" Their talk, however, confessed no wonderings! It was the happy commonplace of companionship: Mrs. Newbolt and her departure for Europe; would Mrs. O'Brien be good to Bingo? what Maurice's business should be. Then Maurice yawned, and said he was glad that the commencement exercises at Fern Hill were over; and she said she was glad, too; she had danced, she said, until she had a pain in her side! After which he read his paper, and she looked out of the window at the flying landscape. Suddenly she said:

"That girl you danced with last night—you danced with her three times!" she said, with sweet reproach—"didn't know we were married!—she wasn't a Fern Hill girl. She told me she had been dancing with my 'nephew.'"

"Did she?... Eleanor, look at that elm tree, standing all alone in the field, like—like a wineglass full of summer!"

For a moment she didn't understand his readiness to change the subject—then she had a flash of instinct: "I believe she said the same thing to you!"

"Oh, she got off some fool thing." The annoyance in his voice was like a rapier thrust of certainty.

"I knew it! But I don't care. Why should I care?"

"You shouldn't. Besides, it was only funny. I was tremendously amused."

She turned and looked out of the window.

Maurice lifted the paper which had been such a convenient shelter for clasping hands, and seemed to read for a while. Then he said, abruptly, "I only thought it was funny for her to make such a mistake."

She was silent.

"Eleanor, don't be—that way!"

"What 'way'? You mean"—her voice trembled—"feel hurt to have you dance *three times*, with a girl who said an uncomplimentary thing about me?"

"But it wasn't uncomplimentary! It was just a silly mistake anyone might make—" He stopped abruptly, for there were tears in her eyes—and instantly his tenderness infolded her like sunshine. But even while he was making her talk of other things—the heat, or the landscape—he was a little preoccupied; he was trying to explain this tiny, ridiculous, lovely unreasonableness, by tracking it back to some failure of sensitiveness on his own part. It occurred to him that he could do this better if he were by himself—not sitting beside her, faintly conscious of her tenseness. So he said, abruptly, "Star, if you don't mind, I'll go and have a smoke."

"All right," she said; "give me the paper; I haven't looked at the news for days!" She was trembling a little. The mistake of a silly girl had had, at first, no significance, it was just, as it always is to the newly married woman, amusing to be supposed not to be married! But that Maurice, knowing of the mistake, had not mentioned its absurdity, woke an uneasy consciousness that he had thought it might annoy her! Why should it annoy her?—unless the reason of the mistake was as obvious to him as to the girl?—whom he had found attractive enough to dance with three times! It was as if a careless hand had pushed open a closed door, and given Maurice's wife a glimpse of a dark landscape, the very existence of which her love had so vehemently denied.

An hour later, however, when Maurice returned, she was serene again. Love had closed the door—bolted it! barred it! and the gray landscape of dividing years was forgotten. And as her face had cleared, so had his. He had explained her annoyance by calling himself a clod! "She hated not to be thought married—of *course!*" What a brute he was not to have recognized the subtle loveliness of a sensitiveness like that! He wanted to tell her so, but he could only push the newspaper toward her and slip his hand under it to feel for hers—which he clutched and gripped so hard that her rings cut into the flesh. She laughed, and opened her pocketbook and showed him the little circle of grass which he had slipped over her wedding ring after fifty-four minutes of married life. At which his whole face radiated. It was as if, through those gay blue eyes of his, he poured pure joy from his heart into hers.

"Be careful," he threatened: "one minute more, and I'll kiss you right here, before people!"

She snapped her purse shut in pretended terror, but after that they held hands under the newspaper, and were perfectly happy—until the moment came of meeting the Houghtons on the platform at the junction; then happiness gave way to embarrassment.

Henry Houghton, obliged to throw away a half-smoked cigar, and, saying under his breath that he wished he was asleep, was cross; but his wife was pleasantly commonplace. She kissed the bride, and the groom, too, and said that Edith was in a great state of excitement about them! Then she condoled with Eleanor about the heat, and told Maurice there were cinders on his hat. But not even her careful matter-of-courseness could make the moment anything but awkward. In the four-mile drive to Green Hill— during which Eleanor said she hoped old Lion wouldn't run away;—the young husband seemed to grow younger and younger; and his wife, in her effort to talk to Mr. Houghton, seemed to grow older and older....

"If I didn't happen to know she was a fool," Henry Houghton said to his Mary, washing his hands before going down to supper, "I should think she was quite a nice woman—she's so good looking."

"*Henry!* At your time of life, are you deciding a woman's 'niceness' by her looks?"

"But tell her she mustn't bore him," he said, ignoring the rebuke. "Tell her that when it comes to wives, every husband on earth is Mr. F.'s aunt—he 'hates a fool'!"

"Why not tell her yourself?" she said: then she sighed; "why *did* she do it?"

"She did it," he instructed her, "because the flattery of a boy's lovemaking went to her head. I have an idea that she was hungry for happiness—so it was champagne on an empty stomach. Think of the starvation dullness of living with that Newbolt female, who drops her g's all over the floor! Edith likes her," he added.

"Oh, Edith!" said Edith's mother, with a shrug; "well; if you can explain Eleanor, perhaps you can explain Maurice?"

"*That's* easy; anything in petticoats will answer as a peg for a man (we are the idealizing sex) to hang his heart on. Then, there's her music—and her pathos. For she is pathetic, Kit?"

But Mary Houghton shook her head: "It is Maurice who is pathetic—my poor Maurice!..."

When they went down to the east porch, with its great white columns, and its broad steps leading into Mrs. Houghton's gay and fragrant garden, they found Edith there before them—sitting on the top step, her arms around her knees, her worshiping eyes fixed on the Bride. Edith had nothing to say; it was enough to look at the "bridal couple," as the kitchen had named them. When her father and mother appeared, she did manage, in the momentary bustle of rising and offering chairs, to say to Maurice:

"Oh, isn't she lovely! Oh, Maurice, let's go out behind the barn after supper and talk! Maurice, *did* she bring her harp? I want to see her play on it! I saw her wedding ring," she ended, in an ecstatic whisper.

"She doesn't play on the harp; she plays on the piano. Did you twig her hair?" Maurice whispered back; "it's like black down!"

Edith was speechless with adoration; she wished, passionately, that Maurice would put his coat down for the Bride to step on, like Sir Walter Raleigh! "for she is a *Queen*!" Edith thought: then Maurice pulled one of her pigtails and she kicked him—and after that she was forgotten, for the grown people began to talk, and say it had been a hot day, and that the strawberries needed rain—but Eleanor hoped there wouldn't be a thunderstorm.

"They *have* to say things, I suppose," Edith reflected, patiently: "but after supper, Maurice and I will talk." So she bore with her father and mother, who certainly tried to be conversational. The Bride, Edith noticed, was rather silent, and Maurice, though grown up to the extent of being married, hadn't much to say—but once he winked at Edith and again tried to pull her hair,—so she knew that he, also, was patient. She was too absorbed to return the wink. She just stared at Eleanor. She only dared to speak to her once; then, breathlessly: "I—I'm going to go to your school, when I'm sixteen." It was as if she looked forward to a pilgrimage to a shrine! It was impossible not to see the worship in her face; Eleanor saw her smile made Edith almost choke with bliss. But, like herself, the Bride had nothing to say. Eleanor just sat in sweet, empty silence, and watched Maurice, twisting old Rover's ears, and answering Mrs. Houghton's maternal questions about his winter underclothing and moths; she caught that wink at Edith, and the occasional broad grin when Mrs. Houghton scolded him for some carelessness, and the ridiculous gesture of tearing his hair when she said he was a scamp to have forgotten this or that. Looking at the careless youth of him, she laughed to herself for sheer joy in the beauty of it!

But Edith's plan for barn conversation with Maurice fell through, because after supper, with an air of complete self-justification, he said to his hosts, "*Now* you must hear Eleanor sing!"

At which she protested, "Oh, Maurice, no!"

The Houghtons, however, were polite; so they all went into the studio, and, standing in the twilight, with Maurice playing her accompaniment, she sang, very simply, and with quite poignant beauty, the song of "Golden Numbers," with its serene refrain:

"*O sweet, O sweet content!*"

"Lovely, my dear," Mrs. Houghton said, and Maurice was radiant.

"Is Mr. F. your father?" Edith said, timidly; and while Eleanor was giving her maiden name, Edith's terrified father said, in a ferocious aside, "Mary! Kill that child!" Late that night he told his wife she really must do something about Edith: "Fortunately, Eleanor is as ignorant of Dickens as of 'most everything else. I bet she never read *Little Dorrit*. But, for God's sake, muzzle that daughter of yours! ... Mary, you see how he was caught?—the woman's voice."

"Don't call her 'the woman'!"

"Well, vampire. Kit, what do you make of her?"

"I wish I knew what to make of her! I feel sure she is really and truly *good*. But, oh, Henry, she's so mortal dull! She hasn't a spark of humor in her."

"'Course not. If she had, she wouldn't have married him. But *he* has humor! Better warn her that a short cut to matrimonial unhappiness is not to have the same taste in jokes! Mary, maybe, her music will hold him?"

"Maybe," said Mary Houghton, sighing.

"'Consider the stars,'" he quoted, sarcastically; but she took the sting out of his gibe by saying, very simply:

"Yes, I try to."

"He is good stuff," her husband said; "straight as a string! When he came into the studio to talk things over he was as sober as if he were fifty, and hadn't made an ass of himself. He took up the income question in a surprisingly businesslike way; then he said that of course he knew I didn't like it—his giving up college and flying off the handle, and getting married without saying anything to me. 'But,' he said, 'Eleanor's aunt is an old hell-cat;—she was going to drag Eleanor abroad, and I had to get her out of her clutches!' ... I think," Henry Houghton interrupted himself, "that's one explanation of Maurice: rescuing a forlorn damsel. Well, I was perfectly direct with him; I said, 'My dear fellow, Mrs. Newbolt is not a hell-cat; and the elopement was in bad taste. Elopements are always in bad taste. But the elopement is the least important part of it. The difference in age is the serious thing.' I got it out of him just what it is—almost twenty years. She might be his mother!—he admitted that he had had to lie about himself to get the license. I said, 'Your age is the dangerous thing, Maurice, not hers; and it's up to you to keep steady!' Of course he didn't believe me," said Mr. Houghton, sighing. "He's in love all right, poor infant! The next thing is for me to find a job for him.... She is good looking, Mary?" She nodded, and he said again, "A pre-Raphaelite woman; those full red lips, and that lovely black hair growing so low on her forehead. And a really good voice. And a charming figure. But I tell you one thing: she's got to stop twitting on facts. Did you hear her say, 'Maurice is so ridiculously young, he doesn't remember'—? I don't know what it was he didn't remember. Something unimportant. But she must not put ideas about his youth into his head. He'll know it soon enough! *You* tell her that."

"Thank you so much!" said Mary Houghton. "Henry, you mustn't say things before Edith! Suppose Eleanor had known her *Little Dorrit*?"

"She doesn't know anything; and she has nothing to say."

"Well, it might be worse," she encouraged him. "Suppose she were talkative?"

He nodded: "Yes; a dull woman is bad, and a talkative woman is bad; but a dull talkative woman is hell."

"My *dear*! I'm glad Edith's in bed. Well, I think I like her."

CHAPTER VI

But the time arrived when Mrs. Houghton was certain that she "liked" Maurice's wife. It would have come sooner if Eleanor's real sweetness had not been hidden by her tiresome timidity ... a thunderstorm sent her, blanched and panting, to sit huddled on her bed, shutters closed, shades drawn; she schemed not to go upstairs by herself in the dark; she was preoccupied when old Lion took them off on a slow, jogging drive, for fear of a runaway.

Everybody was aware of her nervousness. Until it bored him, Henry Houghton was touched by it;—probably there is no man who is so intelligent that the Clinging Vine makes no appeal to him. Mrs. Houghton was impatient with it. Edith, who could not understand fear in any form, tried, in her friendly little way, to reason Eleanor out of one panic or another. The servants joked among themselves at the foolishness of "Mrs. Maurice"; and the monosyllabic Johnny Bennett, when told of some of Eleanor's scares, was bored. "Let's play Indian," said Johnny.

It was only Maurice who found all the scares—just as he found the silences and small jealousies—adorable! The silences meant unspeakable depths of thought; the jealousies were a sign of love. The terrors called for his protecting strength! One of the unfair irrationalities of love is that it may, at first, be attracted by the defects of the beloved, and later repelled by them. Maurice loved Eleanor for her defects. Once, when he and Edith were helping Mrs. Houghton weed her garden, he stopped grubbing, and sat down in the gold and bronze glitter of coreopsis, to expatiate upon the exquisiteness of the defects. Her wonderful mind: "She doesn't talk, because she is always thinking; her ideas are way over *my* head!" Her funny timidity: "She wants me to take care of her!" Her love: "She's—it sounds absurd!—but she's jealous, because she's so—well, fond of me, don't you know, that she sort of objects to having people round. Did you ever hear of anything so absurd?"

"I certainly never did," his old friend said, dryly.

"Well, but"—Maurice defended his wife—"it's because she cares about me, don't you know? She—well, this is in confidence—she said once that she'd like to live on a desert island, just with me!"

"So would I," said Edith. Her mother laughed:

"Tell her desert islands have to have a 'man Friday' — to say nothing of a few 'women Thursdays'!"

Eleanor was, Maurice said, like music heard far off, through mists and moonlight in a dark garden, "full of — of — what are those sweet-smelling things, that bloom only at night?" (Mary Houghton looked fatigued.) "Well, anyway, what I mean is that she isn't like ordinary people, like me —"

"Or Johnny," Edith broke in, earnestly.

"Johnny? Gosh! Why, Mrs. Houghton, things that don't touch most human beings, affect her terribly. The dark, or thunderstorms, or — or anything, makes her nervous. You understand?"

Mrs. Houghton said yes, she understood, but she would leave the rest of the weeding to her assistants ... In the studio, dropping her dusty garden gloves on a fresh canvas lying on the table, she almost wept:

"Henry, it is *too* tragic! She is such a goose, and he is so silly about her! What shall we do?"

"I'll tell you what not to do — spoil my new canvas! If you *really* want my advice: — tell Eleanor that the greatest compliment any husband can pay his wife is contained in four words: 'You never bore me'; and that if she isn't careful Maurice will never compliment her."

Down in the garden, no one was aware of any tragedy. "When I go to Fern Hill," Edith said, "I'm going to tell all the girls *I know Eleanor*! I'm 'ordinary,' too, beside her. And so is mother."

Maurice agreed. "We are all crude, compared to her."

Edith sighed with joy; if she had had any inclination to be contemptuous of Eleanor's timidity, it vanished when it was pointed out to her that it was really a sign of the Bride's infinite superiority.... So the three Houghtons accepted — one with amused pity, and the other with concern, and the third with admiration of such super-refinement, — the fact that Eleanor was a coward. Yet if she had not been a coward, something she did would not have been particularly brave, nor would it have wrung from Mary Houghton the admission: "I *like* her!"

The conquering incident happened in August. The hut up in the woods meant to Maurice and Edith and Johnny that eager grasping at hardship with which Age has no sympathy, but which is the very essence of Youth. Within a week of her arrival at Green Hill, Eleanor (who did not like hardship;) had been carried off for a day of eating smoky food, cooked on a camp fire, and watching cloud shadows drift across the valley and up and over the hills; she had wondered, silently, why Maurice liked this very tiring sort of thing?—and especially why he liked to have Edith go along! "A child of her age is such a nuisance," Eleanor thought. But he did like it, all of it!—the fatigue, and the smoke, and the grubby food—and Edith!—he liked it so much that, just before the time set for their departure for Mercer—and the position in a real-estate office, which had been secured for Maurice—he said:

"Nelly, let's camp out up in the cabin for our last week, all by ourselves!"

Edith's face fell, and so, for that matter, did the Bride's. Edith said, "By yourselves? Not Johnny and me, too?" And Eleanor said, "*At night?* Oh, Maurice!"

"It will be beautiful," he said; "there'll be a moon next week, and we'll sit up there and look down into the valley, and see the treetops lift up out of the mist—like islands from the foam of 'faerylands forlorn'! You'll love it."

"I'm crazy about camping," said Edith, eagerly;—and waited for an invitation, which was not forthcoming. Instead, Maurice, talking his plans over with her, made it quite clear that her room was better than her company. It was Edith's first experience in being left out, and it sobered her a little; but she swallowed the affront with her usual good sense:

"I guess he likes Eleanor more 'an me, so, 'course, it's nice to be by himself with her."

The prospect of being "by themselves" for a week was deeply moving to Maurice. And even Eleanor, though she quaked at the idea of spiders or thunderstorms, thought of the passion of it with a thrill. "We'll be all alone!" she said to herself.

The morning that they started gypsying, everything was very impatient and delightful. The packing, the rolling up of blankets, the stowing of cooking utensils, the consulting of food lists to make sure nothing was being forgotten—all meant much tearing about and bossing; then came the loading the stuff into the light wagon, which, with old Lion, Mr. Houghton had offered to convey the campers (and a temporary Edith) up to the top of the mountain. Edith was, of course, frankly envious, but accepted the privilege of even a day in camp with humble gratitude.

"Rover and Johnny and I will come up pretty often, even if it's only for an hour, because Eleanor must not hurt her hands by washing dishes," she said, earnestly (still fishing for an invitation).

But Maurice only agreed, as earnestly: "No! Imagine Eleanor washing dishes! But I don't want you to stay all night, Buster," he told her, candidly;

then he paused in his work, flung up his arms with a great breath of joyousness. "Great Scott!" he said. "I don't see why gypsies *ever* die!"

Edith felt an answering throb of ecstasy. "Oh, Maurice, I wish you and I were gypsies!" she said. She did not in the least resent his candor as to her presence during the week of camping; though just before they started her feelings really were a little hurt: it happened that in trying to help Eleanor pack, she was close enough to her to notice a thread on her hair; instantly, she put out a friendly and officious thumb and finger to remove it—at which Eleanor winced, and said, "*Ouch!*"

"I thought it was a white thread," Edith explained, abashed.

Eleanor said, sharply, "Please don't touch my hair!" which conveyed nothing to Edith except that the Bride—who instantly ran up to her room— "was mad." When she came back (the "thread" having disappeared) Edith was full of apologies.

"Awfully sorry I mussed your hair," she said.

She went up the mountain with them, walking on the hard grades, and trying to placate Eleanor by keeping a hand on Lion's bridle, so that she might feel sure he wouldn't run away. When at last, rather blown and perspiring, they reached the camp, Eleanor got out of the wagon and said she wanted to "help"; but Edith, still contrite about the "thread," said: "Not I'm not going to have you hurt your lovely hands!" In the late afternoon, having saved Eleanor's hands in every possible way, she left them, and thinking, without the slightest rancor, of the rough bliss she was not asked to share, went running down the mountain with Rover at her heels.

Eleanor, wondering at her willingness to take that long road home with only the lumbering old dog for company, was intensely glad to have her go.

"Girls of that age are so uninteresting," she told Maurice; "and now we'll be all by ourselves!"

"Yes; Adam and Eve," he said; "and twilight; and the world spread out like a garden! Do you see that glimmer over there to the left? That's the beginning of the river—our river!"

He had made her comfortable with some cushions piled against the trunk of a tree, and lighted a fire in a ring of blackened stones; then he brought her her supper, and ate his own on his knees beside her, watching eagerly for ways to serve her, laughing because she cringed when, from an overhanging bough, a spider let himself down upon her skirt, and hurrying to bring her a fresh cup of coffee, because an unhappy ant had scalded himself to death in her first cup. Afterward he would not let her "hurt her hands" by washing the dishes. When this was over, and the dusk was deepening, he went into the woods to the "lean-to" in which Lion was quartered, to see that the old horse was comfortable, but a minute later came crashing back through the underbrush, laughing, but provoked.

"That imp, Edith, didn't hitch him securely, and the old fellow has walked home, if you please—!"

"Lion—gone? Oh, what shall we do?"

"Ill pull the wagon down when I want to go back for food."

"*Pull* it?"

"Won't need much pulling! It will go down by itself. If I put you in it, I'll have to rope a log on behind as a brake, or it would run over me! I bet I give Edith a piece of my mind, when I get hold of her. But it doesn't really matter. I think I like it better to have not even Lion. Just you—and the stars. They are beginning to prick out," he said. He stretched himself on the ground beside her, his hands clasped under his head, and his happy eyes looking up into the abyss. "Sing, Star, sing!" he said. So she sang, softly:

> How many times do I love again?
> Tell me how many beads there are
>   In a silver chain
>   Of evening rain
> Unraveled from the tumbling main
> And threading the eye of a yellow star—
> So many times—

"It looks," she broke off, "a little black in the west? And—was that lightning?"

"Only heat lightning. And if it should storm,—I have you here, in my arms, alone!" He turned and caught her to him, and his mouth crushed hers. Her eyes closed, and her passion answered his, and all that he whispered. Yet while he kissed her, her eyes opened and she looked furtively beyond him, toward that gathering blackness.

They lay there together in the starlit dark, for a long time, his head on her breast. Sometimes she thrilled at his touch or low word, and sometimes she held his hand against her lips and kissed it—which made him protest— but suddenly he said, "By George! Nelly, I believe we are going to have a shower!"

Instantly she was alert with fright, and sat up, and looked down into the valley, where the heat lightning, which had been winking along the line of the hills, suddenly sharpened into a flash. "*Oh!*" she said, and held her breath until, from very far off, came a faint grumble of thunder. "Oh, Maurice!" she said, "it is horrible to be out here—if it thunders!"

"We won't be. Well go into the cabin, and we'll hear the rain on the roof, and the clash of the branches; and we'll see the lightning through the chinks—and I'll have you! Oh, Nelly, we shall be part of the storm!—and nothing in God's world can separate us."

But this time she could not answer with any elemental impulse; she had no understanding of "being part of the storm"; instead, she watched the horizon. "Oh!" she said, flinching. "I don't like it. What shall we do? Maurice, it *is* going to thunder!"

"I think I did feel a drop of rain," he said,—and held out his hand: "Yes, Star, rain! It's begun!" He helped her to her feet, gathered up some of the cushions, and hurried her toward the little shelter. She ran ahead of him, her very feet reluctant, lest the possible "snake" should curl in the darkness against her ankles; but once in the cabin, with a candle lighted, she could not see the lightning, so she was able to laugh at herself; when Maurice went out for the rest of the cushions, she charged him to *hurry*! "The storm will be here in a minute!" she called to him. And he called back:

"I'll only be a second!"

She stood in the doorway looking after him, and saw his figure outlined against the glimmer of their fire, which had already felt the spatter of the coming storm and was dying down; then, even as she looked, he seemed to plunge forward, and fall—the thud of that fall was like a blow on her throat! She gasped, "Maurice—" And again, "*Maurice!* Have you hurt yourself?"

He did not rise. A splash of rain struck her face; the mountain darkness was slit by a rapier of lightning, and there was a sudden violent illumination; she saw the tree and the cushions, and Maurice on the ground—then blackness, and a tremendous crash of thunder.

"Maurice!" she called. "Maurice!" The branches over the roof began to move and rustle, and there was a sudden downpour of rain; the camp fire went out, as if an extinguisher had covered it. She stood in the doorway for a breathless instant, then ran back into the cabin, and, catching the candle from the table, stepped out into the blackness; instantly the wind bore the little flame away!—then seemed to grip her, and twist her about, and beat her back into the house. In her terror she screamed his name; and as she did so, another flash of lightning showed her his figure, motionless on the ground.

"*He is dead*" she said to herself, in a whisper. "What shall I do?" Then, suddenly, she knew what to do: she remembered that she had noticed a lantern hanging on the wall near the door; and now something impelled her to get it. In the stifling darkness of the shack she felt her way to it, held its oily ring in her hand, thought, frantically, of matches, groped along toward the mantelpiece, stumbled over a chair—and clutched at the match box! Something made her open the isinglass slide, strike a match, and touch the blackened wick with the sulphurous sputter of flame,—the next moment, with the lighted lantern in her hand, she was out in the sheeting blackness of the rain!—running!—running!—toward that still figure by the deadened fire. Just before she reached it a twig rolled under her foot, and she said, "A *snake*,"—but she did not flinch. As she gained the circle of stones, a flash of lightning, with its instant and terrific crack and bellow of thunder, showed her a streak of blood on Maurice's face.... He had tripped and fallen, and his head had struck one of the blackened stones.

"He is dead," she said again, aloud. She put the lantern on the ground and knelt beside him; she had an idea that she should place her hand on his heart to see if he were alive. "He isn't," she told herself; but she laid her fingers, which were shaking so that she could not unfasten his coat, somewhere on his left side; she did not know whether there was any pulse; she knew nothing, except that he was "dead." She said this in a whisper, over and over. "He is dead. He is dead." The rain came down in torrents; the trees creaked and groaned in the wind; twice there were flashes of lightning and appalling roars of thunder. Maurice was perfectly still. The smoky glimmer of the lantern played on the thin streak of blood and made it look as though it was moving—trickling—

Then Eleanor began to think: "There ought to be a doctor...." If she left him, to bring help, he might bleed to death before she could get back to him. Instantly, as she said that, she knew that she did not believe that he was dead! She knew that she had hope. With hope, a single thought possessed her. *She must take him down the mountain....* But how? She could not carry him;—she had managed to prop him up against her knee, his blond head lolling forward, awfully, on his breast—but she knew that to carry him would be impossible. And Lion was not there! "I couldn't have harnessed him if he were," she thought.

She was entirely calm, but her mind was working rapidly: The wagon was in the lean-to! Could she get him into it? The road was downhill.... Almost to Doctor Bennett's door....

Instantly she sprang to her feet and, with the pale gleam of the lantern zigzagging across the path, she ran back to the shed; just as she reached it, a glimmer of light fell on the soaked earth, and she looked up with a start and saw the moon peering out between two ragged, swiftly moving clouds; then all was black again—but the rain was lessening, and there had been no lightning for several minutes. "He will die; I must save him," she said, her lips stiff with horror. She lifted the shafts of the wagon, and gave a little pull; it moved easily enough, and, guiding it along the slight decline, she brought it to Maurice's side. There, looking at him, she said again, rigidly:

"He will die; I must save him."

As Henry Houghton said afterward, "It was impossible!—so she did it."

It took her more than an hour to do it, to pull and lift and shove the inert figure! Afterward she used to wonder how she had done it; wonder how she had given the final *push*, which got his sagging body up on to the floor of the wagon! It had strained every part of her;—her shoulder against his hips, her head in the small of his back, her hands gripping his heavy, dangling legs. She was soaking wet; her hair had loosened, and stray locks were plastered across her forehead. She grunted like a toiling animal.

It seemed as if her heart would crack with her effort, her muscles tear; she forgot the retreating rumble of the storm, the brooding, dripping forest stillness; she forgot even her certainty that he would die. She entirely forgot herself. She only knew—straining, gasping, sweating—that she must get the body—the dead body perhaps!—into the wagon. And she did it! Just as she did it, she heard a faint groan. Her heart stood still with terror, then beat frantically with joy.

He was alive!

She ran back to the cabin for the cushions he had saved from the rain, and pushed them under his head; then tied the lantern to the whip socket; then recalled what he had said about "roping a log on behind as a brake." "Of course!" she thought; and managed,—the splinters tearing her hands— to fasten a fairly heavy piece of wood under the rear axle, so that it might bump along behind the wagon as a drag. She pondered as she did these things why she should know so certainly how they must be done? But when they were done, she said, *"Now!"*... and went and stood between the shafts.

It was after midnight when the descent began. The moon rode high among fleecy clouds, but on either side of the road gulfs of darkness lay under motionless foliage. Sometimes the smoky light from the swaying lantern shone on a wet black branch, snapped by the gale and lying in the path, and Eleanor, seeing it, wedging her heels into the mud and sliding stones of the road, and straining backward between the shafts, would say, "A snake.... I must save Maurice." Sometimes she would hear, above the crunching of the wheels behind her, a faint noise in the undergrowth: a breaking twig, a brushing sound, as of a furtive footstep—and she would say, "A man.... I must save Maurice."

The yellow flame of the lantern was burning white in the dawn, as, holding back against the weight of the wagon—the palms of her bleeding hands clenched on the shafts, her feet slipping, her ankles twisted and wrenched—by and by, with the tears of physical suffering streaming down her face, she reached the foot of the mountain. The, thin, cool air of morning flowed about her in crystalline stillness; suddenly the sun tipped the green bowl of the world, and all at once shadows fell across the road like bars. They seemed to her, in her daze of terror and exhaustion, insurmountable: the road was level now, but she pulled and pulled, agonizingly, over those bars of nothingness; then one wheel sank into a rut, and the wagon came to a dead standstill; but at the same moment she saw ahead of her, among the trees, Doctor Bennett's dark, sleeping house. So, dropping the shafts, she went stumbling and running, to pound on the door, and gasp out:

"Come—help—Maurice—come—"

"I think," she said afterward, lying like a broken thing upon her bed, "I was able to do it, because I kept saying, 'I must save Maurice.' Of course, to save Maurice, I wouldn't mind dying."

"My dear, you are magnificent!" Mary Houghton said, huskily. Then she told her husband: "Henry, I *like* her! I never thought I would, but I do."

"I'll never say 'Mr. F.'s aunt' again!" he promised, with real contrition.

It was Eleanor's conquering moment, for everybody liked her, and everybody said she was 'magnificent'—except Maurice, who, as he got well, said almost nothing.

"I can't talk about it," was all he had to say, choking. "She's given her life for mine," he told the doctor.

"I hope not," Doctor Bennett said, "I *hope* not. But it will take months, Maurice, for her to get over this. As for saving your life, my boy, she didn't. She made things a lot more dangerous for you. She did the wrong thing— with greatness! You'd have come to, after a while. But don't tell her so."

"Well, I should say not!" Maurice said, hotly. "She'll never know *that*! And anyway, sir, I don't believe it. I believe she saved my life."

"Well, suit yourself," the doctor said, good-naturedly; "but I tell you one thing: whether she saved your life or not, she did a really wonderful thing—considering her temperament."

Maurice frowned: "I don't think her temperament makes any difference. It would have been wonderful for anybody."

"Well, suit yourself," Doctor Bennett said again; "only, if Edith had done it, say, for Johnny, who weighs nearly as much as you, I wouldn't have called it particularly wonderful."

"Oh, Edith," Maurice said, grinning; "no; I suppose not. I see what you mean." And to himself he added: "Edith is like an ox, compared to Star. Just flesh and blood. No nerves. No soul. Doctor Bennett was right. Eleanor's temperament does make it more wonderful."

CHAPTER VII

It was after this act of revealing and unnecessary courage, that the Houghton family entirely accepted Eleanor. There were a few days of anxiety about her, and about Maurice, too; for, though his slight concussion was not exactly alarming—yet, "Keep your shirt on," Doctor Bennett cautioned him; "don't get gay. And don't talk to Mrs. Curtis." So Maurice lay in his bed in another room, and entered, silently, into a new understanding of love, which, as soon as he was permitted to see Eleanor, he tried stumblingly to share with her.

Physically, she was terribly prostrated; but spiritually, feeding on those stumbling words, she rejoiced like a strong man to run a race! She saw no confession in the fact that everybody was astonished at what she had done; she was astonished herself. "I wasn't afraid!" she said, wonderingly.

"It was because you liked Maurice more than you were scared," Edith said; she offered this explanation the day that Maurice had been allowed to come across the hall, rather shakily, to adore his wife.

His first sight of her was a great shock.... The strain of that terrible night had blanched and withered her face; there were lines on her forehead that never left it.

Edith, sneaking in behind him, said under her breath: "Goodness! Don't she look old!"

She did. But as Maurice fell on his knees beside her, it seemed as if she drank youth from his lips. Under his kisses her worn face bloomed with joy.

"It was nothing—nothing," she insisted, stroking his thick hair with her trembling hand, and trying to silence his words of wondering worship.

"I was not worthy of it.... To think that you—" He hid his face on her shoulder.

Afterward, when he went back to his own room, she lay, smiling tranquilly to herself; her look was the look one sees on the face of a woman who, in that pallid hour after the supreme achievement of birth, has looked upon her child. She was entirely happy. From the open door of Maurice's room came, now and then, the murmur of Edith's honest little voice, or

Maurice's chuckle. They were talking about her, she knew, and the happy color burned in her cheeks. When he came in for his second visit, late that afternoon, she asked him, archly, what he and Edith had been talking about so long in his room?

"I believe you were telling her what a goose I am about thunderstorms," she said.

"I was not!" he declared—and her eyes shone. But when she urged—

"Well, what *were* you talking about?" he couldn't remember anything but a silly story of Edith's hens. He repeated it, and Eleanor sighed; how could he be interested in anything so childish!

As it happened, he was not; he had scarcely listened to Edith. The only thing that interested Maurice now, was what Eleanor had done for him! Thinking of it, he brooded over her, silently, his cheek against hers, then Mrs. Houghton came in and banished him, saying that Eleanor must go to sleep; "and you and Edith must keep quiet!" she said.

He was so contrite that, tiptoeing to his own room, he told poor faithful Edith her voice was too loud: "You disturb Eleanor. So dry up, Skeezics!"

As he grew stronger, and was able to go downstairs, Edith felt freer to talk to him—for down on the porch, or out in the garden, her eager young voice would not reach those languid ears. Then, suddenly, all her chances to talk stopped: "What's the matter with Maurice?" she pondered, crossly; "he's backed out of helping me. Why can't he go on shingling the chicken coop?" For it was while this delightful work was under way that it, and "talk," came to an abrupt end.

The shingling, begun joyously by the big boy and the little girl on Monday, promised several delightfully busy mornings.... Of course the setting out for Mercer had been postponed; there was no possibility of moving Eleanor for the present; so Maurice's "business career," as he called it, with grinning pomposity, had to be delayed—Eleanor turned white at the mere suggestion of convalascing at Green Hill without him! Consequently Maurice, when not worshiping his wife, had nothing to do, and Edith had seized the opportunity to make him useful.... "We'll shingle my henhouse," she had announced. Maurice liked the scheme as much as she did. The September air, the smell of the fresh shingles, the sitting with one leg doubled under you, and the other outstretched on the hot slope of the roof, the tap-tapping of the hammers, the bossing of Edith, the trying to talk of Eleanor, and thunderstorms, while you hold eight nails between your lips; then the pause while Edith climbs down the ladder and runs to the kitchen for hot cookies; all these things would be a delightful occupation for any intelligent person!

"It'll take three mornings to do it," Edith said, importantly; and Maurice said:

"It will, because you keep putting the wrong end up! I wish Eleanor was well enough to do it," he said—and then burst into self-derisive chuckles: "Imagine Eleanor straddling that ridgepole! It would scare her stiff!"

It was after this talk that Maurice "backed out" on the job—but Edith never knew why. She saw no connection between the unfinished roof, and the fact that that same afternoon, sitting on the floor in the Bride's room, she had, in her anxiety to be entertaining, repeated Maurice's remark about the ridgepole. Eleanor, who had had an empty morning, listening to the distant tapping of hammers, had drooped a weary lip.

"I should hate it. Horrid, dirty work!"

"Oh no! It's nice, clean work," Edith corrected her.

"But *you* wouldn't like it, of course," she said, with satisfaction; "you'd be scared! You're scared of everything, Maurice says. You were scared to death, up on the mountain."

Eleanor was silent.

"He thinks it's lovely for you to be scared; it's funny about Maurice," said Edith, thoughtfully; "he doesn't like it when *I'm* scared—not that I ever am, now, but I used to be when I was a child."

The color flickered on Eleanor's cheeks: "Edith, I'll rest now," she said; her voice broke.

Edith looked at her, open-mouthed. "Why, Eleanor!" she said; "what's the matter? Are you mad at anything? Have you a stomachache? I'll run for mother!"

"There's nothing the matter. But—but I wish you'd tell Maurice to come and speak to me."

Edith tore downstairs, and out of the front door: "Maurice! Where are you?"—then, catching sight of him, reading and smoking in a hammock slung between two of the big columns on the east porch, she rushed at him, and pulled him to his astonished feet. "Eleanor wants you! Something's the matter, and—"

Before she could finish, Maurice was tearing upstairs, two steps at a time....

And so it was that Edith, sulkily, worked on the roof by herself.

Yet Maurice had not entirely "backed out." ... The very next morning, before Edith was awake, he had gone out to the henhouse, and, alone, done more than his share of the shingling.

"But, Maurice, why didn't you wake me?" Edith protested, when she discovered what he had done. "I'd have gone out, too!"

"I liked doing it by myself," Maurice evaded.

And for five minutes Edith was sulky again. "He puts on airs, 'cause he's married! Well, I don't care. He can shingle the whole roof by himself if he wants to! I don't like married men, anyhow."

The married man had, indeed, wanted to be by himself—to put the nails in his mouth, and to sit on the cold, slippery shingles in the gray September morning, and to tap-tap-tap—and think, and think.

But he didn't like his thoughts very well....

He thought how he had rushed upstairs, terrified lest Eleanor was fainting or had a "stomachache," or something—and found her sitting up in bed, her cheeks red and glazed with tears, her round, full chin quivering. He thought how he had tried to make out what she was driving at about Edith, and the chicken coop, and the ridgepole!

"You told Edith I was scared!"

Maurice's bewilderment was full of stumbling questions: "Told Edith? When? What?"

And as she said "when" and "what," ending with, "You said I am scared!" Maurice could only say, blankly. "But my darling, you *are*!"

"You may think I am a fool, but to tell Edith so—"

"But Great Scott! I didn't!"

"I won't have you talking me over with Edith; she's a *child*! It was just what you did when you danced three times with that girl who said—Edith is as rude as she was!—and she's a *child*. How can you like to be with a child?" Of course, it was all her fear of Youth,—but Eleanor did not know that; she thought she was hurt at the boy's neglect. Her face, wet with tears, was twitching, her voice—that lovely voice!—was shrill in his astonished ears....

Maurice, on the sloping roof, in the chill September dawn, his fingers numb on the frosty nails, stopped hammering, and leaned his chin on his fist, and thought: "She's sick. She almost killed herself to save me; so her nerve has all gone. That's why she talked—that way." He put a shingle in its place, and planted a nail; "it was because she was scared that what she did was so brave! I couldn't make her see that the more scared she was, the braver she was. It wouldn't have been brave in that gump, Edith, without a nerve in her body. But why is she down on Edith? I suppose she's a nuisance to a person with a wonderful mind like Eleanor's. Talks too much. I'll tell her to dry up when she's with Eleanor." And again he heard that strange voice: "You like to talk to a *child*."

Maurice, pounding away on Edith's roof, grew hot with misery, not because it was so terrible to have Eleanor angry with him; not even because he had finally got mad, and answered back, and said, "Don't be silly!" The real misery was something far deeper than this half-amused remorse. It was that those harmless, scolding words of his held a perfectly new idea: he had said, "Don't be silly." *Was Eleanor silly?*

Now, to a man whose feeling about his wife has been a sort of awe, this question is terrifying. Maurice, in his boy's heart, had worshiped in Eleanor, not just the god of Love, but the love of God. And was she—*silly*? No! Of course not! He pounded violently, hit his thumb, put it into his mouth, then proceeded, mumblingly, to bring his god back from the lower shrine of a pitying heart, to the high alter of a justifying mind: Eleanor was ill.... She was nervous.... She was an exquisite being of mist and music and courage and love! So of course she was sensitive to things ordinary people did not feel. Saying this, and fitting the shingles into place, suddenly the warm and happy wave of confident idealism began to flood in upon him, and immediately his mind as well as his heart was satisfied. He reproached himself for having been scared lest his star was just a common candle, like himself. He had been cruel to judge her, as he might have judged her had she been well—or a gump like Edith! For had she been well, she would not have been "silly"! Had she been well—instead of lying there in her bed, white and strained and trembling, all because she had saved his life, harnessing herself to that wagon, and bringing him, in the darkness, through a thousand terrors—nonexistent, to be sure, but none the less real—to safety and life! Oh, how could he have even thought the word "silly"? He was ashamed and humble; never again would he be cross to her! "Silly? I'm the silly one! I'm an ass. I'll tell her so! I don't suppose she'll ever forgive me. She said I 'didn't understand her'; well, I didn't! But she'll never have cause to say it again! I understand her now," Then, once more, he thought, frowning, "But why is she so down on Edith?"

That Eleanor's irritation was jealousy—not of Edith, but of Edith's years—never occurred to him. So all he said was, "She oughtn't to be down on Edith; *she* has always appreciated her!" Edith had never said that Eleanor was "silly"! But so long as it bothered Eleanor (being nervous) to have the imp round, he'd tell her not to be a nuisance. "You can say anything to Skeezics; she has sense. She understands."

But all the same, Maurice shingled his part of the henhouse before breakfast.

Maurice did not call Eleanor "silly" again for a long time. There was always—when she was unreasonable—the curbing memory that her reasonableness had been shaken by that assault of darkness and fear, and the terrible fatigue of saving his robust young life. Furthermore, Doctor Bennett—telling Henry Houghton that Eleanor had done the worst possible thing, "magnificently"—told Maurice she had "nervous prostration,"—a cloaking phrase which kindly doctors often give to perplexed husbands, so that the egotism of sickly wives may be covered up! So Maurice, repeating to himself these useful words, saw only ill health, not silliness, in Eleanor's occasional tears. It was a week after the shingling of the henhouse, that, leaving her to recuperate still further at Green Hill, he started in on his job of "office boy"—his jocose title for his position in the real-estate office in Mercer. Eleanor did not want to be left, and said so, wistfully.

"I'll come up for Sundays," Maurice comforted her, tenderly.

On these weekly visits the Houghtons were impressed by his tenderness; he played solitaire with his wife by the hour; he read poetry to her until she fell asleep; and he told her everything he had done and every person he had seen, while he was away from her! But the rest of the household didn't get much enjoyment out of Eleanor. Even the adoring Edith had moments when admiration had to be propped up by Doctor Bennett's phrase. As, for instance, on one of Maurice's precious Sundays, he and she and Johnny Bennett and Rover and old Lion climbed up to the cabin to make things shipshape before closing the place for the winter.

"You'll be away from me all day," Eleanor said, and her eyes filled.

Maurice said he hated to leave her, but he had always helped Edith on this closing-up job.

"Oh, well; go, if you want to," Eleanor said; "but I don't see how you can enjoy being with a perfect child, like Edith!"

Maurice went—not very happily. But it was such a fine, tingling day of hard work, in a joyous wind, with resulting appetites, and much yelling at each other—"Here, drop that!" ... "Hurry up, slow poke!"—that he was happy again before he knew it. After the work was over they had a lazy hour before the fire, their eyes stinging with smoke which seemed to envelop them, no matter on which side they sat; an hour in which Rover drowsed at Maurice's feet, and Johnny, in spectacles, read *A Boy's Adventures in the Forests of Brazil,* and Edith gabbled about Eleanor....

"Oh, I wish *I* was married," Edith said; "I'd just love to save my husband's life!"

Maurice said little, except to ask Johnny if he had got to such and such a place in the *Adventures,* or to assent to Edith's ecstasies; but once he sighed, and said Eleanor was awfully pulled down by that—that night.

"I should think," Edith said, "you'd feel she'd just about died for you, like people in history who died for each other."

"I do," Maurice said, soberly.

When they drove home in the dusk, Maurice singing, loudly; Edith, on the front seat of the wagon, snuggling against him; Johnny standing up, balancing himself by holding on to their shoulders, and old Rover jogging along on the footpath,—they were all in great spirits, until a turn in the road showed them Eleanor, sitting on a log, looking rather white.

"Suffering snakes!" said Maurice, breaking off in the middle of a word. Before Lion could quite stop, he was at his wife's side. "Eleanor! How did you get here? ... You *walked*? Oh, Star, you oughtn't to have done such a thing!"

"I was frightened about you. It was so late. I was afraid something had happened. I came to look for you."

Edith and Johnny looked on aghast; then Edith called out: "Why, Eleanor! I wouldn't let anything happen to Maurice!"

Maurice, kneeling beside his wife, had put his arms around her and was soothing her with all sorts of gentlenesses: "Dear, you mustn't worry so! Nelly, don't cry; why, darling, we were having such a good time, we never noticed that it was getting late ..."

"You forgot me," Eleanor said; "as long as you had Edith, you never thought how I might worry!" She hid her face in her hands.

Maurice came back to the wagon; "Edith," he said, in a low voice, "would you and Johnny mind getting out and walking? I'll bring Eleanor along later. I'm sorry, but she's—she's tired."

Edith said in a whisper, "'Course not!" Then, without a look behind her at the crying woman on the log, and the patient, mortified boy bending over her, she, and the disgusted and more deliberate Johnny, ran down the road into the twilight. Edith was utterly bewildered. With her inarticulate consciousness of the impropriety of emotion, naked, *in public!* was the shyness of a child in meeting a stranger—for that crying woman was practically a stranger. She wasn't the Bride—silent and lovely! At Johnny's gate she said, briefly, "'Night!" and went on, running—running in the dusk. When she reached the house, and found her father and mother on the east porch, she was breathless, which accounted for her brevity in saying that Maurice and Eleanor were coming—and she was just starved! In the dining room, eating a very large supper, she listened for the wheels of the wagon and reflected: "Why was Eleanor mad at *me*? She was mad at Maurice, too. But most at me. Why?" She took an enormous spoonful of sliced peaches, and stared blankly ahead of her.

Ten minutes later, hearing wheels grating on the gravel at the front door, and Maurice's voice, subdued and apologetic, she pushed her chair away from the table, rushed through the pantry and up the back stairs. She didn't know why she fled. She only knew that she couldn't face Eleanor, who would sit with Maurice while he bolted a supper for which—though Edith didn't know it!—all appetite had gone. In her room in the ell, Edith shut the door, and, standing with her back against it, tried to answer her own question:

"Why was Eleanor mad?" But she couldn't answer it. Jealousy, as an emotion, in herself or anybody else, was absolutely unknown to her. She had probably never even heard the word—except in the Second Commandment, or as a laughing reproach to old Rover—so she really did not know enough to use it now to describe Eleanor's behavior. She only said, "Maybe it's the nervous prostration? Well, I don't like her very much. I'm glad she won't be at Fern Hill when I go there." To be a Bride—and yet to cry before people! "Crying before people," Edith said, "is just like taking off all your clothes before people—I don't care how bad her nervous prostration is; it isn't nice! But why is she mad at me? That isn't sense."

You can't run other people's feelings to cover, and try to find their cause, without mental and moral development; all this analysis lessened very visibly Edith's childishness; also, it made her rather rudely cold to Eleanor, whose effort to reinstate herself in the glories of the little girl's imagination only resulted in still another and entirely new feeling in Edith's mind—contempt.

"If she had a right to be mad at me yesterday—why isn't she mad to-day?" Edith reasoned.

Eleanor was quick to feel the contempt. "I don't care for Edith," she told Maurice, who looked surprised.

"She's only a child," he said.

Edith seemed especially a child now to Maurice, since he had embarked on his job at Mercer. Not only was she unimportant to him, but, in spite of his mortification at that scene on the road, his Saturday-night returns to his wife were blowing the fires of his love into such a glory of devotion, that Edith was practically nonexistent! His one thought was to take Eleanor to Mercer. He wanted her all to himself! Also, he had a vague purpose of being on his dignity with a lot of those Mercer people: Eleanor's aunt, just back from Europe; Brown and Hastings—cubs! But below this was the inarticulate feeling that, away from the Houghtons, especially away from Edith, he might forget his impulse to use—for a second time—that dreadful word "silly."

So, as the 20th of October approached—the day when they were to go back to town—he felt a distinct relief in getting away from Green Hill. The relief was general. Edith felt it, which was very unlike Edith, who had always sniffled (in private) at Maurice's departure! And her father and mother felt it:

"Eleanor's mind," Henry Houghton said, "is exactly like a drum—sound comes out of emptiness!"

"But Maurice seems to like the sound," Mrs. Houghton reminded him; "and she loves him."

"She wants to monopolize him," her husband said; "I don't call that love; I call it jealousy. It must be uncomfortable to be jealous," he ruminated; "but the really serious thing about it is that it will bore any man to death. Point that out to her, Mary! Tell her that jealousy is self-love, plus the consciousness of your own inferiority to the person of whom you are jealous. And it has the same effect on love that water has on fire. My definition ought to be in a dictionary!" he added, complacently.

"What sweet jobs you do arrange for me!" she said; "and as for your definition, I can give you a better one—and briefer: 'Jealousy is Human Natur'! But I don't believe Eleanor's jealous, Henry; she's only conscious, poor girl! of Maurice's youth. But there is something I *am* going to tell her...."

She told her the day before the bridal couple (Edith still reveled in the phrase!) started for Mercer. "Come out into the orchard," Mary Houghton called upstairs to Eleanor, "and help me gather windfalls for jelly."

"I must pack Maurice's things," Eleanor called over the banisters, doubtfully; "he's a perfect boy about packing; he put his boots in with his collars."

"Oh, come along!" said Mrs. Houghton. And Eleanor yielded, scolding happily while she pinned her hat on before the mirror in the hall.

In the orchard they picked up some apples, then sat down on the bleached stubble of the mowed hillside and looked over at the dark mass of the mountain, behind which a red sun was trampling waist deep through leaden clouds. "How *can* I bring it in?" Mrs. Houghton thought; "it won't do to just throw a warning at her!"

But she didn't have to throw it; Eleanor invited it. "I'm glad we're going to the hotel, just at first," she said; "Auntie says I don't know anything about keeping house, and I get worried for fear I won't make Maurice comfortable. I tell him so all the time!"

"I wouldn't put things into his head, Eleanor," Mrs. Houghton said (beginning her "warning"); "I mean things that you don't want him to feel. I remember when my first baby was coming—the little boy we lost—" she stopped and bit her lip; the "baby" had been gone for nearly twenty years, but he was still her little boy—"I was very forlorn, and I couldn't do anything, or go anywhere; and Henry stayed at home with me like a saint. Well, I told my father that I had told Henry it was hard on him to 'sit at home with an invalid wife.' And father said, 'If you tell him so often enough, he'll agree with you,' There's a good deal in that, Eleanor?"

"I suppose there is," Maurice's wife said, vaguely.

"So, if I were you," Mrs. Houghton said, still feeling her way, "I wouldn't give him the idea that you are any—well, older than he is. A wife might be fifty years older than her husband, and if her *spirit* was young, years wouldn't make a bit of difference!"

Eleanor took this somewhat roundabout advice very well. "The only thing in the world I want," she said, simply, "is to make him happy."

They went back to the house in silence. But that night Eleanor paused in putting some last things into her trunk, and, going over to Maurice, kissed his thick hair. "Maurice," she said, "are you happy?"

"You bet I am!"

"You haven't said so once to-day."

"I haven't said I'm alive," he said, grinning. "Oh, Star, won't it be wonderful when we can go away from the whole caboodle of 'em, and just be by ourselves?"

"That's what I want!" she said; "just to be alone with you. I wish we could live on a desert island!..."

Down in the studio, Mr. Houghton, smoking up to the fire limit a cigar grudgingly permitted by his wife ("It's your eighth to-day," she reproached him), Henry Houghton, listening to his Mary's account of the talk in the orchard, told her what he thought of her: "May you be forgiven! Your intentions are doubtless excellent, but your truthfulness leaves something to be desired: 'Years won't make any difference'? Mary! Mary!"

But she defended herself: "I mean, 'years' can't kill love—the highest love—the love that grows out of, *and then outgrows*, the senses! The body may be just an old glove—shabby, maybe; but if the hand inside the glove is alive, what real difference does the shabbiness make? If Eleanor's mind doesn't get rheumatic, *and if she will forget herself!*—they'll be all right. But if she thinks of herself—" Mary Houghton sighed; her husband ended her sentence for her:

"She'll upset the whole kettle of fish?"

"What I'm afraid of," she said, with a troubled look, "is that you are right:—she's inclined to be jealous, I saw her frown when he was playing checkers with Edith. I wanted to tell her, but didn't dare to, that jealousy is as amusing to people who don't feel it, as it is undignified in people who do."

"My darling, you are a brute," said Mr. Houghton; "I have long suspected it, *in re* tobacco. As for Eleanor, I would never have such cruel thoughts! *I* belong to the gentler sex. I would merely refer her to Mr. F.'s aunt."

CHAPTER VIII

They reached Mercer in the rainy October dusk. It was cold and raw, and a bleak wind blew up the river, which, with its shifting film of oil, bent like a brown arm about the grimy, noisy town. The old hotel, with its Doric columns grimed with years of smoky river fogs, was dark, and smelled of soot; and the manners of the waiters and chambermaids would have set Eleanor's teeth on edge, except that she was so absorbed in the thrill of being back under the roof which had sheltered them in those first days of bliss.

"Do you *remember?*" she said, significantly.

Maurice, looking after suitcases and hand bags, said, absently, "Remember what?" She told him "what" and he said: "Yes. Where do you want this trunk put, Eleanor?"

She sighed; to sentimentalize and receive no response in kind, is like sitting down on a chair which isn't there. After dinner, when she and Maurice came up to their room, which had fusty red hangings and a marble-topped center table standing coldly under a remote chandelier, she sighed again, for Maurice said that, as for this hole of a hotel, the only thing *he* thought of, was how soon they could get out of it! "I can get that little house I told you about, only it's rather out of the way. Not many of your kind of people 'round!"

She knelt down beside him, pushing his newspaper aside and pressing her cheek against his. "*That* doesn't make any difference!" she said; "I'm glad not to know anybody. I just want you! I don't want people."

"Neither do I," Maurice agreed; "I'd have to shell out my cigars to 'em if they were men!"

"Oh, is that your reason?" she said, laughing.

"Say, Star, would you mind moving? I was just reading—"

She rose, and, going over to the window, stood looking out at the streaming rain in one of those empty silences which at first had been so alluringly mysterious to him. She was waiting for his hand on her shoulder, his kiss on her hair—but he was immersed in his paper. "How can he be interested about football, *now*, when we're alone?" she thought, wistfully. Then, to remind him of lovelier things, she began to sing, very softly:

"Art thou poor, yet hast thou golden slumbers?
0 sweet content!
To add to golden numbers, golden numbers,
O sweet content!—0 sweet, O sweet content—"

He dropped his paper and listened—and it seemed as if music made itself visible in his ardent, sensitive face! After a while he got up and went over to the window, and kissed her gently ...

Maurice was very happy in these first months in Mercer. The Weston office liked him—and admired him, also, which pleased his young vanity!— though he was jeered at for an incorrigible and alarming truthfulness which pointed out disadvantages to possible clients, but which—to the amazement of the office—frequently made a sale! As a result he acquired, after a while, several small gilt hatchets, presented by the "boys," and also the nickname of "G. Washington." He accepted these tributes with roars of laughter, but pointed to results: "*I get the goods!*" So, naturally, he liked his work—he liked it very much! The joy of bargaining and his quick and perhaps dangerously frank interest in clients as personalities, made him a most beguiling salesman; as a result he became, in an astonishingly short time, a real force in the office; all of which hurried him into maturity. But the most important factor in his happiness was his adoration of Eleanor. He was perfectly contented, evening after evening in the hotel, to play her accompaniments (on a rented piano), read poetry aloud, and beat her at solitaire. Also, she helped him in his practicing with a certain sweet authority of knowledge, which kept warm in his heart the sense of her infinite superiority. So when, later, they found a house, he entered very gayly upon the first test of married life— house furnishing! It was then that his real fiber showed itself. It is a risky time for all husbands and wives, a time when it is particularly necessary to "consider the stars"! It needs a fine sense of proportion as to the value, relatively, of peace and personal judgment, to give up one's idea in regard, say, to the color of the parlor rug. Maurice's likes and dislikes were emphatic as to rugs and everything else,—but his sense of proportion was sound, so Eleanor's taste,—and peace,—prevailed. It was good taste, so he really had nothing to complain of, though he couldn't for the life of him see why she picked out a *picture* paper for a certain room in the top of the house! "I thought I'd have it for a smoking room," he said, ruefully; "and a lot of pink lambs and green chickens cavorting around don't seem very suitable. Still, if you like it, it's all right!" The memory of the night on the mountain, when Eleanor gave all she had of strength and courage and fear and passion to the saving of his life—made pink lambs, or anything else, "all right"! When the house-furnishing period was over, and they settled down, the "people" Eleanor didn't want to see, seemed to have no particular desire to see them; so their solitude of two (and Bingo, who barked whenever Maurice put his arms around Eleanor) was not broken in upon—which made for domestic, even if stultifying, content. But the thing that really kept them happy during that first rather dangerous year, was the smallness of their income. They had very little money; even with Eleanor's six hundred, it was nearer two thousand dollars than three, and that, for people who had always lived in more or less luxury, was very nearly poverty;—for which, of course, they had reason, so far as married happiness went, to thank God! If there are no children, it is the limited income which can be most certainly relied upon to provide the common interest which welds husband and wife together. This more or less uncomfortable, and always anxious, interest, generally develops in that critical time when the heat of passion has begun to cool, and the friction of the commonplace produces a certain warmth of its own. These are the days when conjugal criticism, which has been smothered under the undiscriminating admiration of first love, begins to raise its head—an ugly head, with a mean eye, in which there is neither imagination nor humor. When this criticism begins to creep into daily life, and the lure of the bare shoulder and perfumed hair lessens—because they are as assured as bread and butter!—it is then that this saving unity of purpose in acquiring bread and butter comes to the rescue.

It came to the rescue of Maurice and Eleanor; they had many welding moments of anxiety on his part, and eager self-sacrifice on her part; of adding up columns of figures, with a constantly increasing total, which had to be subtracted from a balance which decreased so rapidly that Eleanor felt quite sure that the bank was cheating them! Of course they did not appreciate the value of this blessed young poverty—who of us ever appreciates poverty while we are experiencing it? We only know its value when we look back upon it! But they did—or at least Eleanor did—appreciate their isolation, never realizing that no human life can refresh another unless it may itself drink deep of human sympathies and hopes. Maurice could take this refreshment through business contacts; but, except for Mrs. O'Brien, and her baby grandson, Don, Eleanor's acquaintances in Mercer had been limited to her aunt's rather narrow circle.

When Mrs. Newbolt got back from Europe, Maurice was introduced to this circle at a small dinner given to the bride and groom to indicate family forgiveness. The guests were elderly people, who talked politics and surgical operations, and didn't know what to say to Maurice, whose blond hair and good-humored blue eyes made him seem distressingly young. Nor did Maurice know what to say to them.

"I'd have gone to sleep," he told Eleanor, in exploding mirth, on their way home, "if it hadn't been that the food was so mighty good! I kept awake, in spite of that ancient dame who hashed up the Civil War, just to see what the next course would be!"

It was about this time that Maurice began to show a little longing for companionship (outside the office) of a kind which did not remember the Civil War. His evenings of solitaire and music were awfully nice, but—

"Brown and Hastings are in college," he told his wife; "and Mort's on a job at his father's mills. I miss 'em like the devil."

"*I* don't want anyone but you," she said, and the tears started to her eyes; he asked her what she was crying about, and she said, "Oh, nothing." But of course he knew what it was, and he had to remind himself that "she had nervous prostration"; otherwise that terrible, hidden word "silly" would have been on his lips.

Eleanor, too, had a hidden word; it was the word "boy." It was Mrs. Newbolt who thrust it at her, in those first days of settling down into the new house. She had come in, waddling ponderously on her weak ankles, to see, she said, how the young people were getting along: "At least, *one* of you is young!" Mrs. Newbolt said, jocosely. She was still puffing from a climb upstairs, to find Eleanor, dusty and disheveled, in a little room in the top of the house. She was sitting on the floor in front of a trunk, with Bingo fast asleep on her skirt.

"What's this room to be?" said Mrs. Newbolt; then looked at the wall paper, gay with prancing lambs and waddling ducks, and Noah's Ark trees. "What! a *nursery*?" said Mrs. Newbolt; "do you mean—?"

"No," Eleanor said, reddening; "oh no! I only thought that if—"

"You are forehanded," said Mrs. Newbolt, and was silent for almost a minute. The vision of Eleanor choosing a nursery paper, for little eyes (which might never be born!) to look upon, touched her. She blinked and swallowed, then said, crossly: "You're thinner! For heaven's sake don't lose your figger! My dear grandmother used to say—I can see her now, skimmin' milk pans, and then runnin' her finger round the rim and lickin' it. She was a Dennison. I've heard her say to her daughters, I'd rather have you lose your virtue than lose your figger'; and my dear grandfather—your great-grandfather—wore knee breeches; he said—well, I suppose you'd be shocked if I told you what he said? He said, 'If a gal loses one, she—' No; I guess I won't tell you. Old maids are so refined! *He* wasn't an old maid, I can tell you! I brought a chocolate drop for Bingo. Have you a cook?"

Eleanor, gasping with the effort to keep up with the torrent, said, "Yes; but she doesn't know how to do things."

Mrs. Newbolt raised pudgy and protesting hands. "Get somebody who can do things! Come here, little Bingo! Eleanor, if you don't feed that boy, you'll lose him. I remember puffectly well hearin' my dear father say, 'If you want to catch a man's heart, set a trap in his stomach.' Bingo! Bingo!" (The little dog, standing on his hind legs, superciliously accepted a chocolate drop—then ran back to Eleanor.) "Maurice will be a man one of these days, and a man can't live on love; he wants 'wittles and drink.' When I married your uncle Thomas, my dear father said, 'Feed him—and amuse him.' So I made up my mind on my weddin' day to have good food and be entertainin'. And I must say I did it! I fed your dear uncle, and I talked to him, until he died." She paused, and looked at the paper on the wall. "I *hope* the Lord will send you children; it will help you hold the boy—and perhaps you'll be more efficient! You'll have to be, or they'll die. Get a cook." Then, talking all the way downstairs, she trundled off, in angry, honest, forgiving anxiety for her niece's welfare.

Eleanor, planning for the little sunny room, felt bruised by that bludgeon word—which, as it happened, was not accurate, for Maurice, by this time, had gained a maturity of thought and patience that put him practically out of boyhood. When Eleanor repeated her caller's remarks to him, she left that one word out; "Auntie implied," she said, "that you wouldn't love me, if you didn't have fancy cooking."

"She's a peach on cooking herself," declared Maurice; "but, as far as my taste goes, I don't give a hoot for nightingales' tongues on toast."

So, as fancy cooking was not a necessity to Maurice, and as he had resigned himself to an absence of any social life, and didn't really mind smoking in a room with a silly paper on the walls (he had been very much touched when Eleanor told him what the paper meant to her in hope, and unsatisfied longing), he was perfectly contented in the ugly little house in the raw, new street. In point of fact, music and books provided the Bread of Life to Maurice—with solitaire thrown in as a pleasant extra!—so "wittles and drink" did not begin to be a consideration until the first year of married life had passed. Eleanor remembered the date when—because of something Maurice said—she began to realize that they must be considered. It was on the anniversary of their wedding—a cloudy, cold day; but all the same, with valiant sentimentality, they went—Bingo at their heels—to celebrate, in the meadow of those fifty-four minutes of married life. As they crossed the field, where the tides of blossoming grass ebbed and flowed in chilly gusts of wind, they reminded each other of the first time they had come there, and of every detail of the elopement. When they sat down under the locust tree, Eleanor opened her pocketbook and showed him the little grass ring, lying flat and brittle in a small envelope; and he laughed, and said when he got rich he would buy her a circle of emeralds!

"It's confoundedly cold," he said; "b-r-r! ... Oh, I must tell you the news: I got one in on 'em at the office this morning: Old West has been stung on a big block on Taylor Street. Nothing doing. No tenants. I've been working on a fellow for a month, and, by George! I've landed him! I told him the elevator service was rotten—and one or two other pretty little things they've been sliding over, gracefully, at the office; but I landed him! Say, Nelly, Morton asked me to go to a stag party to-morrow night; do you mind if I go?"

She smiled vaguely at his truthtelling; then sighed, and said, "Why, no; if you *want* to. Maurice, do you remember you said we'd come back here for our golden wedding?"

"So I did! I'd forgotten. Gosh! maybe we'll be grandparents by that time!" The idea seemed to him infinitely humorous, but she winced. "What a memory you have!" he said. "You ought to be in Weston's! They'd never catch *you* forgetting where some idiot left the key of the coal bin."

"I sang 'Kiss thy perfumed garments'; remember?"

"'Course I do. Hit 'em again."

She laughed, but ruefully; he had not spoken just that way a year ago. She noticed, suddenly, how much older he looked than on that worshiping day—still the blue, gay eyes, the wind-ruffled blond hair, the hilarious laugh that displayed the very white teeth; but all the same he looked older by more than one year: his mouth had a firmer line; his whole clean-cut face showed responsibility and eager manhood.

Eleanor, clasping her hands around her knees, and watching the grass ebbing and flowing in the wind, sang, "O Spring!" and Maurice, listening, his eyes following the brown ripple of the river lisping in the shallows around the sandbar, and flowing—flowing—like Life, and Time, and Love, sighed with satisfaction at the pure beauty of her voice. "The notes are like wings," he said; "give us a sandwich. I'm about starved."

They spread out their luncheon, and Maurice expressed his opinion of it: "This cake is the limit!" He threw a piece of it at the little dog. "There, Bingo!... Eleanor, he's losing his waist line. But this cake won't fatten him! It's sawdust."

"Hannah *is* a poor cook," she agreed, nervously; "but if I didn't keep her I don't know what she would do, she's so awfully deaf! She couldn't get another place."

"Why don't you teach her to do things? I suppose she thinks we can live on love," he said, chuckling.

She bit her lip,—and thought of Mrs. Newbolt. "Because I don't know how myself," she said.

"Why don't you learn?" he suggested, feeding the rest of his cake to Bingo; "Edith used to make bully cake—"

She said, with a worried look, that she *would* try—

Instantly he was patient and very gentle, and said that the cake didn't matter at all! "But I move we try boarding."

They were silent, watching the slipping gleam on the ripples, until Eleanor said, "Oh, Maurice,—if we only had a child!"

"Maybe we will some day," he said, cheerfully. Then, to tease Bingo, he put his arms around his wife and hugged her,—which made the little dog burst into a volley of barks! Maurice laughed, but remembered that he was hungry and said again, "Let's board."

Eleanor, soothing Bingo, wild-eyed and trembling with jealous love, said no! she would try to have things better. "Perhaps I'll get as clever as Edith," she said—and her lip hardened.

He said he wished she would: "Edith used to make a chocolate cake I'd sell my soul for, pretty nearly! Why didn't Hannah give us hard-boiled eggs?" he pondered, burrowing in the luncheon basket for something more to eat; "they don't take brains!"

Of course he was wrong; any cooking takes brains—and nobody seemed able, in his little household, to supply them. However, boarding was such a terrible threat, that Eleanor, dismayed at the idea of leaving that little room, waiting at the top of the house, with its ducks and shepherdesses; and thinking, too, of a whole tableful of people who would talk to Maurice! made heroic efforts to help Hannah, her mind fumbling over recipes and ingredients, as her hands fumbled over dishes and oven doors and dampers. She only succeeded in burning her wrist badly, and making the deaf Hannah say she didn't want a lady messing up her kitchen.

By degrees, however, "living on love" became more and more uncomfortable, and in October the fiasco of a little dinner for Henry Houghton made Maurice say definitely that, when their lease expired, they would board. Mr. Houghton had come to Mercer on business, bringing Edith with him, as a sort of spree for the child; and when he got home he summed up his experience to his Mary:

"That daughter of yours will be the death of me! There was one moment at dinner when only the grace of God kept me from wringing her neck. In the first place, she commented upon the food—which was awful!—with her usual appalling candor. But when she began on the 'harp'—"

"Harp?" Mary Houghton looked puzzled.

"I won't go to their house again! I detest married people who squabble in public. Let 'em scratch each other's eyes out in private if they want to, the way we do! But I'll be hanged if I look on. She calls him 'darling' whenever she speaks to him. She adores him,—poor fellow! I tell you, Mary, a mind that hasn't a single thought except love must be damned stupid to live with. I wished I was asleep a dozen times."

Maurice, too, at his own dinner table, had "wished he was asleep."

In the expectation of seeing Mr. Houghton, Eleanor had planned an early and extra good dinner, after which they meant to take their guests out on the river and float down into the country to a spot—green, still, in the soft October days—from which they could look back at the city, with its myriad lights pricking out in the dusk, and see the copper lantern of the full moon lifting above the black line of the hills. Eleanor, taught by Maurice, had learned to feel the strange loveliness of Mercer's ugliness, and it was her idea that Mr. Houghton should feel it, too. "Edith's too much of a child to appreciate it," she said.

"She's not much of a child; she's almost fourteen!"

"I think," said Eleanor, "that if she's fourteen, she's too old to be as free and easy with men—as she is with you."

"*Me?* I'm just like a brother! She has no more sense of beauty than a puppy, but she'll like the boat, provided she can row, and adore you."

"Nonsense!" Eleanor said. "Oh, I *hope* the dinner will be good."

It was far from good; the deaf Hannah had scorched the soup, to which Edith called attention, making no effort to emulate the manners of her father, who heroically took the last drop in his plate. Maurice, anxious that Eleanor's housekeeping should shine, thought the best way to affirm it was to say that *this* soup was vile, "but generally our soup is fine!"

"Maurice thinks Edith is a wonderful cook," Eleanor said; her voice trembled.

Something went wrong at dessert, and Edith said, generously, that she "didn't mind a bit!" It was at that point that the race of God kept her father from murdering her, for, in a real desire to be polite and cover up the defective dessert, she became very talkative, and said, wasn't it funny?

When she was little, she thought a harpy played on a harp; "and I thought you had a harp, because father—"

"I'd like some more ice cream!" Mr. Houghton interrupted, passionately.

"But there's salt in it!" said Edith, surprised. To which her father replied, breathlessly, that he believed he'd not go out on the river; he had a headache. ("Mary has got to do something about this child!")

"*I'll* go," Edith announced, cheerfully.

"I think I'll stay at home," Eleanor said; "my head is rather inclined to ache, too, Mr. Houghton; so we'll none of us go."

"Me and Maurice will," Edith protested, dismayed.

Maurice gave an anxious look at Eleanor: "It might do your head good, Nelly?"

"Oh, let's go by ourselves," Edith burst out; "I mean," she corrected herself, "people like father and Eleanor never enjoy the things we do. They like to talk."

"I'd like to choke you!" the exasperated father thought. But he cast a really frightened eye at Eleanor, who grew a little paler. There was some laborious talk in the small parlor, where Eleanor's piano took up most of the space: comments on the weather, and explanations of Bingo's snarling. "He's jealous," Eleanor said, with amused pride, and stroking the little faithful head that pressed so closely against her.

At which Edith began, eagerly, "Father says—" ("What the deuce will she say now?" poor Mr. Houghton thought)—"Father says Rover has a human being's horridest vice—jealousy."

"I don't think jealousy is a vice," Eleanor said, coldly.

Mr. Houghton, giving his offspring a terrible glance, said that he must go back to the hotel and take something for his headache; "And don't keep that imp out too late, Maurice. You want to get home and take care of Eleanor."

"Oh no; he doesn't," Eleanor said, and shook hands with her embarrassed guest, who was saying, under his breath, "*What* taste!"

Out in the street Maurice hurried so that Edith, tucking, unasked, her hand through his arm, had to skip once or twice to keep up with him.... "Maurice," she said, breathlessly, "will you let me row?"

"O Lord—yes! I don't care."

After that Edith did all the talking, until they reached the wharf where Maurice kept his boat; when Edith had secured the oars and they pushed off, he took the tiller ropes, and sat with moody eyes fixed on the water. The mortification of the dinner was gnawing him; he was thinking of the things he might have said to bring Eleanor to her senses! Yet he realized that to have said anything would have added to Mr. Houghton's embarrassment. "I'll have it out with her when I get home," he thought, hotly. "Edith started the mess; why did she say that about Mr. Houghton and Eleanor?" He glanced at her, and Edith, rowing hard, saw the sudden angry look, and was so surprised that she caught a crab, almost keeled over, laughed loudly, and said, *"Goodness!"* which was at that time, her most violent expletive.

"Maurice," she demanded, "did you see that lady on the float, getting into the boat with those two gentlemen?"

Maurice said, absently: "There were two or three people round. I don't know which you mean."

"The young one. She had red cheeks. I never saw such red cheeks!"

"Oh," said Maurice; "*that* one? Yes. I saw her. Paint."

"On her cheeks?" Edith said, with round, astonished eyes. "Do ladies put paint on their cheeks?"

Miserable as Maurice was, he did chuckle. "No, Edith; *ladies* don't," he said, significantly. (Such was the innocent respectability of 1903!)

Edith looked puzzled: "You mean she isn't a lady, Maurice?"

"Look out!" he said, jamming the tiller over; "you were on your right oar."

"But, Maurice," she insisted, "*why* do you say she isn't a lady?... Oh, Maurice! There she is now! See? In that boat?"

"Well, for Heaven's sake don't announce it to the world!" Maurice remonstrated. "Guess I'll take the oars, Edith. I want some exercise."

Edith sighed, but said, "All right." She wanted to row; but she wanted even more to get Maurice good-natured again. "He's huffy," she told herself; "he's mad at Eleanor, and so am I; but it's no sense to take *my* head off!" She hated to change seats—they drew in to shore to do it, a concession to safety on Maurice's part—for she didn't like to turn her back on the red-cheeked lady with the two gentlemen in the following skiff; however, she did it; after all, it was Maurice's boat, and she was his company; so, if he "wanted to row her" (thus her little friendly thoughts ran), "why, all right!" Still, she hated not to look at the lady that Maurice said was not a lady. "She must be twice as old as I am; I should think you were a lady when you were twenty-six," she reflected.

But because her back was turned to the "lady," she did not, for an instant, understand the loud splash behind them, and Maurice's exclamation, "Capsized!" The jerk of their boat, as he backed water, made it rock violently. "Idiots!" said Maurice. "I'll pick you up!" he yelled, and rowed hard toward the three people, now slapping about in not very deep water. "Tried to change seats,"—he explained to Edith. "I'm coming!" he called again.

Edith, wildly excited and swaying back and forth, like a coxswain in a boat race, screamed: "We're coming! You'll get drowned—you'll get drowned!" she assured the gasping, bubbling people, who were, somehow or other, making their muddy way toward the shore.

"Get our skiff, will you?" one of the "gentlemen" called to Maurice, who, seeing that there was no danger to any of the immersed merrymakers, turned and rowed out to the slowly drifting boat.

"Grab the painter!" he told Edith as he gained upon it; she obeyed his orders with prompt dexterity. "You can always depend on old Skeezics," Maurice told himself, with a friendly look at her. He had forgotten Eleanor's behavior, and was trying to suppress his grins at the forlorn and dripping people, who were on land now, shivering, and talking with astonishing loudness.

"Oh, the lady's cheeks are coming off!" Edith gasped, as they beached.

Maurice, shoving the trailing skiff on to its owners, said: "Can I do anything to help you?"

"I'll catch my death," said the lady, who was crying; her trickling tears and her sopping handkerchief removed what remnants of her "cheeks" the sudden bath in the river had left. As the paint disappeared, one saw how very pretty the poor draggled butterfly was—big, honey-dark eyes, and quite exquisite features. "Oh, my soul and body!—I'll die!" she said, sobbing with cold and shock.

"Here," said Maurice, stripping off his coat; "put this on."

The girl made some faint demur, and the men, who were bailing out their half-filled skiff, said, "Oh—she can have our coats."

"They're soaked, aren't they?" Maurice said; "and I don't need mine in the least."

Edith gasped; such reckless gallantry gave her an absolutely new sensation. Her heart seemed to lurch, and then jump; she breathed hard, and said, under her breath, "Oh, *my*!" She felt that she could never speak to Maurice again; he was truly a grown-up gentleman! Her eyes devoured him.

"Do take it," she heard him say to the crying lady, who no longer interested her; "I assure you I don't need it," he said, carelessly; and the "lady" reached out a small, shaking hand, on which the kid glove was soaking wet, and said, her teeth chattering, that she was awfully obliged.

"Get in—get in!" one of the "gentlemen" said, crossly, and as she stepped into the now bailed-out skiff, she said to Maurice, "Where shall I return it to?"

"I'll come and get it," Maurice said—and she called across the strip of water widening between the two boats:

"I'm Miss Lily Dale—" and added her street and number.

Maurice, in his shirt sleeves, lifted his hat; then looked at Edith and grinned. "Did you ever see such idiots? Those men are chumps. Did you hear the fat one jaw at the girl?"

"Did he?" Edith said, timidly. She could hardly bear to look at Maurice, he was so wonderful.

But he, entirely good-natured again, was overflowing with fun. "Let's turn around," he said, "and follow 'em! That fatty was rather happy—did you get on to that flask?"

Edith had no idea what he meant, but she said, breathlessly, "Yes, Maurice." In her own mind she was seeing again that princely gesture, that marvelous tossing of his own coat to the "lady"! "He is *exactly* like Sir Walter Raleigh," she said to herself. She remembered how at Green Hill she had wanted him to spread his coat before Eleanor's feet;—but *that* was commonplace! Eleanor was just a married person, "like mother." This was a wonderful drowning lady! Oh, he *was* Sir Walter! Her eyes were wide with an entirely new emotion—an emotion which made her draw back sharply when once, as he rowed, his hand touched hers. She was afraid of that careless touch. Yet oh, if he would only give *her* some of his clothes! Oh, why hadn't *she* fallen into the water! Her heart beat so that she felt she could not speak. It was not necessary; Maurice, singing a song appropriate to the lady with the red cheeks, was not aware of her silence.

"I bet," he said, "that cad takes it out of the little thing! She looked scared, didn't you think, Edith?"

"Yes, ... *sir*" the little girl said, breathlessly.

Maurice did not notice the new word; "Sorry not to take you down to the Point," he said; "but I ought to keep tabs on that boat. If they capsize again, somebody really might get hurt. She's a—a little fool, of course; but I'd hate to have the fat brute drown her, and he looks capable of it."

However, trailing along in the deepening dusk behind the fat brute, who was rowing hard against the current, they saw the dripping survivors of the shipwreck reach the wharf safely five minutes ahead of them, and scurry off into the darkness of the street.

Maurice, in high spirits, had quite forgiven Eleanor. "I meant to treat you to ice cream, Skeezics," he said, "but I can't go into the hotel. Shirt sleeves wouldn't be admitted in the elegant circles of the Mercer House!"

Instantly a very youthful disappointment readjusted things for Edith; she forgot that strange consciousness which had made her shrink from his careless touch; she had no impulse to say "sir"; she was back again at the point at which the red-cheeked lady had broken in upon their lives. She said, frowning: "My! I did want some ice cream. I *wish* you hadn't given the lady your coat!"

When Maurice got home, he found a repentant Eleanor bathing very red and swollen eyes.

"How's your head?" he said, as he came, in his shirt sleeves, into her room; she, turning to kiss him and say it was better, stopped short.

"Maurice! Where's your coat?"

His explanation deepened her repentance; "Oh, Maurice,—if you've caught cold!"

He laughed and hugged her (at which Bingo, in his basket, barked violently); and said, "The only thing that bothered me was that I couldn't treat Edith to ice cream."

Eleanor's face, passionately tender, changed sharply: "Edith is an extremely impertinent child! Did you hear her, at dinner, talk about jealousy?"

He looked blank, and said, "What was 'impertinent' in that? Say, Star, the girl in the boat was—tough; she was painted up to the nines, and of course it all came out in the wash. And Buster said her 'cheeks came off'! But she was pretty," Maurice ruminated, beginning to pull off his boots.

"I don't see how you can call a painted woman 'pretty,'" Eleanor said, coldly.

Maurice yawned. "She seemed to belong to the fat brute. He was so nasty to her, I wanted to punch his head."

"Poor girl!" Eleanor said, and her voice softened. "Perhaps I could do something for her? She ought to make him marry her."

Maurice chuckled. "Oh, Nelly, you *are* innocent! No, my dear; she'll paint some more, and then, probably, get to drinking; and meet one or two more brutes. When she gets quite into the gutter, she'll die. The sooner the better! I mean, the less harm she'll do."

Eleanor's recoil of pain seemed to him as exquisite as a butterfly's shrinking from some harsh finger. He looked at her tenderly. "Star, you don't know the world! And I don't want you to."

"I'd like to help her," Eleanor said, simply.

"You?" he said; "I wouldn't have you under the same roof with one of those creatures!"

His sense of her purity pleased her; the harem idea is, at bottom, pleasing to women; they may resent it with their intellect, but they all of them like to feel they are too precious for the wind of evil realities to blow upon. So, honestly enough, and with the childlike joy of the woman in love, she played up to the harem instinct, shrinking a little and asking timid questions, and making innocent eyes; and was kissed, and assured she was a lovely goose; for Maurice played up to his part, too, with equal honesty (and youth)—the part of the worldly-wise protector. It was the fundamental instinct of the human male; he resents with his intellect the idea that his woman is a fool; but the more foolish she is (on certain lines) the more important he feels himself to be! So they were both very contented, until Maurice happened to say again that he was sorry to have disappointed Edith about the ice cream.

"She's a greedy little thing," Eleanor said from her pillows; her voice was irritated.

"What nonsense!" Maurice said; "as for ice cream, all youngsters like it. I know I do!"

"I saw her hang on to your arm as you went down the street," Eleanor said. "Mrs. Houghton ought to tell her that nice girls don't paw men!"

"Eleanor! She's nothing but a child, and I'm her brother—"

"You are *not* her brother."

"Oh, Eleanor, don't be so—" he paused; oh, that dreadful word which must not be spoken!—"so unreasonable," he ended, wearily. He lay down beside her in the darkness, and by and by he heard her crying, very softly. "*Oh,* lord!" he said; and turned over and went to sleep.

Thus do the clouds return after rain. Yet each day the sun rises again....

At breakfast Eleanor, with a pitying word for the "poor thing," reminded her husband that he must go and get his coat.

He said, "Gosh! I'd forgotten it!" and added that he liked his eggs softer. He would have "played up" again, and smiled at her innocence, if he had thought of it, but he was really concerned about his eggs, "Hannah seems to think I like brickbats," he said, good-naturedly.

Eleanor winced; "Poor Hannah is so stupid! But she's getting deafer every day, so I *can't* send her away!" Added to her distress at the scorched soup of the night before, was this new humiliation of "brickbats;" naturally she forgot the "poor thing."

Maurice almost forgot her himself; but as he left the office in the afternoon he did remember the coat. At the address which the red-cheeked lady had given him, he found her card—"Miss Lily Dale"—below a letter box in the tiled, untidy vestibule of a yellow-brick apartment house, where he waited, grinning at the porcelain ornateness about him, for a little jerking elevator to take him up to the fourth floor. There, in a small, gay, clean parlor of starched lace curtains, and lithographs, and rows of hyacinth bulbs just started in blue and purple glasses on the window sill, he found the red-cheeked young lady, rather white-cheeked. Indeed, there were traces of hastily wiped-away tears on her pretty face.

"My friend, Mr. Batty, said I upset the boat," she said, taking the coat out of the wardrobe and brushing it briskly with a capable little hand.

The coat reeked with perfumery, and Maurice said, "Phew!" to himself; but threw it over his arm, and said that Mr. Batty had only himself to blame. "A man ought to know enough not to let a lady move about in a rowboat!"

"Won't you be seated?" Lily said; she lighted a cigarette, and shoved the box over to him, across the varnished glitter of the table top.

Maurice, introducing himself—"My name's Curtis";—and, taking in all the details of the comfortable, vulgar little room, sat down, took a cigarette, and said it was a warm day for October; she said she hated heat, and he said he liked winter best.... Then he saw a bruise on her wrist and said: "Why, you gave yourself a dreadful knock, didn't you? Was it on the rowlock?"

Her face dropped into sullen lines: "It wasn't the boat did it."

Maurice, with instant discretion, dropped the subject. But he was sorry for her; she made him think of a beaten kitten. "You must take care of that wrist," he said, his blue eyes full of sympathy. When he went away he told himself he had spotted the big man as a brute the minute he saw him. The "kitten" seemed to him so pathetic that he forgot Eleanor's exquisiteness, and told her about the bruised wrist and the reeking coat, and how pretty the girl was.

"I don't know anything vulgarer than perfumery!" his wife said, with a delicate shrug.

Maurice agreed, adding, with a grin, that he had noticed that when ladies were short on the odor of sanctity, they were long on the odor of musk.

"I always keep dried rose leaves in my bureau drawers," Eleanor said; and he had the presence of mind to say, "You are a rose yourself!"

A husband's "presence of mind" in addressing his wife is, of course, a confession; it means they are not one—for nobody makes pretty speeches to oneself! However, Maurice's "rose" made no such deduction.

CHAPTER IX

It was after Mr. Houghton had swallowed the scorched soup and meditated infanticide, that boarding became inevitable. Several times that winter Maurice said that Hannah "was the limit; so let's board?"

And toward spring, in spite of the cavorting lambs and waddling ducks in the little waiting, empty room upstairs, Eleanor yielded. "We can go to housekeeping again," she thought, "*if—*"

So the third year of their marriage opened in a boarding house. They moved (Bingo again banished to Mrs. O'Brien), on their wedding anniversary, and instead of celebrating by going out to "their river," they spent a hot, grimy day settling down in their third-floor front.

"If people come to see us," said Maurice, ruefully, standing with his hands in his pockets surveying their new quarters, "they'll have to sit on the piano!"

"Nobody'll come," Eleanor said.

Maurice's eyes narrowed: "I believe you need 'em, Nelly? I knock up against people at the office, and I know several fellows and girls outside—"

"What girls?"

"Oh, the fellows' sisters; but you—"

"I don't want anybody but you!"

Maurice was silent. Two years ago, when Eleanor had said almost the same thing: she was willing to live on a desert island, *with him!*—it had been oil on the flames of his love; now, it puzzled him. He didn't want to live on a desert island, with anybody! He needed more than one man "Friday," and any women "Thursdays" who might come along were joyously welcomed. "I am a social beggar, myself," he said; and began to whistle and fuss about, trying to bring order out of a chaos of books and photographs and sheet music. She sat watching him—the alert, vigorous figure; the keen face under the shock of blond hair; the blue eyes that crinkled so easily into laughter. Her face was thinner, and there were rings of fatigue under her dark eyes, and that little nursery in the house they had left, made a swelling sense of emptiness in her heart. ("If I see any awfully pretty nursery paper this winter, I'll buy it, and have it ready, — *in case* we should have to get another house," she thought.) "Oh, do stop whistling," she said; "it goes through me!"

"Poor Nelly!" he said, kindly, and stopped.

The astonishing thing about the "boarding-house marriage," is that it ever survives the strain of the woman's idleness and the man's discomfort! But it does, occasionally. Even this marriage survived Miss Ladd's boarding house, for a time. At first it went smoothly enough because Maurice couldn't blame Eleanor's cook, and Eleanor couldn't say that "nothing she did pleased Maurice"; so two reasons for irritability were eliminated; but a new reason appeared: Maurice's eager interest in everything and everybody — especially everybody! — and his endless good nature, overflowed around the boarding-house table. Everyone liked him, which Eleanor entirely understood; but he liked everyone, — which she didn't understand.

The note of this mutual liking was struck the very first night when Maurice went down into the dingy basement dining room; he and Eleanor made rather a sensation as they entered: Eleanor, handsome and silent, produced the impression of cold reserve; Maurice, amiable and talkative, gave a little shock of interest and pleasure to the fifteen or twenty people eating indifferent food about a table covered with a not very fresh cloth. Before the meal was over he had made himself agreeable to an elderly woman on his left, ventured some drollery to a pretty high-school teacher of mathematics opposite him, and given a man at the end of the table the score. When Eleanor rose, Maurice had to rise, too, though his dessert was not quite devoured; and as the couple left the room there was a murmur of pleasure:

"A real addition to our family," said Miss Ladd.

The bond salesman said, "I wonder if he'll go to the ball game with me on Saturday? I'll get the tickets."

The school-teacher said, "He's awfully good looking."

The widow's comment was only, "Nice boy."

Upstairs in their own room, Maurice said: "What pleasant people! Nelly, let's get some fun out of this; don't dash up here the minute you swallow your food!"

She wondered, silently, how he could call them "pleasant"! To her they were all rather common, pushing persons, who wanted to talk to Maurice. But as her one desire was to do what he liked, she really did try to help him "get some fun out of them." Every night at dinner she smiled laboriously when he teased the teacher, and she listened to the elderly woman in mourning, whose clever talk was so absorbing to Maurice that sometimes he didn't hear his wife speaking to him! Yes; Eleanor tried. Yet, in less than a month Maurice found himself beside a boarder of his own sex, instead of Mrs. Davis, and saw that the school-teacher was too far down the table for jokes. When he asked why their seats had been changed, Eleanor said she had felt a draught—which caused the widow to smile, and write on a piece of paper an arithmetical statement: "Selfishness vanity - humor = jealousy." She handed it to the teacher, who laughed and shrugged her shoulders:

"But she's awfully in love with him," she conceded, under her breath.

The older woman shook her head: "No, my dear; she isn't. No jealous woman knows the meaning of love."

But Eleanor did not see Miss Moore's contemptuous smile, or Mrs. Davis's grave glance. One of the pitiful things about jealous people is that they don't know how amusing—or else boring—or else irritating—they are to an observant and entirely unsympathetic world! Eleanor had no idea that the whole tableful of people knew she was jealous, and found her ridiculous. She only knew that Maurice seemed to like them—which meant that her society "wasn't enough for him "! So she tried to make it enough for him. At dinner she talked to him so animatedly (and so personally) that no one else could get a word in edgewise. Dinner over, she was uneasy until she had dragged her eager-eyed young husband up to the desert island of their third-floor front—a dingy room, with a black-marble mantelpiece, and a worn and frowzy carpet. There were some steel engravings, dim under their old glasses, on the wall,—Evangeline, and Lincoln's Cabinet, and Daniel Webster in a rumpled shirt and a long swallowtail;—all of which Eleanor's looking-glass and the mirrored doors of a black-walnut wardrobe, reflected in multiplying dullness.

Maurice's charming good nature in that first boarding winter never failed. Eleanor's silences—which he had long since discovered were merely empty, not mysterious—were at least no tax on his patience; so he never once called her "silly." He did, occasionally, feel a faint uneasiness lest people might think she was older than he—which was, of course, the beginning of self-consciousness as to what he had done in marrying her. But he loved her. He still loved her. "She isn't very well," he used to defend her to Mrs. Newbolt; "she nearly killed herself, saving my life. She's not been the same girl since."

"'Girl'?" said Mrs. Newbolt; "she's exactly the same *woman*, only more so because she's older. I hope she won't lose her figger; she's gettin' thin.

My dear grandmother—she was a Dennison; fat; I can hear her now talkin' to her daughters: 'Girls! *Don't* lose your figgers!' She had red hair."

Eleanor had not lost her figure; it was still graciously erect, and with lovely curves of bosom and shoulders; but, somehow, she seemed older— older even than she was! Perhaps because of her efforts to be girlish? It was as if she wore clothes she had outgrown—clothes that were too tight and too short. She used Maurice's slang without its virile appropriateness; when they accepted an invitation from one of Maurice's new acquaintances, her anxiety to be of his generation was pathetic—or ludicrous, as one happened to look at it. These friends of Maurice's seemed to have innumerable interests in common with him that she knew nothing about—and jokes! How tired she got of their jokes, which were mostly preposterous badinage, expressed with entire solemnity and ending in yells of laughter. Yet she tried to laugh, too; though she rarely knew what it was all about. There is nothing which divides the generations more sharply than their ideas of humor. But Eleanor tried, very pitifully hard, to be silly with the kind of silliness which Maurice seemed to enjoy; but, alas! she only achieved the silliness which he—like every husband on earth!—hated: the silliness of small jealousies. Once she told Maurice she didn't like those dinner parties that his friends were always asking them to,—"I think it's nicer here," she said.

And he said, cheerfully: "Don't go! I don't mind going alone."

"I know you don't," she said, wistfully…. "Why can't he be satisfied to stay at home with me?" she said once to her aunt; and Mrs. Newbolt told her why:

"Because you don't interest him. Eleanor! if you want to keep that boy, urge him to go out and have a good time, *without you!*" Then she added some poignantly true remarks: "My dear father used to say, 'Just as many men are faithless to their wives because their wives have plain minds, as because other women have pretty faces.' Well, I'm afraid poor dear mother's mind was plain; that's why I always made an effort to talk to your uncle, and be entertainin'. And I'll tell you another thing—for if I have a virtue it's candor—if you let him see you're jealous, he'll make it worth your while! You've got a rip in the back seam of your waist. No man ever keeps on lovin' a jealous woman; he just pretends to, to keep the peace."

Of course this was as unintelligible to Eleanor as it is to all women of her type of mind. So, instead of considering Maurice's enjoyment of society, she committed the absurdity of urging him to enjoy what she enjoyed—a solitude of two. To herself she explained his desire to see other people, by saying it was because they had no children. "When we have a child, he won't want to be with those boys and girls! Oh, why don't we have a baby?"

Her longing for children was like physical hunger. But only Mrs. O'Brien understood it. When Eleanor went, in her faithful way, two or three times a week, to sing to little sickly Don (and pet the boarding and rather pining Bingo), Mrs. O'Brien, listening to the little songs, pretty and silly, would draw a puckery hand over her eyes: "She'd ought to have a dozen of her own! If that boy don't treat her good, I'll iron off every button he's got!"

When Eleanor (hoping for a baby) worried lest Maurice's hopes, too, were disappointed, her gentleness to him was passionate and beseeching; but sometimes, watching his attention to other people, the gentleness grew rigid in an accusation that, because they hadn't a child, he was "getting tired of her"! Whenever she said this foolish thing, there would come, afterward, a rain of repentant tears. But repentance cannot always change the result of foolish words—and the result is so often out of proportion to the words! As Maurice had said that day in their meadow, of Professor Bradley and the banana skin—a very little thing "can throw the switches," in human life!

It was the "little thing" of a lead pencil, in keeping the accounts of their endless games of solitaire, that threw the switches now, for Maurice Curtis.... He happened to produce a very soft pencil, which he had borrowed, he said, "from a darned pretty woman he was showing a house to," and had forgotten to return to her.

Eleanor said it seemed to her bad taste to talk of a strange woman that way: "If she's a lady she wouldn't want a man she didn't know to speak so—so lightly of her."

"I have yet to meet one of your sex who objects to being called pretty," Maurice said, dryly.

To which Eleanor replied that she preferred a hard lead pencil, anyhow,—but *her* wishes seemed to be of no importance! "You're tired of me, Maurice." He said, "Oh, damn!" She said, "I won't have you swear at me!"

He pushed back his chair, toppled the flimsy table over, scattering all the cards on the floor. The falling table struck her knee; she screamed; he flung out of the room—out of the house, into the hot darkness of an August night.... The switches were thrown....

Down on Tyler Street there had been another quarrel—as trivial as the difference of opinion as to hard and soft lead pencils, and again human lives were shifted from one track to another. It was Lily who ran out into the darkness, and wandered through the streets; then strayed down to the bridge that spanned the hurrying black water of that same river which, two years before, had lisped and laughed under Maurice and Eleanor's happy eyes. Lily, watching the current, thought angrily of Batty—then a passing elbow jostled her and some one said, "Beg pardon!" She turned and saw Maurice.

"Well, I do say!" she said; and Maurice, pausing at the voice in the dark, began a brief, "Excuse me; I stumbled—" saw who it was, and said, "Why, Miss Lily! How are you? I haven't seen you for an age!"

She answered with some small jocosity; then suddenly struck her little fist on the railing. "Well, I'm just miserable; that's how I am, if you want to know! Batty—"

Maurice frowned. "Has that pup hurt you?"

She nodded: "I don't know why I put up with him!"

"Shake him!" he advised, good-naturedly.

"I 'ain't got any other friend." She spoke with half-laughing anger; indeed, she was so pretty and so plucky that he forgot, for a moment, the irritation at Eleanor which had driven him out into the night, and it came into his mind that something ought to be done for girls like this. He remembered that Eleanor herself had said so, "Perhaps I could do something for her?" Eleanor had said.

"She isn't bad," he thought, looking at Lily; "she's just a fool, like all of 'em. But there ought to be some way of fishing 'em out of the gutter, before they get to the very bottom. Maybe Eleanor could give her a hand up?" Then he asked her about herself: Had she friends? Where did her family live? Could she do any work? He was rather diverted by his own philanthropy, but it seemed to him that it would be the decent thing to advise the girl, seriously. "I'll talk to her," he thought. "Come on!" he said; "let's hunt up some place and have something to eat."

"I ain't hungry," she said—then saw the careless straightforwardness of his face, and was straightforward herself: "I guess I'd better be going home."

"Oh, come on," he urged her.

She yielded, with a little rollicking chuckle; and as they walked toward a part of town more suitable for such excursions, she confided to him she was twenty, and she'd been "around" for a year.

("Twenty-five, if she's a day," he thought.)

They strolled along for several blocks before discovering, in the purlieus of Tyler Street, a dingy "ice-cream parlor," eminently fitted for interviews with the Lilys of the locality. At a marble-topped table, translucent with years of ice-cream rendezvous, they waited for his order to be filled, and she saw the amused honesty of his face and he saw the good nature of hers; which made him think again of Eleanor's wish to help her.

He urged some indifferent cake upon her, and joked about how many saucers of ice cream they could consume between them; then he became serious: Why didn't she drop Batty?

"Oh," she said, "if I only *could* drop him! I hate him. He's the first friend I've had."

"Was he really the—the first?" Maurice said. His question was the old human interest of playing with fire, but he supposed that it was a desire to raise the fallen.

"Well, except ... there was a man; I expected to marry *him*. Then Batty, he come along."

"I see," said Maurice. "Where's the first man?"

"*I* don't know. I was only sixteen."

"Damn him!" Maurice said, sympathetically. He was so moved that he ordered more ice cream; then it occurred to him that he ought to let her know that he was entirely a philanthropist. "My wife and I'll help you," he said.

"Oh ... you're *married*? You're real young!" she commented.

"I'm no chicken. My wife and I think exactly alike about these things. Of course she's not a prude. She understands life, just as I do. And she'd love to be a real friend to you. She'll put you on your feet, and think none the worse of you. Tell me about yourself," he urged, intimately; he felt some deep satisfaction stir within him, which he supposed was his recognition of a moral purpose. But she drew back into her own reserves.

"They always ask that," she thought; and the momentary reality she had shown hardened into the easy lying of her business: she told this or that—the cruel father of fiction, who tried to drive her into marriage with the rich old man; the wicked lover who destroyed trusting innocence; the inevitable *facilis descensus*—Batty at last. And now the ice-cream parlor in this dirty street, with the clear-eyed, handsome, amused young man, who had forgotten his own anger in the impulse, so frequent in the very young and very upright man, to "save" some little creature of the gutter! As for Maurice, he said to himself, "She's a sweet little thing; and not really bad."

He was right there: Lily was not bad; she was as far from sin as she was from virtue—just a little, unmoral, very amiable animal.

As for Maurice, he continued to discuss her future of rectitude and honor—his imagination reaching in a bound amazing heights. Why not be a trained nurse?—and have a hospital of her own, and gather about her, as assistants, girls who—"well, had had a tough time of it," he said, delicately. As he talked, fatigue at the boredom of his highly moral sentiments crept into her face. She swallowed an occasional yawn, and murmured to most of his statements, "Is that so?" She was sleepy, and wished he would stop talking....

"Guess I'll be going along," she said, good-naturedly.

"I'll come and see you to-morrow," Maurice said, impassioned with the idea of saving her; "then I'll tell you what my wife will do for you."

They went out together and walked toward Lily's rooms; but somehow they both fell silent. Lily was again afraid of Batty, and Maurice's exhilaration had begun to ebb; there came into his mind the bleak remembrance of the overturned table and Eleanor's sobs....

At the door of the apartment house where Lily lived, she said, nervously, "I'd ask you to come in, but he—"

"Oh, I understand; I've no desire to meet the gentleman! What time will I come to-morrow, when he's not around?"

She reflected, uneasily: "Well, I ain't sure—"

Before she could finish, Batty loomed up beside them. He was plainly drunk. "I lost my key," he said; "and I've been waiting—"

"Good night, Miss Lily," Maurice said,—"If he's nasty to her, I'll go back," he thought. He was only halfway down the block when he heard a little piping scream—"O-o-o-w! O-o-o-w!" He turned, and saw her trying to pull her hand away from Batty's twisting grip: he was at her side in a moment: "Here! *Drop* it!" he said, sharply—and landed an extremely neat blow on the drunken man's jaw. Batty, rubbing his cheek, and staring at this very unexpected assailant in profound and giggling astonishment, slouched into the house.

"He 'most twisted my hand off!" Lily said; "oh, ain't he the beast?" She cringed and shook her bruised wrist, then gave Maurice an admiring look. "My soul and body! you lit into him good!" she said; "what am I going to do? I'm afraid to go in."

"If I had a house of my own," Maurice said, "I'd take you home, and my wife would look after you. But we are boarding.... Haven't you some friend you could go to for to-night? ... To-morrow my wife will come and see you," he declared.

"Oh, gracious me, no!" In the midst of her anger she couldn't help laughing. ("He's a reg'lar baby!" she thought.) "No; your wife's a busy society lady, I'm sure. Don't bother about me. I'll just wait round till he goes to sleep." She dabbed at her eyes with a little wet ball of a handkerchief.

"Here, take mine," he said. And with this larger and dryer piece of linen, she did manage to make her face more presentable.

"When he's asleep, I'll slip in," she said.

"Well, let's go and sit down somewhere," Maurice suggested. She agreed, and there was some haphazard wandering about in the darkness, then a weary sitting on a bench in the park, marking time till Batty would surely be asleep.

"You sure handed one out to him," Lily said.

Maurice chuckled at the role of knight-errant which she seemed to discern in him, but he talked earnestly of her future, and once or twice, soothed by his voice, she dozed—but he didn't know it. Indeed, he told himself afterward that her silences showed how his words were sinking in! "It only goes to prove," he thought, when at midnight he left her at her own door, "that the *flower* is in all of them! If you only go about it right, you can bring their purity to the surface! She felt all I said. Eleanor will be awfully interested in her."

He was quite sure about Eleanor; he had entirely forgiven her; he wanted to wake her up, and sit on the edge of her bed, and tell her of his evening, and what a glorious thing it would be to lift one lovely young soul from the gutter.

CHAPTER X

But Eleanor would not "wake up." Within an hour of her foolish outbreak she had begun to listen for his returning step. Then she went to bed and cried and cried, "He doesn't love me," she said, over and over; and once she said, "it is because I am—" But she didn't finish this; she just got up and went over to the bureau and stared into the mirror; she even lit a candle and held it close to the glass; after a while she saw what she was looking for. "Edith tried to make him notice them, that first summer at Green Hill," she thought.

At eleven she went to the window and watched, her eyes straining into the darkness. When, far down the street, a man's figure came in range, she held her breath until it walked into and out of the circling glare of the arc light—not Maurice! It was after twelve when she saw him coming—and instantly she flew back to her bed. When he entered the faintly lighted room, Eleanor was, apparently, sound asleep.

"Star?"

No answer.

He leaned over, saw the droop of her lip and the puffed eyelids—and drew back. Perhaps, if he had kissed her, the soft lead pencil might not have acted as Destiny; she might have melted under the forlorn story he was so eager to tell her. But her tear-stained face did not suggest a kiss.

In the morning Eleanor had what she called a "bilious headache," and when Maurice skirted the subject of the "*flower*," she was too physically miserable to be interested. When she was well again, the opportunity—if it was an opportunity!—was lost; her interest in Lily was not needed, because a call at the apartment house showed Maurice that Batty was forgiven. So he forgot his desire to lift the fallen, in more of those arid moments with Eleanor; reproaches—and reconciliations! Tears—and fire! But fires gradually die down under tears, no matter how one spends one's breath blowing loving words on the wet embers! Enough tears will put out any fire.

Lily, too, was shedding angry tears in those days, and they probably had their effect in cooling Batty's heart; for his unpleasantness finally culminated in his leaving her, and by October she was living in the yellow-brick apartment house alone, and very economically—yet not so economically that she did not buy hyacinth bulbs for the blue and purple glasses on her sunny window sill.

Once Maurice, remembering with vague amusement his reformatory impulse, went to see her; but he did not talk to Eleanor about the call. By this time there were days when he talked as little as possible to Eleanor about anything,—not because he was secretive—he hated secrecy! "It's next door to lying," he thought, faintly disgusted at himself,—but because she seemed to feel hurt if he was interested in anyone except herself. Maurice had passed the point which had seemed so terrible at Green Hill, where he had called his wife "silly." He never called her silly now. He merely, over and over, called himself a fool.

"I've made an ass of myself," he used to think, sorting out his cards for solitaire and looking furtively at the thin face, with its lines of wistful and faded beauty. At forty-two, a happy, busy woman, with a sound digestion, will not look faded; on the contrary, she is at her best—as far as looks are concerned! Eleanor was not happy; her digestion was uncertain; she did not go into society, and she had no real occupation, except to go every day to Mrs. O'Brien's and take Bingo for a walk. Even her practicing had been pretty much given up, for fear of disturbing the people on the floor below her.

"Why don't you have some plants around?" Maurice suggested; "they'd give you something to do! I saw a lot of hyacinths growing in glasses, once; I'll buy some bulbs for you."

"Oh, I'm one of the people flowers won't grow for," she said.

Mrs. Newbolt made a suggestion, too. "Pity you can't have Bingo to keep you company. That's what comes of boarding. I knew a woman who boarded, and she lost her teeth. Chambermaid threw 'em away. Come in and see me any evening when Maurice is out."

As Maurice was frequently out, the invitation was sometimes accepted, and it was on one of these occasions that Mrs. Newbolt, spreading out her cards on the green baize of her solitaire table with fat, beringed hands, made her suggestion:

"Eleanor, you've aged. I believe you're unhappy?"

"No, I'm not! Why should I be?"

"Well, I wouldn't blame you if you were," Mrs. Newbolt said. "'Course you'd have brought it on yourself; I could have told you what to expect! Your dear uncle Thomas used to say that, after a thing happened, I was the one to tell people that they might have expected it. You see, I made a point of bein' intelligent; of course I wasn't *too* intelligent. A man doesn't like that. You're gettin' gray, Eleanor. Pity you haven't children. *He* doesn't look very contented!—but men are men," said Mrs. Newbolt.

"He *ought* to be contented," Eleanor said, passionately; "I adore him!"

"You've got to interest him," her aunt said; "that's more important than adorin' him! A man can buy a certain kind of adoration, but he can't purchase interest."

"I don't know what you're talking about," Eleanor said, trembling.

"Well, if you don't, I'm sure I can't tell you," Mrs. Newbolt said, despairingly; but she made one more attempt: "My dear father used to say that the finest tribute a man could put on his wife's tombstone would be, '*She was interestin' to live with*.' So I tell you, Eleanor, if you want to hold that boy, *make him laugh!*" She was so much in earnest that for a few minutes she actually stopped talking!

Eleanor could not make Maurice laugh—she never made anybody laugh! But for a while she did "hold him"—because he was a gallant youngster, making the best of his bargain. That he had begun to know it was a bad bargain did not lessen his regret for his wife's childlessness, which he knew made her unhappy, nor his pity for her physical forlornness—which he blamed largely on himself: "She almost died that night on the mountain, to save my life!"

But he had ceased to be touched by her reiterated longing for children; he was even a little bored by it. And he was very much bored by her reproaches, her faint tempers and their following ardors of repentant love—bitternesses, and cloying sweetnesses! Yet, in spite of these things, the boarding-house marriage survived the lengthening of the fifty-four minutes of ecstasy into three years. But it might not have survived its own third winter had it not been that Maurice's unfaithfulness enforced his faithfulness. For by spring that squabble about lead pencils, which had turned his careless steps toward the bridge, had turned his life so far from Eleanor's that he had been untrue to her.

He had not meant to be untrue; nothing had been farther from his mind or purpose. But there came a bitter Sunday afternoon in March ...

Eleanor, saying he did not "understand her," cried about something—afterward Maurice was not sure just what—perhaps it was a question from one of the other boarders about the early 'eighties, and she felt herself insulted; "As if I could remember!" she told Maurice; but whatever it was, he had tried to comfort her by joking about it. Then she had reproached him for his unkindness—to most crying wives a joke is unkind. Then she had said that he was tired of her! At which he took refuge in silence—and she cried out that he acknowledged it!

"You can't deny it! You're tired of me because I'm older than you!"

And he said, between his teeth, "If you were old enough to have any sense, I wouldn't be tired of you."

She gave a cry; then stood, the back of her hand against her lips, her eyes wide with terror.

Maurice threw down a book he had been trying to read, got up, plunged into his overcoat, pulled his hat down over his eyes, and, without a word, walked out of the room. A moment later the front door banged behind him. Eleanor, alone, stood perfectly still; she had said foolish things like that many times; she rather liked to say them! But she had not believed them; now, her own words were a boomerang,—they seemed to strike her in the face! *He was tired of her.* Instantly she was alert! What must she do? She sat down, tense with thought; first of all, she must be sweet to him; she mustn't be cross; then she must try (Mrs. Newbolt had told her so!) to "entertain" him. "I'll read things, and talk to him the way Mrs. Davis does!" She must sew on his buttons, and scold poor old O'Brien.... With just this same silent determination she had hurried to act that night on the mountain!

But while she was sitting there in their cheerless room, planning and planning!—Maurice was out, wandering about in the gray afternoon. It had begun to snow, in a fitful, irritating way—little gritty pellets that blew into his face. He had nowhere to go—four o'clock is a dead time to drop in on people! He had nothing to do, and nothing to think of—except the foolish, middle-aged woman, stating, in their dreary third-floor front, an undeniable fact—he was tired of her! Walking aimlessly about in the cold, he said to himself, dully, "Why *was* I such an idiot as to marry her?" He was old enough to curse himself for his folly, but he was young enough to suffer, agonies of mortification, and to pity himself, too; pity himself for the mere physical discomfort of his life: the boarding-house table, with its uninteresting food; the worn shirt cuff which was scratching his wrist; and he pitied himself for his spiritual discomfort—when Eleanor called him "darling" at the dinner table, or exhibited her jealousy before people! "They're sorry for me—confound 'em!" he thought.... Yet how trivial the cuff was, or even—yes, even the impertinence which was "sorry" for him!—how unimportant, when compared to a ring of braided grass, and the smell of locust blossoms, and a lovely voice, rising and falling:

"O Spring!"

"Oh, *damn!*" he said to himself, feeling the scrape of worn linen on the back of his hand. Then he fell into certain moody imaginings with which that winter he frequently and harmlessly amused himself. He used to call these flights of fancy "fool thoughts"; but they were at least an outlet to his smoldering irritation, "Suppose I should kick over the traces some day?" his thoughts would run; and again, "Suppose I should be in a theater fire, and 'disappear,' and never come back, and she'd think I was dead," "Suppose there should be a war, and I should enlist," ... and so forth, and so forth. "Fool thoughts," of course!—but Maurice is not the only man upon whom a jealous woman has thrust such thoughts, or who has found solace in the impossible! So, now, wandering about in the cold, he amused himself by imagining various ways of "kicking over the traces"; then, suddenly, it occurred to him that he wanted something to eat. "By George!" he thought, "I'll get that girl, Lily, and we'll go and have a good dinner!"

Even in the rococo vestibule of the yellow-brick apartment house, while he pressed the bell below Miss Lily Dale's letter box, he began to feel a glow of comfort; and when Lily let him into her little parlor, all clean and vulgar and warm, and fragrant with blossoming bulbs, and gave him a greeting that was almost childlike in its laughing pleasure, his sense of physical well-being was a sort of hitting back at Eleanor.

"Oh," said little Lily, "my! Ain't you cold! Why, your hand's just like ice!"

He let her help him off with his coat, and push him into what had been the vanished Batty's chair; then she saw that his feet were wet, and insisted (to his horror) on unlacing his boots and making him put on a pair of slippers.

"But I was going to take you out to dinner," he remonstrated.

She said: "Oh no! It's cold. I'll cook something for you, and we'll have our dinner right by that fire."

"Can you cook?" he said, with admiring astonishment.

"You bet I can!" she said; "I'll give you a *good* supper: you just wait!" In her pretty, laughing face was very honest friendliness. "I 'ain't forgot that time you handed it out to Batty! He had a bruise on his chin for a week!"

"A steak!" he exclaimed, watching her preparations in the tiny closet of a kitchen that opened into her parlor.

She nodded: "Ain't it luck to have it in the house? A friend of mine gave it to me this afternoon; her father's a butcher; and he's got a dandy shop on the next block; an' Annie run in with it, an' she says" (Lily was greasing her broiler), "'there,' she says, 'is a present for you!'"

Maurice insisted upon helping, and was told where to get the dishes and what to put on the table, and that if he opened that closet he'd see the beer. "I got just one bottle," she said, chuckling; "Batty stocked up. When he lit out, that was all he left behind him."

"Seen him lately?" Maurice asked.

Lily's face changed. "I 'ain't seen—anyone, since November," she said; "I'm a saleslady at Marston's. But I'll have to get out of this flat when Batty's lease runs out. He took it by the year. He was going to 'settle down,' and 'have a home,'—you know the talk? So he took it for the year. Well, he said I could stay till June. So I'm staying. There! It's done!" She put the sizzling steak on a platter and pressed butter and pepper and salt into it with an energetic knife and fork. "I bet," she said, "you wouldn't get a better steak than this at the Mercer House!"

"I bet I wouldn't get one as good," he assured her.

As he ate his extremely well-cooked steak, and drank a cup of extremely well-made coffee, and reflected that the pretty, amber-eyed woman who, after the manner of her kind, had already dropped into the friendliness of a nickname, and who waited on him with a sweet deftness, was a reformed character, owing, no doubt, to his own efforts, Maurice, comfortable in mind and body, felt the intense pleasure of punishing Eleanor by his mere presence in Lily's rooms. For, *if she could know where he was!*... "Gosh!" said Maurice. But of course she never would know. He wouldn't think of telling her where he had spent his evening; which shows how far they had drifted apart since that night when he had come home in his shirt sleeves, and been so eager to tell her how he had given his coat to the "poor thing"!

No; if he told Eleanor of Lily, now, there would be no sympathy for a girl who was really trying to keep straight; no impulse to do any "uplift" work! For that matter, Lily could do something in the way of uplift for Eleanor! ... Look at this tidy, gay little room, and the well-cooked steak, and the bulbs on the window sill! He strolled over and looked at the row of purple hyacinth glasses, full now of threadlike roots and topped with swelling buds. "You're quite a gardener," he said.

"Well, there!" said Lily; "if I hadn't but ten cents, I'd spend five for a flower!"

After they had washed the dishes together she made him comfortable in the big chair, and even put a blossoming hyacinth on the table beside him, so he could smell it now and then. Then she sat down on a hassock at his feet, with her back to the fire, and, flecking off the ashes of her cigarette over her shoulder, she talked a friendly trickle of funny stories; Maurice, smoking, too, thought how comfortable he was, and how pleasant it was to have a girl like Lily to talk to. Once or twice he laughed uproariously at some giggling joke. "She has lots of fun in her," he reflected; "and she's a bully cook; and her hair is mighty pretty.... Say, Lily, don't you want to trim my cuff? It's scratching me to death."

"You bet I do!" Lily said, and got her little shiny scissors and trimmed the broken edge of a worn-out cuff that Eleanor had never noticed.

He felt her small, warm fingers on his hand, and had a sense of comfort that made him almost forget Eleanor. "It would serve her right if I took Lily on," he thought. But he had not the remotest intention of taking Lily on! He only played with the idea, because the impossible reality would serve Eleanor right.

It was a month or two later, on the rebound of another dreariness with Eleanor, that the reality came, and he did "take Lily on." When he did so, no one could have been more astonished—under his dismay and horror—than Maurice.

Unless it was Lily? She had been so certain that he had no ulterior purpose, and so completely satisfied with her own way of living, that her rather snuggling friendliness with him was as honest as a boy's. Her surprise at her own mistake showed how genuine her intention of straightness really was. When he came, once or twice to see her, he called her Lily, and she called him "Curt," and they joked together like two playfellows,—except when he was too gloomy to joke. But it was his gloominess that made her feel sure there was nothing but friendliness in his calls. She was not curious about him; she knew he was married, but she never guessed that his preoccupation—during the spring Maurice was very preoccupied with his own wretchedness and given to those cynical fancies about "theater fires";—was due to the fact that he and his wife didn't get along. She merely supposed that, like most of her "gentlemen friends," "Curt" didn't talk about his wife. But, unlike the gentlemen of her world he was, apparently, a husband whose acquaintance with her had its limits. So they were both astonished....

But when Maurice discovered that such acquaintance had also its risks, the shock was agonizing. He was overwhelmed with disgust and shame. Once, at his desk, brooding over what had happened, his whipping instinct of truthfulness roused a sudden, frantic impulse in him to go home and confess to Eleanor, and ask her to forgive him. She never would, of course! No woman would; Eleanor least of all. But oh, if he only could tell her! As he couldn't, remorse, with no outlet of words, smoldered on his consciousness, as some hidden and infected wound might smolder in his flesh. Yet he knew there would be no further unfaithfulness. He would never, he told himself, see Lily again! *That* was easy! He was done with all "Lilys." If he could only shed the self-knowledge which he was unable to share with Eleanor, as easily as he could shed Lily, how thankful he would be! If he could but forget Lily by keeping away from her! But of course he could not forget. And with memory, and its redeeming pain of shame, was also the stabbing mortification of knowing that he had made a fool of himself, *again*! First Eleanor; then—Lily. Sometimes, with this realization of his idiocy, he would feel an almost physical nausea. It was so horrible to him, that when, a month later, the anniversary which marked his first folly came around again, he made an excuse of having to be away on business. It seemed to Maurice that to go out to their field, with this loathsome secrecy (which was, of course, an inarticulate lie) buried in his soul, would be like carrying actual corruption in his hands! So he went out of town on some trumped-up engagement, and Eleanor, left to herself, took little pining Bingo for a walk. In a lonely; place in the park, holding the dog on her knee, she looked into his passionately loving liquid eyes and wiped her own; eyes on his silky ears....

Those were aging months for Maurice; and though, of course, the poignancy of shame lessened after a while, it left its imprint on his face, as well as on his mind. They speculated about it at the office: "'G. Washington's' got a grouch on," one clerk said; "probably told the truth and lost a transfer! Let's give him another hatchet."

And the friendly people at the boarding house noticed the change in him. He had almost nothing to say, now, at dinner—no more jokes with the school-teacher, no more eager talks with the gray-haired woman....

"Has she forbidden conversation, do you suppose?" Miss Moore asked, giggling; but the widow said, soberly, that she was afraid Mr. Curtis was troubled about something. Mrs. Newbolt saw that there was something wrong with him, and talked of it to Eleanor, without a pause, for an hour. And of course Eleanor felt a difference in him; all day long, in the loneliness of their third-floor front, under the gaze of Daniel Webster, she brooded over it. Even while she was reading magazines and plodding through newspaper editorials on public questions she had never heard of, so that she could find things to talk about to him, she was thinking of the change, and asking herself what she had done—or left undone—to cause it? She also asked him:

"Maurice! Something bothers you! I'm not enough for you. What *is* the matter?"

He said, shortly, "Nothing."

At which she retreated into the silence of hurt feelings. Once, she knelt down, her face hidden on the grimy bed-spread, and prayed: "God, *please* give us a child—that will make him happy. And show me what to do to please him! Show me! Oh, *show* me! I'll do anything!" And who can say that her prayer was not answered? For certainly an idea did spring into her mind: those tiresome people downstairs—he liked to talk to them;—to Miss Moore, who giggled, and tried, Eleanor thought, to seem learned; and to the elderly woman who told stories. How could he enjoy talking to them when he could talk to her? But he did. So, suppose she tried to be more sociable with them? "I might invite Mrs. Davis to come up to our room some evening—and I would sing for her? ... But not Miss Moore; she is *too* silly, with her jokes!" Her mind strained to find ways to be friendly with these people he seemed to like. And circumstances helped her....

That was the month of the great eclipse. For a week Miss Ladd's boarders had talked about it, exchanging among themselves much newspaper astronomical misinformation—which the learned Miss Moore good-naturedly corrected. It was her suggestion that the household should make a night of it: "Let's all go up on the roof and see the show!" So the friendly gayety was planned—a supper in the basement dining room at half past eleven—ginger ale! ice cream! chocolate! Then an adjournment *en masse* to the top of the house. Of course Miss Moore, engineering the affair, invited the Curtises, confident of a refusal—and an acceptance;—both of which, indeed, she secured; but, to her astonishment, it was Mr. Curtis who declined, and his wife who accepted.

"It's a bore," Maurice told Eleanor, listlessly.

She looked worried: "Oh, I am so sorry! I told them at luncheon that we would come. I thought you'd enjoy it" (Her acceptance, which had been a real sacrifice to her, was a bomb to the other boarders. "What *has* happened?" they said to each other, blankly. "She'll be an awful wet blanket," some one said, frowning; and some one else said, "She's accepted because she won't let him out at night, alone!")

When the heterogeneous household gathered in the dining room, and corks popped and jokes were made, Eleanor and Maurice were there; he, watching the other people eat and drink and saying almost nothing; she, talking nervously and trying hard to be slangy about astronomy. Once he looked at her with faint interest—for she was so evidently "trying"! At midnight they all toiled up four flights of stairs from the basement to the garret, where, with proper squeamishness on the part of the ladies, and much gallantry of pushing and pulling on the part of the gentlemen, and all sorts of awkwardnesses and displaying of legs, they climbed a ladder and got out through the scuttle on to the flat roof. Then came the calculating of minutes, and facetiousness as to other people's watches and directions as to what one might expect to see. "It'll look like a bite out of a cookie, when it begins," the bond salesman said; and Miss Ladd tittered, and said what the ladies wanted to see was the man in the moon!

Maurice, intolerably irked, had moved across to the parapet and was staring out over the city. Below him spread the dim expanse of roofs and chimneys, with here and there the twinkle of light in an attic window. Leaning on the coping and looking down, he thought of the humanity under the dark roofs: a horizontal humanity—everybody asleep! The ugly fancy came to him that if that sleeping layer of bodies could be stirred up, there would be instantly a squirming mass of loathsome thoughts—maggots of lust, and shame, and jealousy, and fear. "My God! we're a nasty lot," he thought.

"Look!" a voice said at his shoulder. He sighed, impatiently—and looked. Above him soared the abyss of space, velvet black, pricked faintly here and there by stars; and, riding high—eternal and serene—the Moon.

He heard Miss Moore say, "*It's beginning.*" ... And the solemn curve of the Shadow touched the great disk. No one spoke: they stood—a handful of little human creatures, staring up into immensity; specks of consciousness on a whirling ball that was rushing forever into the void, and, as it rushed, its shadow, sweeping soundless through the emptiness of Space, touched the watching Moon ... and the broad plaque, silver gilt, lessened—lessened. To half. To a quarter. To a glistening line. Then coppery darkness.

No one spoke. The flow of universes seemed to sweep personality out upon eternal tides. Yet, strangely, Maurice felt a sudden uprush of personality! ... Little he was—oh, infinitely little; too little, of course, to be known by the Power that could do this—spread out the heavens, and rule the deeps of Space; and yet he felt, somehow, near to the Power. "It's what they call God, I suppose?" he said. It flashed into his mind that he had said almost exactly the same thing that day in the field (when he was a fool), of the fire of joy in his breast: he had said that Happiness was God! And some people thought this stupendous Energy could know—*us*? Absurd! "Might as well say a man could know an ant." Yet, just because Inconceivable Greatness was great, mightn't it know Inconceivable Littleness? "The smaller I am—the nastier, the meaner, the more contemptible—the greater It would have to be to know me? To say I was too little for It to know about, would be to set a limit to Its greatness." How foolish Reason looks, limping along behind such an intuition—Intuition, running and leaping, and praising

God! Maurice's reason strained to follow Intuition: "If It knows about me, It could help me, ... because It holds the stars. Why! *It* could fix things—with Eleanor!" Looking up into the gulf, his tiny misery suddenly fell away. "It would just prove Its greatness, to help me!" While he groped thus for God among the stars, the order of rushing worlds brought light, just as it had brought darkness: first a gleam; then a curving thread; then a silver sickle; then, magnificently! a shield of light—and the moon's unaltered face looked down at them. Maurice had an overwhelming impulse to drop his weakness into endless, ageless, limitless Power; his glimmer of self-knowledge, into enormous All-Knowledge; his secrecy into Truth. An impulse to be done with silences. "God knows; so Eleanor shall know." The idea of telling the truth was to Maurice—slipping and sinking into bottomless lying—like taking hold upon the great steadinesses of the sky....

People began to talk; Maurice did not hear them. Miss Ladd made a joke; Miss Moore said something about "light miles"; the old, sad, clever woman said, "The firmament showeth his handiwork,"—and instantly, as though her words were a signal—a voice, as silvery as the moon, broke the midnight with a swelling note:

> "The spacious firmament on high,
> With all the blue ethereal sky ..."

A shock of attention ran through the watchers on the roof: Eleanor, standing with her hands clasped lightly in front of her, her head thrown back, her eyes lifted to the unplumbed deeps, was singing:

> "The moon takes up the wondrous tale And nightly to the listening earth Repeats the story of her birth; Whilst all the stars that round her burn, And all the planets in their turn—"

A window was thrown open in a dark garret below, and some one, unseen, listened. Down in the street, two passers-by paused, and looked up. No one spoke. The voice soared on—and ended:

> "Forever singing as they shine...."

Maurice came to her side and caught her hand. There was a long sigh from the little group. For several minutes no one spoke. Miss Moore wiped her eyes; the baseball fan said, huskily, "My mother used to sing that"; the widow touched Eleanor's shoulder. "My—my husband loved it," she said, and her voice broke.

The garret window slammed down; the two people in the street vanished in the darkness. The little party on the roof melted away; they climbed through the scuttle, forgetting to joke, but saying to each other, in lowered voices: "Would you have *believed* it?" "How wonderful!" And to Eleanor, rather humbly: "It was beautiful, Mrs. Curtis!"

In their own room, Maurice took his wife in his arms and kissed her. "I am going to tell her," he said to himself, calmly. The overwhelming grandeur of the heavens had washed him clean of fear, clean even of shame, and left him impassioned with Beauty and Law, which two are Truth. "I will tell her," he said.

Eleanor had sung without self-consciousness; but now, when they were back again in their room—so stifling after those spaces between the worlds!—self-consciousness flooded in: "I suppose it was queer?" she said.

"It was perfect," Maurice said; he was very pale.

"I wanted to do something that they would like, and I thought they might like a hymn? Some of them said they did. But if you liked it, that is all I want."

"I loved it." His heart was pounding in his throat.... "Eleanor" (he could hardly see that terrible path among the stars, but he stumbled upward), "Eleanor, I'm not good enough for you."

"Not good enough? For *me*?" She laughed at such absurdity. He was sitting down, his elbow on his knee, his head in his hand. She came and knelt beside him. "If you are only happy! I did it to make you happy."

She heard him catch his breath. "How much do you love me?" he said.

(Oh, how long it was since he had talked that way—asking the sweet, unanswerable question of happy love!—how long since he had spoken with so much precious foolishness!) "How *much*? Why, Maurice, I love you so that sometimes, when I see you talking to other people—even these tiresome people here in the house, I could just die! I want you all to myself! I—I guess I feel about you the way Bingo feels about me," she said, trying to joke—but there were tears in her eyes.

"I'm not always ... what I ought to be," he said; "I am not—" (the path was very dim)—"awfully good. I—"

"I suppose I'm naturally jealous," she confessed; "I could die for you, Maurice; but I couldn't share your little finger! Do you remember, on our wedding day, you made me promise to be jealous? Well, I *am*." She laughed—and he was dumb. There, on the roof, Truth seemed as inevitable as Law. It did not seem inevitable now. He had lost his way among the stars. He could not find words to begin his story. But words overflowed on Eleanor's lips!... "Sometimes I get to thinking about myself—I *am* older than you, you know, a little. Not that it matters, really; but when I see you with other people, and you seem to enjoy talking to them—it nearly kills me! And you *do* like to talk to them. You even like to talk to—Edith, who is rude to me!" Her words poured out sobbingly: "Why, *why* am I not enough for you? You are enough for me!"

He was silent.

"And ... and ... and we haven't a baby," she said in a whisper, and dropped her face on his knee.

He tried to lift her, but his soul was sinking within him; dropping down—down from the awful heights. Yet still he caught at Truth! "Dear, don't! As for people, I may talk to them; I may even—even be with them, or seem to like them, and—and do things, that—I don't love anybody but you, Eleanor; but I—I—"

It was a final clutch at the Hand that holds the stars. But his entreating voice broke, for she was kissing his confession from his lips. Those last words—"I don't love anybody but you"—folded her in complete content! "Dear," she said, "that's all I want—that you don't love anybody but me." She laid her wet cheek against his in silence.

What could he do but be silent, too? What could he do but choke down the confessing, redeeming words that were on his lips? So he did choke them down, turning his back on the clean freedom of Truth; and the burden of his squalid secret, which he had been ready to throw away forever, was again packed like some corroding thing in his soul....

When, late in August, he and Eleanor went to Green Hill for a few days vacation, the effect of this repression was marked. There were wrinkles on his forehead under the thatch of his blond hair; his blue eyes were dulled, and he was taciturn to the point of rudeness—except to Eleanor. He was very polite to Eleanor. He never, now, amused himself by imagining how he could disappear if he had the luck to be in a theater fire. He knew that because he had enslaved himself to a lie, he had lost the right even to dream freedom. So there were no more "fool thoughts" as to how a man might "kick over the traces." There was nothing for him to do, now (he said), but "play the game." The Houghtons were uneasily aware of a difference in him; and Edith, fifteen now, felt that he had changed, and had fits of shyness with him. "He's like he was that night on the river," she told herself, "when he gave the lady his coat." She sighed when she said this, and it occurred to her that she would be a missionary. "I won't get married," she thought; "I'll go and nurse lepers. He's *exactly* like Sir Walter Raleigh."

But of course she had moments of forgetting the lepers—moments when she came down to the level of people like Johnny Bennett. When this happened, she thought that, instead of going to the South Seas, she would become a tennis star and figure in international tournaments; even Johnny admitted that she served well—for a girl. One day she confessed this ambition to Maurice, but he immediately beat her so badly that she became her old childlike, grumpy self, and said Johnny was nicer for singles; which enabled Maurice to turn her loose on John and go off alone to climb the mountain. He had a dreary fancy for looking at the camp, and living over again those days when he was still young—and a fool, of course; but not so great a fool as now, with Lily living in a little flat in Mercer. Batty's lease had expired, and she had moved into a cheaper, but still ornate, apartment house on the other side of the river. Well! Lily had floated into his life as meaninglessly as a mote floats into a streak of light, and then floated out again. He hadn't seen her since—since that time in May.

"*Ass—ass!*" he said to himself. "If Eleanor *knew*," he thought, "there'd be a bust-up in two minutes." He even smiled grimly to think of that evening of the eclipse when, shaken by the awful beauty of eternal order, he had, for just one high moment, dreamed that he, too, could attain the orderliness of Truth—and tell Eleanor. "Idiot!" he said, contemptuously. Probably Maurice touched his lowest level when he said that; for to be ashamed of an aspiration, to be contemptuous of emotion, is to sin against the Holy Ghost.

When Maurice reached the camp he stood for a while looking about him. The shack had not wintered well: the door sagged on a broken hinge, and the stovepipe had blown over and lay rusting on the roof. In the blackened circle of stones were some charred logs, which made him think of the camp fire on that night of Eleanor's courage and love and terror. He even reverted to those first excuses for her: "She nearly killed herself for me. Nervous prostration, Doctor Bennett said. I suppose a woman never gets over that. Poor Eleanor!" he said, softening; "it would kill her ... if she knew." He sat down and looked off across the valley ... "What am I going to do?" he said to himself. "I can't make her happy; I'd like to, but you can't reason with her any more than if she was a child. Edith has ten times her sense! How absurd she is about Edith. Lord! what would she do if she knew about Lily!"

He reflected, playing with the mere horror of the thought, upon just how complete the "bust-up" would be if she knew! He realized that he had undeserved good luck with Lily; she hadn't fastened herself on him. She was decent about that; if she'd been a different sort, he might have had a nasty time. But Lily was a sport—he'd say that for her; she hadn't clawed at him! And she had protested that she didn't want any money, and wouldn't take it! And she hadn't taken it. He had made some occasional presents, but nothing of any value. He had given her nothing, hardly even a thought (except the thought that he was an ass), since last May. Thinking of her now, he had another of those pangs of shame which had stabbed him so at first, but to which of late he had grown callous. The shame of having been the one—after all his goody-goody talk!—to pull her off the track; still, she was straight again now. He was quite sure of that. "You can tell when they're straight," he thought, heavily. Perhaps, in the winter, he would send her some flowers. He thought of the bulbs on the window sill of Lily's parlor, and tried to remember a verse; something about—about—what was it?

> If of thy store there be
> But left two loaves,
> Sell one, and with the dole
> Buy hyacinths to feed thy soul."

He laughed; *Lily*, feeding her "soul"! "Well, she has more 'soul,' with her flower pots and her good cooking, than some women who wouldn't touch her with a ten-foot pole! Still, *I'm* done with her!" he thought. But he had no purpose of "uplift"; the desire to reform Lily had evaporated. "Queer; I don't care a hoot," he told himself, watching with lazy eyes the smoke from his pipe drift blue between himself and the valley drowsing in the heat. "I'd like to see the little thing do well for herself—but really I don't give a damn." His moral listlessness, in view of the acuteness of that first remorse, and especially of that moment among the stars, when he had stretched out hands passionately eager for the agonizing sacrament of confession, faintly surprised him. How could he have been so wrought up about it? He looked off over the valley—saw the steely sickle of the river; saw a cloud shadow touch the shoulder of a mountain and move down across the gracious bosom of its forests. Below him, chestnuts twinkled and shimmered in the sun, and there were dusky stretches of hemlocks, then open pastures, vividly green from the August rains.... "It ought to be set to music," he thought; the violins would give the flicker of the leaves—"and the harps would outline the river. Eleanor's voice is lovely ... she looks fifty. How," he pondered, interested in the mechanics of it, "did she ever get me into that wagon?" Then, again, he was sorry for her, and said, "Poor girl!" Then he was sorry for himself. He knew that he was tired to death of Eleanor—tired of her moods and her lovemaking. He was not angry with her; he did not hate her;—he had injured her too much to hate her; he was simply unutterably tired of her—what he did hate, was this business of lugging a secret around! "I feel," he said to himself, "like a dog that's killed a hen, and had the carcass tied around his neck." His face twitched with disgust at his own simile. But as for Eleanor, he had been contemptibly mean to her, and, "By God!" he said to himself, "at least I'll play the game. I'll treat her as well as I can. Other fools have married jealous women, and put up with them. But, good Lord!" he thought, with honest perplexity, "can't the women *see* how they push you into the very thing they are afraid of, because they bore you so infernally? If I look at a woman, Eleanor's on her ear.... Queer," he pondered; "she's good. Look how kind she is to old O'Brien's lame child. And she *can* sing." He hummed to himself a lovely Lilting line of one of Eleanor's songs. "Confound it! why did I meet Lily? Eleanor is a million times too good for me...."

Far off he heard a sound and, frowning, looked toward the road: yes; somebody was coming! "Can't a man get a minute to himself?" Maurice thought, despairingly. It was the mild-eyed and spectacled Johnny Bennett, and behind him, Edith, panting and perspiring, and smiling broadly.

"Hello!" she called out, in cheerful gasps; "thought we'd come up and walk home with you!"

"'Lo," Maurice said.

The boy and girl achieving the rocky knoll on which Maurice was sitting, his hands locked about his knees, his eyes angry and ashamed, staring over the treetops, sat down beside him. Johnny pulled out his pipe, and Edith took off her hat and fanned herself. "Mother and Eleanor went for a ride. I thought I'd rather come up here."

"Um—" Maurice said.

"Two letters for you," she said. "Eleanor told me to bring 'em up. Might be business."

As she handed them to him, his eye caught the address on one of them, and a little cold tingle suddenly ran down his spine. Lily had never written to him, but some instinct warned him that that cramped handwriting on the narrow lavender envelope, forwarded from the office, could only be hers. A whiff of perfumery made him sure. He had a pang of fright. At what? He could not have said; but even before he opened the purple envelope he knew the taste of fear in his mouth....

Sitting there on the mountain, looking down into the misty serenities of the sun-drenched valley, with the smoke of Johnny Bennett's pipe in his nostrils, and the friendly Edith beside him, he tore open the scented envelope, and as his eyes fell on the first lines it seemed as if the spreading world below rose up and hit him in the face:

DEAR FRIEND CURT,—I don't know what you'll say. I hope you won't be mad. I'm going to have a baby. *It's yours*....

Maurice could not see the page, a wave of nausea swamped even his horror; he swallowed—swallowed—swallowed. Edith heard him gasp, and looked at him, much interested.

"What's the matter with your hands?" Edith inquired. "Johnny! Look at his hands!"

Maurice's fingers, smoothing out the purple sheet, were shaking so that the paper rustled. He did not hear her. Then he read the whole thing through to its laconic end:

It's yours—honest to God. Can you help me a little? Sorry to trouble you on your vacation.

Your friend,

LILY.

"What *is* the matter with your hands?" Edith said, very much interested.

CHAPTER XI

When, a year after his marriage, Maurice began to awaken to Eleanor's realities, maturity had come to him with a bound. But it was almost age that fell upon him when Lily's realities confronted him. In the late afternoon, as he and Edith and the silent Johnny walked down the mountain, he was dizzy with terror of Lily!

She was blackmailing him.

But even as he said the word, he had an uprush of courage; he would get a lawyer, and shut her up! That's what you do when anybody blackmails you. Perfectly simple. "A lawyer will shut her up!" It was a hideous mess, and he had no money to spend on lawyers; but it would never get out—the newspapers couldn't get hold of it—because a lawyer would shut her up! Though, probably, he'd have to give her some money? How much would he have to give her? And how much would he have to pay the lawyer? He had a crazy vision of Lily's attaching his salary. He imagined a dialogue with his employer: "A case of blackmail, sir." "Don't worry about it, Curtis; we'll shut her up." This brought an instant's warm sense of safety, which as instantly vanished—and again he was walking down the road, with Edith beside him, talking, talking... Eleanor would have to know... No! She wouldn't! He could keep it a secret. But he'd have to tell Mr. Houghton. Then Mrs. Houghton would know! Again a wave of nausea swept over him, and he shuddered; then said to himself: "No: Uncle Henry's white. He won't even tell her."

Edith was asking him something; he said, "Yes," entirely at random—and was at once involved in a snarl of other questions, and other random answers. Under his breath he thought, despairingly, "Won't she ever stop talking! ... Edith, I'll give you fifty cents if you'll keep quiet."

Edith was willing enough to be quiet; "But," she added, practically, "would you mind giving me the fifty cents now, Maurice? You always tear off to Eleanor the minute you get home, and I'm afraid you'll forget it."

He put his hand in his pocket and produced the half dollar. "Anything to keep you still!" he said.

"You don't mind if I talk to Johnny?"

He didn't answer; at that moment he was not aware of her existence, still less Johnny's, for a frightful thought had stabbed him: Suppose it wasn't blackmail? *Suppose Lily had told the truth?* Suppose "it" was his? "She can't prove it—she can't prove it!" he said, aloud.

"Prove what? Who can't?" Edith said, interested.

Maurice didn't hear her. Suddenly he felt too sick to follow his own thought, and go to the bottom of things; he was afraid to touch the bottom! He made a desperate effort to keep on the surface of his terror by saying: "It's all Eleanor's fault. Damnation! Her idiotic jealousy drove me out of the house that Sunday afternoon!"

At this moment Johnny Bennett and Edith broke into shrieks of laughter. "Say, Maurice," Johnny began—

"Can't you children be quiet for five minutes?" Maurice said. Johnny whistled and, behind his spectacles, made big eyes at Edith. "What's *he* got on his little chest?" Johnny inquired. But Maurice was deaf to sarcasm.... "It all goes back to Eleanor!"

Under the chatter of the other two, it was easier to say this than to say, "Is Lily telling the truth?" It was easier to hate Eleanor than to think about Lily. And, hating, he said again, aloud, the single agonized word.

Edith stood stock-still with amazement; she could not believe her ears. *Maurice* had said—? As for Maurice, his head bent as if he were walking in a high wind he strode on, leaving her in the road staring after him.

"Johnny!" said Edith; "did you hear?"

"That's nothing," Johnny said; "I say it often, when mother ain't round. At least I say the first part."

"Oh, *Johnny*!" Edith said, dismayed.

To Maurice, rushing on alone, the relief of hating Eleanor was lost in the uprush of that ghastly possibility: "If it *is* mine?"

Something in him struggled to say: "If it *is*, why, then, I must—But it isn't!" Maurice was, for the moment, a horribly scared boy; his instinct was to run to cover at any cost. He forgot Edith, coming home by herself after Johnny should turn in at his own gate; he was conscious only of his need to be alone to think this thing out and decide what he must do. There was no possible privacy in the house. "If I go up to our room," he thought, frantically, "Eleanor'll burst in on me, and then she'll get on to it that there's something the matter!" Suddenly he remembered the chicken coop. "It's late. Edith won't be coming in." So he skulked around behind the house and the stable, and up the gravel path to the henhouse. Lifting the rusty latch, he stepped quietly into the dusky, feathery shelter. "I can think the damned business out, here," he thought. There was a scuffling "cluck" on the roosts, but when he sat down on an overturned box, the fowls settled into stillness and, except for an occasional sleepy squawk, the place was quiet. He drew a long breath, and dropped his chin on his fist. "Now I'll think," he said. Then, through the cobwebby windows, he saw in the yellowing west the new moon, and below it the line of distant hills. An old pine tree stretched a shaggy branch across the window, and he said to himself that the moon and the hills and the branch were like a Japanese print.

He took the letter out of his pocket—his very fingers shrinking as he touched it—and straining his eyes in the gathering dusk, he read it all through. Then he looked at the moon, which was sliding—sliding behind the pine. Yes, that ragged branch was very Japanese. If he hadn't gone out on the river that night with Edith, he would never have met Lily. The thing he had said on his wedding day, in the meadow, about "switches," flashed into his mind: "A little thing can throw the switches."

"Ten minutes in a rowboat," he said,—"and *this*!" One of the hens clucked. "I'll fight," he said. "Lots of men come up against this sort of thing, and they hand the whole rotten business over to a lawyer. I'll fight. Or I'll move.... Perhaps that's the best way? I'll just tell Eleanor we've got to live in New York. Damn it! she'd ask why? I'll say I have a job there. Lily'd never be able to find me in New York." The moon slipped out below the pine, and hung for a dim moment in the haze. Maurice's mind went through a long and involved plan of concealing his address from Lily when he moved to New York.... "But what would we live on while I was finding a job?" ... Suddenly thought stopped short; he just watched the moon, and listened to a muffled stir among the hens. Then he took out his knife, and began to cut little notches on the window sill. "I'll fight," he said, mechanically.

There were running steps on the gravel path, and instantly he was on his feet. He had the presence of mind to put his hand into a nest, so that when Edith came in she reproached him for getting ahead of her in collecting eggs.

"How many have you got? Two? Griselda was on the nest when I started up the mountain, but I thought there was another egg there?"

"Only one," he said, thickly, and handed it to her.

"Come on in the house," Edith commanded; "I suppose," she said, resignedly, "Eleanor is playing on the piano!" (Edith, as her adoration of Eleanor lessened, was frankly bored by her music.)

"All right," Maurice said, and followed her.

Edith asked no questions; Maurice's "word" on the road had sobered her too much for talk. "He's mad about something," she thought; "but I never heard Maurice say—*that*!" She didn't quite like to repeat what he had said, though Johnny had confessed to saying "part of it." "I don't believe he ever did," Edith thought; "he's putting on airs! But for Maurice to say *all* of it!—that was wrong," said Edith, gravely.

They went out of the henhouse together in silence. Maurice was saying to himself, "I might not be able to get a job in New York... I'll fight." Yet certain traditional decencies, slowly emerging from the welter of his rage and terror, made him add, "If it was mine, I'd have to give her something... But it isn't. I'll fight."

He was so absorbed that before he knew it he had followed Edith to the studio, where, in the twilight. Mr. and Mrs. Houghton were sitting on the sofa together, hand in hand, and Eleanor was at the piano singing, softly, old songs that her hosts loved.

"If," said Henry Houghton, listening, "heaven is any better than this, I shall consider it needless extravagance on the part of the Almighty,"—and he held his wife's hand against his lips. Maurice, at the door, turned away and would have gone upstairs, but Mr. Houghton called out: "Sit down, man! If *I* had the luck to have a wife who could sing, I'd keep her at it! Sit down!" Eleanor's voice, lovely and noble and serene, went on:

"To add to golden numbers, golden numbers!
0 sweet content! O sweet, O sweet content!"

Maurice sat down; it was as if, after beating against crashing seas with a cargo of shame and fear, he had turned suddenly into a still harbor: the faintly lighted studio, the stillness of the summer evening, the lovely voice—the peace and dignity and safety of it all gave him a strange sense of unreality... Then, suddenly, he heard them all laughing and telling Eleanor they were sorry for her, to have such an unappreciative husband!—and he realized that the fatigue of terror had made him fall asleep. Later, when he came to the supper table, he was still dazed. He said he had a headache, and could not eat; instantly Eleanor's anxiety was alert. She suggested hot-water bags and mustard plasters, until Mr. Houghton said to himself: "How *does* he stand it? Mary must tell her not to be a mother to him—or a grandmother."

All that hot evening, out on the porch, Maurice was silent—so silent that, as they separated for the night, his guardian put a hand on his shoulder, "Come into the studio," he said; "I want to show you a thing I've been muddling over."

Maurice followed him into the vast, shadowy, untidy room ("No females with dusters allowed on the premises!" Henry Houghton used to say), glanced at a half-finished canvas, said, "Fine!" and turned away.

"Anything out of kilter? I mean, besides your headache?"

"Well ... yes."

("He's going to say he's hard up—the extravagant cuss!" Henry Houghton thought, with the old provoked affection.)

"I'm bothered about ... something," Maurice began.

("He's squabbled with Eleanor. I wish I was asleep!")

"Uncle Henry," Maurice said, "if you were going to see a lawyer, who would you see?"

"I wouldn't see him. Lawyers make their cake by cooking up other people's troubles. Sit down. Let's talk it out." He settled himself in a corner of the ragged old horsehair sofa which faced the empty fireplace and motioned Maurice to a chair. "I thought it wasn't all headache; what's the matter, boy?"

Maurice sat down, cleared his throat, and put his hands in his pockets so they would not betray him. "I—" he said.

Mr. Houghton appeared absorbed in biting off the end of his cigar.

"I—" Maurice said again.

"Maurice," said Henry Houghton, "keep the peace. If you and Eleanor have fallen out, don't stand on your dignity. Go upstairs and say you're sorry, whether you are or not. Don't talk about lawyers."

"My God!" said Maurice; "did you suppose it was *that*?"

Mr. Houghton stopped biting the end of his cigar, and looked at him. "Why, yes; I did. You and she are rather foolish, you know. So I supposed—"

Maurice dropped his face on his arms on the big dusty table, littered with pamphlets and charcoal studies and squeezed-out paint tubes. After a while he lifted his head: "*That's* nothing. I wish it was that."

The older man rose and stood with his back to the mantelpiece. They both heard the clock ticking loudly. Then, almost in a whisper, Maurice said:

"I've been—blackmailed."

Mr. Houghton whistled.

"I've had a letter from a woman. She says—"

"Has she got anything on you?"

"No proof; but—"

"But you have made a fool of yourself?"

"Yes."

Mr. Houghton sat down again. "Go on," he said.

Maurice reached for a maulstick lying across the table; then leaned over, his elbows on his knees, and tried, with two trembling forefingers, to make it stand upright on the floor. "She's common. She can't prove it's—mine." His effort to keep the stick vertical with those two shaking fingers was agonizing.

"Begin at the beginning," Henry Houghton said.

Maurice let the maulstick drop against his shoulder and sunk his head on his hands. Suddenly he sat up: "What's the use of lying? She's *not* bad all through." The truth seemed to tear him as he uttered it. "That's the worst of it," he groaned. "If she was, I'd know what to do. But probably she's not lying... She says it's mine. Yes; I pretty well know she's not lying."

"We'll go on the supposition that she is. I have yet to see a white crow. How much does she want?"

"She's only asked me to help her, when—it's born. And of course, if it *is* mine, I—"

"We won't concede the 'if.'"

"Uncle Henry," said the haggard boy, "I'm several kinds of a fool, but I'm not a skunk. I've got to be decent"

"You should have thought of decency sooner."

"I know. I know."

"You'd better tell me the whole thing. Then we'll talk lawyers."

So Maurice began the squalid story. Twice he stopped, choking down excuses that laid the blame on Eleanor.... "It wouldn't have happened if I hadn't been—been bothered." And again, "Something had thrown me off the track; and I met Lily, and—"

At last it was all said, and he had not skulked behind his wife. He had told everything, except those explaining things that could not be told.

When the story was ended there was silence. The older man, guessing the untold things, could not trust himself to speak his pity and anger and dismay. But in that moment of silence the comfort of confession made the tears stand in the boy's eyes; he said, impulsively, "Uncle Henry, I thought you'd kick me out of the house!"

Henry Houghton blew his nose, and spoke with husky harshness. "Eleanor has no suspicions?" (He, too, was choking down references to Eleanor which must not be spoken.)

"No. Do you think I ought to—to tell—?"

"No! No! With some women you could make a clean breast... I know a woman—her husband hadn't a secret from her; and I know *he* was a fool before his marriage! He made a clean breast of it, and she married him. But she knew the soul of him, you see? She knew that this sort of rotten foolishness was only his body. So he worshiped her. Naturally. Properly. She meant God to him... Mighty few women like that! Candidly, I don't think your wife is one of them. Besides, this is *after* marriage. That's different, Maurice. Very different. It isn't a square deal."

Maurice made a miserable shamed sound of agreement. Then he said, huskily, "Of course I won't lie; I'll just—not tell her."

"The thing for us to do," said Mr. Houghton, "is to get you out of this mess. Then you'll keep straight? Some fellows wouldn't. You will, because—" he paused; Maurice looked at him with scared eyes—"because if a man is sufficiently aware of having been a damned fool, he's immune. I'll bet on you, Maurice."

CHAPTER XII

Yet Henry Houghton had moments of fearing that he would lose his bet, for Maurice was such a very damned fool! One might have guessed as much when he would not admit that Lily was lying. She might be blackmailing him, he said; she might be a "crow"; but she wasn't lying. When his guardian had talked it all out with him, and written a letter which Maurice was to take to a lawyer ("she'll want to get rid of the child; they always want to get rid of the child; so she may let you off easier if you say you'll see that it is cared for; and we'll have Hayes put it in black and white") when all these arrangements had been made, Maurice almost dished the whole thing (so Mr. Houghton expressed it) by saying—again as if the words burst up from some choked well of truthfulness:

"Uncle Henry, it isn't blackmail; and—and I've got to be half decent!"

Down from the upper hall came a sweet, anxious voice: "Maurice, darling! It's twelve o'clock! What *are* you doing?"

Mr. Houghton called back: "We're talking business, Eleanor. I'll send him up in a quarter of an hour. Don't lose your beauty sleep, my dear. (Mary *must* tell her not to be such an idiot!)" Then he looked at Maurice: "My boy, you can't be decent with a leech. You've got to leave this to Hayes."

"She isn't a leech. I ought to help her, I'll see her myself."

"My dear fellow, don't be a bigger ass than you can help! You can meet what you see fit to call your responsibilities, as a few other conscientious fools have done before you; though," he added, heavily, "I hope she won't suck you dry! How you are going to squeeze out the money, I don't know! I can't help you much. But you mustn't appear in this for a single minute. Hayes will see her, and buy her off."

Maurice shook his head, despairingly: "Uncle Henry, she's common; but she's not vicious. She's a nice little thing. I know Lily! I'll see her. *I'll have to!* I'll tell her I'll—I'll help her." No wonder poor Henry Houghton feared he would lose his bet! "I know you think I'm easy meat," Maurice said; "but I'm not. Only," his face was anguished, "I've *got* to be half decent."

It was after one o'clock when the two men went upstairs, though there had been another summons over the banisters: "Maurice! Why don't you come to bed?" When they parted at Maurice's door, Mr. Houghton struck his ward on the shoulder and whispered, "You're more than half decent. I'll bet on you!" and Maurice whispered back:

"You're *white*, Uncle Henry!"

He went into his room on tiptoe, but Eleanor heard him and said, sleepily, "What on earth have you been talking about?"

"Business," Maurice told her.

"Who was your lavender-colored letter from?" Eleanor said, yawning; "I forgot to ask you. It was awfully scented!"

There was an instant's pause; Maurice's lips were dry;—then he said:

"From a woman... About a house. (My God! I've *lied* to her!)" he said to himself...

Mary Houghton, reading comfortably in bed, looked up at her old husband over her spectacles. "I've heated some cocoa, dear," she said. "Drink it before you undress; you are worn out. What kept you downstairs until this hour?"

"Business."

Mary Houghton smiled: "Might as well tell the truth."

"Oh, Kit, it's a horrid mess!" he groaned; "I thought that boy had got to the top of Fool Hill when he married Eleanor! But he hadn't."

"Can't tell me, I suppose?"

"No. Mary, mayn't I have a cigar? I'm really awfully used up, and—"

"Henry! You are perfectly depraved! No; you may *not*. Drink your cocoa, honey. And consider the stars;—they shine, even above Fool Hill. And 'messes' look mighty small beside the Pleiades!" Then she turned a page of her novel, and added, "Poor Eleanor."

"I don't know why you say 'Poor Eleanor'!"

"Because I know that Maurice isn't sharing his 'mess' with her."

"You are uncanny!" Henry Houghton said, stirring his cocoa and looking at her admiringly.

"No; merely intelligent. Henry, don't let him have any secrets from Eleanor! Tell him to *tell* her. She'll forgive him."

"She's not that kind, Mary."

"Dear, *almost* every woman is 'that kind'! It's deception, not confession, that makes them—the other kind. If Maurice will confess—"

"I haven't said there was anything to confess," he protested, in alarm.

"Oh no; certainly not. You haven't said a word! (Well; you may have just one of those *little* cigars—you poor dear!) Henry, listen: If Maurice hangs a secret round his neck it will drown him."

"If Eleanor would make cocoa for him at one o'clock in the morning there would be no chance for secrets. Kit, I have long known that you are the wisest, as well as the most virtuous and most lovable of your sex, and that I shall only get to heaven by hanging on to your petticoats; but in this one particular I am much more intelligent than you."

"Heaven send you a good opinion of yourself!" his wife murmured.

But he insisted. "On certain subjects women prefer to be lied to."

"Did any woman ever tell you so?" she inquired, dryly.

He shrugged his shoulders, put his cup down, and came over to give her a kiss.

"Which is to say, 'Hold your tongue'?" his Mary inquired.

"Oh, never!" he said, and in spite of his distress he laughed; but he looked at her tenderly. "The Lord was good to me, Mary, when He made you take me."

That talk in the studio marked the moment when Maurice Curtis turned his back on youth. It was the beginning of the retreat of an ardent and gayly candid boy into the adult sophistications of Secrecy. The next day when he and Eleanor returned to Mercer, he sat in the car watching with unseeing eyes the back of her head,—her swaying hat, the softly curling tendrils of dark hair in the nape of her neck—and he saw before him a narrow path, leading—across quaking bogs of evasions!—toward a goal of always menaced safety. Mr. Houghton had indicated the path in that midnight talk, and Maurice's first step upon it would be his promise to relieve Lily of the support of her child—"*on condition that she would never communicate with him again.*" After that, Henry Houghton said, "the lawyer will clinch things; and nobody will ever be the wiser!" Because Eleanor was the woman she was, he saw no way of escape for Maurice, except through this bog of secrecy, where any careless step might plunge him into a lie. He had not dared to point out that other path, which his Mary thought so much safer than the sucking shakiness of the swamp—the rough and terrible path of confession, which lies across the firm aridities of Truth, and leads to that orderly freedom of the stars to which Maurice had once aspired! So now the boy was going back to Mercer to plunge into the pitfalls and limitless shades of concealment. He did it with a hard purpose of endurance, without hope, and also without complaint.

"If I can just avoid out-and-out lying," he told himself, "I can take my medicine. But if I have to lie—!"

He knew the full bitterness of his medicine when he went to see Lily...

He went the very next day, after office hours... There had been a temptation to postpone the taking of the medicine, because it had been difficult to escape from Eleanor. The well-ordered household at Green Hill had fired her with an impulse to try housekeeping again, and she wanted to urge the idea upon Maurice:

"We would be so much more comfortable; and I could have little Bingo!"

"We can't afford it," he said. (Oh, how many things he wouldn't be able to afford, now!)

"It wouldn't cost much more. I'll come down to the office this afternoon and walk home with you, and tell you what I've thought out about it."

Maurice said he had to—to go and see an apartment house at five.

"That's no matter! I'll meet you and walk along with you."

"I have several other places to go."

That hurt her. "If you don't want me—"

He was so absorbed that her words had no meaning to him. "Good-by," he said, mechanically—and the next moment he was on his way.

At the office his employer gave him a keen glance. "You look used up, Curtis; got a cold?" Mr. Weston asked, kindly.

Maurice, sick in spirit, said, "No, sir; I'm all right."

And so the minutes of the long day ticked themselves away, each a separate pang of disgust and shame, until five o'clock came, and he started for Lily's.

While he waited in the unswept vestibule of an incredibly ornate frame apartment house for the answer to his ring, and the usual: "My goodness! Is that you? Come on up!" he had the feeling of one who stands at a closed door, knowing that when he opens it and enters he will look upon a dead face. The door was Lily's, and the face was the face of his dead youth. Carelessness was over for Maurice, and irresponsibility. And hope, too, he thought, and enthusiasm, and ambition. All over! All dead. All lying stiff and still on the other side of a shiny golden-oak door, with its half window hung with a Nottingham lace curtain. When he started up the three flights of stairs to that little flat where he was to look upon his dead, he was calm to the point of listlessness. "My own fault. My own fault," he said.

She was waiting for him on the landing, her fresh cleanness in fragrant contrast to the forlorn untidiness of the stairways. They went into her parlor together and he began to speak at once.

"I got your letter. No; I won't sit down. I—"

"My soul and body! You're all in!" Lily said, startled, "Let me get you some whisky—"

"No, please, nothing! Lily, I'm ... awfully sorry, I—I'll do what I can. I—"

She put her hands over her face; he went on mechanically, with his carefully prepared sentences, ending with:

"There's no reason why we should meet any more. But I want you to know that the—the—*it*, will be taken care of. My lawyer will see you about it; I'll have it placed somewhere."

She dropped her hands and looked at him, her little, pretty face amazed and twitching: "Do you mean you'll take my baby?"

"I'll see that it's provided for."

"I ain't that kind of a girl!" They were standing, one on either side of a highly varnished table, on which, on a little brass tray, a cigarette stub was still smoldering. "*I* don't want anything out of you"—Lily paused; then said, "Mr. Curtis"—(the fact that she didn't call him "Curt" showed her recognition of a change in their relationship)—"I'm not on the grab. I can keep on at Marston's for quite a bit. All I want is just if you can help me in February? But I'll never give my baby up! My first one died."

"Your *first*—"

"So I'll never, never give it up!" Her shallow, honest, amber-colored eyes overflowed with bliss. "I'll just love it!" she said.

Maurice felt an almost physical collapse; neither he nor Henry Houghton had reckoned on maternal love. Mr. Houghton had implied that Lily's kind did not have maternal love. "She'll leave it on a convenient doorstep—unless she's a white blackbird," Henry Houghton had said. Maurice, too, had taken for granted Lily's eagerness to get rid of the child. In his amazement now, at this revelation of an unknown Lily—a white blackbird Lily!—he began, angrily, to argue: "It is impossible for you to keep it! Impossible! I won't permit it—"

"I wouldn't give it up for anything in the world! I'll take care of it. You needn't worry for fear I'll put it onto you."

"But I won't have you keep it! I promise you I'll look after it. You must go away, somewhere. Anywhere!"

"But I don't want to leave Mercer," she said, simply.

In his despairing confusion, he sat down on the little bowlegged sofa and looked at her; Lily, sitting beside him, put her hand on his—which quivered at the touch. "Don't you worry! I'd never play you any mean trick. You treated me good, and I'll never treat you mean; I 'ain't forgot the way you handed it out to Batty! I'll never let on to anybody. Say—I believe you're afraid I'll try a hold-up on you some day? Why, Mr. Curtis, I wouldn't do a thing like that—no, not for a million dollars! Look here; if it will make you easy in your mind, I'll put it down in writing; I'll say it *ain't* yours! Will that make you easy in your mind?" Her kind eyes were full of anxious pity for him. "I'll do anything for you, but I won't give up my baby."

She was trying to help him! He was so angry and so frightened that he felt sick at his stomach; but he knew that she was trying to help him!

"You see," she explained, "the first one died; now I'm going to have another, and you bet I'm going to have things nice for her! I'm going to buy a parlor organ. And I'll have her learned to play. It's going to be a girl. Oh, won't I dress her pretty! But I'll never come down on you about her. Now, don't you worry."

The generosity of her! She'd "put it down in writing"! "I *told* Uncle Henry she was white," he thought. But in spite of her whiteness his blue eyes were wide with horror; all those plans, of Lily in another city, and an unacknowledged child, in still another city—for of course *it* could not be in Mercer any more than Lily could!—all these safe arrangements faded into a swift vision of Lily, in this apartment, with *it*! Lily, meeting him on the street!—a flash of imagination showed him Lily, pushing a baby carriage! For just a moment sheer terror made that dead Youth of his stir.

"You can't keep it!" he said again, hoarsely; "I tell you, I won't allow it! I'll look after it. *But I won't have it here!* And I won't ever see you."

"You needn't," she said, reassuringly; "and I'll never bother you. That ain't me!"

He was dumb.

"An' look," she said, cheerfully; "honest, it's better for you. What would you do, looking after a little girl? Why, you couldn't even curl her hair in the mornings!" Maurice shuddered. "And I'll never ask you for a cent, if you can just make it convenient to help me in February?"

"Of course I'll help you," he said; then, suddenly, his anger fell into despair. "Oh, what a damned fool I was!"

"All gentlemen are," she tried to comfort him. Her generosity made him blush. Added to his shame because of what he had done to Eleanor, was a new shame at his own thoughts about this little, kind, bad, honest woman! "Look here," Lily said; "if you're strapped, never mind about helping me. They'll take you at the Maternity free, if you *can't* pay. So I'll go there; and I'll say I'm married; I'll say my husband was Mr. George Dale, and he's dead; I'll never peep your name. Now, don't you worry! I'll keep on at Marston's for four months, anyway. Yes; I'll buy me a ring and call myself Mrs. Dale; I guess I'll say Mrs. Robert Dale; Robert's a classier name than George. And nobody can say anything to my baby."

"Of course I'll give you whatever you need for—when—when it's born," he said. He was fumbling with his pocketbook; he had nothing more to say about leaving Mercer.

She took the money doubtfully. "I won't want it yet awhile," she said.

"I'll make it more if I can," he told her; he got up, hesitated, then put out his hand. For a single instant, just for her pluck, he was almost fond of her. "Take care of yourself," he said, huskily; and the next minute he was plunging down those three flights of unswept stairs to the street. "My own fault—my own fault," he said, again; "oh, what a cussed, cussed, cussed fool!"

It was over, this dreadful interview! this looking at the dead face of his Youth. Over, and he was back again just where he was when he came in. Nothing settled. Lily—who was so much more generous than he!—would still be in Mercer, waiting for this terrible child. His child!

He had accomplished nothing, and he saw before him the dismaying prospect of admitting his failure to Mr. Houghton. The only comfort in the whole hideous business was that he wouldn't have to pull a lawyer into it, and pay a big fee! He was frantic with worry about expense. Well, he must strike Mr. Weston for a raise!... which he wouldn't tell Eleanor about. A second step into the bog of Secrecy!

When he got home, Eleanor, in the dingy third-floor front, was waiting for him, alert and tender, and gay with purpose: "Maurice! I've counted expenses, and I'm sure we can go to housekeeping! And I can have little Bingo. Mrs. O'Brien says he's just pining away for me!"

"We can't afford it," he said again, doggedly.

"I believe," she said, "you like this horrid place, because you have people to talk to!"

"It's well enough," he said. He was standing with his back to her, his clenched hands in his pockets, staring out of the window. His very attitude, the stubbornness of his shoulders, showed his determination not to go to housekeeping.

"What *is* the matter, Maurice?" she said, her voice trembling. "You are not happy! Oh, what *can* I do?" she said, despairingly.

"I am as happy as I deserve to be," he said, without turning his head.

She came and stood beside him, resting her cheek on his shoulder. "Oh," she said, passionately, "if I only had a child! You are disappointed because we have no—"

His recoil was so sharp that she could not finish her sentence, but clutched at his arm to steady herself; before she could reproach him for his abruptness he had caught up his hat and left the room. She stood there quivering. "He *would* be happier and love me more, if we had a child!" she said again. She thought of the joy with which, when they first went to housekeeping, she had bought that foolish, pretty nursery paper—and again the old disappointment ached under her breastbone. Tears were just ready to overflow; but there was a knock at the door and old Mrs. O'Brien came in with her basket of laundry; she gave her beloved Miss Eleanor a keen look "It's worried you are, my dear? It ain't the wash, is it?"

Eleanor tried to laugh, but the laugh ended in a sob. "No. It's—it's only—" Then she said something in a whisper.

"No baby? Bless you, *he* don't want no babies! What would a handsome young man like him be wanting a baby for? No! And it would take your good looks, my dear. Keep handsome, Miss Eleanor, and you needn't worry about *babies*! And say, Miss Eleanor, never let on to him if you see him give a look at any of his lady friends. I'm old, my dear, but I noticed, with all my husbands—and I've had three—that if you tell 'em you see 'em lookin' at other ladies, *they'll look again!*—just to spite you. Don't notice 'em, and they'll not do it. Men is children."

Eleanor, laughing in spite of her pain, said Mr. Curtis didn't "look at other ladies; but—but," she said, wistfully, "I hope I'll have a baby." Then she wiped her eyes, hugged old O'Brien, and promised to "quit worrying." But she didn't "quit," for Maurice's face did not lighten.

Henry Houghton, too, saw the aging heaviness of the young face when, having received the report of that interview with Lily, he came down to Mercer to go over the whole affair and see what must be done. But there was nothing to be done. Up in his room in the hotel he and Maurice thrashed it all out:

"She prefers to stay in Mercer," Maurice explained; "and she'll stay. There's nothing I can do; absolutely nothing! But she'll play fair. I'm not afraid of Lily."

If Mr. Houghton wished, uneasily, that his ward was afraid of Lily, he did not say so. He only told Maurice again that he was "betting on him."

"You won't lose," Maurice said, laconically.

"Perhaps," Henry Houghton said, doubtfully, "I ought to say that Mrs. Houghton—who is the wisest woman I know, as well as the best—has an idea that in matters of this sort, frankness is the best course. But in your case (of which, of course, she knows nothing) I don't agree with her."

"It would be impossible," Maurice said, briefly. And his guardian, whose belief in secrecy had been shaken, momentarily, by his Mary's opinion, felt that, so long as he had quoted her, his conscience was clear. So he only told the boy again he was *sure* he could bet on him! And because shame, and those bleak words "my own fault," kept the spiritual part of Maurice alive,—(and because Lily was a white blackbird!) the bet stood.

But he made no promises about the future. However much of a liar Maurice was going to be, to Eleanor, he would not, he told himself, lie to this old friend by saying he would never see Lily again. The truth was, some inarticulate moral instinct made him know that there would come a time when he would *have* to see her... During all that winter, when he sat, night after night, at Miss Ladd's dinner table, and Eleanor fended off Miss Moore and the widow, or when, in those long evenings in their own room they played solitaire, he was thinking of Lily, thinking of that inner summons to what he called "decency," which would, he knew, drive him—in three months—in two months—in one month!—to Lily's door. By and by it was three weeks—two weeks—one week! Then came days when he said, in terror, "I'll go to-morrow." And again: "To-morrow, I *must* go. Damn it! I must!" So at last, he went, lashed and driven by that mastering "decency"!

He had bought a box of roses, and, looping two fingers through its strings, he walked twice around the block past the ugly apartment house before he could make up his mind to enter. He wondered whether Lily had died? Women do die, sometimes. "Of course I don't want anything to happen to her; but—" Then he wondered, with a sudden pang of hope, if anything had happened to—*It*? "They're born dead, sometimes!" Nothing wrong in wishing that, for the Thing would be better off dead than alive. He wished he was dead himself! ... The third time he came to the apartment house the string of the box was cutting into his fingers, and that made him stop, and set his teeth, and push open the door of the vestibule. He touched the button under the name "Dale," and called up, huskily, "Is Miss—Mrs. Dale in?" A brisk voice asked his name. "A friend of Mrs. Dale's," he said, very low. There seemed to be a colloquy somewhere, and then he was told to "come right along!" He turned to the stairway, and as he walked slowly up, it came into his mind that this was the way a man might climb the scaffold steps: Step... Step... Step—his very feet refusing! Step... Step—and Lily's door. The nurse, who met him on the landing, said Mrs. Dale would be glad to see him....

She was in bed, very white and radiant, and with a queer, blanketed bundle on one arm; if she was, as the nurse said, "glad to see him," she did not show it. She was too absorbed in some gladness of her own to feel any other kind of gladness. As Maurice handed her the box of roses, she smiled vaguely and said. "Why, you're real kind!" Then she said, eagerly, "He was born the day the pink hyacinth came out! Want to see him?" Her voice thrilled with joy. Without waiting for his answer—or even giving a look at the roses the nurse was lifting out of their waxed papers, she raised a fold of the blanket and her eyes seemed to feed on the little red face with its tightly shut eyes and tiny wet lips.

Maurice looked—and his heart seemed to drop, shuddering, in his breast. "How nasty!" he thought; but aloud he said, stammering, "Why it's—quite a baby."

"You may hold him," she said; there was a passionate generosity in her voice.

Maurice tried to cover his recoil by saying, "Oh, I might drop it."

Lily was not looking at him; it seemed as if she was glad not to give up the roll of blankets, even for a minute. "He's perfectly lovely. He's a reg'lar rascal! The doctor said he was a wonderful child. I'm going to have him christened Ernest Augustus; I want a swell name. But I'll call him Jacky." She strained her head sidewise to kiss the red, puckered flesh, that looked like a face, and in which suddenly a little orifice showed itself, from which came a small, squeaking sound. Maurice, under the shock of that sound, stood rigid; but Lily's feeble arms cuddled the bundle against her breast; she said, "Sweety—Sweety—Sweety!"

The young man sat there speechless.... This terrible squirming piece of flesh—was part of himself! "I wouldn't touch it for a million dollars!" he was thinking. He got up and said: "Good-by. I hope you—"

Lily was not listening; she said good-by without lifting her eyes from the child's face.

Maurice stumbled out to the staircase, with little cold thrills running down his back. The experience of recognizing the significance of what he had done—the setting in motion that stupendous and eternal *Exfoliating*, called; Life; the seeing a Thing, himself, separated from himself! himself, going on in spite of himself!—brought a surge of engulfing horror. This elemental shock is not unknown to men who look for the first time at their first-born; instantly the feeling may disappear, swallowed up in love and pride. But where, as with Maurice, there is neither pride nor love, the shock remains. His organic dismay was so overwhelming that he said to himself he would never see Lily again—because he would not see It!—which was, in fact, "*he*," instead of the girl Lily had wanted. But though his spiritual disgust for what he called, in his own mind, "the whole hideous business," did not lessen, he did, later, through the pressure of those heavy words, "my own fault," go to see Lily—she had taken a little house out in Medfield—just to put down on the table, awkwardly, an envelope with some bills in it. He didn't inquire about It, and he got out of the house as quickly as possible.

Lily had no resentment at his lack of feeling for the child; the baby was so entirely hers that she did not think of it as his, too. This sense of possession, never menaced on Maurice's part by even a flicker of interest in the little thing, kept them to the furtive and very formal acquaintance of giving and receiving what money he could spare—or, oftener, *couldn't* spare! As a result, he thought of Jacky only in relation to his income. Every time some personal expenditure tempted him, he summed up the child's existence in four disgusted and angry words, "I can't afford it." But it was for Lily's sake, not Jacky's, that he economized! He was wretchedly aware that if it had not been for Jacky, Lily might still be a "saleslady" at Marston's, earning good wages. Instead, she was taking lodgers—and it was not easy to get them!—so that she could be at home and look after the baby.

Maurice aged ten years in that first winter of rigid and unexplainable penuriousness, and of a secrecy which meant perilous skirtings of downright lying; for Eleanor occasionally asked why they had so little money to spend? He had requested a raise—and not mentioned to Eleanor the fact that he had got it. When she complained because his salary was so low, he told her Weston was paying him all he was worth, and he *wouldn't* strike for more! "So it's impossible to go to housekeeping," he said—for of course she continued to urge housekeeping, saying that she couldn't understand why they had to be so economical! But he refused, patiently. To be patient, Maurice did not need, now, to remind himself of the mountain and her faithfulness to him; he had only to remind himself of the yellow-brick apartment house, and his faithlessness to her. "I've got to be kind, or I'd be a skunk," he used to think. So he was very kind. He did not burst out at her with irritated mortification when she telephoned to the office to know if "Mr. Curtis's headache was better";—he had suffered so much that he had gone beyond the self-consciousness of mortification;—and he walked with her in the park on Sunday afternoons to exercise Bingo; and on their anniversary he sat beside her in the grass, under the locust tree, and watched the river—their river, which had brought Lily into his life!—and listened to the lovely voice:

"O thou with dewy locks who lookest down!"

CHAPTER XIII

The next fall, however, the boarding did come to an end, and they went to housekeeping. It was Mrs. Houghton who brought this about. Edith was to enter Fern Hill School in the fall, and her mother had an inspiration: "Let her board with Eleanor and Maurice! The trolley goes right out to Medfield, and it will be very convenient for her. Also, it will help them with expenses," Mrs. Houghton said, comfortably.

"But why can't she live at the school?" Edith's father objected, with a troubled look; somehow, he did not like the idea of his girl in that pathetic household, which was at once so conscious and so unconscious of its own instability! "Why does she have to be with Eleanor and Maurice?" Henry Houghton said.

"Eleanor has the refinement that a hobbledehoy like Edith needs," Mrs. Houghton explained; "and I think the child will have better food than at Fern Hill. School food is always horrid."

"But won't Eleanor's dullness afflict Buster?" he said, doubtfully; then—because at that moment Edith banged into the room to show her shuddering mother a garter snake she had captured—he added, with complacent subtlety, "as for food, I, personally, prefer a dinner of herbs with an *interesting* woman, than a stalled ox and Eleanor."

Which caused Edith to say, "Is Eleanor uninteresting, father?"

"Good heavens, no!" said Mr. Houghton, with an alarmed look; "*of course* she isn't! What put such an idea into your head?" And as Buster and her squirming prize departed, he told his Mary that her daughter was destroying his nervous system. "She'll repeat that to Eleanor," he groaned.

His wife had no sympathy for him; "You deserve anything you may get!" she said, severely; and proceeded to write to Eleanor to make her proposition. If they cared to take Edith, she said, they could hire a house and stop boarding—"which is dreadful for both of your digestions; and I will be glad if this plan appeals to you, to feel that Edith is with anyone who has such gentle manners as you."

Eleanor, reading the friendly words at the boarding-house breakfast table, said quickly to herself, "I don't want her... She would monopolize Maurice!" Then she hesitated; "He would be more comfortable in a house of his own... But Edith? Oh, I *don't* want her!"

She turned to show the letter to Maurice, but he was sitting sidewise, one arm over the back of his chair, in vociferous discussion with a fellow boarder. "No, sir!" he was declaring; "if they revise the rules again, they'll revise the guts out of the whole blessed game; they'll make it all muscle and no mind."

"But football isn't any intellectual stunt," the other boarder insisted.

"It *is*—to a degree. The old flying wedge—"

"Maurice!" Eleanor said again; but Maurice, impassioned about "rules," didn't even hear her. She gave his arm a little friendly shake. "Maurice! You are the limit, with your old football!"

He turned, laughing, and took the letter from her hand. As he read it, his face changed sharply. "But Fern Hill is in Medfield!" he exclaimed.

"I suppose she could take the trolley almost to the school grounds," Eleanor conceded, reluctantly.

"Why can't she live out there? It's a boarding school, isn't it?" (She might meet Lily on the car!)

For a moment she accepted his decision with relief; then the thought of his comfort urged her: "I know of an awfully attractive house, with a garden. Little Bingo could hide his bones in it."

"No," he said, sharply; "it wouldn't do. I don't want her."

Instantly Eleanor was buoyantly ready to have Edith ... he *"didn't want her!"* When Maurice rose from the table she went to the front door with him—detaining him—until the pretty school-teacher was well on her way down the street;—with tender charges to take care of himself. Then, in the darkness of the hall, with Maurice very uneasy lest some one might see them, she kissed him good-by. "If we could afford to keep house without taking Edith," she said, "I'd rather not have her. (Kiss me again—no-body's looking!) But we can't. So let's have her."

"In two years I'll have my own money," he reminded her; "this hard sledding is only temporary." But she looked so disappointed that he hesitated; after all, if she wanted a house so much he ought not to stand in the way. Poor Eleanor hadn't much fun! And, as far as he was concerned, he would like to have Edith around. "It's only the Medfield part of it I don't like," he told himself. Yet Lily, on Maple Street, a mile from Fern Hill, was a needle in a haystack! (And even if Edith should ever see her, she wouldn't know her.) ... "If you really want to have her," he told Eleanor, "go ahead."

So that was how it happened that Edith burst in upon Eleanor's dear domesticity of two. Maurice, having once agreed to his wife's wish, was rather pleased at the prospect. "It will help on money," he thought; "another hundred a year will come in handy to Lily. And it will be sort of nice to have Buster in the house."

Lily had not said she must have another hundred. She did not even think so. "*I* can swing it!" Lily had said, sturdily. And she did; but of course, as Maurice, to his intense discomfort, knew only too well, it was hard to swing it. Even with what help he could give her, she couldn't possibly have got along if she had not been astonishingly efficient and thrifty, always looking at both sides of a cent! "I ain't smoking any more," Lily said once; "well, 'tain't *only* to save money; but I don't want Jacky to be getting any funny ideas!" (this when "Ernest Augustus" was only a few months old!) She had a tiny house on Maple Street, with a sun-baked front yard, in which a few shrubs caught the dust on their meager foliage; and she had a border of pansies in the shade under the bay window;—"I *must* have flowers!" Lily said, apologetically;—and she had three roomers, and she had scraped the locality for mealers. She would have made more money if she had not fed her boarders so well. "But there!" said Lily; "if I give 'em nice food, they'll stay!" But, all the same, Maurice knew that two or three dollars more a week would "come in handy." His sense of irritated responsibility about her made him long for that twenty-fifth birthday which would bring him his own money. For, in spite of Lily's thriftiness, her expenses, as well as her toil, kept increasing, and Maurice, cursing himself whenever he thought that but for him she would be "on easy street" at Marston's, had begun the inevitable borrowing. The payment of the interest on his note was a tax on his salary; yet not so taxing as the necessity of being constantly on guard against some careless word which might make Eleanor ask questions about that salary.

But Eleanor asked very few questions about anything so practical as income. Her interest in money matters, now, in regard to Edith, was merely that Edith was a means to an end—Maurice could have his own home! The finding a house, under Mrs. Newbolt's candid guidance—and Maurice's worried reminders that he couldn't "afford" more than so much rent!—gave Eleanor the pleasantest summer she had had since that first summer when, in the meadow, she and Maurice had watched the clouds, and the locust blossoms, and told each other that nothing in heaven or earth, or the waters under the earth, could part them...

The old house they finally secured was in an unfashionable locality; there was a tailor shop next door and an undertaker across the street, and a clanging trolley car screeched on the curve at the end of the block; but the dignity of the pillared doorway, and the carved window casings, had appealed to Maurice; and also the discovery in the parlor, behind a monstrous air-tight stove, of a bricked-up fireplace (which he promptly tore open), all combined to make undertakers and tailors, as neighbors, unimportant! On the rear of the house was an iron veranda—roped with wistaria; below, inclosed in a crumbling brick wall, was the back yard— "*Garden,* if you please!" Maurice announced—for Bingo's bones. Clumps of Madonna lilies had bloomed here, and died, and bloomed again, for almost a century; the yard was shaded by a silver poplar, which would gray and whiten in the wind in hot weather, or delicately etch itself against a wintry sky. A little path, with moss between the bricks and always damp in the shadow of the poplar, led from the basement door to an iron gate; through its rusty bars one could see, a block away, the slipping gleam of the river, hurrying down from "their meadow," to disappear under the bridge. Maurice said he would build a seat around the poplar, "... and we'll put a table under it, and paint it green, and have tea there in the afternoon! Skeezics will like that."

"Edith looks healthy," said Mrs. Newbolt; "my dear father used to say he liked healthy females. Old-fashioned word—females. Well, I'm afraid dear father liked 'em too much. But my dear mother—she was a Dennison— pretended not to see it. She had sense. Great thing in married life, to have sense, and know what not to see! Pity Edith's not musical. Have you a cook? I believe she'd have caught you, Maurice, if Eleanor hadn't got in ahead! I brought a chocolate drop for Bingo. Here, Bingo!"

Bingo, silky and snarly, climbed on to her steeply sloping black-satin lap, ate the chocolate drop—keeping all the while a liquid and adoring eye upon his mistress—then slid down and ran to curl up on Eleanor's skirt.

By September the moving and seat building were accomplished—the last not entirely on Edith's account; it was part of Maurice's painstaking desire to do something—anything!—for "poor Eleanor," as he named her in his remorseful thought. There was never a day—indeed, there was not often an hour!—when his own meanness to his wife (combined with disgust at being a liar) did not ache somewhere in the back of his mind. So he tried, in all sorts of anxious ways, to please her. He almost never saw Lily; but the thought of her often brought Eleanor a box of candy or a bunch of violets. Such expenditures were slightly easier for him now, because he had had another small raise,—which this time he had told Eleanor about. On the strength of it he said to himself that he supposed he ought to give Lily a little something extra? So on the day when Mrs. Houghton and Edith were to arrive in Mercer, he went out to Medfield to tell Jacky's mother that she might count on a few dollars more each month. The last time he had seen her, Lily had told him that Jacky "was fussing with his teeth something fierce. I had to hire a little girl from across the street," she said, "to take him out in the perambulator, or else I couldn't 'tend to my cooking. It costs money to live, Mr. Curtis," Lily had said, "and eggs are going up, awful!" She had never gone back to the familiarity of those days when she called him "Curt." That he, dull and preoccupied, still called her Lily gave her, somehow, such a respectful consciousness of his superiority that she had hesitated to speak of anything so intimate as eggs... "Yes, I must give her something extra," Maurice thought, remembering the "cost" of living. "Talk about paying the piper! I bet *I'm* paying him, all right!"

He was to meet Mrs. Houghton at seven-thirty that night, and it occurred to him that if he told Eleanor he had some extra work to do at his desk he could wedge this call in between office hours and the time when he must go to the station—("and they call me 'G. Washington'!") He felt no special cautiousness in going out to Maple Street; the few people he knew in Mercer did not frequent this locality, and if any of them should chance to see him—a most remote possibility!—why, was he not in the real-estate business, and constantly looking at houses? On this particular afternoon, jolting along in the trolley car, he grimly amused himself with the thought of what he would do if, say, Eleanor herself should see him turning that infernally shrill bell on Lily's door. It was a wild flight of imagination, for Eleanor never would see him—never could see him! Eleanor, who only went to Medfield when their wedding anniversary came round, and she dragged him out to sit by the river and sentimentalize! He thought of the loveliness of that past June—and the contrasting and ironic ugliness of the present September.... Now, the little secret house in the purlieus of Mercer's smoke and grime; then, the river, and the rippling tides of grass and clover, and the blue sky—and that ass, lying at the feet of a woman old enough to be his mother!

He laughed as he swung off the car—then frowned; for he saw that to reach Lily's door he would have to pass a baby carriage standing just inside the gate. He didn't glance into the carriage at the roly-poly youngster. He never, on the rare occasions when he went to see Lily, looked at his child if he could avoid doing so—and she never asked him to. Once, annoyed at Jacky's shrill noisiness, he had protested, frowning: "Can't you keep it quiet? It needs a spanking!" After that indifferent criticism ("For *I* don't care how she brings it up!") Lily had not wanted him to see her baby. She could not have said just why—perhaps it was fear lest Maurice would notice his growing perfection—but when Jacky's father came she kept Jacky in the background! On this September afternoon she said, as she opened the door:

"Why, you're a great stranger! Come right in! Wait a second till I get Jacky. I've just nursed him and I put him out there so I could watch him while I scrubbed the porch." She ran out to the gate, then pushed the carriage up the path.

"Let me help you," Maurice said, politely; adding to himself, "Damn—damn—!" Stepping backward, he lifted the front wheels, and with Lily's help pulled the perambulator on to the little porch and over the threshold into the house—which always shone with immaculate neatness and ugly comfort. He kept his eyes away from the sleeping face on the pillow. Together they got the carriage into the hall—Lily fumbling all the while with one hand to fasten the front of her dress and skipping a button or two as she did so; but he had a glimpse of the heavy abundance of her bosom, and thought to himself that, esthetically, maternity was rather unpleasant.

"Go on into the parlor and sit down," she said; "I'll put him in the kitchen," She pushed the elaborate wicker perambulator, adorned with bows of blue-satin ribbon, down a dark entry smelling of very good soup stock. When she came back she found Maurice, his hat and stick in his hands, standing in her tiny front room, where the sunny window was full of geraniums and scraggly rose bushes. "I got 'em in early. And I dug up my dahlias—I was afraid of frost. (Mercy! I must clean that window on the outside!) Well, you *are* a stranger!" she said, again, good-naturedly. Then she sighed: "Mr. Curtis, Jacky seems kind o' sick. He's been coughing, and he's hot. Would you send for a doctor, if you was me?"

"Why, if you're worried, yes," Maurice said, impatiently; "I was just passing, and—No, thank you; I won't sit down. I was passing, and I thought I'd look in and give you a—a little present. If the youngster's upset, it will come in well," he ended, as his hand sought his waistcoat pocket. Lily's face was instantly anxious.

"What! Did *you* think he looked sick, too? I was kind of worried, but if you noticed it—"

"I didn't in the least," he said, frowning; "I didn't look at him."

"He 'ain't never been what you'd call sick," Lily tried to reassure herself; "he's a reg'lar rascal!" she ended, tenderly; her eyes—those curious amber eyes, through which sometimes a tigress looks!—looked now at Maurice in passionate motherhood.

Maurice, putting the money down on the table, said, "I wish I could do more for you, Lily; but I'm dreadfully strapped."

"Say, now, you take it right back! I can get along; I got my two upstairs rooms rented, and I've got a new mealer. And if Jacky only keeps well, I can manage fine. But that girl that's been wheelin' him has measles at her house—little slut!" Lily said (the yellow eyes glared); "she didn't let on to me about it. Wanted her two dollars a week! If Jacky's caught 'em, I—I'll see to her!"

"Oh, he's all right," Maurice said; he didn't like "it"—although, if it hadn't been for "it" he would probably, long before this, have slipped down into the mere comfort of Lily; "it" held him prisoner in self-contempt; "it," or perhaps the larger It? the It which he had seen first in his glorious, passionately selfish ecstasy on his wedding day; then glimpsed in the awful orderliness of the universe,—the It that held the stars in their courses! Perhaps the tiny, personal thing, Joy, and the stupendous, impersonal thing, Law, and the mysterious, unseen thing, Life, were all one? "Call it God," Maurice had said of ecstasy, and again of order; he did not call Jacky's milky lips "God." The little personality which he had made was not in the least God to him! On the contrary, it was a nuisance and a terror, and a financial anxiety. He shrank from the thought of it, and kept "decent," merely through disgust at the child as an entity—an entity which had driven him into loathsome evasions and secrecies which once in a while sharpened into little lies. But he was faintly sorry, now, to see Lily look unhappy about the Thing; and he even had a friendly impulse to comfort her: "Jacky's all right! But I'll send a doctor in, if you want me to. I saw a doctor's shingle out as I came around the corner."

She said she'd be awfully obliged; and he, looking at his watch, and realizing that Mrs. Houghton's train was due in less than an hour, hurried off.

The doctor's bell was not answered promptly; then the doctor detained him by writing down the address, getting it wrong, correcting it, and saying: "Mrs. Dale? Oh yes; you are Mr. Dale?"

"No—not at all! Just a friend. I happened to be calling, and Mrs. Dale asked me to stop and ask you to come in."

Then he rushed off. On the way to town, staring out of the window of the car, he tingled all over at Doctor Nelson's question: "You are Mr. Dale?"... "Why the devil did I offer to get a doctor? I wish Lily would move to the ends of the earth; or that the brat would get well; or—or something."

There was a little delay in reaching the station, and when he got there, it was to find that Mrs. Houghton's train was in and she and Edith, shifting for themselves, had presumably taken a hack to find their way to Maurice's house. He was mortified, but annoyed, too, because it involved giving

Eleanor some sort of lying explanation for his discourtesy. "I'll have to cook up some kind of yarn!" he thought, disgustedly...

When Edith and her mother had arrived, unaccompanied by Maurice, Eleanor was sharply worried; had anything happened to him? Oh, she was afraid something had happened to him! "Where *do* you suppose he is?" she said, over and over. "I'm always so afraid he's been run over!" And when Maurice, flushed and apologetic, appeared, she was so relieved that she was cross. What on earth had detained him? "How *did* you miss them?"

So Maurice immediately told half of the truth,—this being easier for him than an out-and-out lie. He had been detained because he had to go and see a house in Medfield. "Awfully sorry, Mrs. Houghton!"

Eleanor said she should have thought he needn't have stayed long enough to be late at the station! Well, he hadn't stayed long; but the—"the tenant was afraid her baby had measles and she had asked him to go and get a doctor, and—"

"Of course!" Mrs. Houghton said; "don't give it a thought, Maurice. John Bennett met us—you knew he was at the Polytechnical?—and brought us here. But, anyhow, Edith and I were quite capable of looking out for ourselves; weren't we, Edith?"

Edith, almost sixteen now, long-legged, silent, and friendly, said, "Yes, mother" and helped herself so liberally to butter that her hostess thought to herself, "*Gracious!*"

However, assured that Maurice had not been run over, Eleanor was really indifferent to Edith's appetite, for the sum Mrs. Houghton had offered for the girl's board was generous. So, proud of the new house, and pleased with sitting at the head of her own table, and hoping that Maurice would like the pudding, which, with infinite fussing, she had made with her own hands, she felt both happy and hospitable. She told Edith to take some more butter (which she did!); and tell Johnny to come to dinner some night, "and we'll have some music," she added, kindly.

"Johnny doesn't like music," said Edith; "well, I don't, either. But I guess he'll come. He likes food."

Edith effaced herself a good deal in the few days that, her mother stayed on in Mercer to launch her at Fern Hill; effaced herself, indeed, so much that Maurice, full of preoccupations of his own, was hardly aware of her presence!... He had had a scared note from Lily:

Doctor Nelson says he's *awful* sick, and I've got to have a nurse. I don't like to, because I can't bear to have anybody do for him but me, and she charges so much. Makes me tired to see her all fussed up in white dresses—I suppose it's her laundry I'm paying for! That little girl he caught it from ought to be sent to a Reformatory. I'm afraid my new mealer'll go, if she thinks there's anything catching in the house. I hate to ask you—

The scented, lavender-colored envelope was on Maurice's desk at the office the morning after Mrs. Houghton and Edith arrived. When he had read it, and torn it into minute scraps, Maurice had something else to think of than Edith! He knew Lily wouldn't want to leave "her" baby to go out and cash a money order, and checks were dangerous; so he must take that trip to Medfield again. "Well," said Maurice—pulled and jerked out to Maple Street on the leash of an ineradicable sense of decency—"the devil is getting his money's worth out of *me!*"

He entered No. 16 without turning the clanging bell, for the door was ajar. Lily was in the entry, talking to the doctor, who gave Mrs. Dale's "friend" a rather keen look. "Oh, Mr. Curtis, he's *awful* sick!" Lily said; she was haggard with fright.

Maurice, swearing to himself for having arrived at that particular moment, said, coldly, "Too bad."

"Oh, we'll pull him through," the doctor said, with a kind look at Lily. She caught his hand and kissed it, and burst out crying. The two men looked at each other—one amused, the other shrinking with disgust at his own moral squalor. Then from the floor above came a whimpering cry, and Lily, calling passionately, "Yes, Sweety! Maw's coming!" flew upstairs.

"I'll look in this evening," Doctor Nelson said, and took himself off, rubbing the back of his hand on his trousers. "I wonder if there's any funny business there?" he reflected. But he thought no more about it until weeks afterward, when he happened, one day, in the bank, to stand before Maurice, waiting his turn at the teller's window. He said, "Hello!" and Maurice said, "Hello!" and added that it was a cold day. The fact that Maurice said not a word about that recovering little patient in Medfield made the doctor's mind revert to the possibilities he had recognized in Lily's entry.

"Yet he looks too decent for that sort of thing," the doctor thought; "well, it's a rum world." Then Maurice took his turn at the window, and Doctor Nelson put his notes in his pocket, and the two men nodded to each other, and said, "By," and went their separate ways.

CHAPTER XIV

Edith's first winter in Mercer went pretty well; she was not fussy about what she had to eat; "I can always stoke on bread and butter," she said, cheerfully; and she was patient with the aging Bingo's yapping jealousies; "The smaller a dog is, the more jealous he is!" she said, with good-humored contempt; and she didn't mind Eleanor's speechlessness. "*I* talk!" Edith said. But Maurice?... "I love him next to father and mother," Edith thought; but, all the same, she didn't know what to make of Maurice! He had very little to say to her—which made her feel annoyingly young, and made him seem so old and stern that sometimes she could hardly realize that he was the Maurice of the henhouse, and the camp, and the squabbles. Instead, he was the Maurice of that night on the river, the "Sir Walter Raleigh" Maurice! Once in a while she was quite shy with him. "He's awfully handsome," she thought, and her eyes dreamed. "What a clod Johnny is, compared to him!" ... As for Eleanor, Edith, being as unobservant as most sixteen-year-old girls, saw only the lovely dark eyes and the beautiful brow under the ripple of soft black hair, Eleanor's sterile silences did not trouble her, and she never knew that the traces of tears meant a helpless consciousness that dinner had been a failure. The fact was, she never noticed Eleanor's looks! She merely thought Maurice's wife was old, and didn't "get much fun out of life—she just plays on the piano!" Edith thought. Pain of mind or body was, to Edith—as probably it ought to be to Youth—unintelligible; so she had no sympathy. In fact, being sixteen, she had still the hard heart of a child.

It may have been the remembrance of Sir Walter Raleigh that made her, one night, burst into reminiscent questions:

"Maurice! Do you remember the time that boat upset, and that girl—all painted, you know—flopped around in the water?"

Maurice said, briefly, why, yes; he believed he remembered.

"I remember that girl, too," Eleanor said; "Maurice told me about her."

"Well, what do you suppose?" Edith said; "I saw her to-day."

Maurice, pushing back his chair, got up and went into the little room opening into the dining room, which they called the library. At his desk, his pen in his hand, his jaw set, he sat listening—listening! What in hell would she say next? What she said was harmless enough:

"Yes, I saw her. I was walking home, and on Maple Street who should I see going into a house but this woman! She was lugging a flower pot, and a baby. And,—now, isn't this funny?—she sort of stumbled at the gate, *right by me*! And I grabbed her, and kept the child from falling; and I said—" In the library Maurice's face was white—"I said, 'Why, *I* saw you once— you're Miss Dale. Your boat upset,' And she said, 'You have the advantage of me.' Of course she isn't a lady, you know."

Eleanor smiled, and called significantly to her husband, "Edith says your rescued friend isn't a 'lady,' Maurice!" He didn't answer, and she added to Edith, "No; she certainly isn't a lady! Darling," she called again; "do you suppose she's got married?"

To which he answered, "Where did I put those sheets of blotting paper, Eleanor?"

"Oh yes, she's married," Edith said, scraping her plate; "she told me her name was *Mrs.* Henry Dale. She couldn't seem to remember Maurice giving her his coat, which I thought was rather funny in her, 'cause Maurice is so handsome you'd think she'd remember him. And I said he was 'Mr. Curtis,' and she said she'd never heard the name. I got to talking to her," ("I bet you did," Maurice thought, despairingly); "and she told me that 'Jacky' had had the measles, and been awfully sick, but he was all well now, and she'd taken him into Mercer to get him a cap." ("What's Lily mean by bringing the Thing into town!" Jacky's father was saying through set teeth.) "She was perfectly bursting with pride about him," Edith went on; "said he was 'a reg'lar rascal'! Isn't it queer that I should meet her, after all these years?"

When Eleanor went into the library to hunt for the blotting paper, she, too, commented on the queerness of Edith's stumbling on the lady who wasn't a lady. "How small the world is!" said Eleanor. "Why, Maurice, here's the paper! Right before you!"

"Oh," said Maurice, "yes; thank you." He was saying to himself, "I might have known this kind of thing would happen!" He was consumed with anxiety to ask Edith some questions, but of course he had to be silent.

To show even the slightest interest was impossible—and Edith volunteered no further information, for that night Eleanor took occasion to intimate to her that "Mrs. Dale" must not be referred to. "You can't speak of that kind of person, you know."

"Why not?" Edith said.

"Well, she isn't—nice. She wasn't married. And Edith, it really isn't good taste to tell a man, right to his face, that he's handsome! I don't think any man likes flattery."

"You mean because I said Maurice was handsome? I didn't say it to his face—he was in the library. And it isn't flattery to tell the truth. He is! As for Mrs. Dale, she *is* married; this little Jacky was her baby! She said so. He had the bluest eyes! I never saw such blue eyes—except Maurice's. 'Course she's not a lady; but I don't see what right you have to say she isn't nice."

Eleanor, laughing, threw up despairing hands; "Edith, don't you know *anything?*"

"I know *everything,*" Edith said, affronted; "I'm sixteen. Of course I know what you mean; but Mrs. Dale isn't—that. And," Edith ended, on the spur of the moment, "and I'm going to see her sometime!" The under dog always appealed to Edith Houghton, and when Eleanor left her, appalled by her failure to instill proprieties into her, Edith was distinctly hot. "I'm not going to see her!" she told herself. "I wouldn't think of such a thing. But I won't listen to Eleanor abusing her."

As for Eleanor, she confided her alarm to Maurice. "She mustn't go to see that woman!"

His instant horrified agreement was a satisfaction to her: "Of *course* not!"

"She won't listen to *me,*" Eleanor complained; "you'll have to tell her she mustn't."

"I will," he said, grimly.

And the very next day he did. He happened (as it seemed) to start for his office just as Edith started for school, so they walked along together.

"Edith," he said, the moment they were clear of his own doorway and Eleanor's ears; "that Mrs. Dale; I'd keep away from her, if I were you."

"Goodness!" said Edith; "did you suppose I was going to fall into her arms? Why should I have anything to do with her?"

"Eleanor said you said —"

"Oh, I just said that because Eleanor was down on her, and that made me mad. I couldn't go and see her, if I was dying to—'cause I don't know where she lives—unless it was that house she was going into? Do you know, Maurice?"

"Great Scott! How should I know where she lives?"

"'Course not," said Edith.

But it was many days before Maurice's alarm quieted down sufficiently to let him drift back into the furtive security of knowing that neither Edith nor Eleanor could, by any possibility, get on Lily's track. "And, besides, Lily's too good a sport to give anything away. Pretty neat in her to 'forget' that coat! But she ought to be careful not to forget her husband's name!—it seems to be Henry, now."

CHAPTER XV

A moody Maurice, who puzzled her, and a faultfinding Eleanor, whom she was too generous to understand, drove the sixteen-year-old Edith into a real appreciation of Johnny Bennett. With him, she was still in the stage of unsentimental frankness that pierced ruthlessly to what she conceived to be the realities; and because she was as unselfconscious as a tree, she was entirely indifferent to the fact that Johnny was a boy and she was a girl, Johnny, however, nearsighted and in enormous shell-rimmed spectacles, and still inarticulate, was quite aware of it; more definitely so every week,—for he saw her on Saturdays and Sundays. "And it's the greatest possible relief to talk to you!" Edith told him.

Johnny accepted the tribute as his due. They had been coasting, and now, on the hilltop, were sitting on their sleds, resting. "Gosh! it's hot!" Johnny said: he had taken off his red sweater and tied its sleeves around his neck; "zero? You try pulling both those sleds up here, and you'll think it's the Fourth of July," Johnny said, adjusting his spectacles with a mittened hand. He frequently reverted to the grumpy stage—yet now, looking at Edith, grumpiness vanished. She was breathless from the long climb, and her white teeth showed between her parted, panting lips: her cheeks were burning with frosty pink. Johnny looked, and looked away, and sighed.

"Johnny," Edith said, "why do you suppose Eleanor gives me so many call-downs? 'Course I hate music; and once I said she was always pounding on the piano—and she didn't seem to like it!" Edith was genuinely puzzled. "I can't understand Eleanor," she said; "she makes me tired."

"I should think she'd make Maurice tired!" Johnny said, and added: "That's the worst of getting married. I shall never marry."

"When I was a child," Edith said, "I always said that when I grew up I was going to marry Maurice, because he was just like Sir Walter Raleigh. Wasn't that a joke?"

Johnny saw nothing amusing in such foolishness; he said that Maurice was old enough to be her father! As for himself, he felt, he said, that marriage was a mistake. "Women hamper a man dreadfully. Still—I may marry," Johnny conceded; "but it will be somebody very young, so I can train her mind. I want a woman (if I decide to marry) to be just the kind I want. Otherwise, you get hung up with Eleanors."

Edith lifted her chin. "Well, I like that! Why shouldn't she train your mind?"

"Because," Johnny said, firmly, "the man's mind is the stronger."

Edith screamed with laughter, and threw a handful of snow in his neck. "B-r-r-r!" she said; "it's getting cold! I'll knock the spots out of you on belly bumps!" She got on her feet, shook the snow from the edge of her skirt, flung herself face down on her sled, and shot like a blue comet over the icy slope. Johnny sped after her, his big sled taking flying leaps over the kiss-me-quicks. They reached the bottom of the hill almost together, and Johnny, looking at her standing there, breathless and rosy, with shining eyes which were as impersonal as stars, said to himself, with emotion:

"She's got sense—for a girl." His heart was pounding in his broad chest, but he couldn't think of a thing to say. He was still dumb when she said good-by to him at Maurice's door.

"Why don't you come to dinner next Saturday?" she said, carelessly; "Maurice will be away all week on business; but he'll be back Saturday."

Johnny mumbled something to the effect that he could survive, even if Maurice wasn't back.

"I couldn't," Edith said. "I should simply die, in this house, if it wasn't for Maurice!"

As, whistling, she ran upstairs, Edith thought to herself that Johnny was a *lamb*! "But, compared to Maurice, he's awfully uninteresting." Edith, openly and audibly, compared every male creature to Maurice, and none of them ever measured up to him! His very moodiness had its charm; when he sat down at the piano after dinner and scowled over some new music, or when he lounged in his big chair and smoked, his face absorbed to the point of sternness, Edith, loving him "next to father and mother," watched him, and wondered what he was thinking about? Sometimes he came out of his abstraction and teased her, and then she sparkled into gay impertinences; sometimes he asked her what she thought of this or that phrasing, "...though you are a barbarian, Skeezics, about music"; sometimes he would pull a book from the shelf over his desk and read a poem to her; and he was really interested in her opinion,—ardently appreciative if he liked the poem; if he didn't, it was "the limit."

Maurice was at home that Saturday night for which Edith had thrown the careless invitation to Johnny; and Mrs. Newbolt also dropped in to dinner. It was not a pleasant dinner. Eleanor sat in one of her empty silences; saw Maurice frown at an overdone leg of lamb; heard her aunt's stream of comments on her housekeeping; listened to Edith's teasing chatter to Johnny;—"What *can* Maurice see in her!" She thought. Before dinner was over, she excused herself; she had a headache, she said. "You won't mind, Auntie, will you?"

Mrs. Newbolt said, heartily, "*Not* a bit! My dear mother used to—"

Eleanor, picking up little Bingo, went with lagging step out of the room.

"Children," said Mrs. Newbolt, "why don't you make taffy this evening?"

"*That's* sense," said Edith; "let's! It's Mary's night out. Sorry poor old Eleanor isn't up to it."

Maurice frowned; "Look here, Edith, that isn't—respectful."

Edith looked so blankly astonished that Mrs. Newbolt defended her: "But Eleanor *does* look old! And she'll lose her figger if she isn't careful! My dear grandmother—used to say, 'Girls, I'd rather have you lose your vir—'"

"Don't raise Cain in the kitchen, you two," Maurice said, hastily; "Eleanor hates noise."

Edith, subdued by his rebuke, said she wouldn't raise Cain; and, indeed, she and Johnny were preternaturally quiet until things had been cleared away and the taffy could be started. When it was on the stove, there was at least ten minutes of whispering while they watched the black molasses shimmer into the first yellow rings. Then Johnny, in a low voice, talked for a good while of something he called "Philosophy"—which seemed to consist in a profound disbelief in everything. "Take religion," said Johnny. "I'd like to discuss it with you; I think you have a very good mind—for a woman. Religion is an illustration of what I mean. It's a delusion. A complete delusion. I have ceased to believe in anything."

"Oh, Johnny, how awful!" said Edith, stirring the seething sweetness; "Johnny, be a lamb, and get me a tumbler of cold water, will you, to try this stuff?"

Johnny brought the water ("Oh, how young she is!" he thought), and Edith poured a trickle of taffy into it.

"Is it done?" Edith said, and held out the brittle string of candy; he bit at it, and said he guessed so. Then they poured the foamy stuff into a pan, and put it in the refrigerator. "We'll wait till it gets stiff," said Edith.

"I think," said Johnny, in a low voice, "your hair is handsomer than most women's. I'm particular about a woman's hair."

Edith, sitting on the edge of the table, displaying very pretty ankles, put an appraising hand over the brown braids that were wound around her head in a sort of fillet. "Are you?" she said, and began to yawn—but stopped short, her mouth still open, for Johnny Bennett was *looking at her*! "Let's go into the library," she said, hurriedly.

"I like it out here," Johnny objected.

But as he spoke Maurice lounged into the kitchen. "Stiff?" he said.

"No; won't be for ages," Edith said—and instantly the desire to fly to the library ceased, especially as Mrs. Newbolt came trundling in. With Maurice astride one of the wooden chairs, his blue eyes droll and teasing, and Mrs. Newbolt enthroned in adipose good nature close to the stove, Edith was perfectly willing to stay in the kitchen!

"I say!" Maurice said. "Let's pull the stuff!"

Johnny looked cross. "What," he asked himself, "are Maurice and Mrs. Newbolt butting in for?" Then he softened, for Maurice was teasing Edith, and Mrs. Newbolt was tasting the candy, and the next minute all was in delightful uproar of stickiness and excitement, and Johnny, exploding into wild cackles of laughter, felt quite young for the next hour.

Eleanor, upstairs, with Bingo's little silken head on her breast, did not feel young; she heard the noise, and smelled the boiling molasses, and knew that Mary would be cross when she came home and found the kitchen in a mess. "How can Maurice stand such childishness!" She lay there with a cologne-soaked handkerchief on her forehead, and sighed with pain. "Why *doesn't* he stop them?" she thought. She heard his shout of laughter, and Edith's screaming giggle, and moved her head to find a cool place on the pillow. "She's too old to romp with him." Suddenly she sat up, tense and listening; he was enjoying himself—and she was suffering! "If he had a headache, I would sit with him; I wouldn't leave him alone!" But she was sick in bed,—and he was having a good time—*with Edith.* Her resentment was not exactly jealousy; it was fear; the same fear she had felt when Maurice had told her how Edith had rushed into his room the night of the great storm; *the fear of Youth!* She moved Bingo gently, stroking him until he seemed to be asleep; then sat up, and put her feet on the floor. The folded handkerchief slipped from her forehead, and she pressed her hands against her temples. "I'm going downstairs," she said to herself; "I won't be left out!" She felt a sick qualm as she got on to her feet, and went over to look at herself in the mirror ... her face was pale, and her hair, wet with cologne, was pasted down in straggling locks on her forehead; she tried to smooth it. "Oh, I look old enough to be—his aunt," she said, hopelessly. When she opened her door she heard a little thud behind her; it was Bingo, scrambling off the bed to follow her; as she went downstairs, unsteadily, and clinging to the banisters, he stepped on her skirt, so she had to stoop and pick him up. At the closed kitchen door she paused for a moment, leaning against the wall; her head swam. Bingo, held in one trembling arm, put out his little pink tongue and licked her cheek. "I *won't* be left out," she said again. Just as her hand touched the knob there was an outburst of joyous yells, and a *whack*! as a lump of taffy, flung by one of the roisterers, hit the resounding panel of the door—then Mrs. Newbolt's fat chuckle, and Johnny's voice vociferating that Edith was the limit, and Maurice—"Edith, if you put that stuff in my hair, I'll skin you alive!"

"Boil her in oil!" yelled Johnny.

Eleanor turned around and crept back to the stairs; she caught at the newel post, and stood, gasping; then, somehow, she climbed up to her room. There, lifting Bingo into his basket, she sank on her bed, groping blindly for the damp handkerchief to put across her forehead. "Mary will give notice," she said. After a while, as the throbbing grew less acute, she said, "He's their age." Bingo, crawling out of his basket, scrabbled up on to the bed; she felt his little loving cold nose against her face.

CHAPTER XVI

"What a kid Johnny Bennett is!" Maurice told Eleanor. He was detailing to her, while he was scrubbing the stickiness of the kitchen festivities off his hands, what had happened downstairs. "But do you know, I believe he's soft on Edith! How old is he?"

"He's nearly nineteen. Children, both of them."

"Nineteen?" Maurice said, astounded. Nineteen! Johnny? "Why, *I* was nineteen, when—" He paused. She was silent. Suddenly Maurice felt *pity*. He had run the gamut of many emotions in the last four years—love, and fright, and repentance, and agonies of shame, and sometimes anger; but he had never touched pity. It stabbed him now, and its dagger blade was sawtoothed with remorse. He looked at his wife, lying there with closed eyes, her pillow damp where the wet handkerchief had slipped from her temples, and her beautiful mouth sagging with pain. "Oh, I must be nice to her, poor thing!" he thought. Aloud he said, "Poor Eleanor!"

Instantly her dark eyes opened in startled joy; his tenderness lifted her into indifference to that throbbing in her temples. "I don't mind anything," she said, "if you love me."

"Can't I do something for your head?"

"Just kiss me, darling," she said.

He kissed her, for he was sorry for her. But he was thinking of himself. "I was Johnny Bennett's age, when ... And I *wanted* to kiss her! My God! I may have to keep up this kissing business for—for forty years!" And whenever he was kissing her, he would have to think how he was deceiving her; he would have to think of Lily. Yes; he had been a "kid," like Johnny! How *could* she have done it! Pity sharpened into anger: How could she have taken advantage of a boy? Well; he had had his fling. To be sure, he was paying for it now, not only in anxiety about money, but in shame, and furtiveness, and the corroding consciousness of being a liar, and in the complete shipwreck of every purpose and ambition that a young man ought to have. "And that day, in the field, I called it *love*!" He would have been amused at the cynical memory, if he had not been so bitter. "Love? Rot! Still, I ought to be kinder to her;—but I can't bear to look at her. She's an old woman."

Eleanor put out her hot, trembling hand and groped for his. "Good night, darling," she said; "my head's better."

"So glad," he said.

The next morning, as Eleanor, rather white and shaky, was dressing, she said, "Edith doesn't seem to realize that she is too old to be so free and easy with Johnny Bennett—and you."

"She's getting mighty good looking," Maurice said.

"She has too much color," Eleanor said, quickly.

Maurice was right. During Edith's second winter in Mercer she grew prettier all the time; poor, speechless Johnny, looking at her through his spectacles, was quite miserable. He told some of his intimate friends that life was a bad joke.

"I shall never marry; just do some big work, and then get out. There is nothing really worth while. Mere looks in a woman don't attract me," Johnny said.

But that Maurice found "looks" attractive, began to be obvious to Eleanor, who, night after night, at the dinner table, watched the smiling, shining, careless thing—Youth!—sitting there on Maurice's right, and felt herself withering in the dividing years. As a result, the annoyance which, when Edith was a child, she had felt at her childishness, began to harden into irritation at her womanliness. "I *wish* I could get her out of the house!" she used to think, helplessly.

She felt this irritation especially when they all went, one night, to dine with Tom Morton, who had just married and gone to housekeeping. It was a somewhat looked-forward-to event, although Eleanor thought Edith too young to dine out, and also the shabbiness of Maurice's evening clothes was on her mind. "Do get a new dress suit!" she urged; and he gave the stereotyped answer: "Can't afford it."

They started for the Mortons' gayly enough; but Maurice's gayety went out like a candle in the wind when, as he followed Eleanor and Edith into the parlor, he saw, and after a puzzled moment recognized, the third man in the Morton dinner of six—the man who had stood in Lily's little hall and said that the child would "pull through." ... The spiritual squalor of that scene flashed back in sharp visualization: the doctor; Lily, her amber eyes overflowing with tears, kissing his hand; Jacky's fretful cry from upstairs.... Here he was! that same kindly medical man, "getting off some guff to Mrs. Morton," Maurice told himself, in agonized uncertainty as to what he had better do. Should he recognize him? Or pretend not to know him? It galloped through his mind that if he did "know" him, Eleanor would ask questions. Oh, he knew Eleanor's questions! But if he didn't "know" him, Doctor Nelson would know that questions might be asked. The instant's hesitation between the two risks was decided by Doctor Nelson. He put out his hand and said, "Oh, how are you?" So Maurice said, "Oh, how are you?" as carelessly as anybody else.

Eleanor, when the doctor was introduced, said, a little surprised, "You know my husband?"

"I think I've met Mr. Curtis somewhere," Doctor Nelson said, vaguely.

"He knows so many people I don't," she thought, but she said nothing. No one noticed her silence—or Maurice's, either! The doctor, and Morton, and the handsome bride, were listening to Edith, amused, apparently, at her crudity and ignorance.

"Oh yes," Eleanor heard her say; "Eleanor's voice is perfectly *fine*, father says. I'm not musical. Father says I don't know the difference between 'Yankee Doodle' and 'Old Hundred.' Father say—" and so on.

"She's tiresome!" Eleanor told herself. Later, as she sat at the little dinner table, all gay with flowers and the bride's new candlesticks and glittering bonbon dishes ("Hetty's showing off our loot," the bridegroom said, proudly), Eleanor, looking on, and straining sometimes to be silly like the rest of them, said to herself, bleakly, that the doctor, who looked fifty, had been asked on her account. When he began to talk to her it was all she could do to say, "Really?" or, "Of course!" at the proper places; she was absorbed in watching Edith—the vivid face, the broad smile, the voice so full of preposterous certainties! "I *look* old," she thought; and indeed she did—most unnecessarily! for she was only forty-four. Her throat suddenly ached with unshed tears of longing to be young. Yet if she had not been so bitter she would have seen that Maurice looked almost as old as she did! And no wonder. His consternation at the sight of Doctor Nelson had been panic! He could hardly eat. Naturally, the preoccupation of the two Curtises threw the burden of talk upon the others. Doctor Nelson gave himself up to his hostess, and Morton found Edith's ardors, upon every subject under heaven, most diverting; he teased her and baited her, and her eyes grew more shining, and her cheeks pinker, and her gayety more contagious with every repartee she flung back at him. Mrs. Morton struggled heroically with Maurice's heaviness, but she told her husband afterward, that Mr. Curtis was nearly as dull as his wife! "I *couldn't* make him talk!" she said. After a while she gave up trying to make him talk, and listened to Edith's story of what happened when she was a little girl and came to Mercer with her father:

"A terrible shipwreck!" Edith said; "I remember it because of Maurice's gallantry in giving the flopping girl his coat—he was a perfect Sir Walter Raleigh! Remember, Maurice?"

Maurice said, briefly, that he "remembered"; "if she says Dale, I'm dished," he thought; aloud, he said that the river was growing impossible for boating; which caused them to drop the subject of the flopping girl, and talk about Mercer's increasing dinginess, at which Edith said, eagerly:

"You ought to see our mountains—no smoke there!"

Then, of course, came tales of camping, and, most animatedly, the story of Eleanor's wonderful rescue of Maurice.

"She pulled that great big Maurice all the way down to Doctor Bennett's! And we were all so proud of her!"

Eleanor protested: "It was nothing at all." Maurice, in his own mind, was saying, "I wish she'd left me there!"

When the ladies left the gentlemen to their cigars, Edith was bubbling over with anxiety to confide to Mrs. Morton the joke about the "lady's cheeks coming off," and that gave the married women the chance to express melancholy convictions as to the wickedness of the world, to which Edith listened with much interest.

"I think my painted lady lives in Medfield," she said.

"Why, how do you know?" Eleanor exclaimed, surprised.

"Why, don't you remember the time I saw her, with that blue-eyed baby? She was just going into a house on Maple Street."

It was at this moment that the gentlemen entered, so there was no further talk of painted ladies; and, besides, Maurice was alert to catch Eleanor's eye, and go home! "Edith is capable of saying anything!" he was thinking, desperately.

However, Edith said nothing alarming, and Maurice was able to get her safely away from the powder magazine in the shape of the amiable doctor, who, following them a few minutes later, was saying to himself: "How scared he was! Yet he looks like a good fellow at bottom. A rum world—a rum world!"

The "good fellow" hurried his womenkind down the street in angry preoccupation. As soon as he and Eleanor were alone, he said, "When does Edith graduate?"

"She has two years more."

"Oh, *Lord*!" Maurice said, despairingly; "has she got to be around for two years?" Eleanor's face lightened, but Maurice was instantly repentant. "I ought to be ashamed of myself for saying that! Edith's fine; and she has brains; but—"

"She monopolized the conversation to-night," Eleanor said; "Maurice, it is very improper for her to keep talking all the time about that horrid woman!"

The sharpness of his agreement made her look at him in surprise. "She *mustn't* talk about Mrs. Dale!" he said, angrily.

"Dale? Is that her name?" said Eleanor.

"I don't know. I think so; didn't Edith call her that? Well, anyway, she mustn't keep talking about her!"

His irritation was so marked, that Eleanor's heart warmed; but she said, wearily, "I'll be glad myself when she graduates."

CHAPTER XVII

Edith, reflecting upon her first dinner party, wished Johnny had seen her, all dressed up. Then she pondered the possibilities of her allowance: If she was "going out," oughtn't she to have a real evening dress? But this daring thought faded very soon, for there didn't seem to be any dinner parties ahead. Mrs. Newbolt's supper table was, as Maurice said, sarcastically, the extent of the "Curtises' social whirl"—a fact which did not trouble him in the least! He had his own social whirl. He had made a man-circle for himself; some of the fellows in the office were his sort, he told Edith, and it was evident that their bachelor habits appealed to him, for he dined out frequently; and when he did, he was careful not to tell Eleanor where he was going, because once or twice, when he had told her, she had called up the club or house on the telephone about midnight to inquire if "Mr. Curtis had started home?" ... "I was worried about you, it was so late," she defended herself against his irritated mortification. He used to report these stag parties to Edith, telling her some of the stories he had heard; it didn't occur to him to tell any stories to Eleanor, because, as Henry Houghton had once said, Maurice and his wife didn't "have the same taste in jokes." When Edith chuckled over this or that witticism (or frowned at any opinion contrary to Maurice's opinion!) Eleanor sat in unsmiling silence. It was about this time Maurice fell into the way of saying "we" to Edith: "We" will have tea in the garden; "we" will put in a lot of bulbs on each side of the brick path; "we" will go down to the square and hear the election returns. Occasionally he remembered to say, "Why don't you come along, Eleanor?"

"No, thank you," she said; and sometimes, to herself, she added, "He keeps me out." The jealous woman always says this, never realizing the deeper truth, which is that she keeps herself out! Maurice did not notice how, all that winter, Eleanor was keeping herself out. She was steadily retreating into some inner solitude of her own. No one noticed it, except Mrs. O'Brien—and perhaps fat, elderly, snarling Bingo, who must sometimes, when his small pink tongue lapped her cheek, have tasted tears. By another year, Eleanor's mind had so utterly diverged from Maurice's that not even his remorse (which he had grown used to, as one grows used to some encysted thing) could achieve for them any unity of living. She bored him, and he hurt her; she loved him and tried to please him; he didn't love her, but tried to be polite; he was not often angry with her, he wasn't fond enough of her to be angry! So, forgetful of that security of the Stars—Truth!—to which he had once aspired, he grew dully used to the arid safety of untruth,—though sometimes he swore softly to himself at the tiresome irony of the office nickname which, with an occasional gilt hatchet, still persisted. He would remember that evening of panic at the Mortons', and think, lazily, "She can't possibly get on Lily's track!" So Lily lived in anxious thriftiness at 16 Maple Street; and Maurice, no longer acutely afraid of her, and only seeing her two or three times a year, was more or less able to forget her, in his growing pleasure in Edith's presence in his house—a pleasure quite obvious to Eleanor.

As for Edith, she used to wonder, sometimes, why Eleanor was so "up stage"? (that was her latest slang); but it did not trouble her much, for she was too generous to put two and two together. "Eleanor has nervous prostration," she used to tell herself, with good-natured excuse for some especial coldness; and she even tried, once in a while, "to make things pleasant for poor old Eleanor!" "I lug her in," she told Johnny.

"She's a dose," said Johnny.

"Yes," Edith agreed; "she's stupid. But I'm going to pull off a picnic, some Sunday, to cheer her up. 'Course you needn't come, if you don't want to."

Johnny, looking properly bored, said, briefly, "I don't mind."

This was in mid-September. "Are you game for it, Eleanor?" Edith said one night at dinner; "we can find some pleasant place by the river—"

"I know a bully place," Maurice said, "in the Medfield meadows; remember, Eleanor? We went there on our trolley wedding trip," he informed Edith.

Eleanor, struggling between the pleasure of Maurice's "remember," and antagonism at sharing that sacred remembering with Edith, objected; "It may rain."

"Oh, come on," Edith rallied her: "be a sport! It won't kill you if it does rain!"

But Maurice, after his impulsive recollection of the "bully place," remembered that the trolley car which would take them out to the river, must pass Lily's door; "I hope it will rain," he thought, uneasily.

However, on that serene September Sunday a week later, it didn't rain; and Maurice fell into the spirit of Edith's plans; for, after all, even if the car did pass Lily's ugly little house, it wouldn't mean anything to anybody!

"I'll sit with my back to that side of the street," he told himself. "It's safe enough! And it will give Buster a good time." He didn't realize that he rather hankered for a good time himself; to be sure, he felt a hundred years old! But money was no longer a very keen anxiety (he had passed his twenty-fifth birthday); and the day was glittering with sunshine, and Edith would make coffee, and Eleanor would sing. Yes! Edith should have a good time!

They went clanging gayly along over the bridge, down Maple Street, and through the suburbs of Medfield until they came to the end of the car line, where they piled out, with all their impediments, and started for the river and the big locust.

"You'll sing, Nelly," Maurice said—Eleanor's face lighted with pleasure;—"and I'll tell Edith how a girl ought to behave on her wedding trip, and you can instruct Johnny how to elope."

Then, with little Bingo springing joyously, but rather stiffly, ahead of them, they tramped across the yellowing stubble of the mowed field, talking of their coffee, and whether there would be too much wind for their fire— and all the while Maurice was aware of Lily at No. 16; and Eleanor was remembering her hope of a time when she and Maurice would be coming here, and it would not be "just us"! and Johnny was thinking that Edith was intelligent—for a woman; and Edith was telling herself that *this* kind of thing was some sense!

Eleanor, sitting down under the old locust, watched the three young people. She wondered when Maurice would tell her to sing. "The river is a lovely accompaniment, isn't it?" she hinted. No one replied.

"I'm going in wading after dinner," Edith announced; "what do you say, boys? Let's take off our shoes and stockings, and walk down to the second bridge. Eleanor can sit here and guard our things."

"I'm with you!" Maurice said; and Johnny said he didn't mind; but Eleanor protested.

"You'll get your skirts wringing wet, Edith. And—I thought we were to sit here and sing?"

"Oh, you can sing any old time," Edith said, lifting the lid of the coffee pot and stirring the brown froth with a convenient stick.

"And I'm just to look on?" Eleanor said.

"Why, wade, if you want to," her husband said; "it's safe enough to leave Edith's things here."

After that he was too much absorbed in shooing ants off the marmalade to give any thought to his wife. The luncheon (except to her) was the usual delightful discomfort of balancing coffee cups on uncertain knees, and waving off wasps, and upsetting glasses of water. Maurice talked about the ball game, and Edith gossiped darkly of her teachers, and Johnny Bennett ate enormously and looked at Edith.

Eleanor neither ate nor gossiped; but she, too, watched Edith—and listened. Bingo, in his mistress's lap, had snarled at Johnny when he took Eleanor's empty cup away, which led Edith to say that he was jealous.

"I don't call it 'jealous,'" Eleanor said, "to be fond of a person."

"You can't *really* be fond of anybody, and be jealous," Edith announced; "or if you are, it is just Bingoism."

This brought a quick protest from Eleanor, which was followed by the inevitable discussion; Edith began it by quoting, "'Love forgets self, and jealousy remembers self.'"

Maurice grinned and said nothing—it was enough for him to see Eleanor hit, *hard*! But Johnny protested:

"If your girl monkeys round with another fellow," he said, "you have a right to be jealous."

"Of course," said Eleanor.

"No, sir!" said Edith. "You have a right to be *unhappy*. If the other fellow's nicer than you—I mean if he has something that attracts her that you haven't, of course you'd be unhappy! (though you could get busy and *be* nice yourself.) Or, if he's not as nice as you, you'd be unhappy, because you'd be so awfully disappointed in her. But there's no jealousy about *that* kind of thing! Jealousy is hogging all the love for yourself. Like Bingo! And *I* call it plain garden selfishness—and no sense, either, because you don't gain anything by it. Do you think you do, Maurice? ... For Heaven's sake, hand me the sandwiches!"

Maurice didn't express his thoughts; he just roared with laughter. Eleanor reddened; Johnny, handing the sandwiches, said that, though Edith generally could reason pretty well—for a woman—in this particular matter she was 'way off.

"You are long on logic, Edith," Maurice agreed; "but short on human nature; (she hasn't an idea how the shoe fits!)."

"The reason I'm so up on jealousy," Edith explained, complacently, "is because yesterday, in English Lit., our professor worked off a lot of quotations on us. Listen to this (only I can't say just exactly the words!): *'Though jealousy be produced by love, as ashes by fire, yet jealousy'*—oh, what does come next? Oh yes; I know—'*yet jealousy extinguishes love, as ashes smother flames.*'"

"Who said that?" Maurice said.

Edith said she'd forgotten: "But I bet it's true. I'd simply hate a jealous person, no matter how much they loved me! Wouldn't you, Eleanor? Wouldn't you hate Maurice if he was jealous of you? I declare I don't see how you can be so fond of Bingo!"

Maurice, suddenly ashamed of himself for his pleasure in seeing Eleanor hit, was saying, inaudibly, "Good Lord! what will she say next?" To keep her quiet, he said, good-naturedly, "Don't you want to sing, Nelly?"

She said, very low, "No." Her throat ached with the pain of knowing that the one little contribution she could make to the occasion was not really wanted!

Maurice did not urge her. He and the other two took off their shoes and stockings; and went with squeals across the stubble, down a steep bank, to a pebbly point of sand, round which a sunny swirl of water chattered loudly, then went romping off into sparkling shallows. Edith's lifted skirt, as she stepped into the current, assured her against the wetting Eleanor had foreseen, and also showed her pretty legs—and Eleanor, on the bank, her tensely trembling hand cuddling Bingo against her knee, "guarded" her things! It was at this moment that her old, unrecognized envy of Youth turned into a perfectly recognizable fear of Age. Edith was a woman now, not a child! "And I—dislike her!" Eleanor said to herself. She sat there alone, thinking of Edith's defects—her big mouth, her bad manners, her loud voice; and as she thought,—watching the waders all the while with tear-blurred eyes until a turn in the current hid them—she felt this new dislike flowing in upon her: "He talks to her; and forgets all about me!" ... She was deeply hurt. "He says she has 'brains.' ... He doesn't mind it when she says she 'doesn't care for music,' which is rude to me! And she talks about jealousy! She knows I'm jealous. Any woman who loves her husband is jealous."

Of course this pathetically false opinion made it impossible for her to realize that jealousy is just a form of self-love, nor could she enlarge upon Edith's naïve generalization and say that, if a woman suffers because she is not the equal of the rival who gains her lover's love—*that* is not jealousy! It is the anguish of recognizing her own defects, and it may be very noble. If she suffers because the rival is her inferior, *that* is not jealousy; it is the anguish of recognizing defects in her lover, and it, too, is noble, for she is unhappy, not because he has slighted her, but because he has slighted himself! Jealousy has no such noble elements; it is the unhappiness that Bingo knows—an ignoble agony! ... But Eleanor, like many pitiful wives, did not know this. Sitting there on the bank of the river, without aspiration for herself or regret for Maurice, she knew only the anguish of being neglected. "He wouldn't have left me six years ago," she said; "He doesn't even ask me if I want to wade! I don't; but he didn't *ask* me. He just went off with her!"

Suddenly, her fingers trembling, she began to take off her shoes and stockings. She *would* do what Edith did! ... It was a tremor of aspiration!—an effort to develop in herself a quality he liked in Edith. She went, barefooted, with wincing cautiousness, and with Bingo stepping gingerly along beside her, across the mowed grass; then, haltingly, down the bank to the sandy edge of the river; there, while the little dog looked up at her anxiously, she dipped a white, uncertain foot into the water—and as she hesitated to essay the yielding mud, and the slimy things under the stones, she heard the returning splash of wading feet. A minute later the three youngsters appeared, Edith's skirts now very well above the danger line of wetness, and the two men offering eager guiding hands, which were entirely disdained! Then as, from under the leaning trees, they rounded the bend, there came an astonished chorus:

"Why, look at Eleanor!"

"Your skirt's in the water," Edith warned her; "hitch it up, and 'come on in—the water's fine!'"

She shook her head, and turned to climb up the bank.

"'The King of France,'" Edith quoted, satirically, "'marched *down* a hill, and then marched up again!'"

Eleanor was silent. When the three began to put on their shoes and stockings, Eleanor, putting on her own, her skirt wet and drabbled about her ankles, heard Maurice and Johnny offering to tie Edith's shoestrings—a task which Edith, with condescending giggles, permitted. Both of the boys—for Maurice seemed suddenly as much of a boy as Johnny!—went on their knees to tie, and re-tie, the brown ribbons, Maurice with gleeful and ridiculous deference.

"Want me to tie your shoestrings for you, Nelly?" he said over his shoulder.

"I am capable of tying my own, thank you," she said, so icily that the three playfellows looked at one another and Maurice, reddening sharply, said:

"Give us a song, Nelly!" But she sitting with clenched hands and tensely silent, shook her head. She was too wounded to speak. For the rest of the poor little picnic, with its gathering up of fragments and burning paper napkins—the conversation was labored and conscious.

On the trolley going home, Edith was the only one who tried to talk; Eleanor, holding Bingo in her lap, was dumb; and Johnny—hunting about for an excuse to "get away from the whole blamed outfit!" only said "M-m" now and then. But Maurice said nothing at all. After all, what can a man say when his wife has made a fool of herself?

"Even Lily would have had more sense!" he thought.

CHAPTER XVIII

That dismal festivity of the meadow marked the time when Maurice began to live in his own house only from a sense of duty ... and because Edith was there! A fact which Eleanor's aunt recognized almost as soon as Eleanor did; so, with her usual candor, Mrs. Newbolt took occasion to point things out to her niece. She had bidden Eleanor come to dinner, and Eleanor had said she would—"if Maurice happened to be going out."

"Better come when he's *not* going out, so he can be at home and amuse Edith!" said Mrs. Newbolt. "Eleanor, my dear father used to say that women were puffect fools, because they never could realize that if they left the door *open*, a cat would put on his slippers and sit by the fire and knit; if they locked it, he'd climb up the chimney, but what he'd feel free to prowl on the roof!"

Eleanor preferred to "lock the door"; and certainly during that next winter Edith's gay interest in every topic under heaven was a roof on which Maurice prowled whenever he could! Sometimes he stayed at home in the evening, just to talk to her! When he did, those "brains" which Eleanor resented, made him indifferent to many badly cooked dinners— during which Eleanor sat at the table and saw his enjoyment, and felt that dislike of their "boarder," which had become acute the day of the picnic, hardening into something like hatred. She wondered how he endured the girl's chatter? Sometimes she hinted as much, but Edith never knew she was being criticized! She was too generous to recognize the significance of what she called (to herself) Eleanor's grouch, and Maurice's delight in such unselfconsciousness helped to keep her ignorant, for he held his tongue— with prodigious effort!—even when Eleanor hit Edith over his shoulder. If he defended her, he told himself, the fat *would* be in the fire! So, as no one pointed out to Edith what the grouch meant, she had not the faintest idea that Eleanor was saying to herself, "Oh, if I could *only* get rid of her!" And as no one pointed out to Eleanor that the way to hold Maurice was not to get rid of Edith, but to "open the door," that corrosive thing the girl had called "Bingoism" kept the anger of the day in the field smoldering in her mind. It was like a banked fire eating into her deepest consciousness; it burned all that winter; it was still burning even when the summer vacation came and

Edith went home. Her departure was an immense relief to Eleanor; she told Maurice she didn't want her to come back, ever!

"Why not?" he said, sharply; "*I* like having her here. Besides, think of telling Uncle Henry we didn't want Edith next winter! If you have the nerve for that, *I* haven't." Eleanor had not the nerve; so when, at the end of June, Edith rushed home, it was understood that she would be with Maurice and Eleanor during the next term.... That was the summer that marked the seventh year of their marriage—and the fourth year of Jacky, over in the little frame house on Maple Street. But it was the first year of a knowledge, surprisingly delayed!—which came to Edith; namely, that Johnny Bennett was "queer."

It may have been this "queerness" which made her attach herself to Eleanor, who, in August, went to Green Hill for the usual two weeks' visit. Maurice had to go away on office business three or four times during that fortnight, but he came up for one Sunday. He had insisted upon Eleanor's going, because, he said, she needed the change. "Can't you come?" she pleaded. "Do take some extra time from the office!"

"And be docked? Can't afford it!" he said; "but I'll get one week-end in with you," he promised her, looking forward with real satisfaction to the solitude of his own house. So Eleanor, saying she couldn't understand why he was so awfully economical now that he had his own money!— came alone,—full of remorse at deserting him, and worry because of his loneliness, and leaving a pining Bingo behind her. But, to her silent annoyance, as soon as she arrived at Green Hill she encountered a new and tiresome attentiveness from Edith! Edith was inescapably polite. She did not urge upon Eleanor any of those strenuous amusements to which she and Johnny were devoted; she merely gave up the amusements, and, as Johnny expressed it, "stuck to Eleanor"! Eleanor couldn't understand it, and when Maurice at last arrived, Johnny's perplexity became audible:

"Perhaps," he told Edith, satirically, "you may be able, now, to tear yourself away from Eleanor, and go fishing with me? You fish pretty well— for a woman. Maurice can lug her round."

"I will, if Maurice will go, too," Edith said.

"What do you drag him in for?"—John paused; understanding dawned upon him: "She doesn't want to be by herself with me!" His tanned face slowly reddened, and those brown eyes of his behind the big spectacles grew keen. He didn't speak for quite a long time; then he said, very low, "I'll be here to-morrow morning at four-thirty. Be ready. I'll dig bait."

"All right," said Edith; after which, for the first time in her life, she played a shabby trick on Johnny Bennett; as soon as he had gone home, she invited Eleanor (who promptly declined), and Maurice (who as promptly accepted), to go fishing, too! Then, having got what she wanted, she reproached herself: "Johnny'll be mad as fury. But when he gets to saying things to me he makes me feel funny in the back of my neck. Besides, I want Maurice."

The fishermen were to assemble in the grayness of the August dawn; and Johnny was, as usual, prepared to throw a handful of gravel at Edith's window to hurry her downstairs. But when he loomed up in the mist, who should be on the porch, fooling with a rod, but Maurice!

"What's he butting in for?" Johnny thought, looking so cross that Edith, coming out with the luncheon basket, was really remorseful. "Hullo, Johnny," she said. ("I never played it on him before," she was thinking.) But at that moment her remorse was lost in alarm, for standing in the doorway was Eleanor, her hair caught up in a hurried twist, a wrapper over her shoulders, her bare feet thrust into pink bedroom slippers. (Forty-six looks fifty-six at 4.30 A.M.)

"Darling," Eleanor said, "I believe I'd like to go up to the cabin to-day. Do let's do it—just you and I!"

The three young people all spoke at once:

Johnny said: "Good scheme! We'll excuse Maurice."

Edith said, "Oh, Eleanor, Maurice loves fishing!"

And Maurice said: "I sort of think I'd like to catch a sucker or two in this pool Johnny is always cracking up. I bet he's in for a big jolt about his trout! You come, too?"

"I'd get so awfully tired. And I—I thought we could have a day together up on the mountain," she ended, wistfully.

There was a dead silence. Johnny was thinking: "Gosh! I hope she gets him." And Edith was thinking, "I'd like to choke her!" Maurice's thoughts could not be spoken; he merely said, "All right; if you want to."

"I don't believe I'll go fishing, either," Edith said.

Eleanor, on the threshold, turned quickly: "Please don't stay at home on my account!"

But Maurice settled it. "I'll not go," he said, patiently; "but you must, Edith." He threw down his rod and went into the house; Eleanor, in her flopping pink slippers, hurried after him....

"I did so want to have you to myself," she said; "you don't mind not going fishing with those children, do you?"

He said, listlessly: "Oh no. But don't let's attempt the cabin stunt." Then he stood at the window and watched Johnny and Edith, with fishing rods and lunch basket, disappear down the road into the fog. He was too bored to be irritated; he only counted the hours until he could get back to Mercer, and the office, and the table under the silver poplar. "I'll get hold of the Mortons, and Hannah can give us some sort of grub, and then we'll go to a show," he thought. "I can stick it out here for thirty-six hours more."

He stuck it out that morning by sitting in Mr. Houghton's studio, one leg across the arm of his chair, reading and smoking. Once Eleanor came in and asked him if he was all right. He said, briefly, "Yes."

But she was uneasy: "Maurice, I'll play tennis with you?"

This at least made him chuckle. "*You?* How long since? My dear, you couldn't play a set to save your life!"

After that she let him alone for a while. Early in the afternoon the need to make up to him for what she had done grew intolerable: "Darling, let's play solitaire?"

"I'm going to write letters."

She left him to his letters for an hour, then came again: "Let's walk!"

"Well, if you want to," Maurice said, and yawned. So they trudged off. Eleanor, walking very close to her husband, was thinking, heavily, how far they were apart; but she did her best to amuse him by anxious ponderings of household expenses. He, sheering off to the other side of the road to escape her intimate and jostling shoulder, was thinking of the expenses of another household, and making no effort whatever to amuse her. His silence confessed an irritation which she felt but could not understand; so by and by she fell silent, too, though the helpless tears stood in her eyes. Then, apparently, he put his annoyance, whatever it was, behind him.

"Nelly," he said, "let's go down by the West Branch and meet Edith and Johnny? They'll be coming home that way, 'laden with trout,' I suppose," he ended, sarcastically.

Eleanor began to say, "Oh *no!*" Then something, she didn't know what, made her say, "Well, all right." As they turned into the wood road that ran up toward the mountain, she said another unexpected thing:

"Maurice, I'm tired. I'll go home; you go on by yourself, and—and meet Johnny." She didn't know, herself, why she said it! Perhaps, it was just an effort to make up for what she had done in the morning?

Maurice, astonished, made some half-hearted protest; he would go back with her? But she said no, and walked home alone. Her throat ached with unshed tears. "He *likes* to be with her! He doesn't want me,—and I love him—I love him!"

The two youngsters had made a long day of it. On their way to the brook that morning, crashing through underbrush, climbing rotting rail fences that were hidden in docks and briers, balancing on the precarious slipperiness of mossy rocks, the triumphant Johnny, his heart warm with gratitude to Eleanor, had led his captive and irritated Edith. When they broke through low-hanging boughs and found the pool, the trout possibilities of which Johnny had so earnestly "cracked up," Edith was distinctly grumpy. "Eleanor is a selfish thing," she said. "Gimme a worm."

"I think Maurice would have been cussedly selfish not to do what she wanted," Johnny said; "my idea of marriage is that a man must do everything his wife wants."

"Maurice is never selfish! He's great, simply great!" Edith said.

"Oh, he's decent enough," Johnny admitted, then he paused, frowning, for he couldn't open his bait box; he banged it on a stone, pried his knife under the lid, swore at it—and turned very red. Edith giggled.

"Let me try," she said.

"No use; the rotten thing's stuck."

But she took it, shook it, gave an easy twist, and the maddening lid— loosened, of course, by Johnny's exertions—came off! Edith shrieked with joy; but Johnny, though mortified, was immensely relieved. They sat down on a sloping rock, and talked bait, and the grave and spectacled Johnny became his old self, scolding Edith for talking so loudly. "Girls," he said, "are *born* not fishermen!" Then they waded out into the stream, and began to cast. It was broad daylight by this time, and the woods were filling with netted sunbeams; the water whispered and chuckled.

"Pretty nice?" Johnny said, in a low voice; and Edith, all her grumpiness flown, said:

"You bet it is!" Then, as an afterthought, she called back, "But Eleanor is the limit!"

Johnny, forgetting his gratitude to Eleanor, said, savagely: "*Keep quiet!* You scared him off! Gosh! girls are awful."

So Edith kept quiet, and he wandered up the stream, and she wandered down the stream, and they fished, and they fished—and they never caught a thing.

"I had *one* bite," Johnny said when, at about eleven, fiercely hungry, they met on the bank where they had left their lunch basket; "but you burst out about Eleanor, and drove him off. Girls simply *can't* fish."

Edith was contrite—but doubted the bite. Then they sat down on a mossy rock, and ate stacks of sandwiches and hard-boiled eggs, and watched the water, and talked, talked, talked. At least Edith talked—mostly about Maurice. Johnny lit his pipe, puffed once or twice, then let it go out and sat staring into the green wall of the woods on the other side of the brook. Then, suddenly, quietly, he began to speak....

"I want to say something."

"The mosquitoes here are awful!" Edith said, nervously; "don't you think we'd better go home?"

"Look here, Edith; you've got to be half decent to me—unless, of course, you've soured on me? If you have, I'll shut up."

"Johnny, don't be an idiot! 'Course I haven't soured on you. You're the oldest friend I've got. Older than Maurice, even."

"Well, I guess I am an older friend than Maurice! But lately you've treated me like a dog. You skulk round to keep from being by ourselves. You never give me a chance to open my head to you—"

"Johnny, that's perfectly absurd! I've had to look after Eleanor—"

"Eleanor *nothing*! It's me you want to shake."

"I do *not* want to shake you! I'm just busy."

"Edith, I care a lot about you. I don't care much for girls, as a rule. But you're not girly. And every time I try to talk to you, you sidestep me."

"Now, Johnny—"

"But I'm going to tell you, all the same." He made a clutch at the sopping-wet hem of her skirt. "I *will* say it! I care an awful lot about you. I'm not a boy. I want to marry you."

There was a dead silence; then Edith said, despairingly, "Oh, Johnny, how perfectly horrid you are!" He gasped. "You simply spoil everything with this sort of ... of ... of talk."

"You mean you don't like me?" His face twitched.

"Like you? I like you awfully! That's why I'm so mad at you. Why, I'm *awfully* fond of you—"

"Edith!"

"I mean I never had a friend like you. I've always liked you ten times better than any silly old girl friend I ever had. I've liked you *almost* as much as Maurice. Of course I shall never like anybody as much as Maurice. He comes next to father and mother. But now you go and—and talk ... I just can't bear it," Edith said, and fumbled for her pocket handkerchief; "I *hate* talk." Her eyes overflowed.

"Edith! Look here; now, *don't*! Honestly, I can stand being turned down, but I can't stand—that. Edith, *please*! I never saw you do that—girl stunt. I'll never bother you again, if you'll just stop crying!"

Edith, unable to find her handkerchief, bent over and wiped her eyes on her dress. "I'm *not* crying," she said, huskily; "but—"

"I think," John Bennett said, "honestly, Edith, I think I've loved you all my life."

"And I have loved you," she said; "You are a lamb! Oh, Johnny, I'm perfectly crazy about you!"

His swiftly illuminating face made her add, hastily, "and now you go and spoil everything!"

"I won't spoil things, Skeezics," he said, gently; "oh, say, Edith, let up on crying! *That* breaks me all up."

But Edith, having discovered her handkerchief, was mopping very flushed cheeks and mumbling on about her own woes. "Why can't you be satisfied just to go on the way we always have? Why can't you be satisfied to have me like you almost as much as I like Maurice?"

"Maurice!" the young man said, with a helpless laugh. "Oh, Edith, you are several kinds of a goose! In the first place, Maurice is married; and in the second place, he's old enough to be your father—"

"He isn't old enough to be my father! And I shall *never* like anybody as much as Maurice, because there isn't anybody like him in the entire world. I've always thought he was exactly like Sir Walter Raleigh. Besides, I shall never marry *anybody*! But I mean, I don't see why it isn't enough for you to have me awfully fond of you?"

"Well, it isn't," Johnny said, briefly, "but don't you worry." He was white, but his tenderness was like a new sense. Edith had never seen *this* Johnny. Her entirely selfish impatience turned to shyness. "Edith," he said, very gently, "you don't understand, dear. You're awfully young—younger than your age. I didn't take in how young you were—talking about Maurice! I suppose it's because you know so few girls, that you are so young. Well; I can't hang round with you any more, as if we were ten years old. You see, I—I love you, Edith. That makes the difference ... dear."

"Oh," said Edith, desperately, "how perfectly *horrid*—" She looked really distracted, poor child! (but that was the moment when her preposterous youthfulness ceased.) She jumped to her feet so suddenly that Johnny, who had begun, his fingers trembling, to scrape out the bowl of his pipe, dropped his jackknife, which rolled down the steeply sloping rock into the water. "Oh, I'm so sorry!" Edith said.

John sighed. "Oh, that's nothing," he said, and slid over the moss and ferns to the water's edge; there, lying flat on his stomach, his sleeve rolled up, he thrust his bare white arm into the dark and troutless depths of the pool, and salvaged his knife. Edith, on the bank, began furiously to pack up. When Johnny climbed back to her she said she wanted to go home, "*now!*"

"All right," he said again, gently.

So, silently, they started homeward; and never in her life had Edith been so glad to see any human creature as she was to see Maurice on the West Branch Road! But she let him do all the talking. To herself she was saying, "It's all Eleanor's fault for not letting him come this morning! I just hate her!..."

That night her father said to her mother, rather sadly, "Mary, our little girl has grown up. Johnny Bennett is casting sheep's eyes at her."

"Nonsense!" said Mary Houghton, comfortably; "she's a perfect child, and so is he."

CHAPTER XIX

Curiously enough, though Edith's mother did not recognize what was going on between "the children," Eleanor did. When she came back to Mercer, a week later, she overflowed about it to Maurice. "Calf love!" she summed it up.

"She didn't look down on that kind of love seven years ago," he thought, cynically. But he didn't say so; no matter what his thoughts were, he was always kind to Eleanor. Lily, over in Medfield; Lily, in the small, secret house; Lily, with the good-looking little boy—blue-eyed, rosy-cheeked, blond-haired!—the squalid memory of Lily, said to him, over and over: "You are a confounded liar; so the least you can do is to be decent to Eleanor."

So he was kind.

"*I* couldn't bear myself," he used to think, "if I wasn't—but, O Lord!"

That "O Lord!" was his summing up of a growing and demoralizing sense of the worthlessness and unreality of life. Like Solomon (and all the rest of us, who see the universe as a mirror for ourselves!) he appraised humanity at his valuation of himself. He didn't use Solomon's six words, but the eight of his generation were just as exact—"*The whole blooming outfit is a rotten lie!* If," he reflected, "deceit isn't on my 'Lily' line, it is on a thousand other lines." From the small cowardices of appreciations and admirations which one did not really feel, up through the bread-and-butter necessities of business, on into the ridiculousness of what is called "Democracy" or "Liberty"—on, even, into those emotional evasions of logic and reason labeled "Religion"—all lies—all lies! he told himself. "And I," he used to think, looking back on seven years of marriage, "I am the most accomplished liar of the whole shootin' match!... If they get off that G. Washington gag on me any more at the office, somebody'll get their head punched."

All the same, even if he did say, "O Lord!" he was carefully kind to his boring wife.

But when Edith (suddenly grown up, it seemed to Maurice) came back for the fall term, he said "O Lord!" less frequently. The world began to seem to him a less rotten place. "Nice to have you round again, Skeezics!" he told her; and Eleanor, listening, went up to her room, and sat with her fingers pressed hard on her eyes. "It's dreadful to have her around! How *can* I get rid of her?" she thought. Very often now the flame of jealousy flared up; it scorched her whenever she recognized Edith's "brains," whenever she noticed some gay fearlessness, or easy capability; whenever she watched the girl's high-handed treatment of Maurice: criticizing him! Telling him he was mean because he was always saying he "couldn't afford things"! Declaring that she wished he would stop his everlasting practicing—and apparently not caring a copper for him! If Edith said, "Oh, Maurice, you are a perfect *idiot*!" Eleanor would see him grin with pleasure; but when Eleanor put her arms around him and kissed him, he sighed. To Maurice's wife these things were all like oil on fire; but it never occurred to her to try to develop in herself any of the qualities he seemed to find attractive in Edith. Instead, she thought of that June day in the meadow by the river when he said he loved her inefficiency—he loved her timidity, and, oh, how he had loved her love! He had made her promise to be jealous! Eleanor was not a reasoning person—probably no jealous woman is; but she did recognize the fact that what made him love her then, made him impatient with her now. This seemed to her irrational; and so, of course, it was!—just as the tide is irrational, or the turning of the earth on its axis is irrational. Nature has nothing to do with reason. So, in its deep and beautiful and animal beginnings, Love, too, is irrational. It has to ascend to Reason! But Eleanor did not know these things. All she knew was that Maurice *hurt* her, a dozen times a day.

She was brooding over this one Sunday afternoon in late September, when, at the open window of her bedroom, with Bingo snoozing in her lap, she listened to Edith, down in the garden: "How about a jug of dahlias on the table?"

And Maurice: "Bully! Say, Edith, why couldn't we have a yellow scheme for the grub? Orange cup, and that sort of fussy business you make out of cheese and the yolks of eggs? And yellow cakes?"

"Splendid! I'll mix up some perfectly stunning little sponge cakes, 'Lemon Queens.' Yellow as anything!"

This was all to get ready for a tea under the silver poplar, which was dropping yellow leaves down on the green table, and the mossy brick path, and the chairs for the company. The Mortons were coming, and there would be, Eleanor told herself, wearily, the usual shrieking over flat jokes,—Edith's jokes, mostly. Her dislike of Edith was a burning ache below her breastbone. "Maurice has her, so he doesn't want me," she thought; then suddenly she got up and hurried downstairs. "I'll fix the table!" she said, peremptorily.

"It's all done," Edith said; "doesn't it look pretty? Oh, Eleanor, let me put a dahlia behind your ear! You'll look like a Spanish lady!" She put the gorgeous flower into the soft disorder of Eleanor's dark hair, avoiding Bingo's angry objections, and said, with open admiration, "Eleanor, you *are* handsome! I adore dahlias!" she announced; "those quilly ones, red on the outside and yellow inside! There are some stunning ones on Maple Street, where I saw that Dale woman. Wonder if she'd sell some roots?"

The color flew into Maurice's face. "Did you get your bicycle mended?" he said.

Instantly Edith forgot the dahlias, and plunged into bicycle technicalities, ending with the query, "Why don't you squeeze out some money, and buy one of those cheap little automobiles, Maurice, you mean old thing!"

"Can't afford it," Maurice said.

But Eleanor was puzzled. There had been a hurried note in Maurice's voice when he asked Edith about her bicycle—an imperative changing of the subject! She looked at him wonderingly. Why should he change the subject? Was he annoyed at Edith's bad taste in referring to the creature? But Edith's taste was always bad, and Maurice was not generally so sensitive to it; not as sensitive as he ought to be! Or as he had been in those old days when he had said that Eleanor was too lovely to know the wickedness of the world, and he "didn't want her to"! She was really perplexed; and when Edith rushed off to make the cakes, and Maurice went indoors, she sat there in the garden, looking absently out through the rusty bars of the iron gate at the distant glimmer of the river, and wondered: "Why?"

She was still wondering even when the Mortons arrived, bringing with them—of all people!—Doctor Nelson. (*"Gosh!"* said Maurice.) "We're celebrating his appointment at the hospital; he's the new superintendent!" Mrs. Morton explained.

Eleanor said, mechanically, "So glad to see you, Doctor Nelson!" But she was saying to herself, "*Why* was Maurice provoked when Edith spoke of Mrs. Dale?" When some more noisy and very young people arrived, she was too abstracted to talk to them. She was so silent that most of them forgot her; until Mrs. Morton, suddenly remembering her existence, tried to be conversational:

"I suppose Mr. Curtis told you of our wild adventure on the river in August, when we got beached and spent the afternoon on a mud flat?"

"No," Eleanor said, vaguely. But afterward, when the guests had gone, she said to Maurice, "Why didn't you tell me about your adventure with the Mortons?"

"He told me," Edith said, complacently.

"I forgot, I suppose," Maurice said, carelessly, and lounged off into the house to sit down at the piano—where lie immediately "forgot" not only the adventure on the river—but even his dismay at seeing Doctor Nelson!—who by this time was, of course, quite certain that it was a "rum world."

That winter—although he was not conscious of it—Maurice's "forgetfulness" in regard to his wife became more and more marked, so it was a year of darkening loneliness for Eleanor. She was at last on that "desert island"—which had once seemed so desirable to her;—she had nothing to interest her except her music (and the quality of her voice was changing, pathetically); furthermore, Maurice rarely asked her to sing, so the passion had gone out of what voice she had! She didn't care for books; she didn't know how to sew; and, except for Mrs. Newbolt, there was no one she wanted to see. Often, in her empty evenings, while Edith was in her own room studying, she sat by the fire and cried, and broke her heart upon her desire for a child—"*then* he would be happy, and stay at home!"

It was a dull house; so dull that Edith made up her mind to get out of it for her next winter at Fern Hill. When she went home for the Easter vacation, she expressed decided opinions: "Father, once, ages ago"—she was sitting on her father's knee, and tormenting him by trying to take his cigar away from him—"you got off something about the dinner of herbs and Eleanor's stalled ox—"

"Good heavens, Buster! You haven't said that before Eleanor?"

"Ha! I got a rise out of you!" Edith said, joyfully; "I haven't mentioned it, *yet*; but I shall make a point of doing so unless you order two pounds of candy for me, *at once*. Well, I suppose what you meant was that Eleanor is stupid?"

"Mary," said Henry Houghton, "your blackmailing daughter is displaying a glimmer of intelligence."

"I'm only reminding you of your own remark," Edith said, "to explain why I want to be in one of the dormitories next winter. Eleanor *is* stupid—though she's never fed me on stalled ox! And I think she sort of doesn't like it because I'm not *awfully* fond of music."

"You are an absolute heathen about music," her father said.

"Well, it bores me," Edith explained, cheerfully; "though I adore Maurice's playing. Maurice is a lamb, and I adore just being in the house with him! But she's nasty to him sometimes. And when she is, I'd like to choke her!"

"Edith—Edith—" her mother remonstrated. And her father reminded her that she must *not* lose her temper.

"Let your other parent be a warning to you as to the horrors of an uncontrolled temper," said Henry Houghton; "I have known your mother, in one of her outbursts of fury, so far forget herself as to say, *'Oh, my!'*"

Edith grinned, but insisted, "Eleanor is dull as all get out!"

"Consider the stars," Mrs. Houghton encouraged her.

But Mr. Houghton said, "Mary, you've got to do something about this girl's English! ... You miss John Bennett?" he asked Edith (Johnny was taking a special course in an Eastern institute of technology).

"He did well enough to fill in the chinks," Edith said, carelessly; "but it's Maurice's being away that takes the starch out of me. He's everlastingly tearing off on business. And when he's at home—" Edith was suddenly grave—"of course Maurice is always 'the boy stands on the burning deck'; but you can't help seeing that he's fed up on poor old Eleanor! Sometimes I wonder he ever does come home! If I were in his place, when she gets to nagging *I'd* go right up in the air! I'd say, well,—something. But he keeps his tongue between his teeth."

That evening, when Henry Houghton was alone with his wife, he said what he thought about Maurice: "He *is* standing on the burning deck of this pathetic marriage of his, magnificently. He never bats an eyelash! (Your daughter's slang is vulgar.)"

"Eleanor is the pathetic one," Mary Houghton said, sadly; "Maurice has grown cynical—which is a sort of protection to him, I suppose. Yes; I'm afraid Edith is right; she'd better be out at the school next winter. It isn't well for a girl to see differences between a husband and wife.... Henry, you shan't have another cigar! That's the third since supper! Dear, what *is* the trouble about Maurice?"

"Mary, things have come to a pretty pass, when you snoop around and count up my cigars! I *will* smoke!" But he withdrew an empty hand from his cigar box, and said, sighing, "I wish I could tell you about Maurice; Kit; but I can't betray his confidence."

"If I guessed, you wouldn't betray anything?"

"Well, no. But—"

"I guessed it a good while ago. Some foolishness about a woman, of course. Or—or badness?" she ended, sadly.

He nodded. "I wish I was asleep whenever I think of it! Mary, there are some pretty steep grades on Fool Hill, and he's had hard climbing.... It's ancient history now; but I can't go into it."

"Of course not. Oh, my poor Maurice! Does Eleanor know?"

"Heavens, no! It wouldn't do."

"Honey, the unforgivable thing, to a woman, is not the sin, but the deceit. And, besides, Eleanor loves him enough to forgive him. She would die for him, I really believe!"

"Yet the green-eyed monster looks out of her eyes if he plays checkers with Edith! My darling," said Henry Houghton, "as I have before remarked, your ignorance on this one subject is colossal. *Women can't stand truth.*"

"It's a provision of nature, then, that all men are liars?" she inquired, sweetly; "Henry, the loss of Edith's board won't trouble Maurice much, will it?"

"Not *as* much, of course, now that he has all his money; but he has to scratch gravel to make four ends meet," Henry Houghton said.

"*Four* ends!" she said; "oh, is it as bad as that? He has to support—somebody?"

He said, "Yes; so long as you have guessed. Mary, I really must have a smoke."

"Why *am* I so weak-minded as to give in to you!" she sighed; then handed him the cigar box, and scratched a match for him; he held her wrist—the sputtering match in her fingers—lighted the cigar, blew out the match, and kissed her hand.

"You are a snooper and a porcupine about tobacco; but otherwise quite a nice woman," he said.

CHAPTER XX

When Edith's Easter vacation was over, and she went back to Mercer, she was followed by a letter from Mrs. Houghton to Eleanor, explaining the plan for the school dormitory the following winter. But there was another letter, to Maurice, addressed (discreetly) to his office. It was from Henry Houghton, and it was to the effect that if any "unexpected expenses" came along, and Maurice felt strapped because of the cessation of Edith's board, he must let Mr. Houghton know; then a suggestion as to realizing on certain securities.

"That's considerate in him," Eleanor said; "but I don't know what 'unexpected expenses' we could have?"

It was a chilly April day. Maurice happened to be laid up home with a sore throat; Eleanor, searching for a cook, had stopped at his office for a lease he wanted to see, and brought back with her some mail she found on his desk.

"I knew this letter was from Mr. Houghton, so I opened it," she said, as she handed it to him. His instant and very sharp annoyance surprised her. "I wouldn't open your *business* letters," she defended herself; "but I didn't suppose you'd mind my seeing anything the Houghtons might write—"

"I don't like to have any of my mail opened!" he said, briefly, his eyes raking Henry Houghton's letter, and discovering (of course!) nothing in the fine, precise handwriting which was in the least betraying. ("But suppose he *had* said what the 'unexpected expenses' might be!")

"We shall miss Edith's board," Eleanor said; "but, oh, I'll be so glad to have her go!"

Maurice was silent. "If she lives in Medfield all the time, she'll be sure and run into Lily," he thought. "The devil's in it." He was in his bedroom, wrapped up in a blanket, shivering and hot and headachy. The chance of Edith's "running into Lily" would, of course, be even less if she were at Fern Hill, than it was now when she was going back and forth in the trolley every day; but he was so uncomfortable, physically, that he didn't think of that; and his preoccupation made him blind to Eleanor's hurt look.

"I am willing to have you read all *my* letters," she said.

"I'm not willing to have you read mine!" he retorted.

"Why not?" she demanded—"unless you have secrets from me."

"Oh, Eleanor, don't be an idiot!" he said, wearily.

"I believe you *have* secrets!" she said—and burst out crying and ran out of the room.

He called her back and apologized for his irritability; but as he got better, he forgot that he had been irritable—he had something else to think of! He must get down to the office and write to Mr. Houghton, asking him to address personal letters to a post-office box. And he made things still safer by going out to Medfield to see Lily and give her the number of the box in case she, too, had occasion to write any "personal" letters, which, indeed, she very rarely had. "I say *that* for her!" Maurice told himself. He hoped—as he always did when he had to go to Maple Street, that he would not see It—an It which had, of course, long before this, acquired sufficient personality to its father to be referred to as "Jacky"; a Jacky who, in his turn, had discovered sufficient personality in Maurice to call him "Mr. Gem'man"—a corruption of his mother's title for her very infrequent visitor, "the gentleman."

Jacky's "Mr. Gem'man" found the front door of the little house open, and, looking in, saw Lily in the parlor, mounted on a ladder, hanging wall paper. She stepped down, laughing, and moved her bucket of paste out of his way.

"Won't you be seated?" she said. Her rosy face was beaming with artistic satisfaction; "Ain't this paper lovely?" she demanded; "it's one of them children's papers that's all the rage now. I call it a reg'lar art gallery! Look at the pants on them rabbits! It pretty near broke me to buy it. The swells put this kind of paper in 'nurseries,' and stick their kids off in 'em; but that ain't *me*! I put it on the parlor! Set down, won't you?"

Maurice sat down and, very much bored, listened while Lily chattered on, with stories about Jacky:

"He says to the milkman yesterday, 'I like your shirt,' he says. And Amos—that's his name—he said, 'You can get one like it when you're grown up like me.' And Jacky, he says—oh, just as *sad!*—I'd rather have it now, 'cause when I grow up, maybe I'll be a lady.'"

Maurice smiled perfunctorily.

"Ain't he the limit?" Lily demanded, proudly; "he's a reg'lar rascal! He stuck out his tongue at the grocer's boy, yesterday, 'cause he stepped on my pansy bed. I wish you could 'a' seen him."

Maurice swallowed a yawn. "He's fresh."

"'Course," Lily said, quickly, "I gave him a smack! He's getting a good bringing up, Mr. Curtis. I give him a cent every morning, to say his prayers."

Maurice didn't care a copper about Jacky's manners, or his morals, either; but he said, carelessly, "A kid that's fresh is a bore."

Lily frowned. When Maurice, having explained about the letter box, gave her the usual "present" she made her usual good-natured protest—but this time there was more earnestness in it, and even a little sharpness. "I don't need it; I've got three more mealers—well, one of 'em can't pay me; her husband's out of work; but she don't eat more than a canary, poor thing! I can take care of Jacky *myself*."

The emphasis puzzled Jacky's father for a moment. That Lily, seeing the growing perfection of her handsome, naughty little boy, was becoming uneasy lest Maurice might be moved to envy, never occurred to him. If it had, he would of course have been enormously relieved; he might even have played upon her fear of such an impossibility to induce her to move away from Mercer! As it was, after listening to the account of the pansy catastrophe, he got up to go, thankful that he had not had to lay eyes on the child, whose voice he heard from the back yard.

Lily, friendly enough in spite of that moment of resentment, went to the front door with him. She had grown rather stout in the last year or two, but she was always as shiningly clean as a rose, and her little lodging house was clean, too; she was indefatigably thorough—scrubbing and sweeping and dusting from morning to night! "It's good business," said little Lily; "and it is just honest, too, for they pay me good!" Her only unbusinesslike quality was a generous kindliness, which sometimes considered the "mealers'" purses rather than her own. She had, to be sure, small outbursts of temper, when she "smacked" Jacky, or berated her lodgers for wasting gas; but Jacky was smothered with kisses even before his howls ceased, and the lodgers were placated with cookies the very next day—but that, too, was "good business"! Her "respectability" had become a deep satisfaction to her. She occasionally referred to herself as "a perfect lady." Her feeling about "imperfect" ladies was of most virulent disapproval. But she had no more spirituality than a hen. Her face was as good-humored, and common, and pretty as ever; and she had a fund of not too refined, but always funny, stories to tell Maurice; so he liked her, after a fashion, and she liked him, after a fashion, too, although she was a little afraid of him; his bored preoccupation seemed like sternness to Lily. "Grouchiness," she called it; "probably that's why he don't take to Jacky," she thought; "well, it's lucky he don't, for he shouldn't have him!" But as Maurice, on the little porch, said good-by, she really wondered at his queerness in not taking to Jacky, who, grimy and handsome, was sitting on the ground, spooning earth into an empty lard pail.

"Come in out o' the dirt, Sweety!" Lily called to him.

Jacky rose reluctantly, then stood looking, open-mouthed, at his mother's visitor.

"Say," he remarked; "I kin swear."

"You don't say so!" said Maurice.

"I kin say 'dam,'" Jacky announced, gravely.

"You are a great linguist! Who instructed you in the noble art of profanity?"

"Huh?" said Jacky, shyly.

"Who taught you?"

"Maw," said Jacky.

Maurice roared; Lily giggled,—"My soul and body! Listen to that child! Jacky, you naughty boy, telling wrong stories. One of these days I'm going to give you a reg'lar spanking." Then she stamped her foot, for Jacky had settled down again in the dust; "Do you hear me? Come right in out of the dirt! That's one on me!" she confessed, laughing: then added, anxiously: "Say, Mr. Curtis, I do smack him when he says bad words; honest, I do! He's getting a *good* bringing up, though my mealers spoil him something awful. But I'd just shake his prayers out of him, if he forgot 'em."

Maurice, still laughing, said: "Well, don't become too proficient, Jacobus. Good-by," he said again. And as he said it, Eleanor, in a trolley car, glanced out of the window and saw him.

"Why, there's Maurice!" she said; and motioned to the conductor to stop. Hunting for a cook had brought her to this impossible suburb, where Maurice, no doubt, was trying to buy or sell a house. "I'll get out and walk home with him," she thought, eagerly. But the car would not stop until the end of the second block, and when she hurried back Maurice had disappeared. He had either gone off in another direction, or else entered the house; but she could not remember which house!—those gingerbread tenements were all so much alike that it was impossible to be sure on which of the small porches she had seen her husband, and a fat, common-looking woman, and a child playing in the yard. All she could do was to wander up and down the block, looking at every front door in the hope that he would appear; as he didn't, she finally took the next car into town.

"Did you sell the house this afternoon?" she asked Maurice at dinner that night; and he, remembering how part of his afternoon had been spent, said he hadn't any particular house on the string at the moment.

"Then what took you to Medfield?" Eleanor asked, simply.

"Medfield!"

"I saw you out there this afternoon," she said; "you were talking to a woman. I supposed she was a tenant. I got off the car to walk home with you, but I wasn't sure of the house; they were all alike."

"What were you doing in Medfield?"

"Oh, Hannah has given notice; I was hunting for a cook. I heard of one out on Bell Street."

"Did you find her?"

"No," Eleanor said, sighing, "it's perfectly awful!"

"Too bad!" her husband sympathized.

In the parlor, after dinner, while Eleanor was getting out the cards for solitaire, Maurice, tingling with alarm and irritation, sat down at the piano and banged out all sorts of chords and discords. "Lily'll *have* to move," he was saying to himself. (Bang—*Bang!*) His Imagination raced with the possibilities of what would have happened if Eleanor had found the house which was "like all the other houses," and heard his "good-by" to Lily, or perhaps even caught the latest addition to Jacky's vocabulary! "The jig would have been up," he thought. (Bang—Crash!)... "She'll *have* to move! Suppose Eleanor took it into her head to hunt her up? She's capable of it!" (Crash!)

Eleanor's absorption in the cook she could not find kept her for nearly forty-eight hours from speculation as to what, if not office business, took Maurice to Medfield. When she did begin to speculate she said to herself, "He doesn't tell me things about his business!" Then she was stabbed again by his annoyance because she had opened the letter from Mr. Houghton; then by his secretiveness in regard to that adventure on the river with Mrs. Morton. (He had told Edith!) Then this—then that—and by and by a tiny heap of nothings, that implied reserves. He wasn't confidential. She told him *everything*! She never kept a thing from him! And he didn't even tell her why he was over in Medfield when no real-estate matters took him there. Why should he *not* tell her? And when she said that, the inevitable answer came: He didn't tell her, because he didn't want her to know! Perhaps he had friends there? No. No friends of Maurice's could live in such a locality. Well, perhaps there was some woman? Even as she said this, she was ashamed.

She knew she didn't believe it. Of course there wasn't any woman!... But, at any rate, he had interests in Medfield that he did not tell her about. She hinted this to him at breakfast the next morning. She had not meant to speak of it; she knew she would be sorry if she did. Eleanor was incapable of analysis, but she was, in her pitiful way, aware that jealousy, *when articulate*, is almost always vulgar—perhaps because the decorums of breeding (which insist that, for the sake of others, one's own pain must be hidden) are not propped up by the reserves of pride. At any rate, she was not often publicly bitter to Maurice. This time, however, she was.

"Apparently," she said, "Maurice has acquaintances on Maple Street whom I don't know."

"The élite," Edith remarked, facetiously; "his lovely Mrs. Dale lives there."

Maurice's start was perceptible.

"Perhaps it was Mrs. Dale you went to see?" Eleanor said.

Maurice, trained in these years of furtiveness to self-control, said, "Does she live on Maple Street, Edith?"

"I guess so. The time I rescued her little boy and her flower pot, ages ago, she was going into a house on Maple Street."

"I saw Maurice in Medfield on Thursday," said Eleanor; "and he doesn't seem to want to say what he was doing there!"

"I am perfectly willing to tell you what I was doing," he retorted; "I went from our office to see the woman who rents the house."

Eleanor's slow mind accepted this entirely true and successfully false remark with only the wonder of wounded love. "Why didn't he say that at first?" she thought; "why does he hide things from me?"

Maurice, however, made sure of that "hiding." Eleanor's attack upon him frightened him so badly that that very afternoon, after office hours (Eleanor being safe in bed with a headache), he went to see Lily. Her astonishment at another visit so soon was obvious; she was still further astonished when he told her why he had come. He hated to tell her. To speak of Eleanor offended his taste—but it had to be done. So, stammering, he began—but broke off:

"Send that child away!"

"Run out in the yard, Sweety," Lily commanded.

"Won't," said Jacky.

"Clear out!" Maurice said, sharply, and Jacky obeyed like a shot—but paused on the porch to turn the ferociously clanging doorbell round and round and round. "Well," Maurice began, "I'll tell you what's happened... Lily! Make him stop!"

"Say, now, Jacky, stop," Lily called; but Jacky, seized apparently with a new idea, had already stopped, and was running out on to the pavement.

So again Maurice began his story. Lily's instant and sympathetic understanding was very reassuring. He even caught himself, under the comfort of her quick co-operation, ranging himself with her, and saying *"we."* "We've got to guard against anything happening, you know."

"Oh, my soul and body, yes!" Lily agreed; "it would be too bad, and no sense, either; you and me just acquaintances. 'Course I'll move, Mr. Curtis. But, there! I hate to leave my garden—and I've just papered this room! And I don't know where to go, either," she ended, with a worried look.

"How would you like to go to New York?" he said, eagerly.

She shook her head: "I've got a lot of friends in this neighborhood. But there's a two-family house on Ash Street—"

"Say," said Jacky, in the hall; "I got—"

"Oh, but you must leave Medfield!" he protested; "she"—that "she" made him wince—"she may try to hunt you up."

"She can't. She don't know my name."

Maurice felt as if privacy were being pulled away from his soul, as skin might be flayed from living flesh. "But you see," he began, huskily, "there's a—a girl who lives with us; and she—she mentioned your name." Then, cringing, he told her about Edith.

Lily looked blankly puzzled; then she remembered; "Why, yes, sure enough! It was right at the gate—oh, as much as four years ago; I slipped, and she grabbed Jacky. Yes; it comes back to me; she told me she seen me the time we got ducked. 'Course, I gave her the glassy eye, and said I didn't remember the gentleman in the boat with her. And she caught on that I lived here? Well, now, ain't the world small?"

"Damned small," Maurice said, dryly.

"Say," said Jacky, from the doorway, "I got a—"

"Well, she—I mean this young lady—told my—ah, wife that you lived on Maple Street, and—" He was stammering with angry embarrassment; Lily gave a cluck of dismay. "Confound it!" said Maurice; "what'll we do?"

"Now, don't you worry!" Lily said, cheerfully. "If she ever speaks to me again, I'll say, 'Why, you have the advantage of me!'"

Her mincing politeness made him laugh, in spite of his irritation. "I think you'd like it in New York?" he urged.

Lily's amber eyes were full of sympathy—but she was firm: "I wouldn't live in New York for anything!"

"Mr. Gem'man," said Jacky, sidling crabwise into the room to the shelter of his mother's skirt; "I—"

"Say, now, Sweety, be quiet! No, Mr. Curtis; I only go into real good society, and I've always heard that New York ladies ain't what they should be. And, besides, I want a garden for Jacky. I'll tell you what I'll do! I'll take the top flat in that house on Ash Street. It has three little rooms I could let. There's a widow lady's been asking me to go in on it with her; it has a garden back of it Jacky could play in—last summer there was a reg'lar hedge of golden glow inside the fence! Mr. Curtis, you'd 'a' laughed! He pinched an orange off a hand-cart yesterday, just as cute! 'Course I gave him a good slap, and paid the man; but I had to laugh, he was so smart. And he's got going now, on God—since I've been paying him to say his prayers. Well, I suppose I'll have to be going to church one of these days," she said, resignedly. "The questions he asks about God are something fierce! *I* don't know how to answer 'em. Crazy to know what God eats—I told him bad boys."

"Lily, I don't think—*Thunder and guns!*" said Maurice, leaping to his feet and rubbing his ankle; "Lily, call him off! The little wretch put his teeth into me!"

Lily, horrified, slapped her son, who explained, bawling, "Well, b-b-but he didn't let on he heard me tellin' him that I—"

"I *felt* you," Maurice said, laughing; "Gosh, Lily! He's cut his eyeteeth— I'll say that for him!" He poked Jacky with the toe of his boot, good-naturedly: "Don't howl, Jacobus. Sorry I hurt your feelings. Lily, what I was going to say was, I don't believe that Ash Street place is what you want?"

"Yes, it is. The widow lady is a dressmaker, and she has three children. We were talking about it only yesterday. Her father's feeble-minded, poor old man! I take him in some doughnuts whenever I fry 'em. Mr. Curtis, don't worry; I'll fix it, somehow! And until I get moved, I won't answer the bell here. Look! I'll give you a key, and you can come in without ringing if you want to."

"No—*no!* I don't want a key! I wouldn't take a key for a million dollars!"

Lily's quick flush showed how innocent her offer had been. "I suppose that doesn't sound very high toned—to offer a gentleman a key? But I'll tell you! I ain't giving any door keys to my house. Jacky ain't ever going to feel funny about his mother," she said, sharply.

It was on the tip of Maurice's tongue to say, "Nor about his father!" but he was silent. It was the first time his mind had articulated his paternity, and the mere word made him dumb with disgust. Lily, however, was her kind little self again, full of promises to "clear out," and reassurances that "*she*" would never get on to it.

It was then that the grimness of the situation for Maurice lightened for a ridiculous moment. Jacky, breathing very hard, peered from behind his mother, and stretched out to Maurice an extremely dirty, tightly clenched fist. "I got a—a pre-present for you," he explained, panting. Maurice, in a great hurry to get away, paused to put out his hand, in which his son placed, very gently, a slimy, half-smoked cigar. "Found it," Jacky said, in a stertorous whisper, "in the gutter."

It was impossible not to laugh, and Maurice swallowed his impatience long enough to say, "Jacobus, you overwhelm me!" Then he took his departure, holding the gift between a reluctant thumb and finger. "Funny little beggar," he said to himself, and pitched the stub into the gutter from which Jacky had salvaged it; he didn't look back to see his son hanging over the palings, watching the fate of his present with stricken eyes... So it was that, when the day came that Eleanor did actually begin to search for what was hidden, Maple Street was empty of possibilities; Lily had flitted away into the secrecy of the two-family house on Ash Street.

It was nearly three months before the search began. Edith had gone home, Mrs. Newbolt was at the sea-shore, and Maurice was in and out— away for two or three days at a time on office business, and when at home absent almost every evening with some of those youthful acquaintances who seemed ignorant of Eleanor's existence. So there were long hours when, except for her little old dog, she was entirely alone—alone, to brood over Maurice's queer look when she had accused him of having an "acquaintance on Maple Street"; and by and by she said, "I'll find out who it is!" Yet she had moments of trying to tear from her mind the idea of any concealment, because the mere suspicion was an insult to Maurice! She had occasional high moments of saying, "I *won't* think he has secrets from me; I'll trust him." But still, because suspicion is the diversion of an empty mind, she played with it, as one might play with a dagger, careful only not to let it touch the quick of belief. After a while she deluded herself into thinking that, to exonerate Maurice, she must prove the suspicion false! It was only fair to him to do that. So she must find the woman whom she had seen on the porch with him. If she wasn't Mrs. Dale, that would "prove" that everything was all right, and that Maurice's presence there only meant that he was attending to office business; nothing to be jealous about in *that*! And if the woman *was* Mrs. Dale? Eleanor's throat contracted so sharply that she gasped. But again and again she put off the search for the exonerating proof—for she was ashamed of herself, "I'll do it to-morrow." ... "I'll do it next week."

It was a scorching, windy July day when she took her first defiling step and "did it." There had been a breakfast-table discussion of a vacation at Green Hill, the usual invitation having been received.

"Do go," Maurice had urged. "I'll do what I did last year—hang around here, and go to the ball games, and come up to Green Hill for Sundays." He was acutely anxious to have her go.

She was silent. "*Why* does he want to be alone?" she thought; "why— unless he goes over to Medfield?" Then, in sudden decision, she said to herself, "I will find out why, to-day!" But she was afraid that Maurice would, somehow, guess what she was going to do; so, to throw him quite off the track, she told him that Donny O'Brien was sick again; "I must go and see him this morning," she said.

Maurice, reading the sports page of the morning paper, said, "Too bad!" and went on reading. He had no interest in his wife's movements; the two-family house on Ash Street was beyond her range!

An hour later, Eleanor, giving Bingo a cooky to console him for being left at home, started out into the blazing heat, saying to herself: "I'll recognize her the minute I see her. Of course I *know* she isn't the Dale woman, but I want to *prove* that she isn't!"

Her plan was to ring the bell at every one of the gingerbread houses on that block on Maple Street, and ask if Mrs. Dale lived there? If she was not to be found, that would prove that Maurice had not gone to see her. If she was found, why, then—well, then Eleanor would say that she had heard that the house was in the market? If Mrs. Dale said it was not, that would show that it wasn't "office business" which had brought Maurice to that porch!

On Maple Street the heat blazed up from the untidy pavement, and a harsh wind was whirling little spirals of dust up and down the dry gutter. Eleanor's heart was beating so smotheringly that when her first ring was answered she could scarcely speak: "Does Mrs. Dale live here?"

"No," said the girl who opened the door, "there ain't nobody by that name livin' here."

And at the next door: "Mrs. Dale? No. This is Mrs. Mahoney's house."

It was at the sixth house, where some dusty pansies were drying up under the little bay window, that a woman whose red, soapy hands had just left the wash tub, said:

"Some folks with that name lived here before I took the house. But they moved away. She was real nice; used to give candy to the children round here. She was a widow lady. She told me her husband's name was Joseph. Was it her you was looking for?"

"I don't know her husband's name," Eleanor said.

"Her baby had measles when mine did," the woman went on; "I lived across the street, then. But I took a fancy to the house, because she'd papered the parlor so handsome, so I moved in the first of May, when she got out."

A little cold, prickling thrill ran down Eleanor's back. She had told herself that "Maurice had a secret"; but she had not really believed that the secret was about Mrs. Dale. She had been sure, in the bottom of her heart, that she would be able to "prove" that the woman he had been talking to that day was not Mrs. Dale.

Now, she had proved—that she was.

Eleanor swayed a little, and put her hand out to clutch at the porch railing. The woman exclaimed:

"Come in and sit down! I'll get you a glass of water."

Eleanor followed her into the kitchen and sat down on a wooden chair. She was silent, but she whitened slowly. The mistress of the house, scared at her pallor, ran to draw a tumbler of water from the faucet in the sink; she held it to Eleanor's lips, apologizing for her wet hands:

"I was tryin' to get my wash out.... Where do you feel bad?"

"It's so hot, that's all," Eleanor said, faintly: "I—I'm not ill—thank you very much." She tried to smile, but the ruthless glare of sunshine through the open kitchen door showed her face strained, as if in physical suffering.

"I'm awfully sorry I can't tell you where Mrs. Dale lives," the woman said, sympathetically. "Was she a friend of yours?" Eleanor shook her head. "There! I'll tell you who maybe could tell you—the doctor. He took care of her baby. Doctor Nelson—"

"Nelson!"

"He's the hospital doctor now. Why don't you ask him?"

"Thank you," said Eleanor vaguely. She rose, saying she felt better and was much obliged. Then she went out on to the porch, and down the broken steps to the windy scorching street.

She was certain: Maurice had gone to Medfield to see Mrs. Dale...

Why?

She was quite calm, so calm that she found herself thinking that she had forgotten to get an yeast cake for Mary. "I'll get it as I go home," she thought. But as she stood waiting for the car it occurred to her that she had better think things out before she went home. Better not see Maurice until she had decided just how she should tell him that there was no use having secrets from her! That she *knew* he was seeing Mrs. Dale! Then he would have to tell her *why* he was seeing her... There could be only one reason... For a moment she was suffocated by that "reason"! She let the returning car pass, and signaled the one going out into the country; she would go, she told herself, to the end of the route, and by that time she would know what to do. The car was crowded, but a kindly faced young woman rose and offered her a seat. Eleanor declined it, although her knees were trembling.

"Oh, do take it!" the woman urged, pleasantly, and Eleanor could not resist sinking into it.

"You are very kind," she said, smiling faintly.

The woman smiled, too, and said, "Well, I always think what I'd like anyone to do for my mother, if *she* couldn't get a seat in a car! I guess you're about her age."

Eleanor hardly heard her; she sat staring out of the window—staring at that same landscape on which she and Maurice had gazed in the unseeing ecstasy of their fifty-four minutes of married life! "He said we would come back in fifty years—not by ourselves." As she said that, a thought stabbed her! *There was a child that day, in the yard!*

When she saw that the car was approaching the end of the route, she thought of the locust tree, and the blossoming grass, and the whispering river. "I'll go there, and think," she said.

"All out!" said the conductor; and she rose and walked, stumbling once or twice, and with one hand outstretched, as if—in the dazzling July day—she had to feel her way in an enveloping darkness. She went down the country road, where the bordering weeds were white with dust, toward that field of young love, and clover, and blue sky.

When she reached the river, curving around the meadow, brown and shallow in the midsummer droughts, she saw that the big locust was long past blossoming, but some elderberry bushes, in full bloom, made the air heavy with acrid perfume; the grass, starred by daisies, and with here and there a clump of black-eyed Susans, was ready for mowing, and was tugging at its anchoring roots, blowing, and bending, and rippling in the wind, just as it had that other day!... "And I sat right here, by the tree," she said, "and he lay there—I remember the exact place. And he took my hand—"

Her mind whirled like a merry-go-round: "Well, I knew he was hiding something. I wish I had seen Doctor Nelson, and asked him where she lives. I wonder if he's the Mortons' friend?... If I don't get that yeast cake to Mary before lunch, she can't set the rolls.... Edith saw her with a child five years ago. Why"—her mind stumbled still farther back—"why, the very day Edith arrived in Mercer, Maurice had been looking at some house in Medfield, where the tenant had a sick child. That was why he was late in meeting Mrs. Houghton!... The child had measles. I wish I had gone to see Doctor Nelson! Then I would have known.... I can get some rolls at the bakery, and Mary needn't set them for dinner. I sang 'O Spring.'" She put her hands over her face, but there were no tears. "He kissed the earth, he was so happy. When did he stop being happy? What made him stop?... I wonder if there are any snakes here?—Oh, I *must* think what to do!" Again her mind flew off at so violent a tangent that she felt dizzy. "I didn't tell Mary what to have for dinner.... He gave her his coat, that time when the boat upset.... She was all painted, he said so." She picked three strands of grass and began to braid them together: "He did that; he made the ring, and put it over my wedding ring." Mechanically she opened her pocketbook, and took out the little envelope, shabby now, with years of being carried there. She lifted the flap, and looked at the crumbling circle. Then she put it back again, carefully, and went on with her toilsome thinking: "I'll tell him I know that he went to see the Dale woman. ... He said we had been married fifty-four minutes. It's eight years and one month. He thinks I'm old. Well, I am. That woman in the car thought I was her mother's age, and *she* must have been thirty! Why did he stop loving me? He hates Mary's cooking. He said Edith could make soup out of a paving stone and a blade of grass. Edith is rude to me about music, and he doesn't mind! How vulgar girls are, nowadays. Oh—I *hate* her!... Mary'll give notice if I say anything about her soup."

Suddenly through this welter of anger and despair a small, confused thought struggled up; it was so unexpected that she actually gasped: He hadn't quite lied to her! "There *was* office business!" Some real-estate transfer must have been put through, because—"Mrs. Dale had moved"! In her relief, Eleanor burst into violent crying; he had not *entirely* lied! To be sure, he didn't say that the woman whom he had gone "from the office" to see, the woman who rented the house, was Mrs. Dale; in that, he had not been frank; he kept the name back—but that was only a reserve! Only a harmless secrecy. There was nothing *wrong* in renting a house to the Dale woman! As Eleanor said this to herself, it was as if cool water flowed over flame-licked flesh. Yes; he didn't talk to her as he did to Edith of business matters; he didn't tell her about real-estate transactions; but that didn't mean that the Dale woman was anything to him! She was crying hard, now; "He just isn't frank, that's all." She could bear *that*; it was cruel, but she could bear it! And it was a protection to Maurice, too; it saved him from the slur of being suspected. "Oh, I am ashamed to have suspected him!" she thought; "how dreadful in me! But I've proved that I was wrong." When she said that she knew, in a numb way, that after this she must not play with the dagger of an unbelieved suspicion. She recognized that this sort of thing may be a mental diversion—but it is dangerous. If she allowed herself to do it again, she might really be stabbed; she might lose the saving certainty that he had not lied to her—that he had only been "not frank."

Suddenly she remembered how unwilling he had been, years ago, to talk of the creature to her! She smiled faintly at his foolishness. Perhaps he didn't want to talk of her now? Men are so absurd about their wives! Her heart thrilled at such precious absurdity. As for seeing that doctor—of course she wouldn't see him! She didn't *need* to see him. And, anyhow, she wouldn't, for anything in the world, have him, or anybody else, suppose that she had had even a thought that Maurice wasn't—all right! "He just wasn't quite frank; that was all." ... Oh, she had been wicked to suspect him! "He would never forgive me if he knew I had thought of such a thing, He must never know it."

In the comfort of her own remorse, and the reassurance of his half frankness, she walked back to the station and waited, in the midday heat, for the returning car. Her head had begun to ache, but she said to herself that she must not disappoint little Donny. So she went, in the blazing sun, to the old washerwoman's house, climbed three flights of stairs, and found the boy in bed, flushed with worry for fear "Miss Eleanor" wasn't coming. She took the little feeble body in her arms, and sat down in the steamy kitchen by an open window, where Donny could see, on the clothes lines that stretched like gigantic spiderwebs across a narrow courtyard, shirts and drawers, flapping and kicking and bellying in the high, hot wind. She talked to him, and said that if his grandmother would hire a piano, she would give him music lessons;—and all the while her sore mind was wondering how old the mother of that woman in the car was? Then she sang to Donny—little merry, silly songs that made him smile:

> "The King of France,
> And forty thousand men,
> Marched up a hill—"

She stopped short; Edith had thrown "The King of France" at her, that day of the picnic, when she had cringed away from the water and the slimy stones, and climbed up on the bank where she had been told to "guard the girl's shoes and stockings"! "Oh, I'll be so glad to get her and her 'brains' out of the house!" Eleanor thought. But her voice, lovely still, though fraying with the years—went on:

"Marched up a hill—
And
  then
    marched
      down
        again!"

When, with a splitting headache, she toiled home through the heat, she said to herself: "He ought to have been frank, and told me the woman was Mrs. Dale; I wouldn't have minded, for I know such a person couldn't have interested him. She had no figure, and she looked stupid. He couldn't have said *she* had 'brains'! That girl in the car was impertinent."

CHAPTER XXI

The heat and the wind—and remorse—gave Eleanor such a prolonged headache that Maurice, in real anxiety and without consulting her—wrote to Mrs. Houghton that "Nelly was awfully used up by the hot weather," and might he bring her to Green Hill now, instead of later? Her prompt and friendly telegram, "*Come at once,*" made him tell his wife that he was going to pack her off to the mountains, *quick*!

She began to say no, she couldn't manage it; "I—I can't leave Bingo" (she was hunting for an excuse not to leave Maurice), "Bingo is so miserable if I am out of his sight."

"You can take him,—old Rover's gone to heaven. Think you can start to-morrow?" He sat down beside her and took her hand in his warm young paw; the pity of her made him frown—pity, and an intolerable annoyance at himself! She, a woman twice his age, had married him, when, of course, she ought to have told him not to be a little fool; "...wiped my nose and sent me home!" he thought, with cynical humor. But, all the same, she loved him. And he had played her a damned cheap trick!—which was hidden safely away in the two-family house on Ash Street. "Hidden." What a detestable word! It flashed into Maurice's mind that if, that night among the stars, he had made a clean breast of it all to Eleanor, he wouldn't now be going through this business of hiding things—and covering them up by innumerable, squalid little falsenesses. "There would have been a bust-up, and she might have left me. But that would have been the end of it!" he thought; he would have been *free* from what he had once compared to a dead hen tied around a dog's neck—the clinging corruption of a lie! The Truth would have made him free. Aloud, he said, "Star,"—she caught her breath at the old lovely word—"I'll go to Green Hill with you, and take care of you for a few days. I'm sure I can fix it up at the office."

The tears leaped to her eyes. "Oh, Maurice!" she said; "I haven't been nice to you. I'm afraid I'm—rather temperamental. I—I get to fancying things. One day last week I—had horrid thoughts about you."

"About *me*?" he said, laughing; "well, no doubt I deserved 'em!"

"No!" she said, passionately; "no—you didn't! I know you didn't. But I—" With the melody of that old name in her ears, her thoughts were too shameful to be confessed. She wouldn't tell him how she had wronged him in her mind; she would just say: "Don't keep things from me, darling! Be frank with me, Maurice. And—" she stopped and tried to laugh, but her mournful eyes dredged his to find an indorsement of her own certainties—"and tell me you don't love anybody else?"

She held her breath for his answer:

"You *bet* I don't!"

The humor of such a question almost made him laugh. In his own mind he was saying, "Lily, and *Love*? Good Lord!"

Eleanor, putting her hand on his, said, in a whisper, "But we have no children. Do you mind—very much?"

"Great Scott! no. Don't worry about *that*. That's the last thing I think of! Now, when do you think you can start?" He spoke with wearied but determined gentleness.

She did not detect the weariness,—the gentleness made her so happy; he called her "Star"! He said he didn't love anyone else! He said he didn't mind because they had no children.... Oh, how dreadful for her to have had those shameful fears—and out in "their meadow," too! It was sacrilege.... Aloud, she said she could be ready by the first of the week; "And you'll stay with me? Can't you take two weeks?" she entreated.

"Oh, I can't afford *that*" he said; "but I guess I can manage one...."

Later that day, when she told Mrs. Newbolt—who had come home for a fortnight—what Maurice had planned for her, Eleanor's happiness ebbed a little in the realization that he would be in town all by himself, "for a whole week! He'll go off with the Mortons, I suppose," she said, uneasily.

"Well," said Mrs. Newbolt, with what was, for her, astonishing brevity, "why shouldn't he? Don't forget what my dear father said about cats: '*Open the door!*' Tell Maurice you *want* him to go off with the Mortons!"

Of course Eleanor told him nothing of the sort. But she was obliged, at Green Hill, to watch him "going off" with Edith. "I should think," she said once, "that Mrs. Houghton wouldn't want her to be wandering about with you, alone."

"Perhaps Mrs. Houghton doesn't consider me a desperate character," he said, dryly; "and, besides, Johnny Bennett chaperones us!"

Sometimes not even John's presence satisfied Eleanor, and she chaperoned her husband herself. She did it very openly one day toward the end of Maurice's little vacation. Henry Houghton had said, "Look here; you boys" (of course Johnny was hanging around) "must earn your salt! We've got to get the second mowing in before night. I'll present you both with a pitchfork."

To which Maurice replied, "Bully!"

"Me, too!" said Edith.

And John said, "I'll be glad to be of any assistance, sir."

("How their answers sum those youngsters up!" Mr. Houghton told his Mary.)

Eleanor, dogging Maurice to a deserted spot on the porch, said, uneasily, "Don't do it, darling; it's too hot for you."

But he only laughed, and started off with the other two to work all morning in the splendid heat and dazzle of the field. "Skeezics, don't be so strenuous!" he commanded, once; and Johnny was really nervous:

"It's too hot for you, Buster."

"Too hot for your grandmother!" Edith said—bare-armed, open-throated, her creamy neck reddening with sunburn.

Toward noon, Maurice's chaperon, toiling out across the hot stubble to watch him, called from under an umbrella, "Edith! You'll get freckled."

"When I begin to worry about my complexion, I'll let you know," Edith retorted; "Maurice, your biceps are simply great!"

"*How* she flatters him!" Eleanor thought; "And she knows he is looking at her." He was! Edith, lifting a forkful of hay, throwing the weight on her right thigh and straining backward with upraised arms, her big hat tumbling over one ear, and the sweat making her hair curl all around her forehead, was something any man would like to look at! No man would want to look at Eleanor—a tired, dull, jealous woman, whose eyes were blinking from the glare and whose face sagged with elderly fatigue. She turned silently and went away. "He likes to be with her—but he doesn't say so. Oh, if he would only be frank!" Her eyes blurred, but she would not let the tears come, so they fell backward into her heart—which brimmed with them, to overflow, after a while, in bitter words.

Edith, watching the retreating figure, never guessing those unshed tears, said, despairingly, to herself, "I suppose I ought to go home with her?" She dropped her pitchfork; "I'll come back after dinner, boys," she said; "I must look after Eleanor now."

"Quitter!" Maurice jeered; but Johnny said, "I'm glad she's gone; it's too much for a girl." His eyes followed her as she went running over the field to catch up with Eleanor, who, on the way back to the house, only poke once; she told Edith that flattery was bad taste the cup overflowed! "Men hate flattery," she said.

"Hate it?" said Edith, "they lap it up!"

When the two young men sat down under an oak for their noon hour, with a bucket of buttermilk standing precariously in the grass beside them, John said again, anxiously, "It was too hot for her; I hope she won't have a headache."

"She always has headaches," Maurice said, carelessly.

"What!" said Bennett, alarmed; "she's never said a word to me about headaches."

"Oh, you mean Edith? I thought you meant Eleanor. Edith never had a headache in her life! Some girl, Johnny?"

"Has that just struck you?" said John.

Maurice fished some grass seeds out of the buttermilk, took a deep draught of it, and looked at his companion, lying full length on the stubble in the shadow of the oak. It came to him with a curious shock that Bennett was in love. No "calf love" this time! Just a young man's love for a young woman—sound and natural, and beautiful, and right.... "I wonder," Maurice thought, "does she know it?"

It seemed as if Johnny, puffing at his pipe, and slapping a mosquito on his lean brown hand, answered his thought:

"Edith's astonishingly young. She doesn't realize that she's grown up." There was a pause; "*Or that I have.*"

Maurice was silent; he suddenly felt old. These two—these children!— believing in love, and in each other, were in a world of their own; a world which knew no hidden household in the purlieus of Mercer; no handsome, menacing, six-year-old child; no faded, jealous woman, overflowing with wearisome caresses! In this springtime world was Edith—vigorous, and sweet, and supremely reasonable;—and *never* temperamental! And this young man, loving her.... Maurice turned over on his face in the grass; but he did not kiss the earth's "perfumed garment"; he bit his own clenched fist.

He was very silent for the rest of their day in the field for one thing, they had to work at a high pitch, for then were blue-black clouds in the west! At a little after three Edith came out again, but not to help.

"I had to put on my glad rags," she said, sadly, "because some people are coming to tea. I hate 'em—I mean the rags."

Maurice stopped long enough to turn and look at her, and say, "They're mighty pretty!" And so, indeed, they were—a blue organdie, with white ribbons around the waist, and a big white hat with a pink rose in a knot of black velvet on the brim. "How's Eleanor?" he said, beginning to skewer a bale of hay on to his pitchfork.

"She's afraid there's going to be a thunderstorm," Edith said; "that's why I came out here. She wants you, Maurice."

"All right," he said, briefly; and struck his fork down in the earth. "I've got to go, Johnny."

To do one's duty without love is doubtless better than to fail in doing one's duty, but it has its risks. Maurice's heartless "kindness" to his wife was like a desert creeping across fertile earth; the eager generosity of boyhood had long ago hardened into the gray aridity of mere endurance.

Edith turned and walked back with him; they were both silent until Maurice said, "You've got Johnny's scalp all right, Skeezics."

"Don't be silly!" she said; her annoyance made her look so mature that he was apologetic; was she in love with the cub? He was suddenly dismayed, though he could not have said why. "I don't like jokes like that," Edith said.

"I beg your pardon, Edith. I somehow forget you're grown up," he said, and sighed.

She laughed. "Eleanor and you have my age on your minds! Eleanor informed me that I was too old to be rampaging round making hay with you two boys! And she thinks I 'flatter' you," Edith said, grinning. "I trust I'm not injuring your immortal soul, Maurice, and making you vain of your muscle?"

Instantly he was angry. Eleanor, daring to interfere between himself and Edith? He was silent for the rest of the walk home; and he was still silent when he went up to his wife's room and found her lying on her bed, old Bingo snoozing beside her—windows closed, shades down. "Oh, Maurice!" she said, with a gasp of relief; "I was so afraid you would get caught in a thunderstorm!"

"*Don't* be so absurd!" he said.

"I—I love you; that's why I am 'absurd,'" she said, piteously. It was as if she held to his lips the cup of her heart, brimming with those unshed tears,—but is there any man who would not turn away from a cup that holds so bitter a draught?

Maurice turned away. "This room is insufferably hot!" he said. He let a window curtain roll up with a jerk, and flung open a window.

She was silent.

"I wish," he said, "that you'd let up on Edith. You're always criticizing her. I don't like it."

That night Johnny Bennett, somehow, lured Edith out on to the porch to say good night. The thunderstorm had come and gone, and the drenched garden was heavy with wet fragrance.

"Let's sit down," Johnny said; then, beseechingly, "Edith, don't you feel a little differently about me, now?"

"Oh, Johnny, *dear!*"

"Just a little, Edith? You don't know what it would mean to me, just to hope?"

"Johnny, I am awfully fond of you, but—"

"Well, never mind," he said, patiently, "I'll wait."

He went down the steps, hesitated, and, while Edith was still squeezing a little wet ball of a handkerchief against her eyes, came back.

"Do you mind if I ask you just one question, Edith?"

"Of course not! Only, Johnny, it just about *kills* me to be—horrid to you."

"Have you really got to be horrid?" said John Bennett.

"Johnny, I *can't* help it!"

"Is it because there's any other fellow, Edith? That's the question I wanted to ask you."

She was silent.

"Edith, I really think I have a right to know?"

Still she didn't speak.

"Of course, if there *is*—"

"There isn't!" she broke in.... "Why, Johnny, you're the best friend I have. No; there isn't anybody else. The honest truth is, I don't believe I'm the sort of girl that gets married. I can't imagine caring for *anybody* as much as I care for father and mother and Maurice. I—I'm not sentimental, Johnny, a bit. I'm awfully fond of you; *awfully*! You come next to Maurice. But—but not that way. That's the truth, Johnny. I'm perfectly straight with you; you know that? And you won't throw me over, will you? If I lost you, I declare I—I don't know what I'd do! You won't give me up, will you?"

John Bennett was silent for a long minute; then he said, "No, Edith; I'll never give you up, dear." And he went away into the darkness.

CHAPTER XXII

Edith's flight to one of the schoolhouses was not the entire release that Eleanor expected.

"Look here, Skeezics," Maurice had announced; "you can't turn me down this way! You've got to come to supper every Sunday night!—when I'm at home. Isn't that so, Nelly?"

Eleanor said, bleakly: "Why, if Edith would *like* to, of course. But I shouldn't think she'd care to come in to town at six, and rush out to Medfield right after supper."

"I don't mind," Edith said.

"You bet she won't rush off right after supper!" Maurice said; "I won't let her. And if she doesn't get in here by three o'clock, I'll know the reason why!"

So Edith came in every Sunday afternoon at three—and Eleanor never left her alone with Maurice for a moment! She sat and watched them; saw Edith's unconcealed affection for Maurice, saw Maurice's pleasure in Edith, saw his entire forgetfulness of herself,—and as she sat, silently, watching, watching, jealousy was like a fire in her breast.

However, in spite of Eleanor, sitting on the other side of the fire, in bitter silence, those Sunday afternoons were delightful to Edith. She and Maurice were more serious with each other now. His feeling about her was that she was a mighty pretty girl, who had sense, and who, as he expressed it, "spoke his language." Her feeling about him was a frankly expressed appreciation which Eleanor called "flattery." She had an eager respect for his opinions, based on admiration for what she called to herself his hard-pan goodness. "How he keeps civil to Eleanor, *I* don't know!" Edith used to think. Sometimes, watching his civility—his patience, his kindness, and especially his ability to hold his tongue under the provocation of some laconic and foolish criticism from Eleanor—Edith felt the old thrill of the Sir Walter Raleigh moment. Yes; there was no one on earth like Maurice! Then she thought, contritely, of good old Johnny. "If I hadn't known Maurice, I might have liked Johnny," she thought; "he *is* a lamb." When she reflected upon Eleanor, something in her generous, careless young heart hardened:

"She's not nice to Maurice!" She had no sympathy for Eleanor. Youth, having never suffered, is brutally unsympathetic. Edith had known nothing but love,—given and received; so of course she could not sympathize with Eleanor!

When the Sunday-night suppers were over, Eleanor and Maurice escorted their guest back to Fern Hill; Edith always said, "Don't bother to go home with me, Eleanor!" And Maurice always said, "I'll look after the tyke, Nelly, you needn't go"; and Eleanor always said, "Oh, I don't mind." Which was, of course, her way of "locking the door" to keep her cat from a roof that became more alluring with every bolt and bar which shut him from it.

On these trolley rides through Medfield Maurice was apt to be rather silent, and he had a nervous way of looking toward the rear platform whenever the car stopped to take on a passenger—"although," he told himself, "what difference would it make if Lily did get on board? She's so fat now, Edith wouldn't know her. And as for Lily, she's white. She'd play up, like a 'perfect lady'!"

He was quite easy about Lily. He hadn't seen her for more than a year, and she made no demands on him. She was living in the two-family house on Ash Street, with the dressmaker and her three children and feeble-minded father, in the lower flat. There was the desired back yard for Jacky, where a thicket of golden glow lounged against the fence, and where, tinder stretching clothes lines, a tiny garden overflowed with color and perfume. Every day little Lily would leave her own work (which was heavy, for she had several "mealers") and run downstairs to help Mrs. Hayes wash and dress the imbecile old man. And she kept a pot of hyacinths blooming on his window sill.

Maurice (with grinding economies) sent her a quarterly money order, and felt that he was, as he expressed it to himself, "square with the game," — with the Lily-and-Jacky game. He could never be square with the game he played with Eleanor; and as for his own "game," his steadily pursued secretiveness was a denial of his own standards which permanently crippled his self-respect. Though, curiously enough, these years of careful lying had made him, on every subject except those connected with the household in Medfield, of a most scrupulous truthfulness. Indeed, the office still called him "G. Washington."

Jacky was six that winter—a handsome, spoiled little boy. He looked like Maurice—the same friendly, eager, very bright blue eyes and the same shock of blond hair. Lily's ideas of discipline were, of course, ruining him, to which fact Maurice was entirely indifferent; his feeling about Jacky was nothing but a sort of spiritual nausea; Jacky was not only an economic nuisance, but he had made him a liar! He said to himself that of course he didn't want anything to happen to the brat ("that would break Lily's heart!"), but—

Then in March, something did happen to him. It was on a Sunday that the child came down with scarlet fever, and Lily, in her terror, did the one thing that she had never done, and that Maurice, in his certainty of her "whiteness," felt sure she never would or could do: she sent a telegram—*to his house!*

It had been a cold, sunny day. Just before luncheon Eleanor had been summoned to Mrs. O'Brien's: "*Donny is kind of pining; do please come and sing to him, Miss Eleanor,*" the worried grandmother wrote, and Eleanor hadn't the heart to refuse. "I suppose," she thought, looking at Maurice and Edith, "they'll be glad to get rid of me!" They were squabbling happily as to whether altruism was not merely a form of selfishness; Edith had flung, "*Idiot!*" at Maurice; and Maurice had retorted, "I never expect a woman to reason!" It was the kind of squabbling which is the hall mark of friendship and humor, and it would have been impossible between Eleanor and her husband.... She left them, burning with impatience to get down to Mrs. O'Brien's and back again in the shortest possible time. As soon as she was out of the house Maurice disposed of altruism by a brief laying down of the law:

"There's no such thing as disinterestedness. You never do anything for anybody, except for what you get out of it for yourself.... Let's go skating?"

The suggestion was not the result of premeditation; Maurice, politely opening the front door for his wife, had realized, as he stood on the threshold and a biting wind flung a handful of powdery snow in his face,—the sparkling coldness of the day; and he thought to himself, "this is about the last chance for skating! There'll be a thaw next week." So, when he came back, whistling, to the library, he said: "Are you game for skating? It's cold as blazes!"

And Edith said: "You bet I am! Only we'll have to go to Fern Hill for my skates!"

Maurice said, "All right!" and off they went, the glowing vigor and youth of them a beauty in itself!

So it was that when Eleanor got home, after having gently and patiently sung to poor Donny for nearly an hour, the library was empty; but a note on the mantelpiece said: "We've gone skating.—E. and M." "She waited until I went out," Eleanor thought; "*then* she suggested it to him!" She sat down, huddling over the fire, and thinking how Maurice neglected her; "He doesn't want me. He likes to go off with Edith, alone!" They had probably gone to the river—"our river!"—that broad part just below the meadow, where there was apt to be good skating. That made her remember the September day and the picnic, when Edith had talked about jealousy—"Bingoism," she had called it. "She tried to attract him by being *smart*. I detest smartness!" The burning pain under her breastbone was intolerable. She thought of the impertinent things Edith had said that day—and the ridiculous inference that if the person of whom you were jealous, was more attractive in any way than you were yourself, it was unreasonable to be jealous;—"get busy, and *be* attractive!" Edith had said, with pert shallowness. "She doesn't know what she's talking about!" Eleanor said; and jealousy seared her mind as a flame might have seared her flesh. "I haven't skated since I was a girl.... I—I believe next winter I'll take it up again." The tears stood in her eyes.

It was at that moment that the telegram was brought into the library.

"Mr. Curtis isn't in," Eleanor told the maid; then she did what anyone would do, in the absence of the person to whom the dispatch was addressed; signed for it ... opened it ... read it.

Jacky's sick; please come over quick.

L. D.

"There's no answer," she said. When the maid had left the room, Maurice's wife moistened the flap of the flimsy brown envelope—it had been caught only on one side; got up, went into the hall, laid the dispatch on the table, came back to the library, and fainted dead away.

No one heard her fall, so no one came to help her—except her little dog, scrabbling stiffly out of his basket, and coming to crouch, whining, against her shoulder. It was only a minute before her eyelids flickered open;— closed—opened again. After a while she tried to rise, clutching with one hand at the rung of a chair, and with the other trying to prop herself up; but her head swam, and she sank back. She lay still for a minute; then realized that if Maurice came in and found her there on the floor, he would know that she had read the telegram.... So again she tried to pull herself up; caught at the edge of his desk, turned sick, saw everything black; tried again; then, slowly, the room whirling about her, got into a chair and lay back, crumpled up, blindly dizzy, and conscious of only one thing: she must get upstairs to her own room before Edith and Maurice came home! She didn't know why she wanted to do this; she was even a little surprised at herself, as she had been surprised when, that night on the mountain, "to save Maurice," she had, instinctively, done one sensible thing after another. So now she knew that, when he came home with Edith, Maurice must be saved "a scene." He must not discover, yet, that ... *she knew.*

For of course now, it was knowledge, not suspicion: Maurice was summoned to see a sick boy called Jacky; Jacky was the child of L. D.; and L. D. was the Dale woman, who had lived in the house on Maple Street. Her shameful suspicion had not been shameful! It had been the recognition of a fact.... Clutching at supporting chairs, Eleanor, somehow, got out of the library; saw that brown envelope in the hall, stopped (holding with one hand to the table), to make sure it was sealed. Bingo, following her, whimpered to be lifted and carried upstairs, but she didn't notice him. She just clung to the banisters and toiled up to her room. She pushed open her door and looked at her bed, desiring it so passionately that it seemed to her she couldn't live to reach it—to fall into it, as one might fall into the grave, enamored with death. Down in the hall the little dog cried. She didn't faint again. She just lay there, without feeling, or suffering. After a while she heard the front door open and close; heard Edith's voice: "Hullo, Eleanor! Where are you? We've had a bully time!" Heard Maurice: "Headache, Nelly? Too ba—" Then silence; he must have seen the envelope—picked it up—read it.... That was why he didn't finish that word—so hideously exact!—"*bad.*" After a while he came tiptoeing into the room.

"Headache? Sorry. Anything I can do?"

"No."

He did not urge; he was too engrossed in the shock of an escaped catastrophe; *suppose Eleanor had read that dispatch!* Good God! Was Lily mad? He must go and see her, quick, and say—He grew so angry as he thought of what he was going to say that he did not hear Edith's friendly comments on "poor dear Eleanor."

"Edith," he said, "that—that dispatch: I've got to see somebody on business. Awfully sorry to take you out to Fern Hill before supper, but I'm afraid I've got to rush off—"

"'Course! But don't bother to take me home. I can go by myself."

"No. It's all right. I have time; but I've got to go right off. I hate to drag you away before supper—"

"That's of no consequence!" she said, but she gave Maurice a swift look. What was the matter with him? His forehead, under that thatch of light hair, was so lined, and his lips were set in such a harsh line, that he looked actually *old!* Edith sobered into real anxiety. "I wish," she said, "that you wouldn't go out to Fern Hill; you'll have to come all the way back to town for your appointment!"

He said, "No: the—the appointment is on that side of the river." On the trolley there was no more conversation than there might have been if Eleanor had been present. At Edith's door he said, "'Night—"

But as he turned away, she called to him, "Maurice!" Then ran down the steps and put her hand on his arm: "Maurice, look here; is there anything I can do? You're bothered!"

He gave a grunt of laughter. "To be exact, Edith, I'm damned bothered. I've been several kinds of a fool."

"You haven't! And it wouldn't make any difference if you had. Maurice, you're a perfect *lamb*! I won't have you call yourself names! Why" —her eyes were passionate with tenderness, but she laughed—"I used to call you 'Sir Walter Raleigh,' you know, because you're great, simply great! Maurice, I bet on you every time! Do tell me what's the matter? Maybe I can help. Father says I have lots of sense."

Maurice shook his head. "You do have sense! I wish I had half as much. No, Skeezics; there's nothing anybody can do. I pay as I go. But you're the dearest girl on earth!"

She caught at his hand, flung her arm around his shoulder, and kissed him: "You are the dearest boy on earth!" Before he could get his breath to reply, she flew into the house—flew upstairs—flew into her own room, and banged the door shut. "*Maurice is unhappy!*" she said. The tears started, and she stamped her foot. "I can't *bear* it! Old darling Maurice—what makes him unhappy? I could kill anybody that hurts Maurice!" She began to take off her hat, her fingers trembling—then stopped and frowned: "I believe Eleanor's been nasty to him? I'd like to choke her!" Suddenly her cheeks burned; she stood still, and caught her lower lip between her teeth; "I don't care! I'm *glad* I did it. I—I'd do it again! ... Darling old Maurice!"

CHAPTER XXIII

When Jacky's father—with that honest young kiss warm upon his cheek—reached the little "two-family" house, he saw the red sign on the door: *Scarlet Fever*.

"He's got it," he thought, fiercely; "but why in hell did she send for me?—and a telegram!—to the *house*! She's mad." He was panting with anger as he pressed the button at Lily's door; "I'll tell her I'll never see her again, long as I live!" Furious words were on the tip of his tongue; then she opened the door, and he was dumb.

"Oh, Mr. Curtis—don't—don't let them take Jacky! Oh, Mr. Curtis!" She flung herself upon him, sobbing frantically. "Don't let them—I'll kill them if they touch Jacky! Oh, my soul and body! He'll die if they take him—I won't let them take him—" She was shaking and stammering and gasping. "I won't have him touched.... You got to stop them—"

"Lily, *don't*! What's the matter?"

"This woman downstairs 's about crazy, because she has three children. I hope they all catch it and die and go to hell! She's shut up there with 'em in her flat. She won't put her nose outside the door! She come up here this morning, and saw Jacky, and she said it was scarlet fever. Seems she knew what it was, 'cause she had a boy die of it—glad he did! And she sent—the slut!—a complaint to the Board of Health—and the doctor, he come this afternoon, and said it was! And he said he was going to take Jacky *to-night*!"

Her voice made him cringe; her yellow tigress eyes blazed at him; he had known that Lily, for all her good humor, had occasional sharp gusts of temper, little squalls that raced over summer seas of kindliness! But he had never seen this Lily: A ferocious, raucous Lily, madly maternal! A Lily of the pavements.... "An' I said he wasn't going to do no such thing! An' I said I'd stop it: I said I'd take the law to him; I said I'd get Jacky's father: I—"

"Good God! Lily—"

"Oh, what do I care about *you*? I ain't goin' to kill Jacky to protect *you*! You got to stop them taking him!" She clutched his arm and shook it: "I never asked nothing of you, yet. I ask it now, and you'll *do* it, or I'll tell everybody in town that he's yours—" Her menacing voice broke and failed, but her lips kept moving; those kind, efficient hands of hers, clutching at him, were the claws of a mother beast. Maurice took her arm and guided her into the little parlor, where a row of hyacinths on the window sill made the air overpoweringly sweet; he sat down beside her on the sofa.

"Get steady, Lily, and tell me: I'll see what can be done. But there's to be no *father* business about it, you understand? I'm just a 'friend.'"

So, stammering and breaking into sobs and even whispered screams, and more outrageous abuse of her fellow tenant, she told him: It was scarlet fever, and there were children in the house. The Board of Health, "sicked on by that damned woman," said that Jacky must go to the hospital—to the contagious ward. "And the doctor said he'd be better off there; he said they could do for him better than me—me, his mother! They're going to send a ambulance—I telegraphed you at four o'clock—and here it is six! You *must* have got it by five—why didn't you come? Oh—my God, *Jacky!*" Her suffering was naked; shocking to witness! It made Maurice forget his own dismay.

"I was out," he began to explain, "and—"

But she went on, beads of foam gathering in the corners of her mouth: "I didn't telephone, for fear *she'd* get on to it." He could see that she was angry at her own consideration. "I'd ought to have sent for you when he come down with it!" ... Where had he been all this time, anyway!—and her nearly out of her head thinkin' this rotten woman downstairs was sicking the Board o' Health on to her! "And look how I've washed her father for her! I'll spit on him if—if—if anything happens to Jacky. Yes, I tell you, and you mind what I say: If Jacky dies, I'll kill her—my soul and body, I'll kill her anyway!"

"Lily, get steady. I'll fix things for you. I'll go to the Board of Health and see what can be done; just as—as a friend of yours, you understand."

From the next room came a wailing voice: "Maw—"

"Yes, Sweety; in a minute—" She grasped Maurice's hand, clung to it, kissed it. "Mr. Curtis, I'll never make trouble for you after this! Oh, I'll go to New York, and live there, if you want me to. I'll do *anything*, if you just make 'em leave Jacky! (Yes, darling Sweety, maw's coming.) You'll do it? Oh, I knew you'd do it!" She ran out of the room.

He got up, beside himself with perplexity: but even as he tried to think what on earth he could do, the doctor came. The ambulance would arrive, he said, with bored cheerfulness, in twenty minutes. Lily, rushing from

Jacky's bedside, flew at him with set teeth, her trembling hands gripping the white sleeve of his linen jacket.

"This gentleman's a friend of mine," she said, jerking her head toward Maurice; "he says you *shan't* carry Jacky off!"

The doctor's relief at having a man to talk to was obvious. And while Maurice was trying to get in a word, there came another whimper from the room where Jacky lay, red and blotched, talking brokenly to himself: "Maw!" Lily ran to him, leaving the two men alone.

"Thank Heaven!" the doctor said; "I'd about as soon argue with a hornet as a mother. She's nearly crazy! I'll tell you the situation." He told it, and Maurice listened, frowning.

"What can be done?" he said; "I—I am only an acquaintance; I hardly know Mrs. Dale; but she sent for me. She's frantic at the idea of the boy being taken away from her."

"He'll *have* to be taken away! Besides, he'll have ten times better care in the hospital than he could have here."

"Can she go with him?" Maurice said.

"Why, if she can afford to take a private room—"

"Good heavens! money's no object; anything to keep her from doing some wild thing!"

"You a relation?" the doctor asked.

"Not the slightest. I—knew her husband."

"The thing for you to do," said the doctor, "is to hustle right out to a telephone; call up the hospital. Get Doctor Nelson, if you can—"

"Nelson!"

"Yes; if not, get Baker; tell him I—" then followed concise directions; "But try and get Nelson; he's the top man. They're frightfully crowded, and if you fool with understrappers, you'll get turned down. I'd do it, but I've got to stay here and see that she doesn't get perfectly crazy."

Almost before the doctor finished his directions, Maurice was rushing downstairs.... That next half hour was a nightmare. He ran up the street, slippery with ice; saw over a drug store the blue sign of the public telephone, and dashed in—to wait interminably outside the booth! A girl in a silly hat was drawling into the transmitter. Once Maurice, pacing frantically up and down, heard her flat laugh; then, to his dismay, he saw her, through the glass of the door, instead of hanging up the receiver, drop a coin into the slot....

"Damn! *Another* five minutes!"

He turned and struck his fist on the counter. "Why the devil don't you have two booths here?" he demanded.

The druggist, lounging against the soda-water fountain, smiled calmly: "You can search *me*. Ask the company."

"Can't you stop that woman? My business is important. For God's sake pull her out!"

"She's telephoning her beau, I guess. Who's going to stop a lady telephoning her beau? Not me."

The feather gave a last flirtatious jerk—and the booth was empty.

Maurice, closing its double doors, and shutting himself into the tiny box where the fetid air seemed to take him by the throat and the space was so narrow he could hardly crowd his long legs into it, rushed into another delay. Wrong number! ... When at last he got the right number and the hospital, there were the usual deliberate questions; and the, "I'll connect you with So-and-so's desk." Maurice, sitting with the receiver to his ear, could feel the blood pounding in his temples. His mind whirled with the possibilities of what Lily might say in his absence: "She'll tell the doctor my name—" As his wire was connected, first with one authority and then with another, each authority asked the same question, "Are you one of the family?" And to each he gave the same answer, "No; a friend; the doctor asked me to call you up."

Finally came the voice of the "top man"—the voice which had spoken in Lily's narrow hall six years ago, the voice which had joked with Edith at the Mortons' dinner party, the voice which had burst into extravagant guffaws under the silver poplar in his own garden—Doctor Nelson's voice—curt, impersonal: "Who is this speaking?"

Then Maurice's voice, disguised into a gruff treble, "A friend."

"One of the family?"

"No."

Five minutes later Maurice, coming out of that horrible little booth, the matter arranged at an expense which, later, would give Jacky's father some bad moments, was cold from head to foot. When he reached Lily's house the ambulance was waiting at the door. Upstairs, the doctor said, "Well?"

And Lily said: "Did you do it? If you didn't, I'll—"

"I did," Maurice said. Then he asked if he could be of any further service.

"No; the orderly will get him downstairs. He's too heavy for Mrs. Dale to carry. She's got her things all ready. You—" he said, smiling at Maurice, "Mr.—? I didn't get your name. You look all in!"

Maurice shook his head: "I'm all right. Mrs. Dale will you step in here? I want to speak to you a minute." As Lily preceded him into the dining room, he said, quickly, to the doctor, "I want to tell her not to worry about money, you know." To Lily—when he closed the door—he was briefly ruthless: "I'll pay for everything. But I just want to say, if he dies—"

She screamed out, "No—no!"

"He won't," he said, angrily; "but if he does, you are to say his father's dead. Do you understand? Say his name was—what did you call it?—William?"

"I don't know. My God! what difference does it make? Call it anything! John."

"Well, say his father was John Dale of New York, and he's dead. Promise me!"

She promised—"Honest to God!" her face was furrowed with fright. As they went back to the doctor Maurice had a glimpse of Lily's bedroom, where Jacky, rolled in a blanket, was vociferating that he would *not* be carried downstairs by the orderly.

"Oh, Sweety," Lily entreated; "see, nice pretty gentleman! Let him carry you?"

"Won't," said Jacky.

At which Maurice said, decidedly: "Behave yourself, Jacobus! I'll carry you."

Instantly Jacky stopped crying: "You throwed away the present I give you," he said; "but," he conceded, "you may carry me."

The doctor objected. "It isn't safe—"

"Oh, let's get it over," Maurice said, sharply; "I shan't see any children. It's safe enough! Anything to stop this scene!"

The bothered doctor half consented, and Maurice lifted Jacky, very gently; as he did so, the little fellow somehow squirmed a hand out of the infolding blanket, and made a hot clutch for his father's ear; he gripped it so firmly that, in spite of Maurice's wincing expostulation, he pulled the big blond head over sidewise until it rested on his own little head. That burning grip held Maurice prisoner all the way downstairs; it chained him to the child until they reached the street. There the clutch relaxed, but for one poignant moment, as Maurice lifted Jacky into the ambulance, father and son looked into each other's eyes, and Maurice said—the words suddenly tumbling from his lips:

"Now, my little Jacky, you'll be good, won't you?" Then the ambulance rolled softly away, and he stood on the curbstone and felt his heart swelling in his throat: "Why did I say '*my*'?" As he walked home he tried to explain the possessing word away: "Of course I'd say 'my' to any child; it didn't mean anything! But suppose the orderly had heard me?" Even while he thus denied the Holy Spirit within him, he was feeling again that hot, ridiculous tug on his ear. "*I* was the only one who could manage him," he thought.... "Of course what I said didn't mean anything."

He stopped on the bridge and looked down into the water—black and swift and smooth between floating cakes of ice. Now and then a star glimmered on a slipping ripple; on the iron bridge farther up the river a row of lights were strung like a necklace across the empty darkness.... Somewhere, in the maze of streets at one end of the bridge, was Eleanor, lying in bed with a desperate headache. Somewhere, in the maze of streets at the other end of the bridge, was Lily, taking "his" little Jacky to the hospital. Somewhere, on one of the hillsides beyond Medfield, was Edith in the schoolhouse. And Eleanor was loving him and trusting him; and Lily was "blessing him" (so she had told him) for his goodness; and Edith was "betting on him"! ... "I wonder if anybody was ever as rotten as I am?" Maurice pondered.

Then he forgot his "rottenness," and smiled. "He obeyed *me*! Lily couldn't do a thing with him; what did he mean about the 'present'? I believe it was that old cigar! He must have seen me pitch it into the gutter. He wanted me to carry him; wouldn't look at that orderly! What made him grab my ear?"

When Maurice said that, down, down, under his rage at Lily, under his fear of exposure, under his nauseating disgust at himself—something stirred, something fluttered. The tremor of a moral conception:

Paternal pride.

"*What* a grip!"

CHAPTER XXIV

After a tornado comes quietness; again the sun shines, and birds sing, and many small things look up, unhurt. It was incredible to Maurice, eating his breakfast the next morning, reading his paper, opening his letters, and glancing at a pale Eleanor, heavy-eyed and silent, that his world was still the same world that it had been before he had picked up the sealed telegram on the hall table. He asked Eleanor how she felt; told her to take care of herself; said he'd not be at home to dinner, and went off to his office.... He was safe! Those two minutes in the dining room of Lily's flat, while the white-jacketed orderly was trying to persuade the protesting Jacky to let him carry him downstairs, had removed any immediate alarm; Lily had promised not to communicate with Jacky's father.

So Maurice, walking to the office, told himself that everything was all right—but "a close call!" Then he thought of Jacky, who, at his command, had so instantly "behaved himself"; and of that grip on his ear; and again that pang of something he did not recognize made him swallow hard. "Poor little beggar!" he thought: "I wonder how he is? I wonder if he'll pull through?" He hoped he would. "Tough on Lily, if anything happens." But his anxiety—though he did not know it—was not entirely on Lily's account. For the first time in the child's life, Maurice was aware of Jacky as a possession. The tornado of the night before—the anger and fear and pity—had plowed down below the surface of his mind, and touched that subsoil of conscious responsibility for creation, the realization that, whether through love or through selfishness, the man who brings a child into this terrible, squalid, glorious world, is a creator, even as God is the Creator. So Maurice, sitting at his desk that next day, answering a client on the telephone, or making an appointment to go and "look at a house," was really feeling in his heart—not love, of course, but a consciousness of his own relation to that little flushed, suffering body out in the contagious ward of the hospital in Medfield. "Will he pull through?" Maurice asked himself. It was six years ago that, standing at the door of a yellow-brick apartment house, with two fingers looped through the strings of a box of roses, Jacky's father had said, "Perhaps it will be born dead!" How dry his lips had been that day with the hope of death! Now, suddenly, his lips were dry with fear that the kid wouldn't pull through—which would be "tough on Lily."

His face was stern with this new emotion of anxiety which was gradually becoming pain; he even forgot how scared he had been at the thought that Eleanor *might* have opened that telegram. "I swear, I wish I hadn't hurt his feelings about that cigar stub!" he said. Then he remembered Eleanor: "I could wring Lily's neck!" But Eleanor hadn't opened the telegram; and Maurice hoped Jacky would get well—because "it would be tough on Lily" if he didn't. Thus he dismissed his wife. So long as Lily's recklessness had not done any harm, it was easy to dismiss her—so very far had she receded into the dull, patiently-to-be-endured, background of life!

The Eleanor of the next few weeks, who seemed just a little more melancholy and silent than usual, a little more devoted to old Bingo, did not attract his attention in any way. But when Edith came in on the following Sunday, he had his wife sufficiently on his mind to say, in a quick aside:

"Edith, don't give me away on being sort of upset last Sunday night, will you?" (As he spoke, he remembered that swift kiss. "Nice little Skeezics!" he thought.) But he finished his sentence with perfect matter-of-factness: "it was just a—a little personal worry. I don't want Eleanor bothered, you understand?"

"Of course," said Edith, gravely

And so it was that in another month or two, with reliance upon Edith's discretion, and satisfaction in a recovering Jacky, the track of the tornado in Maurice's mind was quite covered up with the old, ugly, commonplace of furtive security. In the security Maurice was conscious, in a kindly way, that poor old Eleanor looked pretty seedy; so he brought her some flowers once in a while; not as often as he would have liked to, for, though he had more money now, eight weeks of a private room in a hospital "kind o' makes a dent in your income," Maurice told himself; "but I don't begrudge it," he thought; "I'm glad the kid got well."

So, after that night of terror and turmoil,—when Eleanor had fainted—Maurice's life in his own house settled again into the old tranquil forlornness, enlivened only by those Sunday-afternoon visits from Edith.

And Eleanor?... There had been some dumb days, when she moved about the house or sat opposite Maurice at table, or exercised Bingo, like an automaton. Sometimes she sat at her window, looking down through the bare branches of the poplar at the still, wintry garden; the painted table, heaped with grimy snow slowly melting in the chill March sunshine; the dead stalks of the lilies on each side of the icy bricks of the path; the rusty bars of the iron gate, through which, now and then, came the glimmer, a block away, of the river—"their river"! Sometimes for an hour her mind numbly considered these things; then would come a fierce throb of pain:

"He was all the time saying he 'couldn't afford' things; that was so he could give her money, I suppose?" Then blank listlessness again. She did not suffer very much. She was too stunned to suffer. She merely said to herself, vaguely, "I'll leave him." It may have been on the third day that, when she said, "I will leave him; he has been false to me," her mind whispered back, very faintly, like an echo, "He has been false to himself." For just a moment she loved him enough to think that he had sinned. *Maurice has sinned!* When she said that, the dismay of it made her forget herself. She said it with horror, and after a while she added a question: "*Why* did he do it?" Then came beating its way up through anger and wounded pride, and suffering love, still another question: "Was it my fault that he did it? Did he fall in love with that frightful woman because I failed him?" Instantly her mind sheered off from this question: "I did everything I knew how to make him happy! I would have died to make him happy. I adored him! How could he care for that common, ignorant woman I saw on the porch? A woman who wasn't a lady. A—a *bad* woman!" But yet the question repeated itself: "Why? Why?" It demanded an answer: Why did Maurice—high-minded, pure-hearted, overflowing with a love as beautiful, and as perfect as Youth itself—how *could* Maurice be drawn to such a woman? And by and by the answer struggled to her lips, tearing her heart as it came with dreadful pain: "He did it because I didn't make him happy."

Just as Maurice, recognizing the responsibility of creation, had, at the touch of his son's little hand, felt the tremor of a moral conception, so now Eleanor, barren so long! felt the pangs of a birth of spiritual responsibility: "I didn't make him happy, so—Oh, my poor Maurice, it was my fault!"... But of course this divine self-forgetfulness in self-reproach, was as feeble as any new-born thing. When it stirred, and uttered little elemental sounds—"my fault, my fault"—she forgot the wrong he had done her, in seeing the wrong he had done himself.... "Oh, my Maurice—my Maurice!" But most of the time she did not hear this frail cry of the sense of sin! She thought entirely and angrily of herself; she said, over and over, that she was going to leave him. She was absorbed in hideous and poignant imaginings, based on that organic curiosity which is experienced only by the woman who meditates upon "the other woman." When these visions overwhelmed her, she said she wouldn't leave him—she would hold him! She wouldn't give him up to that frightful creature, whom he—kissed.... "Oh, my God! He *kisses* her!" No; she wouldn't give him up; she would just accuse him; just tell him she knew he had been false; tell him there was no use lying about it! Then, perhaps, say she would forgive him?... Yes; if he would promise to throw the vile woman over, she would forgive him. She did not, of course, reflect that forgiveness is not a thing that can be promised; it cannot be manufactured. It comes in exact proportion as we love the sinner more and self less.

And forgiveness is not forgetfulness! It is more love.

Eleanor did not know this. So, except for those occasional cooling and divine moments of blaming herself, she scorched and shriveled in the flames of self-love. And as usual, she was speechless. There were many of these silent hours (which were such a matter of course to Maurice that he never noticed them!) before she gathered herself together, and decided that she would not leave him. She would fight! How? "Oh, I *can't* think!" she moaned. So those first days passed—days of impotent determinations, which whirled and alternated, and contradicted each other.

Once Maurice, glancing at her over his newspaper at breakfast, thought to himself, "She hasn't said a word since she got up! Poor Eleanor!..." Then he remembered how he had once supposed these silences of hers were full of things too lovely and profound for words! He frowned, and read the sporting page, and forgot her silences, and her, too. But he did not forget Jacky. "I'll buy the kid a ball," he was thinking....

So the days passed, and each day Eleanor dredged her silences, to find words: "What shall I say to him?" for of course she must say *something*! She must "have it out with him," as the phrase is. Sometimes she would decide to burst into a statement of the fact: "Somebody called 'L. D.' has a claim upon you, because she sends for you when 'Jacky' is sick. I am certain that 'Jacky' is your child! I am certain that 'L.D.' is Mrs. Dale. I am certain that you don't love me...." And he would say—Then her heart would stand still: What *would* he say? He would say, "I stopped loving you *because you are old.*" And to that would come her own terrible assent: "I had no right to marry him—he was only nineteen. I had no right..." (Thus did that new-born sense of her own complicity in Maurice's sin raise its feeble voice!) And little by little the Voice became stronger: "I didn't make him happy *not* because I was old, but because I was selfish...." So, in alternating gusts of anger and fear, and outraged pride,—and self-forgetting horror for Maurice,—her soul began to awake. Again and again she counted the reasons why he had not been happy, beginning with the obvious reason, his youth and her age: But that did not explain it. "We had no children." That did not explain it! Nor, "I wasn't a good housekeeper"; nor, "I didn't do things with him ... I didn't skate, and walk, and joke with him"; nor, "I didn't entertain him. Auntie always said men must be entertained. I—I am stupid." There was no explanation in such things; neither dullness nor inefficiency was enough to drive a man like Maurice Curtis into dishonor or faithlessness! Then came the real explanation—which jealousy so rarely puts into words: "*I was selfish.*" At first, this bleak truthfulness was only momentary. Almost immediately she was swept from the noble pain of knowing that Maurice had been false to himself; swept from the sense of her own share in that falseness, swept back to the insult to *herself!* Back to self-love. With this was the fear that if she accused him, if she told him that she knew he was false to her, if she made him very angry, he would leave her, and go and live with this woman—who had given him a child ... Yet every morning when she got up, she would say to herself, "I'll tell him to-day." And every night when she went to bed, "To-morrow."

Still she did not "have it out with him." Then weeks pushed in between her and that Sunday afternoon when the resealed telegram had been put on the hall table. And by and by it was a month, and still she could not speak. And after a while it was June—June, and the anniversary (which Maurice happened to forget, and to which Eleanor's suffering love would not permit her to refer!). By that June day, that marked nine of the golden fifty years, Eleanor had done what many another sad and injured woman has done—dug a grave in her heart, and buried Trust and Pride in it; and then watched the grave night and day. Sometimes, as she watched, her thought was: "If he would tell me the truth, even now, I would forgive him. It is his living a lie, every day, every minute, that I can't bear!" Then she would look at Maurice—sitting at the piano, perhaps, playing dreamily, or standing up in front of the fireplace filling his pipe, and poking old Bingo with his foot and telling him he was getting too fat; "You're 'losin' your figger,' Bingo!" Eleanor, looking and listening, would say to herself, "Is he thinking of Mrs. Dale, *now*?" And all day long, when she was alone (watching the grave), she would think: "Where is he *now*? Is he with her? Oh, I think I will follow him,—and *watch*.... Was he with her last night when he said he had gone to the theater? ... Is he lying to me when he says he has to go away on business, and is he really with her? It's the *lying* I can't bear! If only he would not lie to me!... Does she call him 'Maurice'? Perhaps she called him 'darling'?" The thought of an intimacy like *that*, was oil on the vehement flame!

"You look dreadfully, Eleanor," Mrs. Newbolt told her once, her pale, protruding eyes full of real anxiety. "I'd go and see a doctor, if I were you."

"I'm well enough," Eleanor said, listlessly.

"At your age," said her aunt, "you never can tell *what's goin' on inside!* Here's a piece of candy for Bingo—he's too fat. My dear father used to say that a man's soul and his gizzard could hold a lot of secrets. It's the same with women. So look out for your gizzard. Here, Bingo!"

Eleanor was silent. She had just come from Mrs. O'Brien's, where she had given the slowly failing Donny a happy hour, and she was tired. Mrs.

Newbolt found her alone in the garden, sitting under the shimmering silver poplar. The lilies were just coming into bloom, and on the age-blackened iron trellis of the veranda the wistaria had flung its purple scarves among the thin fringes of its new leaves. The green tea table was bare: "I'd give you a cup of tea," Eleanor said, "but Maurice is going out to dinner, so I told Mary not to keep the fire up, just for me."

"Maurice goin' out to dinner! Why, it's your weddin' day! Eleanor, if I have one virtue, it's candor: Maurice oughtn't to be out to dinner so much—and on your anniversary, too! Of course, it's just what I expected when you married him; but that's done, and I'm not one to keep throwin' it up at you. If you want to hold him, *now*, you've got to keep your figger, and set a good table. Yes, and leave the door open! Edith has a figger. She entertains him, just the way I used to entertain your dear uncle—by talkin'. I'd have Bingo put away, if I were you; he's too old to be comfortable. You got to make him *want* to sit by the fire and knit! But here you are, sittin' by yourself, lookin' like a dead fish. A man don't like a dead fish—unless it's cooked! I used to broil shad for your dear uncle." For an instant she had no words to express that culinary perfection by which she had kept the deceased Mr. Newbolt's stomach faithful to her. "Yes, you've got to be entertainin', or else he'll go up the chimney, and out to dinner, and forget what Day it is!"

Eleanor's sudden pallor made her stop midway in her torrent of frankness; it was then she said, again, really alarmed: "See a doctor! You know," she added, jocosely; "if you die, he'll marry Edith; and you wouldn't like that!"

"No," Eleanor said, faintly, "I wouldn't like that."

CHAPTER XXV

When a rather shaky Jacky was discharged from the hospital, Lily notified Maurice of his recovery and added that she had moved.

> I couldn't [Lily wrote] go back to that woman who turned me out when Jacky was sick: so I got me a little house on Maple Street—way down at the far end from where I was before, so you needn't worry about anybody seeing me. My rent's higher, but there's a swell church on the next street. I meant to move, anyway, because I found out that there was a regular huzzy living in the next house on Ash Street, painted to beat the band! And I don't want Jacky to see that kind. I've got five mealers. But eggs is something fierce. I am writing these few lines to say Jacky's well, and I hope they find you in good health. It was real nice in you to fix that up at the hospital for me. I hope you'll come and see us one of these days.
>
> Your friend,
>
> LILY.
>
> P.S.—Of course I'm sorry for her poor old father.

Reading this, Maurice said to himself that it would be decent to go and see Lily; which meant, though he didn't know it, that he wanted to see Jacky. He wasn't aware of anything in the remotest degree like affection for the child; he just had this inarticulate purpose of seeing him, which took the form of saying that it would be "decent" to inquire about him. However, he did not yield to this formless wish until June. Then, on that very afternoon when Mrs. Newbolt had been so shatteringly frank to Eleanor, he walked down to the "far end of Maple Street." And as he walked, he suddenly remembered that it was "The Day"! "Great Scott! I forgot it!" he thought. "Funny, Eleanor didn't remind me. Maybe she's forgotten, too?" But he frowned at the bad taste of such an errand on such a day, and would have turned back—but at that moment he saw what (with an eagerness of which he was not conscious!) he had been looking for—a tow-headed boy, who, pulling a reluctant dog along by a string tied around his neck, was following a hand organ. And Maurice forgot his wedding anniversary!

He freed the half-choked puppy, and told his son what he thought. But Jacky, glaring up at the big man who interfered with his joys, told his father what *he* thought:

"If I was seven years old, I'd lick the tar out of you! But I'm six, going on seven."

Maurice, looking down on this miniature self, was, to his astonishment, quite diverted. "You need a licking yourself, young man! Is your mother at home?"

Jacky wouldn't answer.

Maurice took a quarter out of his pocket and held it up. "Know what that is?"

Jacky, advancing slowly, looked at the coin, but made no response.

"Come back to the house and find your mother, and I'll give it to you."

Jacky, keeping at a displeased distance behind the visitor, followed him to his own gate, then darted into the house, yelled, "Maw!" returned, and held out his hand.

Maurice gave him the quarter and went into the parlor, where the south window was full of plants, and the sunshine was all a green fragrance of rose geraniums. When a shiningly clean, smiling Lily appeared—evidently from the kitchen, for she was carrying a plate of hot gingerbread—she found Maurice sitting down, his hands in his pockets, his long legs stretched out in front of him, baiting Jacky with questions, and chuckling at the courageous impudence of the youngster.

"He's no fool," said Maurice to himself. "This kid is a handful!" he told Lily ... "You're a bully cook!"

"You bet he is!" Lily said, proudly. "Have another piece? I've got to take some over to Ash Street for that poor old man.... Oh yes; I *was* kind of put out at his daughter. Wouldn't you think, if anyone was enough of a lady to wash your father, you wouldn't go to the Board of Health about her? But there! The old gentleman's silly, so I have to take him some gingerbread.... Say, I must tell you something funny—he's the cutest young one! I gave him five cents for the missionary box, and he went and bought a jew's-harp! I had to laugh, it was so cute in him. But I declare, sometimes I don't know what I'm going to do with him, he's that fresh!"

"Spank him," Maurice advised.

Lily looked annoyed; "He suits me—and he belongs to me."

"Of course he does! You needn't think that I—" he paused; something would not let him finish those denying words: "that I—want him." Jacky, standing with stocky legs wide apart, his hands behind him, his fearless blue eyes looking right into Maurice's, made his father's heart quicken. Jacky was Lily's, of course, but—

So they looked at each other—the big, blond, handsome father and the little son—and Jacky said, "Mr. Curtis, does God see everything?"

"Why, yes," Maurice said, rather confused, "He does; Jacky. So," he ended, with proper solemnity, "you must be a very good boy."

"Why," said Jacky, "will He get one in on me if I ain't?"

"So I'm told," said Maurice.

"Does He see *everything*?" Jacky pressed, frowning; and Maurice said:

"Yes, sir! Everything."

Jacky reflected and sighed. "Well," he said, "I should think He'd laugh when he sees your shoes."

"Why! what's the matter with my shoes?" his discomfited father said, looking down at his feet. "My shoes are all right!" he defended himself.

"Big," Jacky said, shyly.

Maurice roared, crushed a geranium leaf in his hand, and asked his son what he was going to be when he grew up; "Theology seems to be your long suit, Jacobus. Better go into the Church."

Jacky shook his head. "I'm going to be a enginair. Or a robber."

"I'd try engineering if I were you. People don't like robbers."

"But *I'll* be a *nice* robber," Jacky explained, anxiously.

"I'll bring you a train of cars some day," Maurice said.

"Say, 'Thank you,' Jacky," Lily instructed him.

Again Jacky shook his head. "He 'ain't gimme the cars yet."

Maurice was immensely amused. "He wants the goods before he signs a receipt! I'll buy some cars for him."

"My soul and body!" said Lily, following him to the door; "that boy gets 'round everybody! Well, what do you suppose? I go to church with him! Ain't that rich? Me! He don't like church—though he's crazy about the music. But I take him. And I don't have to listen to what the man says. I just plan out the food for a week. Sometimes,"—her amber eyes were lovely with anxiously pondering love—"sometimes I don't know but what I'll make a preacher of him? Some preachers marry money, and get real gentlemanly. And then again I think I'd rather have him a clubman. But, anyway, I'm savin' up every last cent to educate him!"

"He's worth it," Maurice said, and there was pride in his voice; "yes, we must—I mean, you must educate him."

On his way home, stopping to buy some flowers for his wife, Maurice found himself thinking of Jacky as a boy ... as a mighty bright boy, who must be educated. As—*his* boy!

"You forgot the day," he challenged Eleanor, good-naturedly, when he handed her the violets.

She said, briefly, "No; I hadn't forgotten."

The pain in her worn face made him wince.... But he was able to forget it in thinking of the toys he had ordered for Jacky on the way home. "I'd like to see him playing with them," he said to himself, reflecting upon the track, and the engine, and the very expensive wonder of a tiny snow plow. But he didn't yield to the impulse to see the boy for a month. For one thing, he was afraid to. The recollection of that day when Lily's doorstep had been the edge of a volcano still made him shiver; and as Eleanor had briefly but definitely refused to take her usual "vacation" at Green Hill without him, there was no time when he could be sure that she would not wander out to Medfield! So it was not until one August afternoon, when he knew that she was going to a concert, that he went to Maple Street. But first he bought a top;—and just as he was leaving the office, he went back and rummaged in a pigeonhole in his desk and found a tiny gilt hatchet; "it will amuse him," he thought, cynically.

Lily was not at home; but Jacky was sitting on the back doorstep, twanging his jew's-harp. He was shy at first, and tongue-tied; then wildly excited on learning that there were "presents" in Mr. Curtis's pocket. When the top was produced, he dropped his jew's-harp to watch it spin on a string held between Maurice's hands; then he devoted himself to the hatchet, and chopped his father's knee, energetically. "Pity there's no cherry tree round," said Maurice; "Look here, Jacobus, I want you always to tell the truth. Understand?"

"Huh?" said Jacky. However, under the spell of his gifts he became quite conversational; he said that one of these here automobiles drooled a lot of oil. "An' it ran into the gutter. An' say, Mr. Curtis, I saw a rainbow in a puddle. An' say, it was handsome." After that he got out his locomotive and its cars. Maurice mended a broken switch for him, and then they laid the tracks on the kitchen floor, and the big father and the little son pushed the train under a table; that was a roundhouse, Maurice told Jacky. ("Why don't they have a square house?" Jacky said); and beneath the lounge—which was a tunnel, the bigger boy announced ("What is a tunnel?" said Jacky)—and over Lily's ironing board stretched between two stools; "That's a trestle." ("What grows trestles?" Jacky demanded.) Exercise, and a bombardment of questions, brought the perspiration out on Maurice's forehead. He took off his coat, and arranged the tracks so that the switches would stop derailing trains. In the midst of it the door opened, and Jacky said, sighing, "Maw."

Lily came in, smiling and good-natured, and very red-faced with the fatigue of carrying a hideous leprous-leaved begonia she had bought; but when she saw the intimacy of the railroad, she frowned. "He'll wear out his pants, crawling round that way," she said, sharply. "Now, you get up, Jacky, and don't be bothering Mr. Curtis."

"He brung me two presents. I like presents. Mr. Curtis, does God eat stars?"

"God doesn't eat," Maurice said, amused; "I'd say 'brought,' instead of 'brung,' if I were you."

"Hasn't He got any mouth?" Jacky said, appalled.

"Well, no," Maurice began (entering that path of unanswerable questions in which all parents are ordained to walk); "You see, God—why, God, He hasn't any mouth. He—"

"Has He got a beak?" Jacky said, intensely interested.

"Lily, for Heaven's sake," Maurice implored, "doesn't he *ever* stop?"

"Never," said Lily, resignedly, "except when he's asleep. And nobody can answer him. But I wish he'd let up on God. I tell him whatever pops into my head. When it comes to God, I guess one thing 's as true as another. Anyway, nobody can prove it ain't."

Just as Maurice was going away, his theological son detained him by a little clutch at his coat. "I'll give you a present next time you come," Jacky said, shyly.

Even the hope of a present did not lure Maurice out to Maple Street very soon. But it was self-preservation, as well as fear of discovery, which kept him away. "If I saw much of him I might—well, get kind of fond of the little beggar."

The same thought may have occurred to Lily; at any rate, when, four weeks later, Jacky's father came again; she didn't welcome him in quite her old, sweet, hospitable way; but Jacky welcomed him!... Jacky knew his mother as his slave; he showed her an absent-minded affection when he wanted to get anything out of her; but he knew Mr. Curtis as "The Man"—the man who "ordered him round," to be sure, but who gave him presents and who,—Jacky boasted to some of his gutter companions,—"could spit two feet farther than the p'leesman."

"Aw, how do you know?" the other boys scoffed.

Jacky, evading the little matter of evidence, said, haughtily, "I *know*."

When "The Man" declared that next fall Jacky was to go to school, *regularly*, and not according to his own sweet will, Jacky waited until he was alone with his mother to kick and scream and say he wouldn't. Lily slapped him, and said, "Mr. Curtis will give you a present if you're on time every morning!"

She told Maurice to what she had committed him: "You see, I'm bound to educate him, and make a gentleman of him, so he can have an automobile, and marry a society girl. No chippy is going to get Jacky—smoking cigarettes, and saying 'La! La!' to any man that comes along. I hate those cheap girls. Look at the paint on 'em. I don't see how they have the face to show themselves on the street! Well, *I* can't make him prompt at school; but he'll be Johnny-on-the-spot if you say so. My soul and body, he'll do anything for you! He's saved up all his prayer money and bought a lot of chewing gum for you."

"Great Scott!" said Maurice, appalled at the experimental obligations which his son's gift might involve.

"So I told him that next winter you'd give him a box of candy every Saturday if he was on time all the week. I ain't asking you to go to any expense," she pleaded; "I'll buy the candy. But you promise him—"

"I'll promise him a spanking if he's *not* on time, once," Maurice retorted; "for Heaven's sake, Lily, let up on spoiling him!"

At which Lily said: "He's my boy! I guess I know how to bring him up!"

Maurice, the next morning, looking across his breakfast table at Eleanor and remembering this remark, said to himself: "Lily needn't worry; I don't want him—and I couldn't have him if I did! But what *is* going to become of him?"

His new, slowly awakening sense of responsibility expressed itself in this unanswerable question, which irritated his mind as a splinter might have irritated his flesh. He thought of it constantly—thought of it when Eleanor sang (with a slurred note once or twice), "O sweet, O sweet content!" Thought of it when his conscience reminded him that he must have tea with her in the garden under the poplar on Sunday afternoons. Thought of it when he and she went up to the Houghtons', to spend Labor Day (she would not go without him!). Perhaps the thing that gave him some moments of forgetfulness was a quite different irritation which he felt when, on reaching Green Hill, he discovered that John Bennett, too, was spending Labor Day in the mountains. Johnny had come he said, to see his father.... "I wouldn't have known it if he hadn't mentioned it!" said Doctor Bennett; for, Johnny practically lived at the Houghtons', where Edith was so painstakingly kind to him that he was a good deal discouraged; but the two families made pleasing deductions! Mary Houghton intimated as much to Maurice.

"What!" he said. "Are they engaged?"

"Well, no; not *yet*."

There was a little pause; then Maurice (this was one of the moments when he forgot Jacky's future!) said, with great heartiness, "Old John's in luck!" He and Mrs. Houghton were sitting on the porch in that somnolent hour after dinner, before she went upstairs to take a nap, and Maurice should go over to the Bennetts' for singles with Johnny; Eleanor was resting. Out on the lawn in the breezy sun and shadow under the tulip tree, Edith, fresh from a shampoo, was reading. Now and then she tossed her head like a colt, to make her fluffy hair blow about in a glittering brown nimbus.

Maurice got up and sauntered over to her. "Coming to see me wallop Johnny?"

"Maybe; if my horrid old hair ever dries."

Maurice looked at the "horrid old hair," and wished he could put out his hand and touch it. He was faintly surprised at himself that he didn't do it! "How mad I used to make her when I pulled her hair!" Now, he couldn't even put a finger on it. He remembered the night of Lily's distracted telegram, when he had taken Edith to Fern Hill, and she had "bet on him," and had been again, just for an instant, so entirely the "little girl" of their old frank past, that she had *kissed him*! "So, why can't I touch her hair, now?" he pondered; "we are just like brother and sister." But he knew he couldn't. Aloud, he said, "Don't be lazy, Skeezics," and lounged off toward Doctor Bennett's. His face was heavy.

At the doctor's, John, sitting on a gate post, waiting for him, yelled, derisively: "You're late! 'Fraid of getting walloped? Where's Buster?"

"She's forgotten all about you. Get busy!" Maurice commanded.

They played, neither of them with much zest, and both of them with glances toward the road. The walloping was fairly divided; but it was

Maurice who gave out first, and said he had to go home. ("Eleanor'll be hunting for me, the first thing I know," he thought.)

"Tell Edith I'll come over to-night," Johnny called after him.

"I'm not carrying *billets-doux*," Maurice retorted. "I suppose," he thought, listlessly, "it will be a short engagement." He went home by the path through the woods, and halfway back Edith met him—the shining hair · dried, but inclined to tumble over her ears, so that her hat slipped about on her head. She said:

"Johnny lick you?"

"Johnny? No! He's not up to it!" They both grinned, and Maurice sat down on a wayside log to put a knot in a broken shoestring. Edith sat down, too, trying to keep her hat on, and cursing (she said) the unreliability of her hair. The shoestring mended, Maurice batted a tall fern with his racket.

"Eleanor's sort of forlorn, Maurice?" Edith said. "Generally is." He slashed at the fern, and she heard him sigh. "That time she dragged me down the mountain took it out of her."

Edith nodded; then she said, with her straight look: "You're a perfect lamb, Maurice! You are awfully"—she wanted to say "patient," but there was an implication in that; so she said, lamely—"nice to Eleanor."

"The Lord knows I ought to be!" he said, cynically.

"Yes; she just about killed herself to save you," Edith agreed.

"Oh, not because of that!"

The misery in his voice startled her; she said, quickly, "How do you mean, Maurice? I don't understand."

"I ought to be 'nice' to her."

"But you are! You are!"

"I'm not."

"Maurice, I'm awfully fond of Eleanor; you won't think I'm finding fault, or anything? But sometimes, when she doesn't feel very well, she—you—I mean, you really *are* a lamb, Maurice!"

Edith was twenty that summer—a strong, gay creature; but her old, ridiculous, incorrigible candor (and that honest kiss in the darkness!) made her still a child to Maurice.... Yet Johnny Bennett was going to marry her!... Maurice rested his chin on his left fist, and batted the fern; then he said:

"I've been infernally mean to Eleanor. It's little enough to be 'nice,' as you call it, now."

She flew to his defense. "Talk sense! You never did a mean thing in your life."

His shrug fired her into a frankness which she regretted the next minute. "Maurice, you are too good for Eleanor—or anybody," she ended, hastily.

He gave her a look of entreaty for understanding—though he knew, he thought, that in her ignorance of life she couldn't understand even if she had been told! Yet for the mere relief of speaking, he skirted the ugly truth:

"I can't be too patient with her when she's forlorn, because I—I haven't played the game with her."

"It's up to her to forgive that!"

"She doesn't know it."

"Maurice! You haven't a secret from Eleanor?"

Her dismay was like a stab. "Edith, I can't help it! It was a long time ago—but it would upset her to know that I'd—well, failed her in any way." His face was so wrung that Edith could have cried; but she said what she thought:

"Secrets are horrid, Maurice. You've made a mistake."

"A 'mistake'?" He almost laughed at the devilish humor of that little word 'mistake,' as applied to his ruined life. "Well, yes, Edith; I made a 'mistake,' all right."

"Oh, I don't mean a 'mistake' as to this thing you say that Eleanor wouldn't like," Edith said. "I mean not telling her."

He shook his head; with that nagging thought of Jacky in the back of his mind, it was impossible not to smile at her dogmatic ignorance.

"Because," Edith explained, "secrets trip you into fibbing."

"You bet they do! I'm quite an accomplished liar."

Edith did not smile; she spoke with impatient earnestness: "That's perfectly silly; you are not a liar! You couldn't lie to save your life, and you know it." Maurice laughed. "Why, Maurice, don't you suppose I know you, through and through? *I* know what you are!—a 'perfec' gentil knight.'"

She laughed, and Maurice threw up his hands.

"Bouquets," Edith conceded, grinning; "but I won't hand out any more, so you needn't fish! Well, I don't know what on earth you've done, and I don't care; and you can't tell me, of course! But one thing I do know; it isn't fair to Eleanor not to tell her, because—"

"My dear child—"

"Because she wouldn't really mind, she's so awfully devoted to you. Oh, Maurice, do tell Eleanor!" Then, even as she spoke, she was frightened; what was this thing that he did not dare to tell Eleanor?—"or me?" Edith thought. It couldn't be that Maurice—was not good? Edith quailed at herself. She had a quick impulse to say, "Forgive me, Maurice, for even thinking of such a horrid thing!" But all she said, aloud, briefly, was, "As I see it, telling Eleanor would be playing the game."

Maurice put his hand over her fist, clenched with conviction on her knee. "Skeezics," he said, "you are the soundest thing the Lord ever made! As it happens, it's a thing I can't talk about—to anybody. But I'll never forget this, Edith. And ... dear, I'm glad you're going to be happy; you deserve the best man on earth, and old Johnny comes mighty darned near being the best!"

Edith, frowning, rose abruptly. "Please don't talk that way. I hate that sort of talk! Johnny is my friend; that's all. So, please never—"

"I won't," Maurice said, meekly; but some swift exultation made him add to himself, "Poor old Johnny!" His face was radiant.

As for Edith, she hardly spoke all the way back to the house. But not because of "poor old Johnny"! She was absorbed by that intuition—which she did not, she told herself, believe. Yet it clamored in her mind: Maurice had done something wrong. Something so wrong, that he couldn't speak of it, even to her! Then it must be—? "No! that's impossible!" But with this recoil from a disgusting impossibility, came an upsurge of something she had never felt in her life—something not unlike that emotion she had once called Bingoism—a resentful consciousness that Maurice had not been as completely and confidentially her friend as she was his!

But Edith hadn't a mean fiber in her! Instantly, on the heels of that small pain came a greater and nobler pain: "I can't bear it if he has done anything wrong! But if he has, it's some wicked woman's fault." As she said that, anger at an injury done to Maurice made her almost forget that first virginal repulsion—and made her entirely forget that fleeting pain of knowing that she had not meant as much to him as he meant to her! "But he hasn't done anything wrong," she insisted; "he wouldn't look at a horrid? woman!"

"For Heaven's sake, Edith," Maurice remonstrated; "this isn't any Marathon! Go slow. I'm not in any hurry to get home."

"I am," Edith said, briefly. She was in a great hurry! She wanted to be alone, and argue to herself that she had been guilty of a dreadful disloyalty to him.... "Maurice? Why! He would be the last man in the world to—to do that,—darling old Maurice! He has simply had a crush on somebody, and likes her better than he likes Eleanor—or me; but *that's* nothing. Eleanor deserves it; and very likely I do, too! But he's so frightfully honorable about Eleanor—he's a perfect crank on honor!—that he blames himself for even that." By this time the possibility that the unknown somebody was "horrid" had become unthinkable; she was probably terribly attractive, and Maurice had a crush on ... "though, of course, she can't be really nice," Edith thought; "Maurice simply doesn't see through her. Boys are so stupid! They don't know girls," Again there was a Bingo moment of hot dislike for the "girl," whoever she was!—and she walked faster and faster.

Maurice, striding along beside her, was thinking of the irony of the "bouquet" she had thrown at him, and the innocence of that "Tell Eleanor"! "What a child she is still! And she's not in love with Johnny—" He didn't understand his exhilaration when he said that, but, except when he reproached her for tearing ahead, it kept him silent...

Supper was ready when they got home, so Edith had no chance to be solitary, and after supper Johnny Bennett dropped in. When he took his reluctant departure ("Confound him!" Maurice thought, impatiently, "he has on his sitting breeches to-night!") Maurice told Edith to come into the garden with him, and listen to the evening primroses; "They 'blossom with a silken burst of sound'—they *do*!" he insisted, for she jeered at the word "listen."

"They don't!" she said, and ran down the steps, flitting ahead of him in the dusk like a white moth. In their preoccupation, they neither of them looked at Eleanor; sitting silently on the porch between Mr. and Mrs. Houghton. They went, between the box hedges, to the primrose border, and Maurice quoted:

> Silent they stood.
> Hand clasped in hand, in breathless hush around!
> And saw her shyly doff her soft green hood,
> And blossom—with a silken burst of sound!

"Let's clasp hands," Maurice suggested.

"No, thank you," said Edith. And so they watched and listened. A tightly twisted bud loosened half a petal—then another half—and another—until it was all a shimmering whorl of petals, each caught at one side to the honeyed crosspiece of the pistil; then: "*There!*" said Maurice. "Did you hear it?"—all the silken disks were loose, and the flower cup, silver-gilt, spilled its fragrance into the stillness!

"It was the dream of a sound," she admitted

Her voice was a dream sound, too, he thought; a wordless tenderness for her flooded his mind, as the perfume of the primroses flooded the night. It seemed as if the lovely ignorance of her was itself a perfume! "'Tell Eleanor'! She doesn't know the wickedness of the world, and I don't want her to." He put his hand on her shoulder in the old, brotherly way—but drew it back as if something had burned him! That recoil should have revealed things to him, but it didn't. So far as his own consciousness went, he was too intent on what he called "the square deal" for Eleanor, to know what had happened to him; all he knew was that Edith, all of a sudden, was grown up! Her childishness was gone. He mustn't even put his hand on her shoulder! He had an uneasy moment of wondering—"Girls are so darned knowing, nowadays!"—whether she might be suspicious as to what that secret was, which she had advised him to "tell Eleanor"? But that was only for a moment; "Edith's not that kind of a girl. And, anyway, she'd never think of such a thing of me—which makes me all the more rotten!" So he clutched at Edith's undeserved faith in him, and said, "She'll never think of *that*." Still, she was grown up ... and he mustn't touch her. (This was one of the times when he was not worrying about Jacky!)

Edith, talking animatedly of primroses, had her absorbing thoughts, too; they were nothing but furious denial! "Maurice—horrid? Never!" Then, on the very breath of "Never," came again the insistent reminder: "But he could tell *me* anything, except—" So, thinking of just one thing, and talking of many other things, she walked up and down the primrose path with Maurice. They neither of them wanted to go back to the three older people: the father and mother—and wife.

Eleanor, on the porch, strained her eyes into the dusk; now and then she caught a glimmer of the dim whiteness of Edith's skirt, or heard Maurice's voice. She was suffering so that by and by she said, briefly, to her hosts—her trembling with unshed tears—"Good night," and went upstairs, alone—an old, crying woman. Eleanor had been unreasonable many times; but this time she was not unreasonable! That night anyone could have seen that she was, to Maurice, as nonexistent as any other elderly woman might have been. The Houghtons saw it, and when she went into the house Mary Houghton said, with distress:

"She suffers!"

Her husband nodded, and said he wished he was asleep. "Why," he demanded, "are women greater fools about this business than men? Poor Maurice ventures to talk to Edith of 'shoes and ships and sealing wax,'— and Eleanor weeps! Why are there more jealous women than men?"

"Because," Mary Houghton said, dryly, "more men give cause for jealousy than women."

"*Touché! Touché!*" he conceded; then added, quickly, "But Maurice isn't giving any cause."

"Well, I'm not so sure," she said.

Up in her own room, Eleanor, sitting in the dark by the open window, stared out into the leafy silence of the night. Once, down in the garden, Maurice laughed;—and she struck her clenched hand on her forehead:

"I can't bear it!" she said, gaspingly, aloud; "I can't bear it—*she interests him*!" His pleasure in Edith's mind was a more scorching pain to her than the thought of Lily's body....

Later, when Maurice and Edith came up from the garden darkness, they found a deserted porch. "Let's talk," he said, eagerly.

Edith shook her head. "Too sleepy," she said, and ran upstairs. He called after her, "Quitter!" But it provoked no retort, and he would have gone back to walk up and down alone, by the primroses, and worry over Jacky's future, if a melancholy voice had not come from the window of their room: "Maurice.... It's twelve o'clock." And he followed Edith indoors....

Edith had been sharply anxious to be by herself. She could not sit on the porch with Maurice, and not burst out and tell him—what? Tell him that nothing he had done could make the slightest difference to her! "He has probably met some awfully nice girl and likes her—a good deal. As for there being anything wrong, I don't believe it! That would be horrible. I'm a beast to have thought of such a thing!" She decided to put it out of her mind, and went to her desk, saying, "I'll straighten out my accounts."

She began, resolutely; added up one column, and subtracted the total from another; said: "Gosh! I'm out thirty dollars!" nibbled the end of her pen, and reflected that she would have to work on her father's sympathies;—then, suddenly, her pen still in her hand, she sat motionless.

"Even if there *was* anything—bad, I'd forgive him. He's a lamb!" But as she spoke, childishness fell away—she was a deeply distressed woman. Maurice was suffering. And she knew, in spite of her assertions to the contrary, that it wasn't because of any slight thing; any "crush" on a girl—nice or otherwise! He was suffering because he had done wrong—and she couldn't tear downstairs and say: "Maurice, never mind! I love you just as much; I don't care what you've done!" Why couldn't she say that? Why couldn't she go now, and sit on the porch steps beside him, and say—anything? She got up and began to walk about the room; her heart was beating smotheringly. "Why shouldn't I tell him I love him so that I'd forgive—*anything*? He knows I've always loved him!—next to father and mother. Why can't I tell him so, now?" Then something in her breast, beating like wings, made her know why she couldn't tell him!

"I love him; that's why."

After a while she said: "There's nothing wrong in it. I have a right to love him! He'll never know. How funny that I never knew—until to-night! Yet I've felt this way for ever so long. I think since that time at Fern Hill, when he was so bothered and wouldn't tell me what was the matter." Yes; it was strange that now, when some stabbing instinct had made her know that Maurice was not her "perfec' gentil knight," that same instinct should make her know that she loved him!... Not with the old love; not with the love that could overflow into words, the love that had kissed him when he had been "bothered"! "I can never kiss him again," she thought. She did not love him, now, "next to father and mother—dear darlings!" And when she said that, Edith knew that the "darlings" were of her past. "I love them next to Maurice," she thought, smiling faintly. "Well, he will never know it! Nobody will ever know it.... I'll just keep on loving him as long as I live." She had no doubt about that; and she did not drop into the self-consciousness of saying, "I am wronging Eleanor." That, to Edith, would not have been sense. She knew that she was not "wronging" anyone. As for the unknown girl, who, perhaps, had "wronged" Eleanor, and about whom, now, Maurice was so ashamed and so repentant—she was of no consequence anyhow. "Of course she is bad," Edith thought, "and the whole thing was her fault!" But it was in the past; he had said so. "He said it was long ago. If," she thought, "he did run crooked, why, I'm sorry for poor Eleanor; and he ought to tell her; there's no question about *that*! It's wrong not to tell her. And of course he couldn't tell me. That wouldn't be square to Eleanor!... But I hate to have him so unhappy.... No; it's right for him to be unhappy. He ought to be! It would be dreadful if he wasn't. But, somehow, the thing itself doesn't seem to touch me. I love him. I am going to love him all I want to! But no one will ever know it."

By and by she knelt down and prayed, just one word: *"Maurice."* She was not unhappy.

CHAPTER XXVI

During the next two days at Green Hill, Eleanor's dislike of Edith had no chance to break into silent flames, for the girl was so quiet that not even Eleanor could see anything in her behavior to Maurice to criticize. It was Maurice who did the criticizing!

"Edith, come down into the garden; I want to read something to you."

"Can't. Have to write letters."

"Edith, if you'll come into the studio I'll play you something I've patched up."

"I'm a heathen about music. Let's sit with Eleanor."

"Skeezics, what's the matter with you? Why won't you come and walk? You're getting lazy in your old age!"

"Busy," Edith said, vaguely.

At this point Maurice insisted, and Edith sneaked out to the back entry and telephoned Johnny Bennett: "Come over, lazybones, and take some exercise!"

John came, with leaps and bounds, so to speak, and Maurice said, grumpily:

"What do you lug Johnny in for?"

So, during the rest of her visit (with John Bennett as Maurice's chaperon!) Eleanor merely ached with dislike of Edith; but, even so, she had the small relief of not having to say to herself: "Is he seeing Mrs. Dale, now? ... Did he go to her house yesterday?" Of course, as soon as she went back to Mercer those silent questions began again; and her audible question nagged Maurice whenever he was in the house: "Did you go to the theater last night? ... Yes? *Did you go alone?* ... Will you be home to-night to dinner? ... No? *Where are you going?*"

Maurice, answering with bored patience, thought, with tender amusement, of Edith's advice, "Tell Eleanor." How little she knew!

He did not see Edith very often that next winter, "which is just as well," he thought. But his analysis stopped there; he did not ask himself why it was just as well. She made flying visits to Mercer, for shopping or luncheons, so he had glimpses of her, and whenever he saw her he was conscious of a little wistful change in her, for she was shy with him—*Edith*, shy!—and much gentler. When they discussed the Eternities or the ball game, she never pounded his arm with an energetic and dissenting fist, nor was there ever the faintest suggestion of the sexless "rough-house" of their old jokes! As for coming to town, she explained that she was too busy; she had taken the burden of housekeeping from her mother, and she was doing a good deal of hard reading preparatory to a course of technical training in domestic science, to which she was looking forward when she could find time for it. But whenever she did come to Mercer, she did her duty by rushing in to see Eleanor! Eleanor's criticisms of her, when she rushed out again, always made Maurice silently, but deeply, irritated. The criticisms lessened in the fall, because Eleanor had the pitiful preoccupation of watching poor Don O'Brien fade out of the world; and when he had gone she had to push her own misery aside while his grandmother's heart broke into the meager tears of age upon her "Miss Eleanor's" breast. But, besides that, she did not have the opportunity to criticize Edith, for the Houghtons went abroad.

So the rest of that year went dully by. To Eleanor, it was a time of spasmodic effort to regain Maurice's love; spasmodic, because when she had visions—hideous visions! of Maurice and the "other woman,"—then, her aspirations to regain his love, which had been born in that agony of recognized complicity in his faithlessness, would shrivel up in the vehement flame of jealousy. To Maurice, it was a time of endurance; of vague thoughts of Edith, but of no mental disloyalty to his wife. Its only brightness lay in those rare visits to Medfield, when Jacky looked at him like a worshiping puppy, and asked forty thousand questions which he couldn't answer! They were very careful visits, made only when Maurice was sure Eleanor would not be going to "look for a cook." He always balanced his brief pleasure of an hour with his little boy by an added gentleness to his wife— perhaps a bunch of violets, bought at the florist's on Maple Street where Lily got her flower pots or her bulbs. He was very lonely, and increasingly bothered about Jacky. ... "Lily will let him go plumb to hell. But I put him on the toboggan! ... I'm responsible for his existence," he used to think. And sometimes he repeated the words he had spoken that night when he had felt the first stir of fatherhood, "My little Jacky."

He would hardly have said he loved the child; love had come so gradually, that he had not recognized it! Yet it had come. It had been added to those other intimations of God, which also he had not recognized. Personal Joy on his wedding day had been the first; and the next had come when he looked up at the heights of Law among the stars, and then there had been the terrifying vision of the awfulness of Life, at Jacky's birth. Now, into his soul, arid with long untruth, came this flooding in of Love—which in itself is Life, and Joy, and the fulfilling of Law! Or, as he had said, once, carelessly, "Call it God."

This pursuing God, this inescapable God! was making him acutely uncomfortable now, about Jacky. Maurice felt the discomfort, but he did not recognize it as Salvation, or know Whose mercy sent it! He merely did what most of us do when we suffer: he gave the credit of his pain to the devil— not to Infinite Love. "Oh," the poor fellow thought, coming back one day from a call at the little secret house on Maple Street, "the devil's getting his money's worth out of me; well, I won't squeal about *that*! But he's getting his money's worth out of my boy, too. She's ruining him!"

He said this once when he had been rather recklessly daring in seeing "his boy." It was Saturday afternoon, and Jacky was free from his detested school. Maurice had given him a new sled, and then had "fallen," as he expressed it, to the little fellow's entreaty: "Mr. Curtis, if you'll come up to the hill, I'll show you how she'll go!" But before they started Maurice had a disagreeable five minutes with Lily. She had told him, tears of laughter running down her rosy cheeks, of some performance of Jacky's. He had asked her, she said, about his paw; "and I said his name was Mr. George Dale, and he died ten or eleven years ago of consumption—had to tell him something, you know! An' he says,—he's great on arithmetic,—'Poor paw!' he says, 'how many years was that before I was born?' I declare, I was all balled up!" Then, as she wiped her laughing eyes, she had grown suddenly angry: "I'm going to take him away from his new Sunday school; the teacher—it was her did the Paul Pry act, and asked him about his father;— well, I guess she ain't much of a lady; I never see her name in the Sunday papers;—she came down on Jacky because he told her a 'lie'; that's what she called it, 'a lie'! Said he'd go to hell if he told lies. I said, 'I won't have you threatening my child!' I declare I felt like saying, 'You go to hell yourself!' but of course I don't say things that ain't refined."

"Well, but Lily, the little beggar must tell the truth—"

"Mr. Curtis, Jacky didn't say anything but what you or me would say a dozen times a day. He just told her he hadn't a library book out, when he had. Seems he forgot to bring it back, so, 'course, he just said he hadn't any book. Well, this teacher, she put the lie onto him. It's a vulgar word, 'lie.' And as for hell, they say society people don't believe there is such a place any more."

When he and his little son walked away (Jacky dragging his magnificent sled), Maurice was nervously anxious to counteract such views.

"Jacobus," he said, "I'm going to tell you something: Big men never say anything that isn't so! Do you get on to that?" (In his own mind he added, "I'm a sweet person to tell him that!") "Promise me you'll never say anything that isn't just exactly so," said Maurice.

"Yes, sir," said Jacky. "Say, Mr. Curtis, have you got teeth you can take out?" When Maurice said, rather absently, that he had not, Jacky's dismay was pathetic. "Why, maw can do *that*," he said, reproachfully. It was the first flaw in his idol. It took several minutes to recover from the shock of disappointment; then he said: "Lookee here!" He paused beside a hydrant, and with his mittened hand broke off a long icicle, held it up and turned it about so that the sun flashed on it. "Handsome, ain't it?" he asked, timidly.

Maurice said yes, it was "handsome";—"but suppose you say *'isn't it'* instead of *'ain't* it.' 'Ain't' is not a nice word. And remember what I told you about telling the truth."

"Yes, sir," said Jacky, and trudged along, pulling his sled with one hand and carrying his icicle in the other.

After this paternal effort, Maurice stood in the snow watching the crowd of children—red-cheeked, shrill-voiced—sliding down Winpole Hill and yelling and snow-balling each other as they pulled their sleds up to the top of the slope again. It was during one of these panting tugs uphill, that Jacky saw fit to slap a fellow coaster, a little, snub-nosed girl with a sniffling cold in her head, and all muffled up in dirty scarves. Instantly Maurice, striding in among the children, took his son by the arm, and said, sharply:

"Young man, apologize! *Quick!* Or I'll take you home!"

Jacky gaped. "Pol'gize?"

"Say you're sorry! Out with it. Tell the little girl you're sorry you hit her."

"But I ain't," Jacky explained, anxiously; "an' you said I mustn't say what ain't so."

"Well, tell her you won't do it again," Maurice commanded, evading, as perplexed fathers must, moral contradictions.

Jacky, bewildered, said to his howling playmate, "I don't like you, but I won't hit you again, less I have to; then I'll lick the tar out of you!" He paused, rummaged in his pocket, produced a horrid precious little gray lump of something, and handed it to her. "Gum," he said, briefly.

Maurice, taking another step into paternal wisdom, was deaf to the statute of limitation in the apology; but walking home with the little boy, he said to himself, "She's ruining him!" and fell into such moody silence that he didn't even notice Jacky's obedient struggles with "isn't." Once, a week later, as a result of this experience, he tried to make some ethical suggestions to Lily. She was displaying her latest triumph—a rosebush, blossoming in *February*! And Maurice, duly admiring the glowing flower, against its background of soot-speckled snowdrift on the window sill, began upon Jacky's morals. Lily's good-humored face hardened.

"Mr. Curtis, you don't need to worry about Jacky! He don't steal, and he don't swear,—much; and he's never been pinched, and he's awful handsome; and, my God! what more do you want? I ain't going to make his life miserable by tellin' him to talk grammar, or do the polite act!"

"Lily, I only mean I want him to turn out well, and he won't unless he tells the truth—"

"He'll turn out good. You needn't worry. Anybody's got to have sense about telling the truth; you can't just plunk everything out! I—I believe I'll go and live in New York."

Instantly Maurice was silenced. "She *mustn't* take him away!" he thought, despairingly.

His fear that she would do so was a constant worry.... His work in the Weston real-estate office involved occasional business trips of a few days, and his long hours on trains were filled with this increasing anxiety about Jacky. "If she takes him away from Mercer, and I can't ever see him, nothing can save him! But, damn it! what can I do?" he would say. He tried to reassure himself by counting up Lily's good points; her present uprightness; her honest friendliness to him; her almost insane devotion to Jacky, and her pathetic aspiration for respectability, which was summed up in that one word of collective emptiness,—"Society." But immediately her bad points clamored in his mind; her ignorance and unmorality and vulgarity. "Truth is just a matter of expediency with her. If he gets to be a liar, I'll boot him!" Maurice would think of these bad points until he got perfectly frantic! His sense of wanting advice was like an ache in his mind—for there was no one who could advise him. Then, quite unexpectedly, advice came....

In the fall the Houghtons got back from Europe. Maurice saw them only between trains in Mercer, for Henry Houghton was in a great hurry to get up to Green Hill, and Edith, too, was exercised about her trunks and the unpacking of her treasures of reminiscence. But Mrs. Houghton said: "We shall be coming down to do some shopping before Christmas. No! We'll *not* inflict ourselves upon Eleanor! We'll go to the hotel; you will both take dinner with us."

They came, and Maurice and Eleanor dined with them, as Mrs. Houghton had insisted that they should; but only Mrs. Houghton accepted Eleanor's repaying hospitality.

"Mother has virtue enough for the family," Edith said; "I'm going to stay here with father."

"It will be a jewel in your crown," Henry Houghton told his Mary.

"Why not collect jewels for your crown?" she inquired. "Henry, Maurice looks troubled. What do you suppose is the matter?"

"He does look seedy," he agreed; "poke about and find out what's wrong. You can do it better if your inelegant offspring isn't around, and if I'm not there, either. He won't open his lips to me! I think it's money. He's carrying a pretty heavy load. But he never peeps.... I wish he wouldn't economize on cigars, though; he offered me one yesterday, and politeness compelled me to smoke it!"

"'Peeps'!" said Edith; "how elegant!"

So that was how it happened that Mary Houghton went alone to dine with Maurice and Eleanor. But she couldn't discover, in Maurice's talk or Eleanor's silences, any hint of financial anxiety. "So," she said to herself, "it isn't money that worries him." When he walked back with her to the hotel after dinner, he was thinking, "She'd know what to do about Jacky." But of course he couldn't ask her what to do! He could never ask anybody— except, perhaps, Mr. Houghton; and what would he, an old man, know about bringing up a little boy? He was listening, not very closely, to Mrs. Houghton's talk of the Custom House; but when she said, "John Bennett met us on the dock," he was suddenly attentive.

"Has Edith—?" he began.

She laughed ruefully. "No. Young people are not what they were in my day. Edith is not a bit sentimental."

Maurice was silent. When they reached the hotel, they went upstairs into a vast, bleak parlor, and steered their way among enormous plush armchairs to a sofa. A few electric bulbs, glaring among the glass prisms of a remote chandelier, made a dim light—but not too dim for Mary Houghton to see that Maurice's face was drawn and worried; involuntarily she said:

"You dear boy, I wish you didn't look so careworn!"

"I'm bothered about something," he said.

"Your uncle Henry told me to 'poke around,' and see if you were troubled about money?" she said, smiling.

"Oh, not especially. I'm always more or less strapped. But money isn't worth bothering about, really."

"If you 'consider the stars,' you will find very few things are worth bothering about! Except, of course, wrongdoing."

And, to his own astonishment, he found himself saying, "I'm afraid that's where I come in!" As he spoke, he remembered that night of the eclipse—oh, those moon-washed depths, those stupendous serenities of Law and Beauty which, together, are Truth! How passionately he had desired Truth. And now Mrs. Houghton was saying "Consider the stars." "If I could only tell her!" he thought.

"If the wrongdoing is behind you," said Mary Houghton, "let it go."

"It won't let me go," he said, with nervous lightness. "Though it's behind me, all right!"

Which made her say, gently, "Maurice, perhaps I know what troubles you?" His start made her add, quickly: "Your uncle Henry has never betrayed your confidence; but ... I guessed, long ago, that something had gone wrong. I don't know how wrong—"

"Oh, Mrs. Houghton," he said, despairingly, "awfully wrong! Awfully—awfully wrong!" He put his elbow on his knee, and rested his chin on his clenched fist; she was silent. Then he said: "You've always been an angel to me. I am glad you guessed. Because—I don't know what to do."

"About the woman?"

"No. The boy."

"Oh!" she said; "a *child*!"

Her dismay was like a blow. "But you said you had 'guessed'?"

"I guessed that there was a woman; but I didn't know—" She put her arm over his shoulders and kissed him. "My poor Maurice!" The tears stood in her eyes.

"I told you it was 'awful,'" he said, simply; "yes, it is my little boy; I'm worried to death about him. Lily—that's her name—is perfectly all right; she means well, and adores him, and all that; but—" Then he told her what Jacky's mother had been and what she was now; and the illustrations he gave of Lily's ignorance of ethical standards made Mary Houghton cringe. "She's ruining the little fellow," he said; "he's not mean nor a coward—I'll say that for him! But he lies whenever he feels like it, and honesty only means not getting 'pinched.' She's awfully ambitious for him; but her idea of success is what she calls 'Society,' Oh, it's such a relief to speak to you, Mrs. Houghton! I haven't a soul I can talk to."

"Maurice, can't you get him?" Her voice was shocked.

He almost laughed. "Wild horses wouldn't drag him from Lily!"

She was silent before the complexity of the situation—the furtive paternity, with its bewildered sense of responsibility, in conflict with the passion of the dam!

"I have to be so infernally secret," Maurice said. "If it wasn't for that, I could train him a little, because he's fond of me," he explained—and for a moment his face relaxed into one of his old charming smiles. "He really is an awfully fine little beggar. I swear I believe he's musical! And he's confoundedly clever. Why, he said—" Mrs. Houghton could have wept with the pitifulness of it! For Maurice went on, like any proud young father, with a story of how his little boy had said this or done that. "But he's fresh, sometimes, and he's the kind that, if he got fresh, ought to be licked. She can't make him mind; but" —here the poor, shamed pride shone again in his blue eyes—"he minds *me!*"

Mary Houghton was silent; she tried to consider the stars, but her dismay at a child endangered, came between her and the eternal tranquillities. "The boy must be saved," she thought, "at any cost! It isn't a question of Maurice's happiness; it's a question of his *obligation.*"

"This thing of having a secret hanging round your neck is hell!" Maurice told her. "Every minute I think—'Suppose Eleanor should find out?'"

Mrs. Houghton put her hand on his knee. "The only way to escape from the fear of being found out, Maurice, *is to be found out.* Get rid of the millstone. Tell Eleanor."

"You don't know Eleanor," he said, dryly.

"Yes, I do. She loves you so much that she would forgive you. And with forgiveness would come helpfulness with the little boy. The child is the important one—not you, nor Eleanor, nor the woman. Oh, Maurice, a child is the most precious thing in the world! You *must* save him!"

"Don't you suppose I want to? But, good God! I'm helpless."

"If you tell Eleanor, you won't be 'helpless.'"

"You don't understand. She's jealous of—of everybody."

"Telling her will prove to her she needn't be jealous of—this person. And the chance to do something for you would mean so much to her. She will forgive you—Eleanor can always do a big thing! Remember the mountain? Maurice! Let her do another great thing for you. Let her help you save your child, by making it possible for you to be open and aboveboard, and see him all you want to—all you *ought* to. Oh, Maurice dear, it would have been better, of course, if you had told Eleanor at first. You wouldn't have had to carry this awful load for all these years. But tell her now! Give her the chance to be generous. Let her help you to do your duty to the little boy. Maurice, his character, and his happiness, are your job! Just as much your job as if he had been Eleanor's child, instead of the child of this woman. Perhaps more so, for that reason. Don't you see that? *Tell* Eleanor, so that you can save him!"

The appeal was like a bugle note. Maurice—discouraged, thwarted, hopeless—heard it, and his heart quickened. This inverted idea of recompense—of making up to Eleanor for having secretly robbed her, by telling her she had been robbed!—stirred some hope in him. He did not love his wife; he was profoundly tired of her; but suppose, now, he did throw himself upon her generosity and give her a chance to prove that love which was a daily fatigue to him? Mere *Truth* would, as Mrs. Houghton said, go far toward saving Jacky. He was silent for a long time. Then Mary Houghton said:

"I ought to tell you, Maurice, that Henry—who is the very best man in the world, as well as the wisest!—doesn't agree with me about this matter of confession. He doesn't understand women! He thinks you ought not to tell Eleanor."

"I know. He said so. That first night, when I told him the whole hideous business, he said so. And I thought he was right. I'm afraid I still think so."

"He was wrong. Maurice, save the child! Tell Eleanor."

"That is what Edith said."

"*Edith!*" Mary Houghton was stupefied.

"Oh, not about this. I only mean Edith said once, 'Don't have a secret from Eleanor.'"

"She was right," Edith's mother said, getting her breath.

Then they were silent again. A distant measure of ragtime floated up from the lobby; once, as a heavy team passed down in the street, the chandelier swayed, and little lights flickered among the faintly clicking prisms. Mrs. Houghton looked at him—and looked away. Maurice was thirty-one; his face was patient and melancholy; the old crinkling laughter rarely made gay wrinkles about his eyes, yet wrinkles were there, and his lips were cynical. Suddenly, he turned and struck his hand on hers:

"I'll do it," he said....

Late that night Henry Houghton, listening to his Mary's story of this talk, looked almost frightened. "Mary, it's an awful risk—Eleanor will never stand up to it!"

"I think she will."

"My dear, when it comes to children, you—with your stars!—get down to the elemental straighter than I do; I know that! And I admit that it is terrible for Maurice's child to be scrapped, as he will be if he is brought up by this impossible person. But as for Eleanor's helping Maurice to save him from the scrap heap, you overlook the fact that to tell a jealous woman that she has cause for jealousy is about as safe as to take a lighted match into a powder magazine. There'll be an explosion."

"Well," she said, "suppose there is?"

"Good heavens, Mary! Do you realize what that means? She'll leave him!"

"I don't believe she will," his wife said, "but if she does, he can at least see all he wants of the boy. He seems to be an unusually bright child."

Her husband nodded. "Yes; Nature isn't shocked at illegitimacy; and God doesn't penalize it."

"But *you* do," she said, quickly, "when you won't admit that Jacky is the crux of the whole thing! It isn't poor Maurice who ought to be considered, nor that sad, tragic old Eleanor; nor the dreadful person in Medfield. But just that little child—*whom Maurice has brought into the world.*"

"Do you mean," her husband said, aghast, "that if Eleanor saw fit to divorce him, you think he should marry this 'Lily,' so that he could get the child?"

She did shrink at that. "Well—" she hesitated.

He saw his advantage, and followed it: "He couldn't get complete possession in any other way! Unless he were legally the father, the woman could, at any minute, carry off this—what did you say his name was?—Jacky?—to Kamchatka, if she wanted to! Or she might very well marry somebody else; that kind do. Then Maurice wouldn't have any finger in the pie! No; really to get control of the child, he'd have to marry her, which, as you yourself admit, is impossible."

"I don't admit it."

"*Mary!* You must be reasonable; you know it would be shocking! So why not keep things as they are? Why run the risk of an explosion, by confessing to Eleanor?"

Mary Houghton pondered, silently.

"Kit," he said, "this is a 'condition and not a theory'; the woman was—was common, you know. Maurice doesn't owe her anything; he has paid the piper ten times over! Any further payment, like ruining his career by 'making an honest woman' of her,—granting an explosion and then Eleanor's divorcing him,—would be not only wrong, but ridiculous; which is worse! Maurice is an able fellow; I rather expect to see him go in for politics one of these days. Imagine this 'Lily' at the head of his table! Or even imagine her as a fireside companion!"

"It would be terrible," she admitted—her voice trembled—"but Jacky's life is more important than Maurice's dinner table. And fireside happiness is less important than the meeting of an obligation! Henry, Maurice made a bad woman Jacky's mother; he owes *her* nothing. But do you mean to say that you don't think he owes the child a decent father?"

"My darling," Henry Houghton said, tenderly, "you are really a little crazy. You are like your stars, you so 'steadfastly pursue your shining,' that you fail to see that, in this dark world of men, there has to be compromise. If this impossible situation should arise—which God forbid!—if the explosion should come, and Eleanor should leave him, of course Maurice wouldn't marry the woman! I should consider him a candidate for an insane asylum if he thought of such a thing. He would simply do what he could for the boy, and that would be the end of it."

"Oh," she said, "don't you see? It would be the *beginning* of it!—The beginning of an evil influence in the world; a bad little boy, growing into a bad man—and his own father permitting it! But," she ended, with a sudden uplifted look, "the 'situation,' as you call it, won't arise; Eleanor will prevent it! Eleanor will save Jacky."

CHAPTER XXVII

Walking home that night, with Mrs. Houghton's "tell Eleanor" ringing in his ears, Maurice imagined a "confession," and he, too, used Mr. Houghton's words, "'there will be an explosion!' But I'll gamble on it; I'll tell her. I promised Mrs. Houghton I would," Then, very anxiously, he tried to decide how he should do it; "I must choose just the right moment," he thought.

When, three months later, the moment came, he hardly recognized it. He had been playing squash and had given his knee a nasty wrench; the ensuing synovitis meant an irritable fortnight of sitting at home near the telephone, with his leg up, fussing about office work. And when he was not fussing he would look at Eleanor and say to himself, "How can I tell her?" Then he would think of his boy developing into a little joyous liar—and thief! The five cents that purchased the jew's-harp, instead of going into the missionary box, was intensely annoying to him. "But the lying is the worst. I can stand anything but lying!" the poor lying father thought. It was then that Eleanor caught his eye, a half-scared, appraising, entreating eye—and stood still, looking down at him.

"Maurice, you want something? What is it?"

"Oh, Nelly!" he said; "I want—" And the thing tumbled from his lips in six words: "I want you to forgive me."

Eleanor put her hand to her throat; then she said, "I know, Maurice."

Silence tingled between them. Maurice said, "You *know*?"

She nodded. He was too stunned to ask how she knew; he only said, "I've been a hound."

Instantly, as though some locked and bolted door had been forced, her heart was open to him. "Maurice! I can bear it—if only you don't lie to me!"

"I have lied," he said; "but I can't go on lying any more! It's been hell. Of course you'll never forgive me."

Instantly she was on her knees beside him, and her lips trembled against his cheek; but she was silent. She was agonizing, not for herself, but for him; *he had suffered.* And when that thought came, Love rose like a wave and swept jealousy away! It was impossible for her to speak. Over in his basket old Bingo growled.

"It was years ago," he said, very low; "I haven't—had anything to do with her since; but—"

She said, gasping, "Do you ... love her still?"

"Good God! no; I never loved her."

"Then," she said, "I don't mind."

His arms went about her, his head dropped on her shoulder. The little dog, unnoticed, barked angrily. For a few minutes neither of them could speak. To him, the unexpectedness of forgiveness was an absolute shock. Eleanor, her cheek against his hair, wept. Happy tears! Then she whispered:

"There is ... a child?"

He nodded speechlessly.

"Maurice, I will love it—"

He was too overcome to speak. Here she was, this irritating, foolish, faithful woman, coming, with outstretched, forgiving arms—to rescue him from his long deceit!

"I have known it," she said, "for nearly two years."

"And you never spoke of it!"

"I couldn't."

"I want to tell you everything, Eleanor. It was—that Dale woman."

She pressed very close to him: "I know."

He wondered swiftly how she knew, but he did not stop to ask; his words rushed out; it was as if the jab of a lancet had opened a hidden wound: "I never cared a copper for her. Never! But—it happened. I was angry about something, and,—Oh, I'm not excusing myself. There isn't any excuse! But I met her, and somehow—Oh, Eleanor!"

"Maurice, ... what does she call you?"

"Call me? What do you mean?"

"What name?"

"Why, 'Mr. Curtis,' of course."

"Not 'Maurice'? Oh—I'm so glad! Go on."

"Well, I never saw her again until she wrote to me about ... this child. Eleanor! I tried to tell you. Do you remember? One night in the boarding house—the night of the eclipse? I thought you'd never forgive me, but I tried to tell you ... Oh, Star, you are wonderful!"

It was an amazing moment; he said to himself: "Mrs. Houghton was right. Edith was right. How I have misjudged her!" He went on, Eleanor still kneeling beside him, sometimes holding his hand to her lips, sometimes pressing her wet cheek against his; once her graying hair fell softly across his eyes ... "Then," he said, "then ... the baby was born."

"Oh, *we* had no children!"

His arms comforted her. "I didn't care. I have never cared. I hated the idea of children, because of ... this child."

"Is his name Jacky?"

"That's what she called him. I never really noticed him, until winter before last; then I kind of—" He paused, then rushed on; it was to be Truth henceforward between them! "I sort of—got fond of him." He waited, holding his breath; but there was no "explosion"! She just pressed his hand against his breast.

"Yes, Maurice?"

"He was sick and she sent for me—"

"I know. That's how I knew. The telegram came, and I—Oh," she interrupted herself, "I wasn't prying!" She was like a dog, shrinking before an expected blow.

The fright in her face went to his heart; what a brute he must have been to have made her so afraid of him!

"It was all right to open it! I'm glad you opened it. Well, he was pretty sick, and I had to get him into the hospital; and after that I began to get sort of—interested in him. But now I'm worried to death, because—" Then he told why he was worried; he told her almost with passion!... "For he's an awfully fine little chap! But she's ruining him." It was amazing how he was able to pour himself out to her! His anxiety about Jacky, his irritation at Lily—yet his appreciation of Lily; he wouldn't go back on Lily! "She wasn't bad—ever. Just unmoral."

"I understand."

"Oh, Eleanor, to be able to talk to you, and tell you!" So he went on telling her: he told her of his faint, shy pride in his little son; told her a funny speech, and she laughed. Told her Jacky had seen a rainbow in the gutter and said it was "handsome." "He really notices Beauty!" Told her of Lily's indignation at the Sunday-school teacher, and his own effort to make Jacky tell the truth, "I have a tremendous influence over him. He'll do anything for me; only, I see him so seldom that I can't counteract poor old Lily's influence. She hasn't any idea of our way of looking at things."

"You must counteract her! You must see him all the time."

"Eleanor," he said, "I have never known you!"

He tried to lift her and hold her in his arms, but she was terrified about his knee.

"No! Don't move! You'll hurt your knee. Maurice, can't I see him?"

"What! Do you really want to?" he said, amazed "Eleanor, you are wonderful!"

That whole evening was entire bliss—as much to Maurice as to Eleanor; to him, it was escape from the bog of secrecy in which, soiled with self-disgust, he had walked for nearly nine years; and with the clean sense of touching the bedrock of Truth was an upspringing hope for his little boy, who "noticed Beauty"! He would be able to see Jacky, and train him, and gain his affection, and make a man of him. He had a sudden vision of companionship. "He'll be in business with me." But that made him smile at himself. "Well, we'll go to ball games, anyway!"

To Eleanor, the evening was a mountain peak; from the sun-smitten heights of a forgiveness that knew itself to be Love, and forgot that it forgave, she looked out, and saw—not that grave where Truth and Pride were buried, but a new heaven and a new earth; Maurice's complete devotion. And his child,—whom she could love.

CHAPTER XXVIII

Those next weeks were full of plans and hopes on Eleanor's part, and gratitude on Maurice's part. But she would not let him say that he was grateful, or that she was generous; he had told her, of course, how Mrs. Houghton had guessed long ago what had happened, and how she had urged him to trust his wife's nobility—but Eleanor would not let him call her "noble"; "Don't say it! And don't be 'grateful,' I just love you," she said; "and if you only knew what it means to me to be able to do anything for you! It's so long since you've needed me, Maurice."

The pathos of her sense of uselessness made his eyes sting. "I couldn't get along without you," he told her.

Once, on a rainy April Sunday morning, when they were talking about Jacky (Maurice had gone to see him the day before, and was gnashing his teeth over some cheerful obliquity on the part of Lily)—Maurice said, emphatically: "Gosh! Nelly, I don't know what I'd do without you!"

She, sitting on a stool at his side (and looking, poor woman! old enough to be his mother), was radiant.

"And you don't enjoy talking to Lily?" she said—just for the happiness of hearing, again, his horrified protest, "I should say *not!* There's nothing she can talk about."

"She doesn't know about books and things? She hasn't—brains?"

"Brains? She probably never read anything in her life! She has lots of sense, but no intellect. She hasn't an idea beyond food and flowers—and Jacky."

"I wish I had her idea about food," Eleanor said, simply.

It was her fairness toward Lily that amazed him; it made him reproach himself for his stupidity in not having confessed to her long ago! "Why was I such a fool, Eleanor, as not to know that you were a big woman? Mrs. Houghton knew it. Why, even Edith knew it! She told me you'd forgive anything."

"*What!*" She rose abruptly and stood looking at him with suddenly angry eyes. "Does Edith know?" she said.

"No! Of course she doesn't know—*this*! But one day she and I were taking a walk, and I was thinking what a devilish mess I was in.... And I suppose Edith saw I was down by the head, and she got to talking about you—"

"You let her talk about me!"

"She was saying how perfectly fine you had been about the mountain—"

"I don't need Edith Houghton's approval of my conduct, Maurice." She was trembling, and her face was quite pale. He rushed in deeper than ever:

"I was only saying I felt so—badly, because I had failed to make you happy. Of course I didn't say how! And she said, 'Don't have any secrets from Eleanor!'"

"So it was Edith who made you—"

For a moment Maurice was too dismayed to speak; besides, he didn't know what to say. What he did say was that she misunderstood him. "Good heavens! Eleanor, you didn't think I'd tell Edith a thing like *that*? Or that I'd tell any woman, when I didn't tell you? But Edith knew you better than I did; she said no matter what I'd done (I just happened to say I was a skunk), you loved me enough to forgive me. And you have forgiven me."

"Yes," she said, in a whisper; "I've forgiven you."

She went over to the window, and stood perfectly silent. It was raining steadily; the river, a block away, was hidden in the yellow fog; down in the yard, the tables and chairs under the poplar dripped and dripped. As for Maurice, it was as if some dark finger had stretched out and touched a bubble.... She was the same Eleanor.

But he did not dwell upon this revealing moment; it was enough that at last he could stop lying, and that Eleanor would help him about Jacky! He called her back from the window and made her sit down again beside him, pretending not to see how her hands were trembling. Then he went on talking about Jacky.

"His latest achievement is an infernal mouth harmonicon."

She said, listlessly, "I wish I could give him music lessons."

"He's crazy about music; trails hand organs all over Medfield!" Maurice said, with a great effort to be cheerfully casual; "but, Heaven knows, I'd be glad if you could give him lessons in anything! Manners, for instance. He hasn't any. Or grammar; I told him not to say 'ain't,' and, if you please! he told his mother *she* mustn't say it! Lily got on her ear."

She smiled faintly. "I wish I could see him," she said.

She had urged this more than once, but it had not seemed practicable. "I can't bring him here," Maurice explained; "he'd blurt out to Lily where he'd been, and she'd get uneasy. Even as it is, I live in dread that she'll pack up and clear out with him."

"She *shan't* take him away!" Eleanor said; she was eager again;—after all, Edith, for all her impertinence in advising Maurice how to treat his wife!—Edith could not break in upon an intimacy like this!

Her incessant talk about Jacky (which might have bored Maurice just a little, if it had not touched him) gave her, in some subtle, spiritual way, a sense of approaching motherhood: *she made preparations!* She planned little gifts for him;—Maurice had told her of Jacky's lively interest in benefits to come; once, she thought, "I suppose he's too old to have one of those funny papers in his room? I saw such a pretty one to-day, little rabbits in trousers!"—For by this time she had determined that, somehow, she would get possession of him! In these maternal moments she feared no rivalry from Edith Houghton. Jacky would save her from Edith!

"Oh, Maurice! I *must* see him," she said once.

"I'll fix it so you can," he told her. But it was two months before he was able to fix it; then "Forepaws" came to town, and the way was clear! He would take Jacky, and Eleanor should go and have a seat near by, and come up and speak to the youngster, as any admiring stranger might, and, indeed, often did, for Jacky was a striking child—his eyes blue and keen, his skin very clear, and his cheeks glowing with health. "If he goes home and tells Lily a lady spoke to him," Maurice said, "she won't think anything of it."

"May I give him some candy?"

"No; he has too much of it as it is; get one of those tin horns for him. He'll raise Cain for Lily, I suppose; but we won't have to listen to him!" (That "we" so fed Eleanor's starved soul, that she thought of Edith Houghton with a sort of gay contempt: "*I'm* not afraid of her!")

The plan for seeing Jacky went through easily enough. "I'll take that boy of yours to the circus," Maurice told Lily, carelessly, one day.

"Why, that's awful kind in you, Mr. Curtis; but ain't you afraid somebody'll see you luggin' a child around?"

"Lots of men take kids to the circus—just as an excuse to go themselves."

So Maurice and the eight-year-old Jacky, in a new sailor suit, and a face so clean that it shone, walked in among the gilded cages, felt the sawdust under their feet, smelled the wild animals, heard the yelps of the jackals, the booming roar of lions, and the screeching chatter of the monkeys. And as Jacky dragged his father from cage to cage, a yard or two behind them came Eleanor.... Now and then, over Jacky's head, she caught Maurice's eye; and they both smiled.

When a speechless Jacky was taken into the central tent to sit on a narrow bench, and drink pink lemonade and eat peanuts, Eleanor was quite near him. He was unconscious of her presence—unconscious of everything! except the blare of the band, the elephants, the performing dogs—especially the poor, strained performing dogs! He never spoke once; his eyes were fixed on the rings; he didn't see his father watching him, amused and proud; still less did he see the lady who had been at his heels in the animal tent, and who now kept her mournful dark eyes on his face. When the last horse gave the last kick and trotted out through the exit, with its mysterious canvas walls, Jacky was in a daze of bliss. He sat, open-mouthed, staring at the empty, trampled sawdust.

"Come along, young man!" Maurice said; "do you want to stay here all night?"

"I'm going to be a circus rider," said Jacky, solemnly.

It was then that the "lady" spoke to him—her voice broke twice: "Well, little boy, did you like the circus?" the lady said. She was so pale that Maurice put his hand on her arm.

"Better sit down, Nelly," he said, kindly, under his breath.

She shook her head. "No ... Jacky, don't you want to tell me your name?"

"But you *know* my name," said Jacky, with a bored look.

Maurice gave her a warning glance, and she tried to cover her blunder: "I heard your father—I mean this gentleman—call you 'Jacky,'" she explained—panting, for Maurice's quick frown frightened her. "Here's a present for you," she said.

"*Present!*" said Jacky—and made a joyous grab at the horn, which he immediately put to his lips; but before it could emit its ear-piercing screech, Maurice struck it down.

"Where are your manners? Say 'Thank you' to the lady."

Jacky sighed, but murmured, "'Ank you."

Eleanor, her chin trembling, said: "May I kiss him?"

"'Course," Maurice said, huskily.

She bent down and kissed him with trembling lips—"Ach!—you make me all wet," Jacky said, frowning at her tears on his rosy cheek.

Later, as Maurice pulled his reluctant son out on to the pavement, he was so moved that he almost forgot that she was still the old Eleanor; he didn't even listen to his little boy's passionate assertion that he would be a flying-trapeze man. As he walked along beside his wife to put her on the car he spoke with great tenderness:

"I'll leave him at Lily's, and then I'll come right home, dear, and we'll talk things over."

When he and his son got back to Maple Street, Jacky was blowing that infernal horn so that the whole neighborhood was aware of his ecstasy. Lily, waiting for them at the gate, put her hands over her ears.

"My soul and body! For the land's sake, stop! Who give you that horrid thing?"

"An old lady," said Jacky—and blew a shattering screech on Eleanor's horn.

CHAPTER XXIX

From the day of the circus, Jacky became, to Eleanor, not a symbol of Maurice's unfaithfulness, but a hope for the future. The thought of his mother was only the scar of a wound, which Maurice, in some single slashing moment, had made in her heart. She was crippled by it, of course. But the wound had healed so she could forget the scar—because Maurice had never loved Lily, never found her "interesting," never wanted to wander about with *her*, in a dark garden, and talk

Of shoes—and ships—and sealing wax— And cabbages— and kings ...

To be sure the scar ached dully once in a while; but Eleanor knew that if she could get possession of Jacky she would be protected against other wounds—wounds which would never heal! She said to herself that Maurice would never think of Edith Houghton if he had Jacky! But how should she get Jacky?

For months she revolved countless schemes to persuade Lily to resign him; schemes so futile that Maurice, listening to them every night when he got home from the office, was touched, of course; but by and by he was also a little uneasy. He had told her where Lily lived, then regretted it, for once she walked up and down before the house on Maple Street for an hour, hoping to see "the woman," but failing, because Lily and Jacky happened to be in town that afternoon.

"I have a great mind to steal him for you!" she said, telling Maurice of her fruitless effort.

He protested, too disturbed at her mere presence on Lily's street to notice her attempt at a joke. "If Lily should imagine that we were interested in Jacky, she'd run!" he explained; "it's dangerous, Nelly, really. You mustn't go near her!"

She promised she wouldn't; but every day of that Mercer winter of low-hanging smoke and damp chilliness, she longed to get possession of the child—first to make Maurice happy; then with the craving, driving, elemental desire for maternity; and then for self-protection,—Jacky would vanquish Edith!

So she brooded: *a child!*

"If I could only get him, it wouldn't be 'just us'!" ... "A boy's clothes are not as pretty as a girl's, but a little rough suit would be awfully attractive.... I'd give him music lessons.... We could go out to our field in June. And he would take off his shoes and stockings and wade!" How foolish Edith's grown-up childishness of wading looked, compared to the scene which she visualized—a little, handsome boy, standing in the shallow rippling water, bareheaded, probably; the sunshine sifting down through the locust blossoms and touching that thatch of yellow hair, and glinting into those blue eyes. "He would call me 'Mamma'!" Then she hummed to herself, "'O Spring!' Oh, I *must* have him!" Her hope became such an obsession that its irrationality did not strike her. It was so in her mind that she even spoke of it once to Mrs. Houghton. "I know you *know*?" she said; "Maurice told me he told you."

Mary Houghton said, hesitatingly, "I think I know what you mean."

This was in March. Mrs. Houghton and Edith were in town for a few days' shopping, and of course they meant to see Eleanor. "I'll go to the dressmaker's," Edith had told her mother, "and then I'll corral Maurice, and we'll drop in on Mrs. Newbolt, and *then* I'll meet you at Eleanor's. I don't hanker for a long call on Eleanor." Edith's gayly candid face hardened.

So it was that Mrs. Houghton had arrived ahead of her girl, and the two older women were alone before a little smoldering fire in the library. Eleanor had left her tea tray to go across the room and give little helpless Bingo a lump of sugar. "He only eats what I give him," she said; "dear old Bingo! I think he actually suffers, he's so jealous." Then, pouring Mrs. Houghton's tea, she suddenly spoke: "I know you—know?" When Mary Houghton said, gravely, yes, she "*knew*," Eleanor said, "Oh, Mrs. Houghton, Maurice and I are nearer to each other than we ever were before!"

"That's as it should be. And as I knew it would be, too. You've done a noble thing, Eleanor."

"No! No! Don't say that! It was nothing. Because I—love him so. And he never cared for that woman. She has no brains, he says. But what I want is to get the boy for him. Oh, he must have the boy!" Then she told Mrs. Houghton how Maurice went to see the child. "He goes once a week, though he says she's jealous if he makes too many suggestions; so he has to be very careful or she would get angry. But he has managed it so I have seen him; last summer he took him to the circus, and I sat near them. And twice he's had him in the park and I spoke to him. And on Christmas he took him to the movies; I sat beside him. And I buttoned his coat when he went out!" Her eyes were rapt.

Mary Houghton, listening, said to herself, "*Now* what will Henry Houghton say about the 'explosion'? I shall rub it into him when I get home!" ... "Eleanor, you are magnificent!" she said.

"But how could I do anything else—if I loved Maurice?" Eleanor said. "Oh, I do want him to have Jacky! We must make a man of him. It would be wicked to let Lily ruin him! And I want to give him music lessons. He has Maurice's blue eyes."

It was infinitely pathetic, this woman with gray hair, telling of her young husband's joy in his little son—who was not hers. And Eleanor's sense of the paramount importance of the child gave Mrs. Houghton a new and real respect for her. Aloud, she agreed heartily with the statement that Jacky must be saved from Lily.

"She isn't bad," Eleanor explained; "but she's just like an animal, Maurice says. Devoted to Jacky, but no more idea of right and wrong than—than Bingo!" She was so happy that she laughed, and looked almost young—but at that moment the street door opened, closed, and in the hall some one else laughed. Instantly Eleanor looked old. "It's Edith," she said, coldly.

It was—with Maurice in tow. "I haled him forth from his office," Edith said; "and we went to see your aunt, Eleanor. She's a lamb!"

"Tea?" Eleanor said, briefly.

"Yes, indeed!" Edith said. She looked very pretty—cheeks glowing and brown hair flying about the rounded brim of a brown fur toque.

Maurice, keeping an eye on her, was gently kind to his wife. "Head better, Nelly?" Then, having secured his tea, he drew Edith over to the window and they went on with some discussion which had paused as they entered the house.

Eleanor, watching them, and making another cup of tea for Mrs. Houghton, spilled the boiling water on the tray and on her own hand.

"My dear!" said Mrs. Houghton, "you have scalded yourself!"

And, indeed, Eleanor whitened with the pain of her smarting, puffing fingers. But she said, her eyes fixed on Edith, "What *are* they talking about?" Mrs. Houghton's look of surprise made her add: "Edith seems so interested. I just wondered...." She had caught a phrase or two:

"I can take the spring course,—it's three months. I think our University Domestic Science Department is just every bit as good as any of the Eastern ones."

"Where did you two meet each other?" Eleanor called, sharply.

"Why, I told you," Edith said, coming over to the tea table; "I dragged him from his desk!"

"Come, Edith, we must go," Mrs. Houghton said, rising.

"Why don't you stay to dinner?" Maurice urged—but Eleanor was silent. "If you are in town next week, Skeezics, you've got to put up here. Understand? Tell her so, Eleanor!"

Eleanor said nothing. Mrs. Houghton said she was afraid it wouldn't be convenient.

Eleanor said nothing.

"Of course you will come here!" Maurice said; he was sharply angry at his wife.

In the momentary and embarrassing pause, the color flew into Edith's face, but she was elaborately indifferent. "Good-by, Eleanor; good-by, Maurice!"

"I'm going to escort you to the hotel," Maurice said; and, over his shoulder to Eleanor: "I've got to rush off to St. Louis to-night, Eleanor. That Greenleaf business. Has Mrs. O'Brien brought my things home?"'

"I'll see," she said, mechanically....

Nobody had much to say on that walk to the hotel; but when Maurice had left them, and the two ladies were in their room, Edith faced her mother:

"What *is* the matter?"

"You mean with Eleanor? She has a headache, I suppose."

"Mother, don't squirm! You know just as well as I do that she doesn't want me to stay with them. Why not?" She did not wait for an answer, which, indeed, her mother could not immediately find. "Well, Heaven knows I'm not pining to be with her! I shall run in to-morrow morning, and tell her that Mrs. Newbolt asked me to stay with her.... Mother, how *could* Maurice have fallen in love with Eleanor?" Her voice trembled; she went over to the window and stood looking down into the street; her hands were clenched behind her, and her soft young chin was rigid. "He was just a boy," she said; her eyes were blurring so that the street was a gray fog; "how *could* Eleanor?" It seemed as if her own ardent, innocent body felt the recoil of Maurice's youth from Eleanor's age! She thought of that dark place in his past, which she had accepted with pain, but always with defending excuses; she excused him again, now, in her thoughts: "Eleanor was *impossible*! That's why somebody else ... caught him. And it was long ago. And Eleanor's old enough to be his mother. He never could have loved her!" Suddenly she had a fleeting, but real, pity for Eleanor: "Poor thing!" Aloud she said, huskily, over her shoulder, "If she had really loved him, she wouldn't have done such a terrible thing as marry him."

Mrs. Houghton, reading the evening paper, said, briefly, "She loves him *now*, my dear."

"Oh!" Edith said, passionately, "sometimes I am sorry for Eleanor—and then the next minute I perfectly hate her!"

"She was only forty when she married him," Mary Houghton said; "that isn't old at all! And I have always been sorry for her." She looked up over her spectacles at the tense young figure by the window, outlined against the yellow sunset; saw those clenched hands, heard the impetuous voice break on a word,—and forgot Eleanor in a more intimate anxiety: "Of course," she said, "such a difference in age as there is between Maurice and Eleanor is a pity. But Maurice is devoted to her, and with reason. She has been generous when he has been unkind. I happen to know that."

"Maurice couldn't be unkind!"

Her mother ignored this. "And remember another thing, Edith: It isn't years that decide whether a marriage is a failure. One of the happiest marriages I ever knew was between a woman of fifty and a man of thirty. You see—" she paused, and took off her spectacles, and tapped the arm of her chair, thoughtfully: "You see, Edith, you don't understand. You are so appallingly young! You think Love speaks only through the senses. My dear, Love's highest speech is in the Spirit; the language of the senses is only it's pretty, stammering, divine baby-talk!" Edith was silent. Her mother went on: "Yes, it isn't age that decides things. It's selfishness or unselfishness. At present Eleanor is extraordinarily unselfish, so I believe they may yet be very happy."

"Oh, I hope so, of course," Edith said—and put up a furtive finger to wipe first one cheek, and then the other.... "Poor Maurice!" she said.

CHAPTER XXX

When Maurice got back to the firelit library, he said, filling his pipe with rather elaborate attention, and trying to speak with good-natured carelessness, "I'm afraid Edith thought you didn't want her, Nelly." He was sorry the next moment that he had said even as much as that: Eleanor was breathing quickly, and her dark, sad eyes were hard with anger.

"I don't," she said

Maurice said, sharply, "You have never liked her!"

"Why should I like her? She talks to you incessantly. And now, she *looks* at you; here—before me! Looks at you."

"Eleanor, what on earth—"

"Oh, I saw her, when you were talking over there by the window; I watched her. She looked at you! I am not blind. I understand what it means when a girl looks at a man that way. And now she's planning to be in Mercer for three months? Well, that's simply to be near you. She'd like to live in the same house with you, I suppose! If it wasn't for me, she'd be in love with you—perhaps she is, anyhow? Yes, I think she is." There was a sick silence. "And, perhaps," she said, with a gasp, "you are in love with her?"

He was dumb. The suddenness of the attack completely routed him— its suddenness; but more than its suddenness was a leaping question in his own mind. When she said, "You are in love with her?" an appalled "Am I?" was on his lips. Instantly he knew, what he had not known, at any rate articulately, that he was in love with Edith. His thoughts broke in galloping confusion; his hand, holding the hot bowl of his pipe, trembled. He tried to speak, stammered, said, with a sort of gasp, "Don't—don't say a thing like that!" Then he got his breath, and ended, with a composure that kept his words slow and his voice cold, "It is terrible to say a thing like that to me."

She flung out her hands. "What more can I do for you than I have done? Oh, Maurice—Maurice, no woman could love you more than I do?... *Could they?*"

"I am grateful; I—" He tried to speak gently, but his voice had begun to shake with angry terror; it was abominable, this thing she had said! (But ...

it was true.) "No; no woman could have done more for me than you have, Eleanor; I am grateful."

"Grateful? Yes. You give me gratitude." Maurice was speechless. "I thought, perhaps, you loved me," she said. A minute later he heard her going upstairs to her own room.

He stood staring after her, open-mouthed. Then he said, under his breath, "Good God!" After a while he went over to the fireplace, and, standing with one hand on the mantelpiece, he kicked the charred logs on the hearth together. "This room is cold. I must build the fire up.... Yes, it's true.... The wood is too green to burn. I'll order from another man next time.... I suppose I've been in love with her for a good while. I wonder if it began that night Jacky was sick ... and she kissed me? No; it must have been before that." He stooped and mended the fire, piling the logs together with slow exactness: "What life might have been!" He took up the bellows and urged a little flame to rise and flicker and lap the wood, then burst to crackling blaze. After a while he said, "Poor Nelly!" But he had himself in hand by that time, and, though this terrifying knowledge was surging in him, he knew that his voice would not betray him. He went upstairs to comfort her with kindly assurances that she was wrong. ("More lies," he thought, wearily.)

But apparently she didn't need comforting! She was smoothing her hair before the glass, and seemed perfectly calm. He had expected tears, and violent reproaches, which he was prepared to meet with either good-natured ridicule or quiet falsehood, as the occasion might demand. But nothing was demanded. She continued to brush her hair; so he found it quite easy to come up behind her and lay a hand on her shoulder, and say, "Nelly, dear, that wasn't a nice thing to say!"

She did not meet his eyes in the mirror; she only said (she was trembling), "I suppose it wasn't."

Maurice was puzzled, but he said, casually, that he was sorry to have to rush off that night. "I've got to take the Limited for St. Louis. Mr. Weston wants some papers put through. I hate to leave you."

She made no answer.

"I shall be gone a week, maybe more; because if I don't pull the chestnut out of the fire in St. Louis, I'll have to go to some other places."

She hardly heard him; she was saying to herself: "I *oughtn't* to have told him she was in love with him; it may make him think so, himself!"

"Guess I'll pack my grip now," he said.

"Maurice," she said, breathlessly, "I didn't mean—" She was so frightened that she couldn't finish her sentence; but he said, with kindly understanding:

"Of course you didn't!"

It flashed into her mind that if she left him alone, he would know that what she had said was so meaningless that she didn't think it worth talking about. "I—I'm going to Auntie's to dinner," she told him, on the spur of the moment. "Do you mind?"

"No; of course not. Wait a second, and I'll walk round with you."

She said, unsteadily, "Oh no; you've got your packing to do—" Then she kissed him swiftly, and hurried downstairs.

"But Eleanor, wait!" he called; "I'll go with—"

She had gone. He heard the front door close. He stood still in his perplexity. What was the matter? She had got over that jealousy of Edith in an instant; got over it, and accepted his departure without all those wearying protestations of love and loneliness to which he was accustomed. "Is she angry," he told himself; "or just ashamed of having been so foolish?" Mechanically, he picked out some neckties from his drawer, and paused.... "But she wasn't foolish. I do love Edith.... How did she get on to it? She is so good to me about Jacky—and I love Edith!" He went on packing his grip. "I wonder if any man ever paid as I am paying?—I'll call her up at Mrs. Newbolt's, before I go, and say good-by."

No doubt he would have done so, but when he went downstairs he found Johnny Bennett, smoking comfortably before that very cheerful little fire.

"I dropped in," said Johnny, "to ask for some dinner."

"If you'll take pot luck," said Maurice; "Eleanor isn't at home, and I don't know what the lady below stairs will work off on us." (It would be a relief, he thought, to have somebody at table, so that he would not be alone with his own confusion.)

"I came," Johnny said, "to tell you I'm off."

"Off? When? Where to? I thought your electric performances were panning out so well—"

"Oh, they're panning out all right," John said; "but they'll pan out better in South America. I'm going the first of the month."

"South America! What's the matter with Pennsylvania?"

"Well," Johnny said; "I thought I'd light out—"

Then they began to talk climate, and consulates, which carried them through dinner, and went on in the library, and Maurice's surface interest in Johnny's affairs, at least kept him from thinking of his own dismay.

"But I supposed," he said, and paused, "I sort of thought you—had reasons for staying round here?"

"There's no use hanging round," John said; "it's better to pull out altogether. It's easier that way," he said, simply. "So I'm off for a year. They wanted me to sign for three years, but I said, 'one.' Things may look better for me when I get home."

Maurice, standing with his back to the fire, his hands in his pocket, looked down at the steady youngster—looked at the mild eyes behind those large spectacles, looked at the clean, strong lines of the jaw and forehead. A good fellow. A very good fellow. He wondered why Edith wouldn't take him? ("It couldn't make any difference to me," he thought; "and I want her to be happy.")

"Johnny," he said, "you can say, 'Mind your business,' before I begin, if you want to. But I don't think anybody's cutting you out? Better 'try, try again.'"

Johnny took his pipe from his mouth, bent forward to shake the ashes out of it, and stared into the fire. Then he said, clearing his throat once or twice: "I've bothered her, 'trying,' I thought I'd start on a new tack."

"You'll get her yet!" Maurice encouraged him. He wondered, as he spoke, how he could speak so lightly, urging old Johnny to go ahead and make another stab at it, and, maybe, "get her"! He wondered if he was looking at things the way the dead look at the living? He was not, he thought, suffering, as he had suffered in those first moments when Eleanor had flung the truth at him. "You'll get her yet," he said, vaguely.

Johnny took out his tobacco pouch, and began to fill his pipe, poking his thumb down into the bowl with slow precision, then holding it on a level with his eyes and squinting at it, to make sure it was smooth; he seemed profoundly engrossed by that pipe—but he put it in his mouth without lighting it.

"Well, I don't know," he said; "I haven't an awful lot of hope that I'll ever get her. But I thought I'd try this way. Maybe, if she doesn't see me for a year...."

"There's nobody ahead of you, anyway," Maurice said, absently.

"Well, I don't know," John Bennett said again.

His voice was so harsh that Maurice's preoccupation sharpened into uneasy attention. Johnny's hopes and fears had not really touched him. His encouraging platitudes were only a way of smothering his own thoughts. But that, "Well, I don't know—" woke a keenly attentive fear: *was* there anybody else? ("Not that that could make any difference to me.")

"You 'don't know'?" he said; "how do you mean? You think there *is* somebody?"

Johnny Bennett was silent; he had an impulse to say "you are several kinds of a fool, old man." But he was silent.

"Why, Great Scott!" Maurice protested. "Buried up there in the mountains, she hardly knows a fellow—except you!—and me," he added, with a laugh.

"I think," said John, huskily, "she has ... some kind of an ideal up her sleeve. And I don't fill the bill. Imagination, you know. A—a sort of Sir Walter Raleigh business. Remember how she was always sort of dotty on Sir Walter Raleigh? An ideal, don't you know"; Johnny rambled on: "Girls are that way. Only Edith's the kind that sticks to things."

"'Try, try again,'" said Maurice, mechanically; but his blood suddenly pounded in his ears.

"I'm going to," Johnny said, calmly; and began to talk South America. Indeed, he talked so long that Maurice, catching sight of the clock, exclaimed that he would have to run!

"Johnny, get Eleanor on the wire, will you; at Mrs. Newbolt's, and tell her I'd have called her up, but I got delayed, and had to leg it to catch the train? Or maybe you wouldn't mind going round there, and walking home with her?"

"Glad to," said Johnny.

When Maurice, swinging on to the last platform of the last Pullman, was able to sit down in his section, he was absorbed in Johnny Bennett's affairs.

"What did he mean by saying that? Did he mean—" Johnny's enigmatical words rang in his ears; "I said to 'try again; nobody was cutting him out.' And he said 'She has some kind of an ideal up her sleeve.' ... 'A Sir Walter Raleigh business' ..."

Johnny Bennett, walking toward Mrs. Newbolt's, was also thinking, in his calm way, of just what he had said there by Maurice's fireside. "Of course he doesn't see why she hasn't fallen in love with anybody else. Any decent fellow would be stupid about that sort of thing. But it's been that way ever since she was a child. And I've loved her ever since then, too. All the same, I'll only sign up for a year. Then I'll make another stab at it ..."

When he rang Mrs. Newbolt's doorbell, and was told that Eleanor had not been there, he was perplexed. "I must have misunderstood Maurice," he thought.

CHAPTER XXXI

Eleanor had no intention of going to Mrs. Newbolt's. "She'd talk Edith to me!" she said to herself; "I *can't* understand why she likes her!" Instead of dining with her aunt, she meant to walk about the streets until she was sure that Maurice had started for the train; then she would go back to her own house. So she wandered down the avenue until, tired of looking with unseeing eyes into shop windows, it occurred to her to go into the park; there, on a bench on one of the unfrequented paths, she sat down, hoping that no one would recognize her; it was cold, and she shivered and looked at her watch. Only six o'clock! It would be two hours before Maurice would leave the house for the station. It seemed absurd to be here in the dampness of the March evening; but she couldn't go home and get into any discussion with him; she might burst out again about Edith!—which always made him angry. She wished that she had not told him that Edith was in love with him. "It ought to disgust him, but it might flatter him!" And she oughtn't to have said that other thing; she oughtn't to have accused him of caring for Edith. "Of course he doesn't. And it was a horrid thing to say. I was angry, because I was jealous; but it wasn't true. I wish I hadn't said it. I'll write to him, and ask him to forgive me." But the other thing *was* true: "I saw it in her eyes! She loves him. But I oughtn't to have put the idea into his head!"

The more she thought of what she had put into Maurice's head, the more uneasy she became. Oh, if she only had Jacky! Then, Edith could be as brazen as she pleased, and Maurice would never notice her! "Of course he doesn't love her; I'm certain of *that*!" she said again and again,—and all her schemes, wise and foolish, for getting possession of the boy, began to crowd into her mind.

Then an idea came to her which fairly took her breath away! A perfectly wild idea, which she dared not stop to analyze: suppose, instead of sitting here in the cold, she should go, now, boldly, to Lily, and ask for Jacky? "I believe *I* could persuade her to give him to us! She wouldn't do it for Maurice, but she might for me!"

She got on her feet with a spring! Her spiritual energy was like her physical energy that night on the mountain. Again she was lifting—lifting! This time it was the weight of a Love which might die! She was dragging it, carrying it! her very soul straining under her purpose of keeping it alive by the touch of a child's hand! ... Why not go and see Lily *now*? "She'll have finished her supper by the time I get to her house; it's at the very end of Maple Street!" If Lily consented, Eleanor might even get back to her own house in time to see Maurice, and tell him what she had accomplished before he started for his train! But she would have to hurry....

She actually ran out of the park toward the street; then stood for an endless five minutes, waiting for the Medfield car. "Perhaps I can make her let me bring Jacky home with me!" she said—which showed to what heights beyond common sense she had risen.

At the little house on Maple Street she rang the bell, though she had a crazy impulse to bang upon the door to hurry Lily! But she rang, and rang again, before she heard a child's voice: "Maw. Somebody at the door."

"Well, go open it, can't you?"

She heard little scuffing steps on the oilcloth in the hall; then the door opened, and Jacky stood there. He fixed his blue, impersonal eyes upon her, and waited.

"Is your mother in?" Eleanor said, breathlessly.

"Yes, ma'am," said Jacky.

"Who is it?" Lily called to him; she was somewhere in the back of the house, and Eleanor could hear the clatter of dishes being gathered up from an unseen supper table. Jacky, unable to answer his mother's question, was calmly silent.

"My land! That child's a reg'lar dummy! Jacky, who *is* it?"

"*I* do' know," Jacky called back.

"I am Mrs. Curtis," Eleanor said; "I want to see your mother."

"She says," Jacky called—then paused, because it occurred to him to hang on to the door knob and swing back and forth, his heels scraping over the oilcloth; "she says," said Jacky, "she's Mrs. Curtis."

The noise of the dishes stopped short. In the dining room Lily stood stock-still; "My God!" she said. Then her eyes narrowed and her jaw set; she whipped off her apron and turned down her sleeves; she had made up her mind: "*I'll lie it through.*"

She came out in the hall, which was scented with rose geraniums and reeked with the smell of bacon fat, and said, with mincing politeness, "Were you wishing to see me?"

"Yes," Eleanor said.

"Step right in," said Lily, opening the parlor door. "Won't you be seated?" Then she struck a match on the sole of her shoe, lit the gas, blew out the match, and turned to look at her visitor. She put her hand over her mouth and gasped. Under her breath she said, "His *mother*!"

"Mrs. Dale," Eleanor began—

"Well, there!" said Lily, pleasantly (but she was pale); "I guess you have the advantage of me. What did you say your name was?"

"My name is Curtis. Mrs. Dale, I—I know about your little boy."

"Is that so?" Lily said, with the simper proper when speaking to strangers.

"I mean," Eleanor said, "I know about—" her lips were so dry she stopped to moisten them—"about Mr. Curtis and you."

"I ain't acquainted with your son."

Eleanor caught her breath, but went on, "I haven't come to reproach you."

Lily tossed her head. "Reproach? *Me?* Well, I must say, I don't see no cause why you should! *I* don't know no Mr. Curtis!" She was alertly on guard for Maurice; "I guess you've mixed me up with some other lady."

"Please!" Eleanor said; "I *know*. He told me—about Jacky."

Instantly Lily's desire to defend Maurice was tempered by impatience with him; the idea of him letting on to his mother! Then, noticing her boy, who was silently observing the caller from the doorway, she said:

"Jacky! Go right out of this room."

"Won't," said Jacky. "She gimme the horn," he remarked.

"Aw, now, sweety, go on out!" Lily entreated.

Jacky said, calmly, "Won't."

At which his mother got up and stamped her foot. "Clear right out of this room, or I'll see to you! Do you hear me? Go on, now, or I'll give you a reg'lar spanking!"

Jacky ran. He never obeyed her when he could help it, but he always recognized the moment when he couldn't help it. Lily closed the door, and stood with her back against it, looking at her caller.

"Well," she said, "if you *are* on to it, I'm sure you ain't going to make trouble for him with his wife."

"I am his wife."

"His *wife*?" They looked at each other for a speechess moment. Then the tears sprang to Lily's eyes. "Oh, you poor soul!" she said. "Say, don't feel bad! It's pretty near ten years ago; he was just a kid. Since then—honest to God, I give you my word, he 'ain't hardly said 'How do you do' to me!"

"I know," Eleanor said; her hands were gripped hard together; "I know that. I know he has been ... perfectly true to me—lately. I am not saying a word about that. It's the child. I want to make a proposition to you about the child." Her lips trembled, but she smiled; she remembered to smile, because if she didn't look pleasant Lily might get angry. She was a little frightened; but she gave a nervous laugh. She spoke with gentleness, almost with sweetness. "I came to see you, Mrs. Dale, because I hope you and I can make some arrangement about the little boy. I want to help you by relieving you of—of his support. I mean," said Eleanor, still smiling with her trembling lips, "I mean, I will take him, and bring him up, so as to save you the expense." Lily's amazed recoil made her break into entreaty; "My husband wants him, and I do, too! I thought perhaps you'd let him go home with me to-night? I—I promise I'll take the best of care of him!"

Lily was too dumfounded to speak, but her thoughts raced. "For the land's sake!" she said under her breath. She was sitting down now, but her hands in her lap had doubled into rosy fighting fists.

Her silence terrified Eleanor. "If you'll give him to me," she said, "I will do anything for you—anything! If you'll just let Mr. Curtis have him." She did not mean to, but suddenly she was crying, and began to fumble for her handkerchief.

"Well, if this ain't the limit!" said Lily, and jumped up and ran to her, and put her arms around her. ("Here, take mine! It's clean.") "Say, I'm that sorry for you, I don't know what to do!" Her own tears overflowed.

Eleanor, wincing away from the gush of perfumery from the little clean handkerchief, clutched at Lily's small plump hand—"*I'll* tell you what to do," Eleanor said; "*Give me Jacky!*"

Lily, kneeling beside her, cried, honestly and openly. "There!—now!" she said, patting Eleanor's shoulder; "don't you cry! Mrs. Curtis, now look,"—she spoke soothingly, as if to a child, with her arm around Eleanor—"you know I *can't* let my little boy go? Why, think how you'd feel yourself, if you had a little boy and anybody tried to get him. Would you give him up? 'Course you wouldn't! Why, I wouldn't let Jacky go away from me, even for a day, not for the world! An' he ain't anything to Mr. Curtis. Honest! That's the truth. Now, don't you cry, dear!"

"You can see him often; I promise you, you can see him."

In spite of her pity, Lily's yellow eyes gleamed: "'See' my own child? Well, I guess!"

"I'll give you anything," Eleanor said; "I have a little money — about six hundred dollars a year; I'll give it to you, if you'll let Mr. Curtis have him."

"Sell Jacky for six hundred dollars?" Lily said. "I wouldn't sell him for six thousand dollars, or six million!" She drew away from Eleanor's beseeching hands. "How long has Mr. Curtis thought enough of Jacky to pay six hundred dollars for him? You can tell Mr. Curtis, from me, that I ain't no cheap trader, to give away my child for six hundred dollars!" She sprang up, putting her clenched fists on her fat hips, and wagging her head. "Why," she demanded, raucously, "didn't you have a child of your own for him, 'stead of trying to get another woman's child away from her?"

It was a hideous blow. Eleanor gasped with pain; and instantly Lily's anger was gone.

"Say! I didn't mean that! 'Course you couldn't, at your age. I oughtn't to have said it!"

Eleanor, dumb for a moment after that deadly question, began, faintly: "Mr. Curtis will do so much for him, Mrs. Dale; he'll educate him, and —"

"I can educate him," Lily said; "you tell Mr. Curtis that; you tell him I thank him for nothing! — I can educate my child to beat the band. I don't want any help from him. But —" she was on her knees again, stroking Eleanor's shoulder — "but if he's mean to you because you haven't had any children, I—I—I'll see to him! Well—I've always thought, what with him fussing about 'grammar,' and 'truth,' he'd be a hard man to live with. But if he's been mean to you he'd ought to be ashamed of himself!"

"Oh, he doesn't even know that I have come!" Eleanor said; "he mustn't know it. Oh, please!" She was terrified. "Don't tell him, Mrs. Dale. Promise me you won't! He would be angry."

Her frightened despair was pitiful; Lily was at her wits' end. "My soul and body!" she thought, "what am I going to do with her?" But what was all this business? Mrs. Curtis asking for Jacky—and Mr. Curtis not knowing it? What was all this funny business? "Now I tell you," she said; "you and me are just two ladies who understand each other, and I'm going to be straight with you: if Mr. Curtis is trying to get my child away from me, he'll have a sweet time doing it! There's other places than Medfield to live in. I have a friend in New York, a society lady; she's always after me to come and live there. Mind! I'm not mad at *you*, you poor woman that couldn't have a baby—it's him I'm mad at! He knows Jacky is mine, and I'll go to New York before I'll—"

"Oh, don't say that!" Eleanor pleaded; "my husband hasn't tried to get Jacky; it's just I!"

She saw, with panic, that what Maurice had said was true—Lily might "run"! If she did, there would be no hope of getting Jacky ... and Edith would be in Mercer....

"Mrs. Dale, *promise* me you'll stay in Medfield? It was only I who was trying to get Jacky; Mr. Curtis never thought of such a thing! I wanted him. I'd do everything for him; I'd—I'd give him music lessons."

"Honest," said Lily, soberly, "I believe you're crazy."

She looked crazy—this poor, gray-haired woman of pitiful dignity and breeding. ("I bet she's sixty!" Lily thought)—this old, childless woman, with a "Mrs." to her name, pleading with a mother to give up her boy, so he could have "music lessons"! "And Mr. Curtis's up against *that*," Lily thought, and instantly her anger at Maurice ebbed. "There, dear," she said, touching Eleanor's wet cheeks gently with that perfumed handkerchief; "I don't believe you've had any supper. I'm going to get you something to eat—"

"No, please; *please* no!" Eleanor said. She had risen. She thought, "If she says 'dear' again, I'll—I'll die!" ... "I promise you on my word of honor," she said, faintly, "that I won't try to take Jacky away from you, if—" she paused; it was terrible to have a secret with this woman; it put her in her power, but she couldn't help it—"I won't try to get him, if you won't tell Mr. Curtis that I ... have been here? *Please* promise me!"

"Don't you worry," Lily said, reassuringly; "I won't give you away to him."

Eleanor was moving, stumbling a little, toward the door; Lily hesitated, then ran and caught her own coat and hat from the rack in the hall.

"Wait!" she said, pinning her hat on at a hasty and uncertain angle; "I'm going with you! It ain't right for you to go by yourself ... Jacky," she called out to the kitchen, "you be a good boy! Maw'll be home soon."

Eleanor shook her head in wordless protest. But Lily had tucked her hand under her arm, and was walking along beside her. "He ought to look out for you!" Lily said; "I declare, I've a mind to tell that man what I think of him!" On the car, while Eleanor with shaking hands was opening her purse, Lily quickly paid both fares, saying, politely, in answer to Eleanor's confused protest, "*That's* all right!" There was no talk between them. Lily was too perplexed to say anything, and Eleanor was too frightened. So they rode, side by side, almost to Maurice's door. There, standing on the step while Eleanor took her latch key from her pocketbook, Lily said, cheerfully, "Now you go and get a cup of tea—you're all wore out!" Then she hurried off to catch a Medfield car. "I declare," said little Lily, "I don't know which is the worse off, him or her!"

CHAPTER XXXII

Eleanor, letting herself into her silent house, saw, with relief, that the library was dark, and knew that Maurice had gone to the station and she could be alone. She felt her way into the room, blundering against his big chair; the fire was almost out, and without waiting to turn on the light she thrust some kindling under a charred log and knelt down and took up the bellows. A spark brightened, ran backward under the film of ashes, then a flame hesitated, caught—and there was a little winking blaze.

"Another failure," Eleanor said. She remembered with what eager hope she had started for Lily's house; "I was going to 'bring him home' with me! What a fool I was! ... I always fail," she said. Once more, she had "marched up a hill—and—then—marched—down—again"! Her sense of failure was like a dragging weight under her breastbone! She had not made Maurice happy; she had not given him children; she had not kept Edith out of his life. Failure! Failure! "But he loves me; he said so, when I told him I forgave him about Lily. Of course I oughtn't to have married him. But I loved him ... so much. And I did want to have just a little happiness! I never had had any." She sat there, the bellows in her white, ineffectual hands, looking into the fire; how capable Lily's hands were! She remembered the sturdy left hand, and that shiny band of gold ... Then she looked at her own slender wedding ring, and that made her think of the circle of braided grass; and the locust blossoms; and the field—and the children who were to come there on the wedding anniversaries! And now—Maurice's child called another woman "mother"!... Well, she had tried to bring him back to Maurice; tried, and failed, with hideous humiliation—for, instead of bringing Jacky back, this "mother" had brought her back!... "*And she paid my car fare!*" It was intolerable. "I must send her five cents, somehow!"

She sat on the floor, leaning against Maurice's chair, until midnight; the log burned through, broke apart, and smoldered into ashes. Once she put her cheek down on the broad arm of the chair, then kissed it—for his hand had rested on it!—his dear young hand—In the deepening chilliness, watching the ashes, she ached with the sense of her last failure; but most of the time she thought of Edith, and of what she believed she had read in those humorous, candid eyes. "She dared, *before me!*—to show him that she was in love with him! He doesn't care for her—I know that. But I won't have her come here, to my own house, and make love to him. How can I keep her from coming? Oh, if I could only get Jacky!"

But she couldn't get him. She had accepted that as final. The talk in Lily's parlor proved that there was not the slightest hope of getting Jacky. So the only thing for her to do was to keep Edith out of her house. When, at nearly one o'clock, shivering, she went up to her room, she was absorbed in thinking how she could do this. With any other girl it would have been simple enough; never invite her! But not Edith. Edith came without an invitation. Edith had, Eleanor thought, "no delicacy." She had always been that way. She had always lacked ordinary refinement! From the very first, she had run after Maurice. "She is capable of *kissing* him," Eleanor told herself; "and saying she did it because he was like a brother!" Strangely enough, in this blaze of jealousy she had no flicker of resentment at Lily! Lily (now that she had seen her) was to Eleanor merely the woman to whom Jacky belonged. Looking back on those months that followed her discovery of Lily, and contrasting the agony she had felt then with her despair about Edith now, she was faintly surprised at the difference in her pain. This was probably because faithlessness of the body is not so deadly an insult to Love as faithlessness of the mind. But Eleanor did not, of course, make any such explanation. She just said to herself that Maurice had been a boy when he had been untrue to her, and she herself had been, in some ways, to blame; and he had confessed, and been forgiven. So Lily was now of no consequence—except as she interfered with Eleanor's passionate wish to have Jacky. So she did not hate Lily, or fear her (though she was humiliated at that car fare!). But she did hate Edith, and fear of her was agony.... So she would, somehow, keep her out of the house!

Just as she was getting into bed, she wiped her eyes, then cringed at a gust of perfumery—and realized that she had brought Lily's handkerchief back with her! It was a last abasement: the woman's horrible handkerchief. She burst into hysterical weeping.... The next morning, when she came down to breakfast, her face was haggard with those ravaging tears, and with the fatigue of hating. Even before she had her coffee, she burned the scented scrap of machine-embroidered linen, pressing it down between the logs in the library fireplace; but she could not burn her hate; it burned her!

She was so worn out that when, a little before luncheon, Edith suddenly came breezily in, she was, at first, too confused to know what to say to her.... It was an incredibly mild day; on the shady side of the back yard there was still a sooty heap of melting snow, but the sky was turquoise, soaring without a cloud and brimmed with light, so that the shadows of the bare branches of the poplar, clear-cut like jet, crisscrossed on the brick path; in the border, the brown fangs of the tulips had bitten up through the wet earth, and two militant crocuses had raised their tight-furled purple standards. Eleanor, tempted by the sunshine, had come here, muffled up in an elderly white shawl, to sit by the little painted table—built so long ago for Edith's pleasure! She had put old Bingo's basket in the sun, and stroked him gently; he was very helpless now, and ate nothing except from her hands.

"Poor little Bingo!" Eleanor said; "dear little Bingo!" Bingo growled, and Eleanor looked up to see why—Edith was on the iron veranda.

"Hullo!" Edith said, gayly; "isn't it a wonderful day? I just ran in—" She came down the twisted stairway and, unasked and smiling, sat down at the table. "Bingo! Don't you know your friends? One would think I was a burglar! Oh, Eleanor, the tulips are up! Do you remember when Maurice and I planted them?"

Eleanor's throat tightened. She made some gasping assent.

"I came 'round," Edith said—her frank eyes looked straight into Eleanor's eyes, dark and agonized—"I ran in, because I'm afraid you thought, yesterday, that I wanted to quarter myself on you? And I just wanted to say, don't give it a thought! I perfectly understand that sometimes it's inconvenient to have company, and—"

"It's not inconvenient to have company," Eleanor said.

Edith stopped short. ("What a dead give-away!" she thought; "she dislikes me!") Then she tried, generously, to cover the "give-away" up: She said something about guests and servants: "We're having an awful time at Green Hill—servants are the limit! When a maid stays six weeks, we call her an old family retainer!"

Eleanor said, "I have no difficulty with maids. That is not why I prefer not to have ... company."

By this time, of course, Edith's one thought was to get away, with dignity; but dignity, when you've had your face slapped, is almost impossible. So Edith (being Edith!) chose Truth, and didn't trouble herself with dignity! "Eleanor," she said, "I know it's me you don't want. I felt it last night. I'm afraid I've done something that has offended you. Have I? Truly, Eleanor, I haven't meant to! What is it? Let's talk it out. Eleanor, what *have* I done?" She put her hands down on Eleanor's, clasped rigidly on the table.

"Please!" Eleanor said, and drew her hands away.

"Oh," Edith said, pitifully, "you are troubled!"

Eleanor said, with a gasp: "Not at all ... Edith, I am afraid I must ask you to ... excuse me. I'm busy."

Edith was too amazed to speak; she could not, indeed, think of anything to say! This wasn't "dislike." "Why, she *hates* me!" she thought. "Why does she hate me? Shall I not notice it? Shall I talk about something else?" But she could not talk of anything else; she could only speak her swift, honest thought: "Eleanor, why do you dislike me? Maurice and I have been friends—we have been like brother and sister—ever since I can remember. Oh, Eleanor, I want *you* to like me, too! Please don't keep me away from you and Maurice!"

Eleanor said, rapidly: "He's not your brother; and it would be difficult to keep you away from him. You go to his office to find him."

There was a dead silence. Edith grew very pale. At last she understood. Eleanor was jealous ... Of her! They looked at each other, the angry woman and the dumfounded girl. "Jealous? Of *me?*" Edith thought. "Why *me?* Maurice only cares for me as if I was his sister! ... And I don't do Eleanor any harm by—loving him." ... Eleanor was gasping out a torrent of assailing words:

"Girls are different from what they were in my day. Then, they didn't openly run after men! Now, apparently, they do. Certainly *you* do. You always have. I'm not blind, Edith. I have known what was going on; when you were living with us and I had a headache, you used to talk to him, and try and be clever—to make him think I was dull, when it was only that—I was too ill to talk! And you kept him down in the garden until midnight, when he might have been sitting with me on the porch. And you made him go skating. And now you *look* at him! I know what that means. A girl doesn't look that way at a man, unless—"

There was dead silence.

"Unless she's in love with him. But don't think that, though you are in love with him, he cares for *you!* He does not. He cares for no one but me. He told me so."

Silence.

"Can you deny that you care for my husband?" Edith opened her lips—and closed them again. "You don't deny it," Eleanor said; "you *can't.*" She put her head down on her arms on the table; her fifty years engulfed her. She said, in a whisper, "He doesn't love me."

Instantly Edith's arms were around her. "Eleanor, dear! Don't—don't! He does love you—he does! I'd perfectly hate him if he didn't! Oh, Eleanor, poor Eleanor! Don't cry; Maurice *does* love you. He doesn't care a copper for me!" The tears were running down her face. She bent and kissed Eleanor's hands, clenched on the table, and then tried to draw the gray head against her tender young breast.

Eleanor put out frantic hands, as if to push away some suffocating pressure. Both of these women—Lily, with her car fare and her handkerchief; Edith, with her impudent "advice" to Maurice not to have secrets from his wife—pitied her! She would not be pitied by them!

"Don't touch me!" she said, furiously; "*you love my husband.*"

Edith heard her own blood pounding in her ears.

"Don't you?" said Eleanor; her face was furrowed with pain; "Don't you?"

It was a moment of naked truth. "I have loved Maurice," Edith said, steadily, "ever since I was a child. I always shall. I would like to love you, too, Eleanor, if you would let me. But nothing—*nothing!* shall ever break up my ... affection for Maurice."

"You might as well call it love."

Edith, rising, said, very low: "Well, I will call it love. I am not ashamed. I am not wronging you. You have no need to be jealous of me, Eleanor. He cares nothing for me."

Eleanor struck the table with her clenched fists. "You shall never have him!" she said.

Edith turned, silently, and went up the veranda stairs and out of the house.

CHAPTER XXXIII

When Eleanor got her breath, after that crazy outbreak, she rushed up to her own room, bolted the door, fell on her knees at her bedside, and told herself in frantic gasps, that she would *fight* Edith Houghton! Grapple with her! Beat her away from Maurice! "I must *do* something—do something—"

But what? There was only one weapon with which she could vanquish Edith—Maurice's love for his son. *Jacky!* She must have Jacky ...

But how could she get him?

She knew she couldn't get him with Lily's consent. Frantic with jealousy as she was, she recognized that! Yet, over and over, during the week that followed that hour in the garden with Edith, she said to herself, "If Maurice had Jacky, Edith would be nothing to him." ... It was at this point that one day something made her add, "*Suppose he had Lily, too?*" Then he could have Jacky.

"If I were dead, he could marry Lily."

At first this was just one of those vague thoughts that blew through her mind, as straws and dead leaves blow down a dreary street. But this straw caught, so to speak, and more straws gathered and heaped about it. The idea lodged, and another idea lodged with it: If, to get his child, he married Jacky's mother, Edith would never reach him! And if, by dying, Eleanor gave Maurice his child, he would always love her for her gift; she would always be "wonderful." And Edith? Why, he couldn't, he *couldn't*—if his wife died to give him Jacky—think of Edith again! Jacky, Eleanor thought, viciously, "would slam the door in Edith's face!"

Perhaps, if Maurice had been at home, instead of being obliged to prolong that western business trip, the sanity of his presence would have swept the straws and dead leaves away and left Eleanor's mind bleak, of course, with disappointment about Jacky and dread of Edith—but sound. As it was, alone in her melancholy, uncomfortable house, tiny innumerable "reasons" for considering the one way by which Maurice could get Jacky, heaped and heaped above common sense: ten years ago Mrs. Newbolt said that if Eleanor had not "caught" Maurice when he was young, he would have taken Edith; that was a straw. Two years ago a woman in the street car offered her a seat, because she looked as old as *her* mother. Another straw! Lily supposed she was Maurice's mother! A straw.... Edith admitted—had impudently flung into Eleanor's face!—the confession that she was "in love with him!"—and Edith was to be in town for three months. Oh, what a sheaf of straws! Edith would see him constantly. She would "look at him"! Could Maurice stand that? Wouldn't what little love he felt for his old wife go down under the wicked assault of those "looks"?—unless he had Jacky! Jacky would "slam the door."

Eleanor said things like this many times a day. Straws! Straws! And they showed the way the wind was blowing. Sometimes, in the suffocating dust of fear that the wind raised she even forgot her purpose of making Maurice happy, in a violent urge to make it impossible for Edith Houghton to triumph over her. But the other thought—the crazy, nobler thought!— was, on the whole, dominant: "Maurice would be happy if he had a child. I couldn't give him a child of my own, but I can give him Jacky." Yet once in a while she balanced the advantages and disadvantages of the one way in which Jacky could be given: *Lily?* Could Maurice endure Lily? She thought of that parlor, of Lily's vulgarity, of the raucous note in her voice when those flashes of anger pierced like claws through the furry softness of her good nature; she thought of the reek of scent on the handkerchief. Could he endure Lily? Yet she was efficient; she would make him comfortable. "I never made him comfortable," she thought. "And he doesn't love her; so I wouldn't so terribly mind her being here—any more than I'd mind a housekeeper. But I wouldn't want her to call him 'Maurice.' I think I'll put that into my letter to him. I'll say that I will ask, as a last favor, that he will not let her call him 'Maurice.'"

For by this time she had added another straw to the pile of rubbish in her mind: *she would write him a letter.* In it she would tell him that she was going to ... die, so that he could marry Lily and have Jacky! Then came the mental postscript, which would not, of course, be written; she would make it possible for him to marry Lily—*and impossible for him to marry Edith!* And by and by she got so close to her mean and noble purpose—a gift in one dead hand and a sword in the other!—that she began to think of ways and means. How could she die? She couldn't buy morphine without a prescription, and she couldn't possibly get a prescription. But there were other things that people did,—dreadful things! She knew she couldn't do anything "dreadful." Maurice had a revolver in his bureau drawer, upstairs—but she didn't know how to make it "go off"; and if she had known, she couldn't do it; it would be "dreadful." Well; a rope? No! Horrible! She had once seen a picture ... she shuddered at the memory of that picture. *That* was impossible! Sometimes any way—every way!—seemed impossible. Once, wandering aimlessly about the thawing back yard, she stood for a long time at the iron gate, staring at the glimmer, a block away, of the river—"our river," Maurice used to call it. But in town, "their" river—flowing!—flowing! was filmed with oil, and washed against slimy piles, and carried a hideous flotsam of human rubbish; once down below the bridge she had seen a drowned cat slopping back and forth among orange skins and straw bottle covers. The river, in town, was as "dreadful" as those other impossible things! Back in the meadows it was different—brown and clear where it rippled over shallows and lisped around that strip of clean sand, and darkly smooth out in the deep current;—the deep current? Why! *that* was possible! Of course there were "things" in the water that she might step on—slimy, creeping things!—which she was so afraid of. She remembered how afraid she had been that night on the mountain, of snakes. But the water was clean.

She must have stood there a long time; the maids, in the basement laundry, said afterward that they saw her, her white hands clutching the rusty bars of the gate, looking down toward the river, for nearly an hour. Then Bingo whined, and she went into the house to comfort him; and as she stroked him gently, she said, "Yes, ... our river would be possible." But she would get so wet! "My skirts would be wet ..."

So three days went by in profound preoccupation. Her mind was a battlefield, over which, back and forth, reeling and trampling, Love and Jealousy—old enemies but now allies!—flung themselves against Reason, which had no support but Fear. Each day Maurice's friendly letters arrived; one of them—as Jealousy began to rout Reason and Love to cast out Fear— she actually forgot to open! Mrs. Newbolt called her up on the telephone once, and said, "Come 'round to dinner; my new cook is pretty poor, but she's better than yours."

Eleanor said she had a little cold. "Cold?" said Mrs. Newbolt. "My gracious! don't come near *me*! I used to tell your dear uncle I was more afraid of a cold than I was of Satan! He said a cold *was* Satan; and I said—" Eleanor hung up the receiver.

So she was alone—and the wind blew, and the straws and leaves danced over that battlefield of her empty mind, and she said:

"I'll give him Jacky," and then she said, "Our river." And then she said, "But I must hurry!" He had written that he might reach home by the end of the week. "He might come to-night! I must do it—before he comes home." She said that while the March dawn was gray against the windows of her bedroom, and the house was still. She lay in bed until, at six, she heard the creak of the attic stairs and Mary's step as she crept down to the kitchen, the silver basket clattering faintly on her arm. Then she rose and dressed;

once she paused to look at herself in the glass: those gray hairs! ... Edith had called his attention to them so many years ago! It was a long time since it had been worth while to pull them out. ... All that morning she moved about the house like one in a dream. She was thinking what she would say in her letter to him, and wondering, now and then, vaguely, what it would be like, *afterward*? She ate no luncheon, though she sat down at the table. She just crumbled up a piece of bread; then rose, and went into the library to Maurice's desk... She sat there for a long time, making idle scratches on the blotting paper; her elbow on the desk, her forehead in her hand, she sat and scrawled his initials—and hers—and his. And then, after about an hour, she wrote:

> ... I want you to have Jacky. When I am dead you can get him, because you can marry Lily. Of course I oughtn't to have married you, but—

Here she paused for a long time.

> I loved you. I'd rather she didn't call you Maurice. But I want you to have Jacky; so marry her, and you will have him. I am not jealous, you see. You won't call me jealous any more, will you? And, besides, I love little Jacky, too. See that he has music lessons.

Another pause... Many thoughts... Many straws and dead leaves... "Edith will never enter the house, if Lily is here—with Jacky.... Oh—I hate her."

> You will believe I love you, won't you, darling? I wish I hadn't married you; I didn't mean to do you any harm. I just loved you, and I thought I could make you happy. I know now that I didn't. Forgive me, darling, for marrying you...

Again a long pause....

> I don't mind dying at all, if I can give you what you want. And I don't mind your marrying Lily. I am sure she can make good cake—tell her to try that chocolate cake you liked so much. I tried it twice, but it was heavy. I forgot the baking powder. Make her call you "Mr. Curtis." Oh, Maurice—you will believe I love you?—even if I am—

She put her pen down and buried her face in her arms folded on his desk; she couldn't seem to write that word of three letters which she had supposed summed up the tragedy, begun on that June day in the field and ending, she told herself, on this March day, in the same place. So, by and by, instead of writing "old," she wrote

"a poor housekeeper."

Then she pondered on how she should sign the letter, and after a while she wrote:

"STAR."

She looked at the radiant word, and then kissed it. By and by she got up—with difficulty, for she had sat there so long that she was stiff in every joint—and going to her own desk, she hunted about in it for that little envelope, which, for nearly twelve of the fifty golden years which were to find them in "their field," had held the circle of braided grass. When she opened it, and slid the ring out into the palm of her hand it crumbled into dust. She debated putting it back into the envelope and inclosing it in her letter? But a rush of tenderness for Maurice made her say: "No! It might hurt him." So she dropped it down behind the logs in the fireplace. "When the fire is lighted it will burn up." Lily's scented handkerchief had turned to ashes there, too. Then she folded the letter, slipped it into an envelope, sealed it, addressed it, and put it in her desk. "He'll find it," she thought, "*afterward.*" Find it,—and know how much she loved him!—the words were like wine to her. Then she looked at the clock and was startled to see that it was five. She must hurry! He might come home and stop her!...

She was perfectly calm; she put on her coat and hat and opened the front door; then saw the gleam of lights on the wet pavement and felt the March drizzle in her face; she reflected that it would be very wet in the meadow, and went back for her rubbers.

When the car came banging cheerfully along, she boarded it and sat so that she would be able to see Lily's house. "She's getting his supper," Eleanor thought; "dear little Jacky! Well, he will be having his supper with Maurice pretty soon! I wonder how she'll get along with Mary? Mary will call her 'Mrs. Curtis,' Mary would leave in a minute if she knew what kind of a person 'Mrs. Curtis' was!" She smiled at that; it pleased her. "But she mustn't call him 'Maurice,'" she thought; "I won't permit *that!*"

The car stopped, and all the other passengers got out. Eleanor vaguely watched the conductor pull the trolley pole round for the return trip; then she rose hurriedly. As she started along the road toward the meadow she thought. "I can walk into the water; I never could jump in! But it will be easy to wade in." That made her think of the picnic, and the wading, and how Maurice had tied Edith's shoestrings; and with that came a surge of triumph. "When he reads my letter, and knows how much I love him, he'll forget her. And when she hears he has married Lily, she'll stop making love to him by getting him to tie her shoestrings!"

It was quite dark by this time, and chilly; she had meant to sit down for a while, with her back against the locust tree, and think how, *at last*, he was going to realize her love! But when she reached the bank of the river she stooped and felt the winter-bleached grass, and found it so wet with the small, fine rain which had begun to fall, that she was afraid to sit down. "I'd add to my cold," she thought. So she stood there a long time, looking at the river, leaden now in the twilight. "How it glittered that day!" she thought. Suddenly, on a soft wind of memory, she seemed to smell the warm fragrance of the clover, and hear again her own voice, singing in the sunshine—

"Through the clear windows of the morning!"

"I'll leave my coat on the bank," she said; "but I'll wear my hat; it will keep my hair from getting messy. ... Oh, Maurice mustn't let her call him 'Maurice'! I wish I'd made that clearer in my letter. Why didn't I tell him to give her that five cents? ... I wonder how many 'minutes' we have had now? We had had fifty-four, that Day. I wish I had calculated, and put the number in the letter. No, that might have made him feel badly. I don't want to hurt him; I only want him to know that I love him enough to die to make him happy. Oh—will it be cold?"

It was then that she took, slowly, one step—and stood still. And another—and paused. Her heart began to pound suffocatingly in her throat, and suddenly she knew that she was afraid! She had not known it; fear had not entered into her plans; just love—and Maurice; just hate—and Edith! Nor had "Right" or "Wrong" occurred to her. Now, old instincts rose up. People called this "wicked"? So, if she was going to do it, she must do it quickly! She mustn't get to thinking or she might be afraid to do it, because it would be "wicked." She unfastened her coat, then fumbled with her hat, pinning it on firmly; she was saying, aloud: "Oh—oh—oh—it's wicked. But I must. Oh—my skirts will get wet ... 'Kiss thy perfumed garments' ... No; I'll hold them up. Oh—oh—" And as she spoke her crazy purpose drove her forward; she held back against it—but, like the pressure of a hand upon her shoulder, it pushed her on down the bank—slowly—slowly— her heels digging into the crumbling clay, her hands clutching now at a tuft of grass, now at a drooping branch; she was drawing quick breaths of terror, and talking, in little gasps, aloud: "He'll forget Edith. He'll have Jacky. He'll know how much I love him...." So, over the pebbles, out on to the spit of sand; on—on—until she reached the river's edge. She stood there for a minute, listening to the lisping chatter of the current. Very slowly, she stepped in, and was ankle deep in shallow water,—then stopped short—the water soaked through her shoes, and suddenly she felt it, like circling ice, around her ankles! Aloud, she said, "Maurice,—I give you Jacky. But don't let Lily call you—" She stepped on, into the stream; one step—two—three. It was still shallow. "Why doesn't it get *deep*?" she said, angrily; another step and the water was halfway to her knees; she felt the force of the current and swayed a little; still another step—above her knees now! and the *rip*, tugging and pulling at her floating skirts. It was at the next step that she slipped, staggered, fell full length—felt the water gushing into the neck of her dress, running down her back, flowing between her breasts; felt her sleeves drenched against her arms; she sprang up, fell again, her head under water, her face scraping the pebbly sharpness of the river bed,—again got on to her feet and ran choking and coughing, stumbling and slipping, back to the sand-spit, and the shore. There she stood, soaking wet, gasping. Her hat was gone, her hair dripping about her face. "*I can't*," she said.

She climbed up the bank, catching at the grass and twigs, and feeling her tears running hot over the icy wetness of her cheeks. When she reached the top she picked up her coat with numb, shaking hands and, shivering violently, put it on with a passionate desire for warmth.

"I tried; I *tried*," she said; "but—I can't!"

CHAPTER XXXIV

It was after ten o'clock that night when Eleanor's icy fingers fumbled at Mrs. Newbolt's doorbell. The ring was not heard at first, because her aunt and Edith Houghton and Johnny Bennett were celebrating his departure the next day for South America, by making a Welsh rabbit in a chafing dish before the parlor fire. Mrs. Newbolt, entering into the occasion with voluble reminiscences, was having a very good time. She liked Youth, and she liked Welsh rabbits, and she liked an audience; and she had all three! Then the doorbell rang. And again.

"For Heaven's sake!" said Mrs. Newbolt; "at this time of night! Johnny, the girls have gone to bed; you go and answer it, like a good boy."

"Dump in some more beer, Edith," Johnny commanded, and went out into the hall, whistling. A moment later the other two heard his startled voice, "Why, come right in!" There was no reply, just shuffling steps; then Eleanor, silent, without any hat, her hair plastered down her ghastly cheeks, her face bruised and soiled with sand, stood in the doorway, the astonished John Bennett behind her. Everybody spoke at once:

"Eleanor! What has happened?"

"*Eleanor!* Where is your hat?"

"Good gracious! Eleanor—"

She was perfectly still. Just looking at them, during that blank moment before everything became a confusion of jostling assistance. Edith rushed to help her off with her coat. Johnny said, "Mrs. Newbolt, where can I get some whisky?" Mrs. Newbolt felt the soaking skirt, and tried to unfasten the belt so that the wet mass might fall to the floor.

Eleanor was rigid. "Get a doctor!" Edith commanded.

Johnny ran to the telephone.

"No," Eleanor whispered.

But nobody paid any attention to her. Johnny, at the telephone, was telling Mrs. Newbolt's doctor to *hurry*! Mrs. Newbolt herself had run, wheezing, to open the spare-room bed and get out extra blankets, and fill hot-water bottles; then, somehow or other, she and Edith got Eleanor upstairs, undressed her, put her into the big four-poster, and held a tumbler of hot whisky and water to her lips. By the time Doctor James arrived she had begun to shiver violently; but she was still silent. The trolley ride into town, with staring passengers and a conductor who thought she had been drinking, and tried to be jocose, had chilled her to the bone, and the gradual dulling of thought had left only one thing clear to her: She mustn't go home, because Maurice might possibly be there! And if he was, then he would *know*! So she must go—somewhere. She went first to Mrs. O'Brien's, climbing the three long flights of stairs and feeling her way along dark entries to the old woman's door. She stood there shuddering and knocking; a single gas jet, wavering in the draughty entry, made her shadow lurch on the cracked plaster of the wall; it occurred to her that she would like to put her frozen hands around the little flame to warm them. Then she knocked again. There was no answer, so, shaking from head to foot, she felt her way downstairs again to the street, where the reflection of an occasional gas lamp gleamed and flickered on the wet asphalt. "I'll go to Auntie's," she thought.

She had just one purpose—to get warm! But she was so dazed that she could never remember how she reached Mrs. Newbolt's; probably she walked, for there were no cabs in that part of town and no car line passed Mrs. Newbolt's door. The time after she left Mrs. O'Brien's was a blank. Even when she had swallowed the hot whisky, and began to feel warmer, she was still mentally benumbed, and couldn't remember what she had done. She did not notice Johnny Bennett; she saw Edith, but did not, apparently, understand that she was staying in the house. When the doctor came she was as silent to him as to everybody else.

He asked no questions. "Keep her warm," he said, "and don't talk to her."

Mrs. Newbolt, going to the door with him, palpitating with fright, said, "*We* don't know a thing more about what's happened than you do! She just appeared, drippin', wet!"

"She has evidently fallen into some water," he said; "but I wouldn't ask her about it, yet. Of course we don't know what the result will be, Mrs. Newbolt. I can't help saying I'm anxious. Mr. Curtis had better be sent for. Telegraph him in the morning." He went off, thinking to himself, "She must have gone into the country to do it. If she'd tried the river, here, and scrambled out, she wouldn't have been so frightfully chilled. I wonder what's up?"

Everybody wondered what was up, but Eleanor did not enlighten them; so the three interrupted revelers could do nothing but think. Johnny's thoughts, as he sat down in the parlor among the Welsh-rabbit plates, keeping the fire up, and waiting in case he might be needed, were even briefer than the doctor's: "Tried to commit suicide."

Edith, standing in the upper hall, listening to Mrs. Newbolt at Eleanor's bedside, exclaiming, and repeating her dear mother's ideas about catching cold, and offering more hot-water bottles, had her thoughts: "I won't go into the room—she would hate to see me! The doctor said she had fallen into some water. Did she—do it on purpose? Oh, *was* it my fault?" Edith's heart pounded with terror: "Was it what I said to her in the garden that made her do it?"

Mrs. Newbolt, in a blue-flannel dressing gown, and in and out of the spare room with sibilant whispers of anxiety, had, for once, more thoughts than words; her words were only, "I've always expected it!" But her thoughts would have filled volumes! Mrs. Newbolt had put her hair in order for the night, and now her crimping pins made the shadow of her head, bobbing on the ceiling, look like a gigantic spider.

Eleanor had just one hazy thought: "I tried ... I tried—and I failed."

Other people, however, didn't feel so sure that she had failed. She "looks like death," Mrs. Newbolt told Edith the next morning. "We've got to find Maurice! Edith, why do you suppose she—did it?"

"Oh, but she *didn't!*" Edith said. "What sense would there be—"

"Don't talk about 'sense'! Eleanor never had any. I've telegraphed your mother to come. I wonder how Bingo is? She understands her. The ashman has broken my new ash barrel; I don't know what this country is comin' to!"

Then she went upstairs to try to understand Eleanor herself. "Eleanor, what happened?"

"Nothing. I'm going home this afternoon."

"Indeed you are not! You're not goin' out of this house till Maurice comes and gets you! *What* happened?" she demanded again.

"I fell. Into some water."

"How could you 'fall'? And what 'water'?"

"I had gone out to the river—up in Medfield. To—take a walk; and I ... slipped...."

"Now, Eleanor, look here; if I have a virtue, it's candor, and I'll tell you why; it saves time. That's what my dear father used to say: 'Lyin' wastes time.' I know what you tried to do; and it was very wicked."

"But I didn't do it!"

"You tried to. If you and Maurice have quarreled, I'll stand by *you*."

Eleanor covered her face with her hands—and Mrs. Newbolt burst out, "He's treated you badly! You needn't try to deceive me,—he's been flirtin' with some woman?" Her pale, prominent eyes snapped with anger.

"Oh, Auntie, don't! He hasn't! Only, I—wanted to make him happier; and so I—" She broke into furious crying. Despairing crying.

Instantly Mrs. Newbolt was all frightened solicitude. "There! Don't cry! Have a hot-water bag. They say there's a new kind on the market. I must get a new pair of rubbers. Your face is awfully bruised. He's puffectly happy! He worships the ground you walk on! Eleanor, don't cry. How's your cold? The ashman—"

Eleanor, gasping, said her cold was better, and repeated her determination of going home.

It was the doctor—dropping in, he said, to make sure Mrs. Curtis was none the worse for her "accident"—who put a stop to that.

"I slipped and fell," Eleanor told him; she was very hoarse.

He said yes, he understood. "But you got badly chilled, and you had a cold to start with. So you must lie low for two or three days. When will Mr. Curtis be back?"

Eleanor said she didn't know; all she knew was she didn't want him sent for. She was "all right."

But of course he had been sent for! "I don't know that it was really necessary," Mrs. Newbolt told Mrs. Houghton, who appeared late in the afternoon; "but I wasn't goin' to take the responsibility—"

"Of course not!" Mrs. Houghton said. "Mr. Weston has telegraphed him, too, I hope?" Then, before taking her things off, she went upstairs to Eleanor. "Well!" she said, "I hear you had an accident? Sensible girl, to stay in bed!" She took Eleanor's hand, and its hot tremor made her look keenly at the haggard face on the pillow.

"Oh," Eleanor said, with a gasp of relief, "I'm so glad you're here! There are some things I want attended to. I owe—I mean, somebody paid my car fare. And I *must* send it to her! And then I want something from my desk; but I can't have Bridget get it, and I don't want to ask Auntie to. It's—it's a letter to Maurice. I wanted to tell him something.... But I've changed my mind. I don't want him to see it. He mustn't see it! Oh, Mrs. Houghton, would you get it for me? I'd be *so* grateful! ... And then,—oh, that five cents! I don't know how I'm going to send it to her—"

"Tell me who it is, and I'll get it to her; and I'll get the letter," Mary Houghton told her; and went on with the usual sick-room encouragement: "The doctor says you are better. But you must hurry and get well, so as to help Maurice with the little boy!"

Her words were like a push against some tottering barrier.

"I tried to help him; I tried to get Jacky! I went to the woman's, but she wouldn't give him to me! I *tried*—so hard. But she wouldn't! She paid my car fare—"

Mrs. Houghton bent over and kissed her: "Tell me about it, dear; perhaps I can help."

"There is no help! ... She won't give him up. She insisted on coming home with me, and she paid my car fare! Then I thought, if—I were not alive, Maurice could get him, because he could marry her ..."

Instantly, with a thrill of horror and admiration, Mrs. Houghton understood the "accident"! "Eleanor! What a mad, mad thought! As if you could help Maurice by giving him a great grief! Oh, I do thank God he has been spared anything so terrible!"

"But," Eleanor said, excitedly, "if I were dead, it would be his duty to marry her, wouldn't it? Jacky is his child! Oughtn't he to marry Jacky's mother? Oh, Mrs. Houghton, I owe her five cents—"

The older woman was trembling, but she spoke calmly: "Eleanor, dear, you must live for Maurice, not—die for him."

"Promise me," said Eleanor, "you won't tell him?"

"Of course I won't!" said Mrs. Houghton, with elaborate cheerfulness. She kissed her, and went downstairs, feeling very queer in her knees. She paused at the parlor door to say to Mrs. Newbolt and Edith that she was going out to do an errand for Eleanor; "I hope Maurice will get back soon," she said. "I don't like Eleanor's looks." Then she went to get that letter which Maurice "must not see." As she walked along the street she was still tingling with the shock of having her own theories brought home to her. "Thank God," Mary Houghton said, "that nothing happened!"

The maid who opened the door at Maurice's house was evidently excited, but not about her mistress. "Oh, Mrs. Houghton!" she said, "we done our best, but he wouldn't take a bite!—and I declare I don't know what Mrs. Curtis will say. He just *wouldn't* eat, and this morning he up and died—and me offering him a chop!" Bridget wept with real distress. "Mrs. Houghton, please tell her we done our best; he just smelled his chop—and died. You see, he hasn't eat a thing, without she gave it to him, for—oh, more 'n a month!"

Mary Houghton went into the library, where the fire was out, and the dust on tables and chairs bore witness to the fact that Bridget had devoted herself to Bingo; the room was gloomy, and smelled of soot. Little Bingo lay, stiff and chill, on the sofa; on a plate beside him was a chop rimmed in cold grease,—poor little, loving, jealous, old Bingo! "I hope it won't upset Mrs. Curtis," Mrs. Houghton told the maid; then gave directions about the stark little body. She found the letter in Eleanor's desk, and went back to Mrs. Newbolt's. "Love," she thought, "*is* as strong as death; stronger! Bingo—and Eleanor."

CHAPTER XXXV

Maurice, followed by telegrams that never quite overtook him, did, some forty-eight hours later, get the news that Eleanor had "had an accident," and was at Mrs. Newbolt's, who thought he had "better return immediately." His business was not quite finished, but it did not need Mr. Weston's laconic wire, "Drop Greenleaf matters and come back," to start him on the next train for Mercer. He had been away nearly two weeks—two terrible weeks, of facing himself; two weeks of rebellion, and submission; of tumultuous despair and quiet acceptance. He had looked faithfully—and very shrewdly—into the "Greenleaf matters"; he had turned one or two sharp corners, with entirely honest cleverness, and he was taking back to Mercer some concessions which old Weston had slipped up on! Yes, he had done a darned good job, he told himself, lounging in the smoking compartment of one parlor car or another, or strolling up and down station platforms for a breath of air. And all the while that he was on the Greenleaf job—in Pullmans, sitting in hotel lobbies writing letters, looking through title and probate records—his own affairs raced and raged in his thoughts; they were summed up in one word: "Edith." He could not get away from Edith! He tripped a Greenleaf trustee into an admission (and he thought, "so long as she never suspects that I love her, there's no harm in going along as we always have"). Then he conceded a point to the Greenleaf interests (and said to himself, "her hair on her shoulders that day on the lawn was like a nimbus around the head of a saint. How she'd hate that word 'saint'!"). His chuckle made one of the Greenleaf heirs think that Weston's representative was a good sort;—"pleasant fellow!" But Maurice, looking "pleasant," was thinking: "I'd about sell my soul to kiss her hair ... Oh, I *must* stop this kind of thing! I swear it's worse than the Lily and Jacky business...." Then he signed a deed, and the Greenleaf people felt they had made a good thing of it—but Maurice's telegram that the deed was signed, caused rejoicing in the Weston office! "Curtis got ahead of 'em!" said Mr. Weston. While he was writing that triumphant telegram Maurice was wondering: "Was John Bennett a complete idiot? ... If things had been different would Edith have ... cared?" For himself, he, personally, didn't care "a damn," whether

Weston got ahead of Greenleaf or Greenleaf beat Weston. His own affairs engrossed him: "my job," he was telling himself, "is to see that Eleanor doesn't suffer any more, poor girl! And Edith shall never know. And I'll make a decent man of Jacky—not a fool, like his father." So he wrote his victorious dispatch, and the Weston office congratulated itself.

Maurice had been very grateful for his fortnight of absence from everybody, except the Greenleaf heirs; grateful for a solitude of trains and lawyers' offices. Because, in solitude, he could, with entirely hopeless courage, face the future. He was facing it unswervingly the day he reached Chicago, where he was to get some final signatures; he came into the warm lobby of the hotel, glad to escape the rampaging lake wind, and while he was registering the hotel clerk produced the telegrams which had been held for him. The first, from Mr. Weston, "Drop Greenleaf," bewildered him until he read the other, "Eleanor has had an accident." Then he ran his pen through his name, asked for a time-table, and sent a peremptory wire to Mrs. Newbolt saying that he was on his way home, and asking that full particulars be telegraphed to him at a certain point on his journey. "Let me know just what happened, and how she is," he telegraphed. "It must be serious," he thought, "to send for me!"

It was hardly an hour before he was on a train for another day of travel, during which he experienced the irritation common to all of us when we receive an alarming dispatch, devoid of details. "Economizing on ten cents! What kind of an 'accident'? How serious is it? When was it? Why didn't they let me know before?" and so on; all the futile, anxious, angry questions which a man asks himself under such circumstances. But suddenly, while he was asking these questions, another question whispered in his mind; a question to which he would not listen, and which he refused to answer; but again and again, over and over, it repeated itself, coming, it seemed, on the rhythmical roll of the wheels—the wheels which were taking him back to Eleanor! "If—if—if—" the wheels hammered out; "*if* anything happens to Eleanor—"? He never finished that sentence, but the beginning of it actually frightened him. "Am I as low as this?" he said, frantically, "speculating on the possibility of anything happening to her?" But he was not so low as that—he only heard the jar of the wheels: "If—if—if—if—"

When he reached the station to which he had told Mrs. Newbolt to reply, he rushed out of the car into the telegraph office, and clutched at the message before the operator could put it into its flimsy brown envelope; as he read it he said under his breath, "Thank God!" It was from Mary Houghton:

Accident slight. Slipped into water. All right now except bad cold.

Maurice's hand shook as he folded the message and stuffed it into his pocket. He had the sense of having escaped from a terror—the terror of intolerable remorse. For if she had not been "all right," if, instead of just "a bad cold," the dispatch had said "something had happened"!—then, for all the rest of his life he would have had to remember how the wheels had beaten out that terrible refrain: "If—if—if—"

So he said, "Thank God."

All that day, while Maurice was hurrying back to Mercer, Eleanor lay very still, and when Mrs. Newbolt or Mrs. Houghton came into the room she closed her eyes and pretended to be asleep. Edith did not come into the room; so, in a hazy way, Eleanor took it for granted that she had left the house. "I should think she would!" Eleanor thought; "she could hardly have the face to stay in the same house with me." But she did not think much about Edith; she was absorbed in deciding what she should say to Maurice. Should she tell him the truth?—or some silly story of a walk to their meadow? The two alternatives flew back and forth in her mind like shuttlecocks. There was one thing she felt sure of: that letter—which Mrs. Houghton had brought from her desk, which Maurice was to have read when she had done what she set out to do, but which now she kept clutched in her hand, or hidden under her pillow—*Maurice must not see that letter!* If he read it, now, while she was (she told herself) still half sick from those drenched hours of the trolley ride and the dark wanderings from Mrs. O'Brien's to Mrs. Newbolt's, the whole thing would seem simply ridiculous. Some time, he must know that she loved him enough to buy Jacky for him, by dying—or trying to die! She would tell him, *some time*; because her purpose (even if it had failed) would measure the heights and depths of her love as nothing else could; but he must not know it now, because she hadn't carried it out. That first night, when she had found herself safe and warm (oh, warm! She had thought she never would be warm any more!)—when she had found herself in Mrs. Newbolt's spare room in the four-poster with its chintz hangings and its great soft pillows, she had been glad she had not carried it out. Glad not to be dead. As she lay there, shivering slowly into delicious comfort, and fending off Mrs. Newbolt's distracted questions, she had had occasional moments of a sense of danger escaped; perhaps it *would* have been wrong to—to lie down there in the river? People call it wicked Mrs. Newbolt, for a single suspicious instant ("She forgot it right off," Eleanor said; "she just thought we'd quarreled!"); but Mrs. Newbolt had said it was "wicked." "But I didn't do it!" Eleanor told herself in a rush of gratitude. She hadn't been "wicked"! Instead, she was in Mrs. Newbolt's spare room, looking dreamily at the old French clock on the mantelpiece, whose tarnished gilt face glimmered between two slender black-marble columns; sometimes she counted the tick-tock of the slowly swinging pendulum; sometimes, toward dawn, she watched the foggy yellow daylight peer between the red rep curtains; but counting, and looking, and drowsing, she was glad to be alive. It was not until the next afternoon that she began to be faintly mortified at being alive. It was then that she had felt that she *must* get that letter— Maurice mustn't see it! Little by little, humiliation at her failure to be heroic, grew acute. Maurice wouldn't know that she loved him enough to give him Jacky; he would just know that she was silly. She had got wet; and had a cold in her head. Snuffles—not Death. He might—*laugh*!... It was then that she implored Mrs. Houghton to get the letter out of her desk.

Yet when it was given to her she held it in her hand under the bedclothes, saying to herself that she would not destroy it, yet, because, even though she *had* failed, there might come a time when it would prove to Maurice how much she loved him. She was so absorbed in this thought that she did not grieve much for Bingo. "Poor little Bingo," she said, vaguely, when Mrs. Houghton told her that the little dog was dead; "he was so jealous." Now, with Maurice coming nearer every hour, she could not think of Bingo; she was face to face with a decision! What should she tell him about the "accident"?

It was in the afternoon of the day that Maurice was to arrive,—he had telegraphed that he would reach Mercer in the evening;—that she had a sudden panic about Edith. "She was here that night and saw me. I know she laughed at me because I hadn't any hat on! She may—suspect? If she does, she'll tell him! What shall I do to stop her?" She couldn't think of any way to stop her! She couldn't hold her thoughts steady enough to reach a decision. First would come gladness of her own comfort and safety, and the warm, warm bed; then shame, that she had faltered and run away from a chance to do a great thing for Maurice; then terror that Edith would make her ridiculous to Maurice. Then all these thoughts would whirl about, run backward: First, terror of Edith! then shame! then comfort! Suddenly the terror thought held fast with a question. "Suppose I make her promise not to tell Maurice anything? I think she would keep a promise...." It would be dreadful to ask the favor of secrecy of Edith—just as she had asked the same sort of favor of Lily—but to seem silly to Maurice would be more dreadful than to ask a favor! She held to this purpose of humiliating self-protection, long enough to ask Mrs. Houghton when Edith was coming down from Green Hill.

"Why, she's here, now, in the house!" Edith's mother said.

"*Here?*" Eleanor said, despairingly. If Edith was here, then Maurice, when he came, would see her and she would tell him! "She would make a funny story of it," Eleanor thought; "I know her! She would make him laugh. I can't bear it! ... I would like to speak to Edith," she told Mrs. Houghton, faintly.

Edith, summoned by her mother, stood for a rigid moment outside Eleanor's door, trying to get herself in hand. In these anxious days, Edith's youth had been threatened by assailing waves of a remorse that at times would have engulfed it altogether, but for that unflinching reasonableness which made her the girl she was. "It may be," Edith had said to herself; "it *may* be that what I said to her in the garden made her so angry that she tried to kill herself; but why should it have made her angry? I didn't injure her. Besides, she dragged it out of me! I couldn't lie. She said, 'You love him.' I *would* not lie, and say I didn't! But what harm did it do her?" So she reasoned; but reason did not keep her from suffering. "Did *I* drive her to it?" Edith said, over and over. So when her mother told her Eleanor wanted to speak to her, she grew a little pale. When she entered Eleanor's room her heart was beating so hard she felt smothered, but she was perfectly matter of fact. "Anything I can do for you, Eleanor?" she said. She stood at the foot of the bed, holding on to the carved bed post.

Eleanor looked at her for a silent moment, then gathered herself together. "Edith," she said (she was very hoarse and spoke with difficulty), "I don't want to bother Maurice about—about my accident. So I am going to ask you, please, not to refer to it to him. Not to tell him anything about it. *Anything.* Promise me."

"Of course I won't!" Edith said. As she spoke she forgot herself in pity for the scared, haggard face. ("Oh, *was* it my fault?" she thought, with a real pang.) And before she knew it her coldness was all gone and she was at Eleanor's side; she sat down on the edge of the bed and caught her hand impulsively. "Eleanor," she said, "I've been awfully unhappy, for fear anything I said—that morning—troubled you? Of course there was no sense in talking that way, for either of us. So please forgive me! Was it what I said, that made you—that bothered you, I mean? I'm so unhappy," Edith said, and caught her lip between her teeth to keep it steady; her eyes were bright with tears. "Eleanor, truly I am *nothing* to—to anybody. Nobody cares a copper for me! Do be kind to me. Oh—I've been awfully unhappy; and I'm *so* glad you're better."

Instantly the smoldering fire broke into flame: "I'm *not* better," Eleanor said, "and you wouldn't be glad if I were."

It was as if she struck her hand upon those generous young lips. Edith sprang to her feet. "Eleanor!"

Eleanor sat up in bed, her hands behind her, propping her up; her cheeks were dully red, her eyes glowing. "All this talk about making me unhappy means nothing at all. You have always made me unhappy. And as for anybody's caring for you—they *don't*; you are quite right about that. Quite right! And I want to tell you something else: If anything happens to me, I *want* Maurice to marry again. But he won't marry you."

"Eleanor," Edith said, "you wouldn't say such a thing, or think such a thing, if you weren't sick. I'm sorry I came in. I'll go right away, and—"

"No," she said; "don't go away,"—her arms had begun to tremble with strain of supporting her, she spoke in whispered gasps: "I am going to speak," she said; "I prefer to speak. I want you to know that if I die—"

"You are not going to die! You are going to get well."

"Will you *please* not keep interrupting? It is so hard for me to get my breath. I want you to know that he will marry—that Dale woman. Because it is right that he should. Because of the little boy. His little boy."

Edith was dumb.

"So you see, he can't marry *you*," Eleanor said, and fell back on her pillows, her eyes half closed.

There was a long silence, just the ticking of the Empire clock and the faint snapping of the fire. Edith felt as if some iron hand had gripped her throat. For a moment it was impossible for her to speak; then the words came quietly: "Eleanor, I'm glad you told me this. You are going to get well, and I'm glad, *glad* that you are! But I must tell you: If anything had happened to you, I would have moved heaven and earth to have kept Maurice from marrying that woman. Oh, Eleanor, how can you say you love him, and yet plan such terrible unhappiness for him?"

She turned and ran out of the room, up another flight of stairs to her own bedroom. There she fell down on her bed and lay tense and rigid, her face hidden in her hands. This, then, was what Maurice had meant? She saw again the wood path, and the tall fern breaking under Maurice's racquet; she saw the flecks of sunshine on the moss—she heard him say he "hadn't played the game with Eleanor." Oh, he hadn't, he hadn't! Then she thought of the Dale woman. The accident on the river. The stumble at the gate and of Maurice's child in Lily's arms. "Oh, poor Eleanor! poor Eleanor! ... All the same, she is wicked, to be so cruel to him. She is taking her revenge. Jealousy has made her wicked. But, oh, I wish I hadn't hurt her in the garden! But how *could* Maurice—that little, common woman! How *could* he?" She shook with sobs: "Poor, poor Eleanor ..."

Eleanor, on her big bed, lay panting with anger and fright. "*Now* she'll know I'm hiding something from him!" she thought; "I've put myself in her power by having a secret with her; just as I put myself in Lily's power by asking her not to tell Maurice I had been there. Well, Edith is in *my* power!— because I've made her know he'll never care for her. And she'll keep her word; she'll not tell him about the river."

The relief of this was so great that she could almost forget her humiliation; she gave herself up to thinking what she herself must do to keep Maurice in ignorance. "Auntie will be sure to say something. But he knows how silly she is. She thought we'd quarreled, and that I had tried ... I might tell Maurice that? And he'll make fun of her, and won't believe anything she says! I might say that I went out to—to see our river, and slipped and got wet, and that Auntie thought we'd quarreled, and that I had ... had tried to ... to—And he'll say, 'What a joke!' But maybe he'll say, 'Why did you go out to Medfield so late?' And I'll say, 'Oh, well, I got delayed.' ... Yes, that's the thing to do."

So, around and around, her poor, frantic thoughts raced and trampled one another. When Mrs. Newbolt interrupted them with a tray and some supper, Eleanor, with eyes closed, motioned her away: "My head aches. I can't eat anything. I'm going to try and get a little sleep."

By and by, through sheer fatigue, she did drowse, and when the wheels of Maurice's cab grated against the curb, she was asleep.

Edith, upstairs in her own room, heard the front door close sharply. "I *can't* see him!" she said; "I mustn't see him." But she wanted to see him; she wanted to say to him: "Maurice, you can make it all up to Eleanor! You can make her happy. *Don't* despair about it—we'll all help you make it up to her!" She wanted to say: " Oh, Maurice, you *will* conquer. I know you will!" If she could only see him and tell him these things! "If I didn't love him, I could," she thought....

Maurice came hurrying into the parlor, with the anxious, "How is she?" on his lips; and Mrs. Newbolt and Mrs. Houghton were full of reassurances, and suggestions of food, which he negatived promptly. "Tell me about Eleanor! What happened?"

"She's asleep," Mrs. Newbolt said. "You must have something to eat—" She was in such a panic of uncertainty as to what must and must not be said to Maurice that she clutched at supper as a perfectly safe topic. "I—I—I'll go and see about your supper," said Mrs. Newbolt, and trundled off to hide herself in the dining room.

Mary Houghton could not hide, but she would have been glad to! "Eleanor is sleepy, now, Maurice," she said; "but she'll want to have just a glimpse of you—"

"I'll go right up!"

"Maurice, wait one minute. If I were you, I wouldn't get Eleanor to talking, to-night; she's a little feverish—"

"Mrs. Houghton!" he broke in, "Eleanor's all right, isn't she?" His face was furrowed with alarm. (If that wicked rhythm of the wheels should begin again!)

"Oh yes; I—I think so. She hasn't quite got over the shock yet, but—"

"What shock? Nobody's told me yet what it was! Your dispatch only said she'd slipped into the water. What water?"

"We don't really know," said Mrs. Houghton; "and she mustn't be worried with questions, the doctor says. You see, she got dripping wet, somehow, and then had a long trolley ride—and she had a cold to start with—"

"I'll just crawl upstairs, and see if she's awake," said Maurice. "I won't disturb her."

As he started softly upstairs, Mrs. Newbolt opened the dining-room door a crack, and peered in at Mary Houghton. "Did you tell him?" she said, in a wheezing whisper.

Mrs. Houghton shook her head.

"Well, I can tell you who won't tell him," said Eleanor's aunt; "me! To tell a man that his wife—"

"Hush-sh!" said Mrs. Houghton; "he's coming downstairs. Besides, we don't know that she did—"

The dining-room door closed softly on the whispered words: "Puffect nonsense. Of course we know."

Maurice, tiptoeing into Eleanor's room, thought she was asleep, and was backing out again, when she opened drowsy eyes and said, faintly, "Hullo."

He bent over to kiss her. "Well, you're a great girl, to cut up like this when I'm away from home!"

She smiled, closed her eyes, and he tiptoed out of the room....

Back again in the parlor, he began, "Mrs. Houghton, for Heaven's sake, tell me the whole thing!" He wasn't anxious now; as far as he could see, Eleanor was "all right"—just sleepy. But what on earth—

She told him what she knew; what she suspected, she kept to herself. But she might as well have told it all. For, as he listened, his face darkened with understanding.

"The river? In Medfield? But, why—?"

"Edith says you and she had a good deal of sentiment about the river, and—"

"At six o'clock, on a March evening?" said Maurice. He put his hands in his pockets and began to walk up and down. Mrs. Houghton had nothing more to say; the room was so silent that the dining-room door opened a furtive crack—then closed quickly! Mrs. Houghton began to talk about Maurice's journey, and Maurice asked whether Eleanor could be taken home the next day—at which the dining-room door opened broadly, and Mrs. Newbolt said:

"If you ask *me*, I'd say 'no'! If you want to know what I think, I think she's got a temperature! And she oughtn't to stir out of this house till it's normal."

"Mrs. Newbolt," said Maurice, pausing in his tramping up and down the room; "why did Eleanor go out to Medfield?"

"Perhaps she was lookin' for a cook! I—I think I'll go to bed!" said Mrs. Newbolt—and almost ran out of the room.

Maurice looked down at Mrs. Houghton, and laughed, grimly: "You might as well tell me?"

"My dear fellow, we have nothing to tell! We don't know anything—except that Eleanor has added to her cold, and is very nervous," She paused; could she give him an idea of the extent of Eleanor's "nervousness," and yet not tell him what they all felt sure of? "Why, Maurice," she said; "just to show you how hysterical Eleanor is, she told me—" Mrs. Houghton dropped her voice, and looked toward the dining-room door; but Mrs. Newbolt's ponderous step made itself heard overhead. "She said—Oh, Maurice, this is too foolish to repeat; but it just shows how Eleanor loves you. She implied that she didn't want to get well, so that you could—could get the little boy, by marrying his mother!"

Maurice sat down and stared at her, open-mouthed. "*Marry?* I, marry Lily?" He actually gasped under the impact of a perfectly new idea; then he said, very softly, "Good God."

Mrs. Houghton nodded. "Her one thought," she said (praying that, without breaking her word to Eleanor, and betraying what was so terribly Eleanor's own affair, she might make Maurice's heart so ready for the pathos that he would not be repelled by the folly), "her one desire is that you should have your little boy."

Maurice walked over to the fireplace and kicked two charred pieces of wood together between the fire irons. In the crash of Mary Houghton's calm words, the rhythm of the wheels was permanently silenced.

It was about four o'clock the next morning that the change came: Eleanor had a violent chill.

"I thought we were out of the woods," the doctor said, frowning; "but I guess I was too previous. There's a spot in the left lung, Mr. Curtis."

CHAPTER XXXVI

When Maurice saw his wife the next morning, it was with Mrs. Houghton's warning—emphasized by the presence of a nurse—that he must not excite her. So he sat at her bedside and told her about his trip, and how he had got ahead of the Greenleaf heirs, and how he rushed back to Mercer the minute those dispatches came saying that she was ill—and he never asked her why she was ill, or what took her out to the river in the cold dusk of that March afternoon. She didn't try to tell him. She was very warm and drowsy—and she held in her hand, under the bedclothes, that letter which proved how much she loved him, and which, some time, when she got well, she would show him. All that day the household outside her closed door was very much upset; but Eleanor, in the big bed, was perfectly placid. She lay mere watching the tarnished gilt pendulum swing between the black pillars of the clock on the mantelpiece, thinking—thinking. "You'll be all right to-morrow!" Maurice would say; and she would smile silently and go on thinking. "When I get well," she thought, "I will do—so and so." By and by, still with the letter clutched in her hot hand, she began to say to herself, "*If* I get well." She had ceased worrying over how she was going to explain the "accident" to Maurice; that "*if*" left a door open into eternal reticence. So, instead of worrying, she made plans for Jacky: "He must see a dentist," she told Maurice. On the third day she stopped saying, "*If* I get well," and thought, "When I die." She said it very tranquilly, "When I die Maurice must get him a bicycle." She thought of this happily, for dying meant that she had not failed. She would not be ridiculous to Maurice— she would be his wife, giving him a child—a son! So she lay with her eyes closed, thinking of the bicycle and many little, pleasant things; and with the old, slipping inexactness of mind she told herself that she had not "done anything wrong"; she had *not* drowned herself! She had just caught a bad cold. But she would die, and Maurice would love her for giving him Jacky. Toward evening, however, an uneasy thought came to her: if Maurice knew that, to give him Jacky, she had even tried to get drowned, it might distress him? She wished she hadn't written the letter! It would hurt him to see it.... Well, but he *needn't* see it! She held out the crumpled envelope. "Miss Ryan," she said to the nurse, huskily, "please burn this."

"Yes, indeed!" said Miss Ryan....

There was a burst of flame in the fireplace, and the little, pitiful letter, with its selfishness and pain and sacrifice, vanished—as Lily's handkerchief had vanished, and the braided ring of blossoming grass—all gone, as the sparks that fly upward. Nobody could ever know the scented humiliation of the handkerchief, or the agony of the faded ring, or the renouncing love which had written the poor foolish letter. Maurice wouldn't be pained. As for her gift to him of Jacky, she would just tell him she wanted him to marry Lily, so he could have his child.... And Edith? Oh, he would never think of Edith!

So she was very peaceful until, the next day, she heard Edith's voice in the hall, then she frowned. "She's here! In the house with him! Don't let her come in," she told Maurice; "she takes my breath." But, somehow, she couldn't help thinking of Edith.... "That morning in the garden she cried," Eleanor thought. It was strange to think of tears in those clear, careless eyes. "I never supposed she *could* cry. I've cried a good deal. Men don't like tears." And there had been tears in Edith's eyes when she came in and sat on the bed and said she was "unhappy...." "She believed," Eleanor meditated, her own eyes closed, "that it was because of *her* that I went out to the river." She was faintly sorry that Edith should reproach herself. "I didn't do it because she made me angry; I did it to make Maurice happy. I almost wish she knew that." Perhaps it was this vague regret that made her remember Edith's assertion that she would do "anything on earth" to keep Maurice from marrying Lily. "But that's the only way he can be sure of getting Jacky," Eleanor argued to herself, her mind clearing into helpless perplexity—"and it's the only way to keep him from Edith. But I wish Lily wasn't so vulgar. Maurice won't like living with her." Suddenly she said, "Maurice, do send the nurse out of the room. I want to tell you something, darling." She was very hoarse.

"Better not talk, dear," he said, anxiously.

She smiled and shook her head. "I just want to tell you: I don't mind not getting well, because then you'll marry Lily."

"Eleanor! Don't—don't—"

"And you can give little Jacky the kind of home he ought to have."

She drowsed. Maurice sat beside her with his face buried in his hands. When she awoke, at dusk, she lay peacefully watching the firelight flickering on the ceiling, and, thinking—thinking. Then, into her peace, broke again the memory of Edith's distress. "Perhaps I ought to tell her that I went to the river for Maurice's sake? *Not* because I was angry at her." She thought of Edith's tears, and said, "Poor Edith—" And when she said that a strange thing happened: pity, like a soft breath, blew out the vehement flame. It is always so; pity and jealousy are never together....

The next morning she remembered her words about Jacky—"the kind of home he ought to have"—and again uneasiness as to the kind of "home" it would be for Maurice rose in her mind. Her head whirled with worry. "It won't be pleasant for him to live with her, even if she can cook. He loves that chocolate cake; but he couldn't bear her grammar. Edith said I was 'unkind' to him. Am I? I suppose she thought he'd be happier with her? Would he? *She* can make that cake, too. Yes; he would be happier with her than with Lily;—and Jacky would call her 'Mother,'" Then she forgot Edith.

After a while she said: "Maurice, can't I see Jacky? Go get him! And give Lily the car fare."

Maurice went downstairs and called Mrs. Houghton out of the parlor; in the hall he said: "I think Eleanor's sort of mixed up. She is talking about 'Lily's car fare'! What do you suppose she means? Is she—delirious? And then she says she 'wants to see Jacky.' What must I do?"

"Go and get him," she said.

For a bewildered minute he hesitated. If Mrs. Newbolt should see Jacky, she ... would *know*! And Edith ... would she suspect? Still he went—like a man in a dream. As he got off the car, a block from Lily's door, a glimpse of the far-off end of the route where "Eleanor's meadow" lay, made his purpose still more dreamlike. But he was abruptly direct with Lily: he had come, he said, to tell her that his wife wanted—

"My soul and body!" she broke in; "if she's sent you—" They were in the dining room, Maurice so pale that Lily, in real alarm, had put her hand on his arm and made him sit down. But she was angry. "Has she got on to that again?"

His questioning bewilderment brought her explanation.

"She didn't tell you she'd been here? Well, I promised her I wouldn't give her away to you, and I *wouldn't*,—but so long as she's sent you, now, there's no harm, I guess, telling you?" So she told him. "What possessed you to let on to her?" she ended. She was puzzled at his folly, but she was sympathetic, too. "I suppose she ragged it out of you?"

Maurice had listened, silently, his elbow on his knee, his fist hard against his mouth; he did not try to tell her why he had "let on"; he could not say that he wanted to defend his son from such a mother; still less could he make clear to her that Eleanor had not "ragged it out of him," but that, to his famished passion for truth, confession had been the Bread of Life. He looked at her once or twice as she talked; pretty, yet; kindly, coarse, honest—and Eleanor had supposed that he would marry her! Then, sharply, his mind pictured that scene: his wife, his poor, frightened old Eleanor, pleading for the gift of Jacky! And Lily—young, arrogant, kind.... The pain of it made his passion of pity so like love that the tears stood in his eyes. "Oh, she *mustn't* die," he thought; "I won't let her die!"

When Lily had finished her story he told her his, very briefly: his wife's forgiveness of his unfaithfulness; her desire to do all she could for Jacky: "Help me—I mean help you—to make a man of him, because she loves me. Heaven knows I'm not worthy of it."

Lily gulped. "She ain't young; but, my God, she's some woman!" She threw her apron over her face and cried hard; then stopped and wiped her eyes. "She wants to see him, does she? Well, you bet she shall see him! I'll get him; he's playing in at Mr. Dennett's—he's all on being an undertaker now. Mr. Dennett's a Funeral Pomps Director. But he's got to put on his new suit." She ran out on to the porch, and Maurice could hear the colloquy across the fence: "You come in the house, quick!"

"Won't. We're going to in-in-inter a hen."

"Yes, you will! You're going to put on your new suit and go and see a lady—"

"Lady? Not on your life."

"It's Mr. Curtis wants you—" Then Jacky's yell, "*Mr. Curtis?*" and a dash up the back steps and into the dining room—then, silent, grimy adoration!

Maurice gave his orders. "Change your clothes, young man. I'll bring him back, Lily, as soon as she's seen him."

While he waited for the new suit Maurice walked up and down the little room, round and round the table, where on a turkey-red cloth a hideous hammered brass bowl held some lovely maidenhair ferns. The vision of Eleanor abasing herself to Lily was unendurable. To drive it from his mind, he went to the window and stood looking out through the fragrant greenness of rose geraniums, into the squalid street where the offspring of the Funeral Pomps Director were fighting over the dead hen; from the bathroom came the sound of a sputtering gush from the hot-water faucet; then splashes and whining protests, and maternal adjurations: "You got to look decent! I *will* wash behind your ears. You're the worst boy on the street!"

"Eleanor tried to save him," he thought; "she came here, and begged for him!"

Above the bathroom noises came Lily's voice, sharp with efficiency, but shaking with pity and a quick-hearted purpose of helping: "Say, Mr. Curtis! Could she eat some fresh doughnuts? (Jacky, if you don't stand still I'll give you a regular spanking! I *didn't* put soap in your eyes!) If she can, I'll fry some for her to-morrow."

Maurice, tramping back and forth, made no answer; he was saying to himself, "If she'll just live, I will make her happy! Oh, she *must* live!" It was then that, suddenly, agonizingly, in the midst of splashings, and Jacky's whines, and Lily's anxiety about soap and doughnuts, Maurice Curtis prayed ...

He did not know it was prayer; it was just a cry: "Do something— oh, *do* something! *Do you hear me?* She tried so hard to save Jacky. Make her get well!" So it was that, in his selfless cry for happiness for Eleanor, Maurice found all those differing realizations—Joy, and Law, and Life, and Love—and lo! they were one—a personality! God. In his frantic words he established a relationship with *Him*—not It, any longer! "Please, please make her get well," he begged, humbly.

At that moment, at the door of the dining room, appeared an immaculate Jacky in his new suit, his face shining with bliss and soap. He came and stood beside Maurice, waiting his monarch's orders, and listening, without comprehension, to the conversation:

"Nothing will be said to him that will ... give anything away. She just wants to see him. His presence in the room—"

Jacky gave a little leap. "Did you say *presents*!"

"—his merely being there will please her. She loves him, Lily. You see, she's always wanted children, and—we've never had any."

Jacky's mother said, in a muffled voice, "My land!" Then she caught Jacky in her arms and kissed him all over his face.

"Aw, stop," said Jacky, greatly embarrassed; to have Mr. Curtis see him being kissed, "like a kid!" was a cruel mortification. "Aw, let up," said Jacky.

When he and Mr. Curtis started in to town his eyes seemed to grow bluer, and his face more beaming, and his voice, asking endless questions, more joyous every minute. In the car he shoved up very close to Maurice, and tried to think of something wonderful to tell him. By and by, breathing loudly, he achieved: "Say, Mr. Curtis, our ash sifter got broke." Then he shoved a little closer. Just before they reached Mrs. Newbolt's house the haggard, unhappy father gave his son orders:

"There is a lady who wants to see you, Jacky. She's my wife. Mrs. Curtis. You are to be very polite to her, and kiss her—"

"Kiss a lady!"

"Yes. You'll do what I tell you! Understand?"

"Yes, sir," Jacky said, sniffling.

"You are to tell her you love her; but you are not to speak unless you are spoken to. Do you get on to that?"

"Yes, sir. No, sir," poor Jacky said, dejectedly.

It was Edith who, watching for Maurice from the parlor window, opened the front door to him. She looked up into his eyes, then down into Jacky's, who, at that moment, took the opportunity, sighing, to obey orders; be reached up and gave a little peck at Edith's cheek.

"I love you," he said, gloomily. "I done it," he told Maurice. "*He* said I got to," he explained to Edith, resignedly, as she, startled but pleased, took his little rough hand in hers.

Just as she did so Mrs. Newbolt, coming downstairs, saw him and stopped short in the middle of a sentence—the relationship between the man and the child was unmistakable. When she got her breath she said, coldly: "There's a change, Maurice. Better go right upstairs."

He went, hurriedly, leading his little boy by the hand.

"Well, upon my word!" said Mrs. Newbolt, looking after the small, climbing figure in the new suit. "I wouldn't have believed such a thing of Maurice Curtis—oh, my poor Eleanor!" she said, and burst out crying. "I suppose she knows? Did she want to see the child? I always said she was a puffect angel! But I don't wonder she—she got wet ..."

Eleanor was very close to the River now, yet she smiled when Jacky's shrinking lips touched her cheek.

"Take her hand," Maurice told him, softly, and the little boy, silent and frightened, obeyed; but he kept his eyes on his father.

Eleanor, with long pauses, said: "Dear ... Jacky. Maurice, did you give her ... five cents? He must have ... music lessons."

"Yes, Star," he said, brokenly. "Jacky," he said, in a whisper, "say 'I love you.'"

But Jacky whispered back, anxiously, "But I said it to the other one?"

"*Say it!*" his father said.

"I love you," said Jacky, trembling.

Eleanor smiled, slept for a moment, then opened her eyes. "He doesn't look ... like *her*?"

"Not in the least," Maurice said.

Jacky, quailing, tried to draw his hand away from those cool fingers; but a look from his father stopped him.

"No," Eleanor murmured; "I see ... it won't do for" — Maurice bent close to her lips, but he could not catch the next words — "for you to marry her."

After that she was silent for so long that Maurice led the little boy out of the room. As he brought him into the parlor, Henry Houghton, who had just come in, looked at the father and son, and felt astonishment tingle in his veins like an electric shock. He gripped Maurice's hand, silently, and gave Jacky's ear a friendly pull.

"Edith," Maurice Said, "I would take him home, but I mustn't leave Eleanor. Will you get one of the maids to put him on a Medfield car—"

"I'll take him," Edith said.

Maurice began to say, sharply, "*No!*" then he stopped; after all, why not? "She must know the whole business by this time. Jacky's face gives it all away." She might as well, he thought, know Jacky's mother, as she knew his father.

Jacky, in a little growling voice, said, "Don't want *nobody* to put me on no car. I can—"

"Be quiet, my boy," Maurice said, gently. He gave Edith Lily's address and went back upstairs.

Henry Houghton, watching and listening, felt his face twitch; then he blew his nose loudly. "I'll look after him," he told Edith. "I—I'll take him to—the person he lives with. It isn't suitable for a girl—"

In spite of the gravity of the moment his girl laughed. "Father, you *are* a lamb! No; I'll take him." Then she gave Jacky a cooky, which he ate thoughtfully.

"We have 'em nicer at our house," he said. On the corner, waiting for the Medfield car, Edith offered a friendly hand, which he refused to notice. The humiliation of being taken home, "by a woman!" was scorching his little pride. He made up his mind that if them scab Dennett boys seen him getting out of the car with a woman, he'd lick the tar out of them! All the way to Maple Street he sat with his face glued to the window, never speaking a word to the "woman." When the car stopped he pushed out ahead of her and tore down the street. Happily no Dennett boys saw him!—but he dashed past his mother, who was standing at the gate, and disappeared in the house.

Lily, bareheaded in the pale April sunshine, had been watching for him rather anxiously. In deference to the occasion she had changed her dress; a string of green-glass beads, encircling her plump white neck, glimmered through the starched freshness of an incredibly frank blouse, and her white duck skirt was spotless. Her whole little fat body was as fresh and sweet as one of her own hyacinths, and her kind face had the unchanging, unhuman youthfulness of flesh and blood which has never been harried by the indwelling soul. But she was frowning. She had begun to be nervous; Jacky had been away nearly two hours! "Are they playing a gum game on me?" Lily thought; "Are they going to try and kidnap him?" It was then that she caught sight of Jacky, tearing toward home, his fierce blue eyes raking the street for any of them there Dennett boys, who must have the tar licked out of 'em! Edith was following him, in hurrying anxiety. Instantly Lily was reassured. "One of Mrs. Curtis's lady friends, I suppose," she thought. "Well, it's up to me to keep her guessing on Jacky!" She was very polite and simpering when, at the gate, Edith said that Mr. Curtis asked her to bring Jacky home.

"Won't you come in and be seated?" Lily urged, hospitably.

Edith said no; she was sorry; but she must go right back; "Mrs. Curtis is very ill, I am sorry to say."

At this moment Jacky came out to the gate; he had two cookies in his hand. He said, shyly: "Maw's is better 'an yours. You can have"—this with a real effort—"the *big* one."

Edith took the "big one," pleasantly, and said, "Yes, they are nicer than ours, Jacky."

But Lily was mortified. "The lady'll think you have no manners. Go on back into the house!"

"Won't," said Jacky, eating his cooky.

His mother tried to cover his obstinacy with conversation: "He's crazy about Mr. Curtis. Well, no wonder. Mr. Curtis was a great friend of my husband's. Mr. Dale—his name was Augustus; I named Jacky after him; Ernest Augustus. He died three years ago; no, I guess it was two—"

"Huh?" said Jacky, interested, "You said my paw died—"

Lily, with that desire to smack her son which every mother knows, cut his puzzled arithmetic short. "Yes. Mr. Dale was a great clubman. In

Philadelphia. I believe that's where he and Mr. Curtis got to be chums. But I never met *her*."

Edith said, rigidly, "Really?"

"Jacky's the image of Mr. Dale. He died of—of typhus fever. Mr. Curtis was one of the pallbearers; that's how I got acquainted with him. Jacky was six then," Lily ended, breathlessly. ("I guess *that's* fixed her," she thought.)

Edith only said again, "Really?" Then added, "Good afternoon," and hurried away. So *this* was the woman Eleanor would make Maurice marry! "Never!" Edith said. "Never! if *I* can prevent it!"

Upstairs in Mrs. Newbolt's spare room, as the twilight thickened, there was silence, except for the terrible breathing, and the clock ticking away the seconds; one by one they fell—like beads slipping from a string. Maurice sat holding Eleanor's hand. The others, speaking, sometimes, without sound, or moving, noiselessly, stood before the meek majesty of dying. Waiting. Waiting. It was not until midnight that she opened her eyes again and looked at Maurice, very peacefully.

"Tell Edith it wasn't what she said, made me try ... our river ... Jacky will call her ... Tell Edith ... to be kind to Jacky."

She did not speak again.

CHAPTER XXXVII

"I have an uneasy feeling," said Mr. Houghton, "that he is thinking of marrying the woman, just to carry out Eleanor's wish. Poor Eleanor! Always doing the wrong thing, with greatness." This was in September. Maurice was to come up to Green Hill for a Sunday, and the Houghtons were in the studio talking about the expected guest. Later Edith was to drive over to the junction and meet him....

It was not only Green Hill which talked about Maurice. In the months that followed Eleanor's death, a good many people had pondered his affairs, because, somehow, that visit of Jacky's to Mrs. Newbolt's house, got noised abroad, so Maurice's friends (making the inevitable deductions) told one another exactly what he ought to do.

Mrs. Newbolt expressed herself in great detail: "I shall never forgive him," she said; "my poor Eleanor! *She* forgave him, and sent for the child. More than *I* would do for any man! But I could have told her what to expect. In fact, I did. I always said if she wasn't entertainin', she'd lose him. Yes; she had a hard time—but she kept her figger. Should Maurice marry the—boy's mother? *'Course not!* Puffect nonsense. You think he'll make up to Edith Houghton? She would have too much self-respect to look at him! And if she did, her father would never consent to it."

The Mortons' opinion was just as definite: "I hope Maurice will marry again; Edith's just the girl for him—*What!*" Mrs. Morton interrupted herself, at a whisper of gossip, "he had a mistress? I don't believe a word of it!"

"But I'm afraid it's true," her husband told her, soberly; "there's a boy." His wife's shocked face made him add: "I think Curtis will feel he ought to legitimatize the youngster by marrying his mother. Maurice is good stuff. He won't sidestep an obligation."

"I never heard of such an awful idea!" said Mrs. Morton, dismayed. "I hope he'll do nothing of the kind! You can't correct one mistake by making another. Don't you agree with me?" she demanded of Doctor Nelson; who displayed, of course, entire ignorance of Mr. Curtis's affairs.

He only said, "Well, it's a rum world."

Johnny Bennett, in Buenos Aires, reading a letter from his father, said: "Poor Eleanor!" ... Then he grew a little pale under his tan, and added something which showed his opinion—not, perhaps, of what Maurice *ought* to do, but of what he would do! "I might as well make it a three-years' contract," Johnny said, bleakly, "instead of one. Of course there 11 be no use going back home. Eleanor's death settles *my* hash."

Even Mrs. O'Brien, informed by kitchen leakage as to what had happened, had something to say: "He ought to make an honest woman of the little fellow's mother. But to think of him treating Miss Eleanor that way!"

And now, in the studio, the Houghtons also were saying what Maurice ought—and ought not!—to do: "I'm afraid he's thinking of marrying her," Mr. Houghton had said; and his wife had said, quickly, "I hope so—for the sake of his child!"

"But, Mary," he protested, "look at it from the woman's point of view; this 'Lily' would be wretched if she had to live Maurice's kind of life!"

Edith, standing with her back to her father and mother, staring down into the ashes of the empty fireplace, said, over her shoulder, "Maurice may marry somebody who will help him with Jacky—just as Eleanor would have done, if she had lived."

"My dear," her father said, quickly, "he has had enough of your sex to last his lifetime! As a mere matter of taste, I think Maurice won't marry anybody."

"I don't see why, just because he—did wrong ten years ago," Edith said, "he has got to sidestep happiness for the rest of his life! But as for marrying that Mrs. Dale, it would be a cat-and-dog life."

"Edith," said her father, "when you agree with me I am filled with admiration for your intelligence! Your sex has, generally, mere intuition—a nice, divine thing, and useful in its way. But indifferent to logic. My sex has judgment; so when you, a female, display judgment, I, as a parent, am gratified. 'Cat-and-dog life' is a mild way of putting it;—a quarrelsome home is hell,—and hell is a poor place in which to bring up a child! Mary, my darling, you can derail any train by putting a big enough obstacle on the track; the fact that the obstacle is pure gold, like your idealism, wouldn't prevent a domestic wreck—in which Jacky would be the victim! But in regard to Maurice's marrying anybody else"—he paused and looked at his daughter—"*that* seems to me undesirable."

Edith's face hardened. "I don't see why," she said; then added, abruptly, "I must go and write some letters," and went quickly out of the room.

They looked after her, and then at each other.

"You see?" Mary Houghton said; "she cares for him!"

"I couldn't face it!" her husband said; "I couldn't have Edith in such a mess. Morally speaking, of course he has a right to marry; but he can't have my girl! Let him marry some other man's girl—and I'll give them my blessing. He's a dear fellow—but he can't have our Edith."

She shook her head. "If it were not for his duty to Jacky, I would be glad to have Edith marry him. And as for saying that she 'can't,' these are not the days, Henry, when fathers and mothers decide whom their girls may marry."

While his old friends were thus talking him over, Maurice was traveling up to the mountains. He had seen Mr. and Mrs. Houghton in Mercer several times since Eleanor's death, but he had not been able to face the associations and recollections of Green Hill. This was largely because, though his friends had, with such ease, reached decisions for him, he was himself so absorbed in indecision that he could not go back to the careless pleasantness of old intimacies, (As for that question of the wheels,—"if—if—if anything happens to Eleanor?"—Eleanor herself had answered it in one word: *Lily.*) So, since her death Maurice's whole mind was intent on Jacky. What must he do fear him? His occasional efforts to train the child had been met, more than once, by sharp rebuffs. Whenever he went to see Jacky, Lily was perfectly good humored—*unless* she felt she was being criticized; then the claws showed through the fur!

"You can give me money, if you want to, to send him to a swell school." She said, once; "but I tell you, Mr. Curtis, right out, *I ain't going to have you come in between me and Jacky by talking up things to him that I don't care about.* All these religious frills about Truth! They say nowadays hardly any rich people tell the truth. And talking grammar to him! You set him against me," she, said, and her eyes filled with angry tears.

"I wouldn't think of setting him against you," he said; "only, I want to do my duty to him."

"'Duty'!" said Lily, contemptuously; "I'm not going to bring him up old-fashioned. And this thing of telling him not to say 'ain't,' I say it, and what else would he say? There ain't any other word. He's my child—and I'll bring him up the way I like! Wait; I'll give you some fudge; I've just made it..."

Maurice, now, on his way up to Green Hill, looking out of the car window, and remembering interviews like this with his son's mother, wondered if Edith had seen Lily the day she took Jacky home? That made him wonder what Edith would think of the whole business? To a woman like Edith it would be simply disgusting. "I'll just drop out of her life," he said. He thought of the day he brought Jacky to Mrs. Newbolt's door, and Edith had looked at him—and then at Jacky—and then at him again. *She understood!* Would she understand now? Probably not. "Of course old Johnny'll get her ... But, oh, what life might have been!"

Edith had driven over to the junction earlier than was necessary, because she had wanted to get away from her father and mother. "They are afraid he'll fall in love with me," she thought, hotly; "if he ever does, nothing they can say shall separate us. Nothing! But mother'll try to influence him to marry that dreadful creature, and father will say things about 'honor,' so he'll feel he ought never to marry—anybody. Oh, they are lambs," she said, setting her teeth; "but they mustn't keep Maurice from being happy!" At the station, as she sat in the buggy flecking her whip idly, and waiting for Maurice's train, her whole mind was on the defensive. "He has a right to be happy. He has a right to marry again ... but they needn't worry about *me!*" she thought. "I've never grown up to Maurice. But whatever happens, he shan't marry that woman!"

When Maurice got off the train there was a blank moment when she did not recognize him. As a careworn man came up to her with an outstretched hand and a friendly, "This is awfully nice in you, Skeezics!" she said, with a gasp, "*Maurice!*" He had aged so that he looked, she thought, as old as Eleanor. But they were both laboriously casual, until the usual remarks upon the weather, and the change in the time-table, had been exhausted.

It was Edith who broke into reality—Maurice had taken the reins, and they were jogging slowly along. "Maurice," she said, "how is Jacky?" His start was so perceptible that she said, "You don't mind my asking?"

"I don't mind anything you could say to me, Edith. I'm grateful to you for asking."

"I want to help you about him," she said.

He put out his left hand and gripped hers. Then he said: "I'm going to do my best for the little fellow. I've botched my own life, Edith;—of course you know that? But he shan't botch his, if I can help it!"

"I think you can help it," Edith said.

His heart contracted; yet it was what he had expected. The idealism of an absolutely pure woman. "Well," he said, heavily, "of course I've got to do what I honestly think is the light thing."

"Are you sure," she said, "that you know what the right thing is? You mustn't make a mistake."

"I may be said to have made my share," he told her, dryly.

She did not answer that; she said, passionately, "Maurice, I'd give anything in the world if I could help you!"

"Don't talk that way," he commanded, harshly. "I'm human! So please don't be kind to me, Edith; I can't stand it."

Instantly her heart pounded in her throat: "He *cares*. Oh, they can't separate us. But they'll try to." ... The rest of the drive was rather silent. On the porch at Green Hill the two older friends were waiting to welcome him. ("Don't let's leave them alone," Henry Houghton had said, with a worried look; which made his wife, in spite of her own uneasiness, smile, "Oh, Henry, you are an innocent creature!") After dinner Mrs. Houghton, determinedly commonplace, came to the rescue of what threatened to be a somewhat conscious occasion, by talking books and music. Her husband may have been "innocent," but he did his part by shoving a cigar box toward the "boy," and saying, "How's business? We must talk Weston's offer over," he said.

Maurice nodded, but got up and went to the piano; "Tough on you, Skeezics," he said once, glancing at Edith.

"Oh, I don't mind it, *much*," she said, drolly.

So the evening trudged along in secure stupidity. Yet it was a straining stupidity, and there was an inaudible sigh of relief from everybody when, at last, Mary Houghton said, "Come, good people! It's time to go to bed."

"Yes, turn in, Maurice," said his host; "you look tired." Then he got on his feet, and said good night with an alacrity which showed how much he "wished he was asleep"! But he was not permitted to sleep. Maurice, swinging round from the piano, said, with a rather rigid face:

"Would you mind just waiting a minute and letting me tell you something about myself, Uncle Henry?"

"Of course not!" Mr. Houghton said, with great assumption of cheerfulness. He went back to the sofa—furtively achieving a cigar as he did so—and saying to himself, "Well, at least it will give me a chance to let him see how I feel about his ever marrying again."

Edith was standing by the piano, one hand resting on the keyboard and drumming occasionally in disconnected octaves. ("If it's business," she thought, "I'll leave them alone; but if they are going to 'advise' him, I'll stay—and fight.")

Maurice came and sat on the edge of the big table, his hands in his pockets, and one foot swinging nervously. "I hope you dear people don't think I'm an ungrateful cuss, not to have come to Green Hill this summer; but the fact is, I've been awfully up against it, trying to make up my mind about something."

Henry Houghton looked at the fire end of his cigar with frowning intentness and said yes, he supposed so. "Weston's offer seems to me fair," he said (this referred to a partnership possibility, on which Maurice had consulted him by letter); but his remark, now, was so obviously a running to cover that, in spite of himself, Maurice grinned. "Weston's a very square fellow," said Henry Houghton.

"If you are going to talk 'offers,'" said Edith, "do you want me to clear out?"

"It isn't business," Maurice said, quietly; "it's my ... little son. No; don't clear out, Edith. I'd rather talk to your mother and Uncle Henry before you."

"All right," said Edith, and struck some soft chords; but her young mouth was hard.

"Of course," Maurice said, "as things are now—I mean poor Eleanor gone—I have thought a good deal of what I ought to do for Jacky. It was Nelly's wish that I should do the straight thing for him. There wasn't any question, I think, of the 'straight thing' for Lily—"

"Of course not!" Mary Houghton agreed. And her husband said, "Any such idea would be nonsense, Maurice."

"And I myself don't count," Maurice went on.

Again Mrs. Houghton agreed—very gravely: "Compared to the child, dear Maurice, you don't."

"You *do!*" Edith said; but nobody heard her.

"So at first," Maurice said, "I kept thinking of how Eleanor had wanted me to have him—legally, you know; wanted it so much that she—" there was a silence in the studio; "that she was glad to die, to make it possible." He paused, and Mary Houghton saw his cheek twitch. "Well, I felt that clinched it. I felt I *must* carry out her wish, and ask Mrs. Dale to—marry me."

"Morbid," said Henry Houghton.

Edith, listening, said nothing; but she was ready to spring!

"Perhaps it was morbid," Maurice said; "but just at first it seemed that way to me. Then I began to realize that what poor Nelly wanted, wasn't to have me marry Lily—that was only a means to an end; she wanted Jacky taken care of"; (Edith nodded.) "And she thought marrying his mother was the best way to do that." (Edith shook her head.)

"Well; I thought it all over ... I kept myself and my own feelings out of it." Behind those laconic words lay the weeks of struggle, of which even these good friends could have no idea! Weeks in which, while Mercer was deciding what he ought to do, Maurice, "keeping himself out of it," had put aside ambition and smothered taste, and thrown over, once for all, personal happiness. As a wrestler strips from his body all hampering things, so he had stripped from his mind every instinct which might interfere with a straight answer to a straight question: "What will be best for my boy?" He gave the answer now, in Henry Houghton's studio, while Edith, over in the shadows, at the piano, looked at him. Her face was quite pale.

"So all I had to do," said Maurice, "was to think of Jacky's welfare. That made it easier to decide. I find," he said, simply, "that you can decide things pretty easily if you don't have to think of yourself. So I said, 'If I marry Lily, though Jacky couldn't be taken away from me, physically, spiritually'—you know what I mean, Mrs. Houghton?—'he might be removed to—to the ends of the earth!' I might lose his affection; and I've got to hold on to *that*, at any cost, because that's how I can influence him." He was talking now entirely to Edith's mother, and his voice was harsh with entreaty for understanding. He didn't care very much whether Henry Houghton understood or not. And of course Edith could never understand! But that this serene woman of the stars should misjudge him was unbearable. "You see what I mean, Mrs. Houghton, don't you? I know Lily;—and I know that if she thought I had any *right* to say how he must be brought up, it would mean nothing but perfectly hideous controversies all the time! So long as she thinks she has the upper hand, she'll be generous; she doesn't mind his being fond of me, you know. But she'd fight tooth and nail if she thought I had any *rights*! You see that, don't you?"

"I see it!" Edith said.

"Yet from a merely material point of view," said Mrs. Houghton, "in spite of 'controversies,' legitimacy would give Jacky advantages, which—oh, Maurice, don't you see?—*your son* has a right to!"

But her husband said, quickly, "Mary, living with a quarreling father and mother is spiritual illegitimacy; and the disadvantages of that would be worse than the material handicap of being a—a fatherless child."

His daughter flashed a passionately grateful look at him.

Maurice, still speaking to Edith's mother, said: "That's the way I looked at it, Mrs. Houghton. So it seemed to me that I could do more for him if I didn't marry Lily."

Mary Houghton was silent; it was very necessary to consider the stars.

"I put myself out of it," Maurice said. "I just said, 'If it's best for Jacky, I'll ask her to marry me,' My honest opinion was that it would be bad for him."

Edith struck two chords—and sat down on the piano stool, swallowing hard.

"You don't agree with me, I'm afraid, Mrs. Houghton?" he said, anxiously.

"My dear boy," she said, "I am sure you are doing what you believe to be right. But it does not seem right to me."

He flinched, but he was not shaken; "It isn't going to be easy, whatever I do. I want to educate him, and see him constantly, and influence him as much as possible. And Lily will be less jealous of me, in her own house, than she would be in mine."

Edith got up and came and sat on the arm of the sofa by her father. "I can see," she said, "how much easier it would be for Maurice to do the hard thing."

Maurice looked at her with deep tenderness. "You *are* a satisfying person!" he said.

Henry Houghton took his girl's hand, and held it in a grip that hurt her. "Maurice is right," he said; "things are *not* going to be easy for him. For, though he won't marry Jacky's mother, he won't, I think, marry anybody else."

"Why won't he?" said Edith.

"There is no *moral* reason why he shouldn't," her father conceded; "it is a question of taste; one might perhaps call it a question of honor"—Maurice whitened, but Henry Houghton went on, calmly, "Maurice will, of necessity, be so involved with this woman—and God knows what annoyances she may make for him, that—it distresses me to say so—but I can see that he will not feel like asking any woman to share such a burden as he has to carry."

"If he loves any woman," Edith said, "let him ask her! If she turns him down, it stamps her for a coward!"

"Don't you think I'm right, Maurice?" her father said.

"Yes," Maurice said. "You are right. I've faced that."

Edith sprang to her feet, and stood looking at her father and mother, her eyes stern with protecting passion. "It seems to me absurd," she said,—"like standing up so straight you fall over backward!—for Maurice to feel he can't marry—somebody else, just because he—he did wrong, ever so many years ago! He's sorry, now. Aren't you sorry, Maurice?" she said.

His eyes stung;—the simplicity of the word was like a flower tossed into the black depths of his repentance! "Yes, dear," he said, gently; "I'm 'sorry.' But no amount of 'sorrow' can alter consequences, Edith."

"Oh," she said, turning to the other two, "don't you want Maurice *ever* to be happy?"

"I want him to be good," said her mother.

"I can't be happy, Edith," Maurice told her; "don't you see?"

She looked straight in his eyes, her own eyes terror-stricken. ... They would drive him away from her! "You *shall* be happy," she said.

They saw only each other, now.

"No," Maurice said; "it's just as your father says; I have no right to drag any girl into the kind of life I've got to live. I'll have to see Lily a good deal, so as to keep in with her—and be able to look after Jacky. Personal happiness is all over for me."

She caught at his arm; "It isn't! Maurice, don't listen to them!" Then she turned and stood in front of him, as though to put her young breast between him and that tender, menacing parental love. "Oh, mother—oh, father! I *do* love you; I don't want to do anything you don't approve of;—but Maurice comes first. If he asks me to marry him, I will."

Under his breath Maurice said, "*Edith!*"

"My darling," Henry Houghton said, "consider: people are bound to know all about this. The publicity will be a very painful embarrassment—"

Edith broke in, "As if that matters!"

"But the serious thing," her father went on, "Is that this woman will be a millstone around his neck—"

"She shall be around my neck, too!" she said. There was a breathless moment; then Truth, nobly naked, spoke: "Maurice, duty is the first thing in the world;—not happiness. If you thought it was your duty to marry Lily, I wouldn't say a word. You would never know that I cared. Never! I'd just stand by, and help you. I'd live in the same house with her, if it would help you! But—" her voice shook; "you *don't* think it's your duty. You know it isn't! You know that it would make things worse for Jacky,—not better, as Eleanor wanted them to be. So why shouldn't you be happy? Oh, it's *artificial*, to refuse to be happy!" Before he could speak, she added, quite simply, the sudden tears bright in her eyes, "I know you love me."

He looked at the father and mother: "You wouldn't have me lie to her, would you?—even to save her from herself! ... Of course I love you, Edith,— more than anything on earth,—but I have no right—"

"You have a right," she said.

"I *want* you," he said, "God knows, it would mean life to me! But—"

"Then take me," she said.

Mrs. Houghton came and put her arms around her girl and kissed her. "Take her, Maurice," she said, quietly. Then she looked at her husband: "Dear," she said, and smiled—a little mistily; "wisdom will not die with us! The children must do what *they* think is right ... Even if it is wrong." She had considered the stars.